THE FIN(
OF GOD

MW00654855

THE FINGERPRINTS
OF GOD

Exciting Evidence that God Exists,
Jesus Is Alive and the Bible Can Be Trusted

BRAD CUMMINGS

Pleasant W●rd

© 2004 by Brad Cummings. All rights reserved

Packaged by Pleasant Word, PO Box 428, Enumclaw, WA 98022. The views expressed or implied in this work do not necessarily reflect those of Pleasant Word. The author(s) is ultimately responsible for the design, content and editorial accuracy of this work.

No part of this publication may be reproduced, stored in a retrieval system or transmitted in any way by any means—electronic, mechanical, photocopy, recording or otherwise—without the prior permission of the copyright holder, except as provided by USA copyright law.

Scripture verses and commentary are taken from Rev. C.I. Scofield, D.D. The Scofield Study Bible, Authorized King James Version, (1945 edition) and are used by permission of the Oxford University Press, NY.

Quotation from *God and the New Physics* by Paul Davies © 1983 by Paul Davies reprinted with the permission of Simon and Schuster Adult Publishing Group.

All photos taken by Brad, Ann and Loraine Cummings

"Sweeping Under the Rug Graphic," appearing in Chapter 1 taken from page 36 of John D. Morris, The Young Earth. August 2000. Used by permission of Master Books, Green Forest, AR.

All cartoons appearing in Chapter 10 are used by permission of Josh McDowell Ministries

ISBN 1-4141-0294-1
Library of Congress Catalog Card Number: 2004097303

Table of Contents

Acknowledgements

First, I would like to acknowledge my lovely wife, Ann Marie, for her patience and persistent support during the many long, laboring hours required to research and write this book. She has been, and continues to be a wonderful helper. Special thanks also go out to Roy, Jeff, David, D. Allen and Jim Shanks; Jean, Tom and Loraine Cummings; Larry Page; Pastors Donn Hauser and Lloyd Vaughn for their valuable contributions toward the completion of this text. I also am appreciative of those friends and family members who offered words of support and encouragement along the way. Last, but not least, thanks belong to the one and only God of the Universe . . . to Him this book is humbly dedicated . . . may any and all glory that results from this publication be given to the Ultimate Author of creation and eternal salvation.

Preface

In *The Atheist Debater's Handbook*, B.C. Johnson gave this challenge, "If God exists, there will be evidence of this; signs will emerge which point to such a conclusion."[1] In this book, I'll provide many "signs" that God exists, showing how His fingerprints are present everywhere. The unmistakable fingerprint evidence in these pages is certain to blow you away. I'll lay down this evidence, acting as the attorney, God is on the witness stand and you are the judge and jury. The verdict is in your hands. (I remind you that even the worst criminals receive a trial . . . all I'm asking is that you allow God a trial before condemning him.)

After listening carefully to the evidence, your verdict must include the answers to a few questions, including, What or Who is the originator of life?; What is the purpose of life?; Does God exist?; Is the Bible reliable, or it is just a fairy tale?; Are there good reasons to believe that one faith is superior over all others?; Who is Jesus . . . is there overwhelming evidence that He really lived, died, was buried and rose three days later?; Finally, if God does exist, Jesus is really who He claimed to be and the Bible can be trusted beyond a shadow of a doubt, then what do these facts mean to my life today . . . can God really change my life for the better, or is He just a distant God . . . can He really give me eternal life in a place that far exceeds my best dreams?

I can remember asking myself these questions at one time. But now, after ten years and literally thousands of hours of research in hundreds of scholarly works written by both Christians and those opposed to Christianity, I am convinced that today, perhaps more than ever, the answers to these questions are obvious. My inspiration for writing this book was to let you know what I now know to be true. I've discovered that there are many concrete and common sense reasons to believe. Becoming a Christian does not require that you commit intellectual suicide . . . we don't believe in spite of the evidence, for the evidence is on our side. Christianity is not a blind leap of faith into the dark, but is founded firmly on verifiable historical facts. The truth of Christianity can be checked out, and it has passed the test. It is a well-founded faith based on facts, not feelings. As Clarence McCartney said, "Any kind of evidence that a reasonable mind could ask for, Christianity has to present."[2]

I strongly believe that it's logically impossible to deny the existence of God the Creator, reliability of the Bible and resurrection of Jesus Christ from the tomb if you understand the facts I'm about to present. My hope is that through carefully considering the evidence, you will personally meet the God of creation, and that this meeting will change your life positively both now and forever.

In chapters 1–8, I will thoroughly destroy the 'theory of evolution' and will provide abundant evidence for the existence of God by leading you on a fairly detailed journey from the largest thing we know . . . the Universe, to the smallest . . . quarks, leptons and bosons. In between, we'll scale the high mountain peaks, submarine to the lowest ocean depths, stroll through a vibrant forest community and examine the complex architecture of the human body in search of God's signature on the canvas of creation.

In chapters 9 and 10, I will reveal why we can be confident that the God of the Bible is the only Divine Designer, Creator and Sustainer of the entire Universe. In Chapter 11, we will also consider what impact this fact can have on our lives today, and for all eternity. Please join me on this information packed journey . . . if you carefully consider all the evidence with an open mind, I'm certain that the verdict you reach will lead to a life-transforming experience, enabling you to confidently answer the most important questions in life. I now challenge you to read on and declare with boldness and confidence that it is time for the trial to begin!

PART I:

God Exists

CHAPTER 1

Big God
or Big Bang?

THE CREATION VS. EVOLUTION DEBATE

S ome believe that this world was created by a divine Designer. Others believe that evolution is the reason for
life as we know it . . . a few may secretly or openly hold to
some other unproven theory. Yet only one of these beliefs can answer the most fundamental question of how life began. No one can
reasonably deny that we exist, and must have gotten here somehow
. . . what is the best explanation for how we got here? How can we
know for sure which belief is correct?

Has science proven that evolution is a fact? Many people are under
the false impression that it has, thinking that scientists have all the
answers . . . the fact is that they do not have all the answers. As
Henry Morris, a former evolutionary scientist, and now director of
the Institute for Creation Research said, "Many believe in evolution
for the simple reason that they think science has proven it to be a
'fact' and, therefore, it must be accepted . . . In recent years, a great
many people, having finally been persuaded to make a real
examination of the problem of evolution, have become convinced of
its fallacy, and are now convinced anti-evolutionists."[1] Paul Ackerman

exposed the true state of affairs, saying, "The challenge that creation scientists have raised against Darwinian evolution has been carried forward with increasing success in every quarter. (The battle has been) carried into bastions of the educational and scientific establishment where Darwinism in its modern form has had dominance for many decades. These debates have been a triumph for the cause of creationism and an embarrassment for evolutionists."[2]

As Robert F. Smith, a member of the Western Missouri Affiliate of the American Civil Liberties Union (ACLU), said in 1980: "For the past 5 years, I have closely followed creationist literature and have attended lectures and debates on related issues . . . Based solely on the scientific arguments pro and con, I have been forced to conclude that scientific creationism is not only a viable theory, but that it has achieved parity with (if not superiority over) the normative theory of biological evolution. That this should now be the case is somewhat surprising, particularly in view of what most of us were taught in primary and secondary school. In practical terms, the past decade of intense activity by scientific creationists has left most evolutionist professors unwilling to debate the creationist professors. Too many of the evolutionists have been publicly humiliated in such debates by their own lack of erudition and by the weakness of their theory."[3]

The ACLU is certainly no friend of creationists, so Smith's quote is a highly significant, eye-opening reminder that the beliefs contained in the theory of evolution are not nearly as certain as evolutionists would like the world to believe they are. Since Smith made this statement, the situation has only gotten worse for those who still embrace the theory. With the use of improved technology, scientific discoveries in the past 25 years have greatly strengthened the case for creation by a divine Being and hopelessly weakened the theories of the evolutionists' camp.

The general public has been kept in the dark and fed the unproven lies of evolution as assumed fact for far too long. The purpose of this first chapter is to expose these unproven lies with scientific fact from the world surrounding us. In this and following chapters, you will see that while evolution has no scientific support, there is an avalanche of evidence that this world was created by a supremely intelligent Being. While doing my research, I was careful to be certain the conclusion that this world was created by an intelligent Being is solidly and solely based on the evidence. If the evidence were not overwhelmingly obvious, I would not have written this book. As you read on, I'd ask you to throw your personal bias out the window and let the evidence be the basis for your verdict in the Creation vs. Evolution debate. After exploring the evidence for yourself, I have no doubt that you will become a "convinced anti-evolutionist" and confident creationist.

Before disproving the theory of evolution, we must first understand what it's all about. The theory states that the Universe began 13–20 billion years ago as a tiny hot ball of hydrogen the size of a pinhead, which evolutionists admit came from nothing and nowhere. This ball, they believe, cooled to many billions of degrees as it grew to the size of a football. Then, in a split second, during the largest explosion of all time (called the 'Big Bang'), all matter, time, space, energy and all other known forces began to form into the Universe we know today. The self created atoms then joined into huge clouds of dust and gas, which eventually broke apart to form galaxies, stars and planets, including Earth. Earth, they say, formed about 4.6 billion years ago, and was originally a dense, chaotic 'primordial soup' of dead particles and energy. From this chaotic primordial soup of dead particles evolved, mainly through mutations and natural selection, all of the intricately ordered organisms (including you) that we observe in the natural world today. This, in a nutshell, is the theory of evolution.

Following are several scientific reasons why the theory of evolution can be disregarded as a valid belief. I will start with convincing evidence and work up to the most convincing evidence (Evidence #8). (Although I've tried my best to explain the scientific concepts I'm about to present, I realize that some of them may still be difficult to understand . . . but you really don't need to understand the intricacies of each concept to get the main point that the theory of evolution is impossible and creation by an intelligent Designer is the best explanation for our existence. The cumulative weight of evidence will make this fact overwhelmingly obvious.)

EVIDENCE #1 - THE 2ND LAW OF THERMODYNAMICS

The second law of thermodynamics is one of the best proven facts of science. P.W. Bridgman confirms this while saying, "The two laws of thermodynamics are accepted by physicists as perhaps the most secure generalizations from experience that we have."[4] J.P. Moreland said, "There is no region of the universe that escapes the second law."[5]

The well proven 2nd law states that organisms can't progress from a lower to a higher order.

Everything in the Universe tends to become less ordered and eventually will break down if there is no energy input from the outside to maintain it. The 2nd Law explains why new machines will eventually end up rusting away in a junk pile, why a once sturdy barn will someday collapse to the ground, why a cup of hot coffee cools instead of heating up and is the reason why we must eat to \ maintain order in our body. (If we didn't, our bodies would break down and die within a few weeks to a month for the strongest among us.) The 2nd Law also explains why a complex living organism won't evolve from a dense, chaotic 'primordial soup' of dead particles and energy, even if given a few billion years.

Evolutionist Isaac Asimov has said: "Another way of stating the second law then is, 'The universe is constantly getting more disorderly!' Viewed that way we can see the second law all about us. We have to work hard to straighten a room, but left to itself it becomes a mess again very quickly and very easily. In fact, all we have to do is nothing, and everything deteriorates, collapses, breaks down, wears out, all by itself—and that is what the second law is all about."[6]

Could the Power of the Sun make Evolution Possible?

Evolutionists have tried to sidestep this serious problem by asserting that the second law does not work for open systems like the Earth. They claim that energy input from the sun was capable of powering the process of turning primordial soup into a human being. This however, is false. As respected scholar Norman Geisler observed, "It is easy to pump a lot of energy into a system at random if all you want to do is make it hot, but if you want to organize it—that is, put it in order and create information—that requires intelligence."[7] Evolutionist Dr. John Ross of Harvard University explicitly said, "There are no known violations of the second law of thermodynamics. Ordinarily, the second law is stated for isolated systems, but the second law applies equally well to open systems. There is somehow associated with the field of far-from-equilibrium thermodynamics the notion that the second law of thermodynamics fails for such systems. It is important to make sure that this error does not perpetuate itself."[8]

In support of the validity of the second law for the entire Universe (including isolated, closed and open systems) Asimov further admits, "What the Second Law tells us, then, is that in the great game of the Universe, we not only cannot win; we cannot even break even."[9] Yet, while explaining the complexity of the human brain, he stated, "In man is a three pound brain, which, as far as we know, is the most complex and orderly arrangement of matter in the Universe."[10] So, in essence, Asimov believed that the super complex human brain evolved from nothing and nowhere, even though this has proven to be impossible by the scientific second law of thermodynamics. Unscientific 'reasoning' like this is common within the evolutionists' camp.

Former evolutionist Henry Morris explained, "It would hardly be possible to conceive of two more completely opposite principles than this principle of entropy increase (2nd Law) and the principle of evolution. Each is precisely the converse of the other. As Huxley defined it, evolution involves a continual increase of order, of organization, of size, of complexity. It seems axiomatic that both cannot possibly be true. But there is no question whatever that the second law of thermodynamics is true."[11] The evolutionary belief that our complex, intricately ordered Earth arose from a 'Big Bang' explosion and a chaotic 'primordial soup' of dead particles is an unscientific, irrational belief that directly contradicts the well proven scientific and physical 2nd Law of Thermodynamics.

Is the Universe Eternal?

As a last ditch attempt to validate their theory, some evolutionists have postulated that the universe is eternal. Yet if the second law of thermodynamics is true throughout the universe, as the evidence overwhelming shows, and as even the evolutionists admit, then the universe cannot possibly be eternal, for it would have run out of fuel in the past. Since our universe *is* running down, it will not and could not have existed forever. There had to be a beginning point for this universe. A beginning point requires a beginning creative event. A creative event involving such complex and orderly heavenly bodies and living creatures requires the existence of an eternal, super-intelligent Creator, the first cause of the Universe. (I will discuss this last point in more detail under Evidence #3.)

EVIDENCE #2 - LIFE FROM CHANCE ?

By stating that life resulted by chance from non-life, evolutionists are also contradicting statistics and known biological fact. (Before proving this, I must take a moment to dispel a notion that evolutionists have long clung to as evidence that life can come from non-life . . . In 1953, Stanley Miller and his mentor, Harold Urey, simulated a highly speculative early Earth 'primordial soup' and declared that they had created life from this soup. Nothing could be further from the truth. In fact, not only did they fail to create a complex living creature, but the vast majority of the components produced in their experiments were destructive tars, which would have effectively eliminated any possibility of early life. As former evolutionist Gary Parker discovered, "What Miller actually produced was a seething brew of potent poisons that would absolutely destroy any hope for the chemical evolution of life."[12] The true findings of this famous experiment are often ignored by evolutionists, who have been successful in brainwashing several generations of unsuspecting biology students into believing that science has created life from dead particles, therefore making evolution from a primordial soup feasible. The truth is that the Miller-Urey experiments were highly unscientific and unsuccessful attempts to create life from non-life.)

All truly *scientific* observation concludes that life does not arise by chance from non-life. For life to arise from much simpler non-living components such as amino acids requires organization by an intelligent being (as in the case of recent cloning efforts). These facts kill the theory of evolution by chance from the non-intelligent, upredictable forces of nature. The argument really stops there, but let's play along for a moment and imagine that the amino acids which make up life were somehow created from the chaotic 'primordial soup' of primitive Earth which came from a primeval explosion that came from nothing and nowhere.

The statistical and biological problems I'll mention below are enough to make sure that the dead theory of evolution never moves. (If you have trouble understanding the next section, that's OK since life *is* extremely complex, and hard for even the best biologists to describe. My goal is not necessarily for you to understand the biological terms and relationships, but that you will be overwhelmed by the complexity of life and the statistical impossibility that it came about by pure chance.)

Statistical and Biological Problems Due to the Complexity of Life[13]

Amino acids are the building blocks of proteins, which are one of the main building blocks of life. The average protein is among the most complex of all known chemical structures, containing 400 amino acids of 20 different kinds arranged in precise sequences. Just 100 amino acids can be arranged in 20^{100} (10^{130}) different ways. To appreciate how large this number is, consider that there are only

10^{84} subatomic particles (baryons) in the entire Universe. It has been calculated that if just 100 amino acids were arranged randomly a trillion times per second for 4.6 billion years (the evolutionary estimation of the Earth's age), the probability of them being arranged *even 1 time* in an order capable of producing *just one protein* is statistically zero. [(Statistically speaking, scientists regard anything with less than 1 chance in 10^{50} of occurring randomly as impossible or absurd (without supernatural input.)]

Adding to this impossibility, remember that the average protein contains 400, not only 100 amino acids, and even the smallest living creatures have *hundreds of proteins*, which must also be precisely ordered to make DNA. Evolutionists claim that the first living creature that arose from the primordial soup was a single-celled bacterium having about 100,000 base pairs of DNA nucleotides and 10,000 amino acids with at least 100 functional protein chains. As I've just shown, it's impossible for even one of the 100 proteins within this simple bacterium to be formed by pure chance over a 4.6 billion year time period. Statistically, evolution by pure chance is impossible. But the problems do not end there for the evolutionist.

The issue of chirality presents further statistical difficulties for evolutionists and their hypothetical first bacterium. Chirality explains the fact that all nucleotides in a DNA or RNA chain (I'll unravel the amazing mystery of these chains in a later chapter) must have a specific molecular conformation for the chain to work. *All* nucleotides *must be* on the right-handed side of the DNA chain. In addition, *all* 20 amino acid types *must be* arranged in a specific order on the left hand side for the protein chain to work. In other words, to create the first cell, *all* of the thousands of amino acids in the one hundred-plus functional protein chains would have had to suddenly combine at *exactly* the right time in an *exact* sequence, all on the left-handed side.

Also, *all* 100,000+ nucleotides of the evolutionist's hypothetical bacterium would have had to combine at *exactly* the right time in a specific right-handed sequence to form a functioning DNA molecule that directs cellular activity. The chance of getting 100,000+ properly oriented nucleotides is similar to the chance you'd have of flipping a coin 100,000 times and getting 100,000 heads in a row. To get the specific sequence of amino acids needed for life would require flipping 10,000 tails in a row. Getting both situations to occur is equal to the chances of correctly calling the side of 110,000 flips in a row. The odds of this happening are a staggering 1 in $10^{33,113}$ (1 with 33,113 zeros behind it). This is the same chance you would have of winning 4700 state lotteries in a row with a single ticket for each. The chances of correctly sequencing all 110,000 nucleotides and amino acids in a primordial soup is also equal to properly choosing a single marked particle from nearly 400 Universes as large as ours while being blindfolded. Forming the correct chirality in a primordial soup, or any other environment, even if all the necessary parts can be found, is clearly not only statistically impossible, but logically absurd as well.

Chirality alone is an insurmountable problem for evolutionists, but there are still other factors to consider in the formation of the first simple cell. The first of these would be the need for the correct sequencing of only life-specific amino acids, since only 20 of the 80 amino acids on Earth are life-specific. The chance of this correct sequencing occurring in the first cell is 1 in 10^{6021}. Also, since there are 20 different life-specific amino acids, there would be a 1 in 20 chance of randomly getting the right amino acid in the right spot on each of the 100+ protein chains, each including hundreds of amino acids. (Chirality only considered the orientation of amino acids, not the specific sequence.) The chance of each life-specific amino acid randomly appearing in the proper spot on the proper chain is 1 in $10^{13,010}$.

To further complicate things, the proper material for each gene must come together so that each gene is capable of carrying out its necessary body function. The most simple, single-celled bacterium contains between 265–350 genes vital to life. With 100,000 base pairs, the simplest bacterium requires about 377 base pairs to be correctly sequenced per gene. The chance of this happening in 265 genes is 1 in $10^{60,155}$. Adding to this, for DNA to properly direct the life function of a cell, the genes must also be sequenced correctly on the DNA chain. With 265 genes, the chance of this occurring is 1 in 10^{528}.

Adding together all the probabilities mentioned above, we'll discover that there is a 1 in $10^{112,827}$ chance for the simplest conceivable life form to randomly arise from a primordial soup assuming (and that's an impossibly *HUGE* assumption) that all the necessary ingredients were present. This is the same probability you'd have of winning 16,119 state lotteries in a row with a single ticket for each or picking a single marked electron out of more than 1300 Universes our size, while blindfolded!

The Problem of Irreducible Complexity

Michael Behe, Associate Professor of Biochemistry at Lehigh University, championed the concept of "irreducible complexity"[14] in his landmark book, *Darwin's Black Box—The Biochemical Challenge to Evolution*. This concept basically states that there are too many small cellular parts necessary in the very beginning for a cell to be the product of evolutionary chance. As B.G. Ranganathan explained, "The cell needs all its basic parts within their various functions for survival; therefore, if the cell had evolved, it would have meant that billions of parts would have had to come into existence at the same time, in the same place, and then simultaneously come together in a precise order."[15] If even one microscopic part is removed, or unordered, the first organism would have collapsed before life even started. The simultaneous intricate ordering of billions of tiny parts in a single cell is inconceivable without an Intelligent Organizer . . . a chaotic primeval explosion that came from nowhere and nothing is incapable of creating and ordering the intricate parts of the machinery of life.

The problems of irreducible complexity become even more profound when we consider the relationship between proteins and DNA. Proteins and DNA are two of the most vital parts that would have been needed in the first cell, and both need each other to exist. Proteins are formed from DNA and DNA is formed from proteins. Due to this fact, even evolutionary biologists have now conceded that it is impossible for either to have formed in a primordial soup. Since one cannot be formed without the existence of the other, this means that a Creator was required to make *at least* one of these to begin the process. There is no way around it for evolutionists . . . the DNA-protein complex proves undoubtedly that a Creator must exist . . . if He didn't, then neither DNA nor protein would exist. The fact that they do requires an act of creation by a Creator.

24

What are Some Evolutionists Saying about these Problems?

Evolutionists Sir Frederick Hoyle and Chandra Wickramasinghe reached similar conclusions during independent experiments designed to mathematically analyze the probability that life could have resulted from time, chance and the properties of matter. Following their research, they compared this probability to the chances that "a tornado sweeping through a junkyard might assemble a Boeing 747 from the materials therein."[16] (A Boeing 747 contains approximately 4.5 million non-flying parts that combine to produce flight. A human cell is far more complex and advanced than an airplane, containing at least billions of parts that must be perfectly coordinated to produce life, so the improbabilities are even greater than they described.) Further, they admitted that, "There must be a God."[17] Their research is powerful, positive evidence for the existence of an Intelligent Designer.

The probability of life arising from a primordial soup is an insurmountable problem for evolutionists even if all the necessary ingredients were there, but it is absolutely incredulous when you consider that this material must have come from a chaotic, primeval explosion that admittedly came from nowhere and nothing. The following are two theories that typify the radical 'explanations' given by some evolutionists for how the Universe originated from a primeval 'Big Bang' and how life originated from a primordial soup. One theory was described in this excerpt from *The American Spectator* . . . "From historic Newborn, Michigan comes more evidence in support of the Big Bang theory of creation. On July 12th, an abandoned ranger headquarters at Tahquahemon Falls State Park blew skyward, sending debris a hundred feet into the atmosphere and alarming campers 14 miles away. The explosion now has been traced to bat manure that for decades had been generating methane gas until, in mid-July it became highly volatile and Kaboom! Scientists believe that a similar cataclysm eight million years ago gave us the beginnings of the Universe, though even scientists cannot account for those early bats . . . a world created by bat dung is too depressing to contemplate."[18]

25

As part of another theory, some evolutionists have suggested that perhaps aliens from another planet, galaxy or Universe evolved and then sent the materials needed for life on a rocket ship to Earth, where it evolved here. But, even by their own admission, noted atheists Carl Sagan and Francis Crick, while attempting to build the case for extraterrestrial engineering of human life, estimated that the chance of this actually happening is 1 in $10^{2,000,000,000}$ even if aliens do exist.[19] Evolutionists are clearly grasping at straws when trying to explain the origins of life.

It seems clear that belief in evolution is based purely on faith, since there is no evidence to support their position. While Christians also hold to faith in God, we have a more reasonable case since all the evidence is on our side. Molecular biology, which studies the microscopic complexity of living things, has led to amazing discoveries about the structure and function of cells and their parts. With the electron microscope, X-ray crystallography, and nuclear magnetic resonance imaging technology of today, we have been able to probe further into the intricacies of life than ever before, and what we've found is simply magnificent and astounding. Each new cellular level discovery is creating another hurdle that evolutionists can't overcome or explain away. The information in this second evidence has mentioned just a few of these hurdles.

The hard science of molecular biology, along with mathematics and statistics has made it obvious that the chance of life arising randomly from a primordial soup of amino acids is zero. The incredible cellular level designs that have been discovered by molecular biology are making it equally obvious that a supremely intelligent Designer who has orchestrated the symphony of life must exist. (We will delve deeper into the molecular design that exists in our own bodies in a chapter 8.)

EVIDENCE #3 - YOU CAME FROM SOMEWHERE

Evolutionists go even further than to say the complex and intricately ordered heavenly bodies and living creatures on Earth arose by pure chance from non-living particles. In addition, they believe these non-living particles resulted from nothing that came from nowhere. By admitting that a tiny hot ball existed before the 'Big Bang,' they are actually promoting the idea that matter resulted from nothing. Professor Donald DeYoung said that, "Since every secular origin theory begins with preexisting matter, none is really an *origin* theory at all! Aside from accepting supernatural creation from nothing, science must begin with material from an unknown source."[20] The evolutionary belief that matter resulted from nothing is an absolutely ridiculous theory that has no basis whatsoever in science. The scientific truth is that matter does not result from nothing . . . it simply does not create itself. The Universe can't be self-caused, since matter would need to exist before it created itself into existence. This evolutionary belief is not only scientifically absurd, but is logically absurd as well.

Your body, along with everything else in the Universe, is made entirely of matter. Did you come from nothing? Did the chair you're sitting on or floor you're standing on come from nothing? Did everything you see come from nothing? This is what evolutionists would like you to believe. Clearly, it takes *A LOT* more faith to believe that non-existent, non-intelligent matter is your creator than it does to believe that an Intelligent, Almighty God is your Creator.

Some may ask, 'Where did God come from?' Prominent scholar Norman Geisler answered the question by saying, (please read carefully) "If something exists and if nothing cannot cause something, then it follows that something must necessarily and eternally exist. It must exist eternally since, if nothing ever was, then nothing could now be. But something undeniably now is. Therefore, something always has been. Likewise, something must always have been because nothing cannot cause something. But if something is and if nothing cannot cause something, then it follows that something must necessarily always have been. And, since the cause must bear some significant similarity to its effect, which is an intelligent moral being,

27

then it is reasonable to posit an intelligent, moral cause of everything else that exists. If this is so, then the theistic argument for God is sound."[21] Geisler continued, "God, since he never began to exist, would not require a cause, for he never came into being. This is not a special pleading for God, since this is exactly what the atheist has always claimed about the universe: that it is eternal and uncaused."[22] He continued, "Asking 'What caused the first cause?' is like asking 'What does a square triangle look like?' or 'What is the smell of blue?' It is a meaningless question. Triangles can't have four sides; colors don't smell; and first causes don't have causes because they are first."[23]

The existence of a supreme, eternal Creator is a logical necessity. This eternal Creator must be superior to His mortal creation or He would not have been capable of creating and sustaining the Universe. This God is not bound by time, space and the forces of the Universe like we are, since He is the One Who made it all. God is timeless, eternal and no space or force can contain Him. His life, unlike ours, has no beginning or end . . . He always has and always will be alive. He needed no Creator, since He is the Creator.

Despite the logical certainty of the existence of an eternal Creator, I realize that His existence is still hard to fathom with our finite minds. But even with finite minds, it still seems far more reasonable and satisfying to put faith in an all-powerful, always existent, supremely intelligent God as Creator than it is to place faith in non-existing, non-intelligent matter as the creator. The ultimate question is this . . . what or Who will you place your faith in . . . dead matter or a living God?

EVIDENCE #4 - FLIMSY FINDS

Evolutionists have presented many of their 'missing link' discoveries as compelling and factual explanations to human origins. But in reality, they have based their conclusions on the flimsiest of finds, and have twisted the facts from these flimsy finds to fit their theories. Some of the 'compelling finds' of evolutionists have later proven to be remains of a pig, donkey, or the result of a hoax. Other 'finds' have included an assortment of bone fragments found miles apart, which were pieced together to look like they've come from the same individual. Sometimes, simple backyard rocks have been pictured in textbooks and proclaimed to be tools of pre-human ancestors, while recently made footprints have been photographed and declared pre-human. Clearly, we can't automatically believe the evolutionary community when they profess they've found a 'missing link.'

Is Your Father an Ape? Part I - The Genetic and Social Evidence

One of the most common evolutionary misconceptions is that humans evolved from apes. Based on the speculation that human and ape DNA is 96–99% similar (although the genome of apes has not been fully mapped as in humans), evolutionists claim this as proof that humans evolved from apes. But are humans really that similar to apes, and even if we are, does that prove that we evolved from them? (Interestingly, milk chemistry tests indicate that the donkey is our closest relative, cholesterol level tests demonstrate that the garter snake is our next of kin, tear enzyme chemistry tests conclude that the chicken is humankind's closest relative and certain blood chemistry tests proclaim that the butter bean is our nearest genetic relative. Did we evolve from them?)

The amount of information contained in the 3.2 billion base pairs of a DNA molecule has been estimated to be equivalent to that found in 1,000 books, each with 500 pages. Evolutionists try to hide the fact that if human DNA is even 1% different from ape DNA, this still means there is a 30 million base pair difference, which is equal to the information found in 10 large books of information, containing a total of 3 million words. As we will see later, mutations and natural selection, the proposed primary shaping factors of evolution, are incapable of adding information, which is exactly what is required for an ape to evolve into a human. Evolution simply cannot span the at least 30 million base pair difference, nor any difference, between apes and humans.

It also can't explain the massive social gap between apes and humans. Evolutionist Roger Lewin admitted this gap when stating, "Our intelligence, our reflective consciousness, our extreme technological facility, our complex spoken language, our sense of moral and ethical values . . . each of these is apparently sufficient to separate us from nature."[24] Mark P. Cosgrove said, "If we are honest, we will face the facts and admit that we can find no evolutionary development to explain our unique speech center."[25] Other leading evolutionists have expressed the fact that there seems to be no evolutionary explanation for the existence of human language and in admitted embarrassment say that the evidence is something to be ignored. While evolutionists may try to ignore the vast gulf between apes and humans, any objective person seeking the truth should not. The bottom line is that you did not evolve from an ape.

Is Your Father an Ape? Part II - The Fossil Evidence

Despite what you may have learned in school and/or from the mouths of evolutionists speaking publicly, the fossil evidence concludes that we are not highly evolved apes. While evolutionists have declared that the fossil record provides evidence that humans evolved from apes or one of their 'ancestors,' the real story is completely different. Here is the real story on just a few of their 'missing link finds':

1) 'Ramapithecus' was considered the first 'hominid' (human-like creature) based on only a set of teeth. Further research proved that this fossil belonged to an extinct relative of the orangutan.

2) The famous 'Piltdown' fossil was discovered in 1953 and declared to be a half-human, half-ape skull. Evolutionists determined the fossil to be 500,000 years old, called it 'Dawn Man,' and wrote about 500 books on it. What they didn't know is that this 'discovery' was nothing more than a hoax involving the placement of an ape's jaw with a human skull. The hoax was deliberately placed to see how deeply evolutionists research their 'finds.' Apparently they didn't perform a detailed scientific analysis, since this hoax fooled paleontologists for forty-five years. Other examples highlighting the evolutionists' utter inability to accurately interpret their finds include:

3) 'Hesperithecus,' which was created from a single pig's tooth. Paleontologists and even dental experts were fooled into believing that it was a human tooth for nearly 14 years.

4) 'OCR man' was later proven to be based on the skull cap of a donkey.

5) 'Boise man' was the reconstruction of 400 separate bone fragments that were pieced together to make one supposedly genuine and homogeneous skull.

6) 'Dryopithecus man' was based only on a lower jaw fragment which was later shown to belong to an extinct ape.

7) 'Oreopithecus man' was built from only teeth and pelvis remains.

8) While trying to prove that the famous 'Lucy' fossil walked upright, evolutionists resorted to uncovering a knee joint found more than 200 feet deeper in the Earth and over two miles away. They tried to fool the world by declaring that this knee joint belonged to the same individual. In fact, they were only deluding themselves.

9) 'Australopithecus Africans' and 10) 'Australopithecus Robustus' have proven to be completely ape.

11) 'Homo Erectus,' 12)'Neanderthal Man,' and 13)'Cro Magnon Man' have proven to be completely human.

Clearly, neither genetic research nor fossil 'finds' prove that you evolved from an ape. Jerry Adler and John Carey summed up the true state of fossil evidence by saying, "The missing link between man and the apes . . . is merely the most glamorous of a whole hierarchy of phantom creatures. In the fossil record, missing links are the rule . . . the more scientists have searched for the transitional forms between species, the more they have been frustrated."[26]

Following 25 years of research in the field, Marvin Lubenow said, "The human fossil record is strongly supportive of the concept of Special Creation. On the other hand, the fossil evidence is so contrary to human evolution as to effectively falsify the idea that humans evolved. This is not the message we hear from a hundred different voices coming at us from a dozen different directions. But the human fossils themselves tell the real story."[27] Lubenow continued, "The popular myth is that the hominid fossil evidence virtually proves evolution. The reality is that this evidence has been a disappointment to evolutionists and is being de-emphasized (by evolutionists). In actuality, the human fossil evidence falsifies the concept of human evolution . . . On the other hand, since humans have been humans as far as one can go in the fossil record with no evidence of evolutionary ancestors, that fact constitutes positive evidence that we were created."[28]

Do Similarities Among Creatures Prove that We Came From A Common Ancestor?

Evolutionists also proclaim that since many creatures have similar biological features (although many biological and physiological differences exist between species) they must have arisen from a common primordial ancestral cell. This is pure speculation with absolutely no scientific evidence, but evolutionists still support the idea.

I must take the time to expose another evolutionary fraud which began in the late nineteenth century, and although it has been dismissed by evolutionists, still persists to a certain degree today. A common expression still written in High School and College textbooks is "ontogeny recapitulates phylogeny." This theory was promoted by the German biologist Ernst Haeckle who went to a fraudulent extreme to show that all life has a common ancestor by creating drawings that 'prove' the similarity of physical form in embryos from several distinct species. Later, these drawings were proven to be mythical misrepresentations and his conclusions were dismissed by the scientific community, even among evolutionists. Evolutionists have conclusively shown that Haeckle faked his drawings . . . but while they were a proven lie, still many generations were taught that Haeckle's drawings were concrete proof that all species evolved from a common ancestor.

This brings up another excellent point concerning the drawings some evolutionists use to depict what they think transitional animals (such as between a fish and frog) may have looked like. While these drawings are often presented as fact to the unsuspecting public and school children, they are really much closer to conceptual fantasies, as even many evolutionists now admit. There is no hard core evidence for the existence of these animals, yet sadly, many reconstructive drawings of speculative animals are still shown in our high schools and colleges today. Not knowing any better, these students accept what their teachers are saying as fact, while it really is not.

Rather than trusting in evolutionary fraud and speculation as the reason for homologous physical features in creatures, it is more plausible to believe that an intelligent Creator designed creatures with many of the same features, since He knew that they would cause His creation to be successful on this Earth. Just as an engineer applies wheels to roller-skates, bicycles and cars because they work, God has designed creatures with similar features that make them well-tuned to thrive on planet Earth.

More Evolutionary Failures From the Fossil Record

To expose another false evolutionary claim, I will return to the fossil record. Evolutionists claim that the order in the fossil record shows a steady progression of simpler life forms on the bottom to the most complex on the top, and declare this as evidence for evolution. Nothing could be further from the truth. In fact, the order of life forms in the fossil record is often the exact opposite to what evolutionists proclaim. Walter E. Lammerts, an expert in the field, has observed that, "The actual percentage of area showing this progressive order from the simple to the complex is surprisingly small. Indeed formations with very complex forms of life are found resting directly on the basic granites. Furthermore, I have in my own files a list of over 500 cases that attest to a reverse order, that is, simple forms of life resting on top of more advanced forms."[29] Evolutionists can't reasonably explain away these facts.

Another major embarrassment for evolutionists involves the existence of numerous 'living fossils.' These include the coelacanth, a fish species that was thought to be a link between fish and amphibians, which supposedly became extinct 70 million years ago, based on the evolutionary interpretation of the geologic column. Much to the shock of evolutionists, a living coelacanth identical in form to fossils from 70 million years ago was found in the waters near Madagascar in 1958. Jacques Millot, then director of the Madagascan Institute of Scientific Research, highlighted the importance of this find by saying, "Throughout the hundreds of millions of years, the coelacanths have kept the same form and structure. Here is one of the great mysteries of evolution."[30] Since then, hundreds of coelacanths have been found. Also based on the geologic interpretations of evolutionists, the tuatara should have died out 135 million years ago, the deep-sea mollusk 280 million years ago and a bacteria species found in the Gunflint Iron Formation of Southern Ontario, 1.9 billion years ago. Yet remarkably, and despite the evolutionary theory, all these creatures and more have been found alive today, with no change in their form or structure. These 'living fossils' are a powerful testimony of evolutionary stagnation throughout history. If these creatures have not evolved at all in a 70 million-1.9 billion year span, then nothing but faith can persuade someone that they ever did in the past or will in the future.

Evolutionist Roger Lewin reported this remarkable conclusion about fossil evidence for evolution following a conference of the world's leading evolutionists in Chicago . . . "Evidence from fossils now points overwhelmingly away from the classical Darwinism which most Americans learned in high school."[31] This conference took place in 1980 . . . evolutionists have known for nearly 25 years that the fossil record does not support the Darwinian theory of evolution, yet very sadly, the fossil record is still taught as positive evidence for evolution in our high schools and colleges today. I think it's time for the public to be made aware of this information.

Unfortunately, in many cases, evolution-biased high school teachers and college professors are trusted by their students as an absolute authority on the facts. In this fascinatingly honest admission, an evolutionary physicist professor discussed how he uses the trust of his students to spread his false message . . . "And I use that trust to effectively brainwash them . . . our teaching methods are primarily those of propaganda. We appeal—without demonstration—to evidence that supports our position. We only introduce arguments and evidence that supports the currently accepted theories and omit or gloss over any evidence to the contrary."[32] This evolutionary 'brainwashing' is far too common in our school systems, colleges and universities today. As I said before, it's time for the world to be made aware of the persistent lies of evolution, and to then completely reject and banish the theory.

EVIDENCE # 5 - NO CONCLUSIVE TRANSITIONAL FORMS

For either traditional Darwinian evolutionists or those holding to the more recent Punctuated Equilibrium theory of evolution (or any other conceivable branch of evolutionary theory) to be correct, the fossil record *must* contain transitional forms, where we can obviously see that one species is changing into another. In fact, if the 'theory of evolution' is true, there would be museums full of conclusive transitional fossils. But *there are absolutely none.* Evolutionists have been searching for a convincing fossil link for over 130 years since Darwin proposed his theory, but have found nothing at all. Marvin Lubenow said, "For a hundred years evolutionists paraded the fossils they had found as evidence for evolution. They promised more and better fossils in the future . . . (But by) the early 1970's, when it became obvious that we had more than an adequate sampling of the fossil record, the grim reality dawned that those transitional fossils were not to be found."[33] Even Darwin admitted that "if there are no intermediate forms, then I have devoted my life to a fantasy."[34] Sadly, that is exactly what Darwin did, since his theory bears no evidence.

The scientific fact is that every fossil ever found in the geologic record is a fully formed creature, without even a hint of the formation of transitional features. There are no reptiles with bird feathers or evidence of fish turning into frogs, which would be the case if evolution were true. Even the well known 'Archaeopteryx' fossil that is commonly used to support the evolution of birds from reptiles has failed to become a conclusive missing link, as now admitted by some evolutionists.

The crushing weight of fossil evidence prompted evolutionary paleontologist, George Gaylord Simpson to state, "The regular absence of transitional forms is not confined to mammals, but is an almost universal phenomenon, as has been long noted by paleontologists. It is true of almost all orders of all classes of animals, both vertebrate and invertebrate. A fiorti (even more strongly), it is also true of the classes, and of the major animal phyla, and it is apparently also true of analogous categories of plants."[35] David Kitts, a prominent evolutionary paleontologist from the University of Oklahoma, admitted, "Despite the bright promise that paleontology provides a means of 'seeing' evolution, it has presented some nasty difficulties for evolutionists, the most notorious of which is the presence of 'gaps' in the fossil record. Evolution requires intermediate forms between species and paleontology does not provide them."[36]

The "Cambrian Explosion"

Not only is every fossil found non-transitional, complex and similar to species today, but a large majority appears abruptly and together in the fossil record during the first (lowest) layer in the geologic column, called the Cambrian. Evolutionists Marshall Kay and Edwin H. Colbert observed, "The introduction of a variety of organisms in the early Cambrian, including such complex forms of the arthropods as the trilobites, is surprising . . . The introduction of abundant organisms in the record would not be so surprising if they were simple. Why should such complex organic forms be in rocks about 6 hundred million years old and be absent or unrecognized in the records of the preceding 2 billion years? . . . If there has been evolution of life, the absence of the requisite fossils in the rocks older than the Cambrian is puzzling."[37] Fellow evolutionists R.S.K. Barnes, P. Calow, P.J.W. Olive and D.W. Golding added, "Most of the animal phyla that were represented in the fossil record first appear, fully formed, in the Cambrian."[38] DuNouy noted, "In brief, each group, order or family seems to be born suddenly . . . when we discover them, they are already completely differentiated."[39] Richard Dawkins said, "It is as though they (Cambrian fossils) were just planted there, without any evolutionary history."[40] Respected Christian apologist Norman Geisler explained, "The fossil evidence clearly gives a picture of mature, fully functional creatures suddenly appearing and staying very much the same."[41]

It is also interesting that more species are found in the Cambrian strata than are present today. In fact, while there are currently only 38 different animal phyla (distinct groups), 50 different phyla have been discovered in Cambrian rock. There were actually more animals present in the beginning of geologic time than there are right now, which is an impossibility for evolutionists. According to their theory, there should be many more species today than in the beginning, but this is clearly not the case. Charles Darwin explained the significance of the fact that there are a massive number of well formed, non transitional species that appear first in the fossil record by saying, "If numerous species, belonging to the same genera or families, have really started into life at once, the fact would be fatal to the theory of evolution."[42] The barrage of evidence has prompted leading evolutionist Stephen Gould to admit that, "The Cambrian explosion was the most remarkable and puzzling event in the history of life."[43]

While puzzling and fatal to the theory of evolution, the fact that massive amounts of life forms appear suddenly and fully formed at the very beginning fits perfectly with the predictions of creationists. The explosive worldwide fossil evidence found in the Cambrian layer powerfully contradicts the evolutionary premise that all life arose gradually from a single cell, and suggests that a dramatic event occurred during which all creatures were formed and then buried at once. The concrete fossil evidence firmly rejects the theory of evolution and correlates perfectly with God's creative act and the worldwide flood as described in Genesis, the first book in the Bible.

EVIDENCE #6 - YOUNG EARTH EVIDENCE

Determining the exact age of the Earth and the Universe is not essential in an argument destroying the 'theory of evolution,' since there is so much other great evidence. But it is an issue that many in the world seem intrigued by, and I do believe the evidence strongly refutes the evolutionary timetable while supporting the biblical timeline, so I've decided to tackle the issue briefly here.

There certainly is a wide gulf between the age proposed by evolutionists and biblical creationists. Evolutionists generally believe the Earth is about 4.6 billion years old, although they admit they know little about what happened during the first 4 billion years of their timetable. Biblical creationists, in contrast, generally believe the Earth is less than 10,000 years old based on the known events of history. A study of the evidence will show that the biblical age is more reasonable than the evolutionary age. The following is a sampling of evidence that rebukes the hypothetical evolutionary timescale and supports the biblical age:

The Inaccuracy of Dating Methods

Carbon-14 and potassium-argon dating methods (two of the most popular methods used by evolutionists) have proven to have many inconsistencies, as admitted by scientists, and should not be relied upon as absolutely precise and reliable measures of the Earth's age. Admittedly, errors and assumptions are common with these dating methods, giving unbelievable dates in some cases. As a few of many examples, evolutionists using the potassium-argon dating method tested volcanic material from Hawaii that was *known* to less than 200 years old, but determined with this method that it was between 160 million and 3 billion years old. Using the Carbon-14 (radiocarbon) method, a shell from a *living* snail was found to be *dead for 26,000 years,* a freshly killed seal was considered dead for 1,300 years, and a 1 year old leaf was determined to be 400 years old! Concerning this method, evolutionist Robert Lee observed that, "The troubles of the radiocarbon dating method are undeniably deep and serious. No matter how 'useful' it is, the radiocarbon method is still not capable of yielding accurate and reliable results. There are gross discrepancies, the chronology is uneven and relative, and the accepted dates are actually selected dates."[44]

Marvin Lubenow said, "A very popular myth is that the radioactive dating methods are an independent confirmation of the geologic time scale and the concept of human evolution . . . The radioactive dating methods are a classic example of self-deception and circular reasoning. It is another of the myths of human evolution."[45] It is self-deceptive because evolutionists actually select a range of 'acceptable' dates for their specimens before they are tested, and throw out any dates that fall outside their selected dates. They only accept data that seems to support their timescale, and dismiss anything that doesn't . . . the dating schemes of evolutionists are biased and 'self-deceptive.' Sadly, they have been successful in persuading the general public to believe that their biased dates are correct. The methods of evolutionists are also circular since they use the fossil record to date the geologic strata they see and use the geologic strata they see to date the fossil record. So, again, they've already predetermined the date a fossil or geologic strata 'should' be before any testing is done. In reality, they don't know the actual date of either the fossils or the strata they appear in, so the dates they proclaim are arbitrary, biased and unreliable.

More Wrong Assumptions

Evolutionists insist that it takes millions of years for coal and oil to form and for trees to petrify. They declare that since these things exist, it proves the Earth is at least millions of years old. As usual, the evolutionists are wrong . . . they are simply spinning a tale to provide 'proof' for their philosophy. In fact, coal can be formed in 20 minutes in a laboratory and oil in about 2 hours. And given the right conditions, such as those which would be provided by a worldwide flood, there is no reason to believe that millions of years are required in nature. Trees can be petrified in the lab in two years, and many verified reports prove that wood can be petrified in nature within 25–50 years.

Do Dinosaurs Still Walk Among Us?

Dinosaurs are assumed to have become extinct about 65 million years ago, which is long before humans supposedly evolved on Earth, but the evidence suggests otherwise. First, the Bible, as well as many ancient history books in various libraries around the world give detailed descriptions of dinosaurs and their encounters with people. (Dinosaurs were called "dragons" before the word dinosaur was invented in 1841.) Very interestingly, evidence suggests that dinosaurs may still be alive. Australian Aborigines and natives in the Congo have recently reported seeing live dinosaurs, and have consistently pointed to pictures of dinosaurs when asked what these creatures looked like. There are also a very small, yet growing number of professional scientists who have documented sightings. Among those are biologist Marcellin Agnagna. Agnagna claims that he and his team saw a blackish-brown animal that was 16 feet long with a wide back, long neck and small head in the Congo. He wrote following the sighting, "It can be said with certainty that the animal we saw was Makele-mbembe (the native Congolese word for dinosaur); that it was quite alive, and furthermore, that it is known to many inhabitants of the Likonlala region."[46] Unfortunately, no one has been able to provide photographic evidence to date, but since expeditions are still occurring, we may have solid evidence in the near future.

If you don't believe this word of mouth evidence, then consider the concrete fact that dinosaurs and other creatures have been excavated and were found to still include soft body parts, red blood cells, hemoglobin and DNA. Why is this significant? Because these soft parts could not last for more than a few thousand years buried in the soil, even if carefully preserved . . . certainly not 65 million years. According to Scott R. Woodward, "Under physiological conditions, it would be extremely rare to find preserved DNA that was tens of thousands of years old."[47] This evidence strongly suggests that dinosaurs may have died out only a few thousand years ago, not millions of years ago, as evolutionists believe. While this exciting evidence presents serious problems for evolutionists, it fits very nicely with the timeline of the Bible.

Fascinating Fossil Discoveries Point Towards A Worldwide Flood

Evolutionists have also been shocked at the discovery of thousands of fossilized jellyfish, many bigger than a large dinner plate, and all with freshly preserved body parts. Also, fairly recently, fossilized catfish have been discovered in the 'Green River Formation.' H.P. Buchheim and R.C. Surdam, who conducted research at the site, found that "fossil catfish are distributed in the Green River basin over an area of 16,000 km^2 . . . the catfish range in length from 11 to 24cm, with a mean of 18cm. Preservation is excellent. In some specimens, even the skin and other soft parts, including the adipose fin, are well preserved."[48] This finding destroys the theories of the evolutionists . . . according to them, these fish must have remained exposed for at least hundreds to perhaps millions of years before they were completely buried. It defies both science and common sense to believe that these fish remained exposed that long without being decayed. The evidence clearly concludes that the fish were buried quickly, before scavengers could devour the carcasses.

Other examples abound, including the discovery of many fossil fish caught in the act of swallowing their last meal. Fish have also been found with smaller fish fossilized in their stomach cavities, and one ichthyosaur mother was fossilized while giving birth. These, and thousands of other awkwardly buried plant and animal fossils *worldwide*, provide rock solid evidence that the burial of creatures was quick and complete. It was quicker than swallowing, digestion and birth. It was also complete enough to perfectly preserve soft body parts, which would otherwise be decomposed if left exposed. It was also massive enough to bury in their tracks *billions* of creatures *worldwide*. This collection of creatures includes everything from tiny insects to behemoth dinosaurs. The evidence seems to clearly support the fact of a worldwide flood.

There are many more examples of fragile structures found perfectly preserved in rock layers that are supposedly millions of years old, including those discovered by Dr. Heribert Nilsson, former director of the Swedish Botanical Institute. He observed that ". . . insects and parts of flowers are preserved, even the most fragile structures. It is further astonishing that in certain cases the leaves have been deposited and preserved in a fully fresh condition. The chlorophyll is so well preserved that it has been possible to recognize the alpha and beta types. An extravagant fact, comparable to the preservation of the chlorophyll, was the occurrence of preserved soft parts of the insects; muscles, corium, epidermis, keratin, colour stuffs as melanin and lipochrome, glands and the contents of the intestines."[49] Dr. N.O. Newell, paleontologist at the American Museum of Natural History, adds, "More than 6 thousand remains of vertebrate animals and a great number of insects, mollusks and plants were found in these deposits. The compressed remains of soft tissues of many of the animals showed details of cellular structure and some of the specimens had undergone but little chemical modification . . . well preserved bits of hair, feathers and scales are among the oldest known examples of essentially unmodified preservation of these structures. The stomach content of beetles, amphibians, fishes, birds and mammals provide direct evidence about eating habits. Bacteria of two kinds were found in the excrement of crocodiles and another was found on the trachea of a beetle. Fungi were identified on leaves and the original plant pigments chlorophyll and coproporphyrin were found preserved in some of the leaves."[50] Newell continued, "There are innumerable well-documented records of preservation of tissues of animals and plants in pre-Quaternary rocks."[51] Nilsson stated, "Just as in the case of the chlorophyll, we are dealing with things that are easily destroyed, disintegrating in but a few days or hours. The incrustation must therefore have been very rapid."[52] What Nilsson is saying is that it is impossible to find such fragile biological parts in exquisitely preserved detail unless they were covered up quickly and completely before scavengers could tear them apart. They certainly could not exist undecomposed for millions of years while they were slowly covered, as evolutionists propose.

Nilsson makes another interesting statement concerning the insects he observed, "The insects are of modern types and their geographical distribution can be ascertained. It is then quite astonishing to find that they belong to all regions of the Earth, not only to the Paleoarctic regions, as was expected."[53] Nilsson's insects are not an isolated case either . . . it is a worldwide phenomenon that demands a worldwide cause, since this is not a typical natural occurrence. How did all these various species from different parts of the world end up being buried in the same place at the same time?

Even more striking is the existence of diverse, well-preserved fossil graveyards spanning depths up to 1500 feet thick in certain locations, and averaging hundreds of feet thick worldwide. South African paleontologist Robert Broom estimated, "that there are eight hundred thousand million skeletons of vertebrate animals in the Karoo formation."[54] Henry S. Ladd of the U.S. Geological Survey described the fossilized herring fossil beds of California by saying that "more than a billion fish, averaging 6 to 8 inches in length, died on 4 square miles of bay bottom."[55] Other sites which exemplify the finding of massive animal graveyards worldwide include the La Brea Pits in Los Angeles, which contains tens of thousands of animals from all over the world, both living and extinct. (According to

42

evolutionary theory, each of these animals, collectively *representing all regions of the world*, have fallen into the sticky pits by accident over time.) Other examples include the Sicilian hippopotamus beds, which are so extensive that they've been mined by bulldozers as a source of commercial charcoal; the great mammal beds of the Rockies, as well as dinosaur beds of the Black Hills, Gobi Desert, and Dinosaur National Monument in Utah and Colorado.[56]

It's not just great depths of animal remains that have been discovered either, since 300–400 feet of plant remains have been found compressed into coal. How is it possible for such great thicknesses of diverse plant and animal remains to accumulate worldwide for millions of years without decomposition, as evolutionists contend? The answer is that it is impossible by the evolutionary timetable. Nilsson, an evolutionist for 40+ years, gives us the only reasonable answer . . . "The geologic and paleobiological facts are impossible to understand unless the explanation is accepted that they are the final result of an allochthonous (flood transport, sedimentation and burial) process, *including the whole earth.*"[57] (Emphasis mine) Many other scientists have confirmed that the worldwide flood, as described in Genesis is necessary for the fossil record we see today. And if a worldwide flood occurred, as the evidence strongly suggests, then the earth is not billions of years old as the evolutionists proclaim.

The worldwide discovery of thousands of well preserved tracks from a wide array of creatures has also been uncovered. Many other fragile features such as fine, water-formed ripple marks and even raindrop impressions have been found encased and perfectly preserved in rock. How could these intricate features survive unless they were preserved quickly? Even if impressed on a hard rock surface, markings such as animal tracks and ripple marks will erode within a few decades. These fragile features certainly could not have lasted millions of years while another soil layer was slowly laid down, as evolutionists say. I would suggest to you that the only way for fragile footprints, ripple marks and raindrops to be found well preserved worldwide is the reality of a worldwide flood that quickly covered these features with sediment and water. There is no other plausible explanation.

More Fascinating Fossil Discoveries

The fossil record is full of many other problems for evolutionists. Consider the following . . . in a lab, 30–40 dormant bacteria species were removed from the intestines of bees encased in amber in the Dominican Republic. When cultured, the bacteria actually grew, much to the shock of evolutionists, who claim, based on their dating methods, that the amber and the bacteria in it, is 25–40 million years old. The same bacteria species, *Bacillus,* has been found encased in '250–650 million year old' rocks, and was still alive! Bacteria can remain dormant for a long time, but even they don't have zero metabolism . . . they would starve to death long before 250 million years were up. In another failure for evolutionists, coal beds have been found containing fossilized flowering plants, which supposedly didn't evolve until 100 million years *after* the coal bed formed. In a similar case, cocoons of wasps have been found fossilized inside '270 million year old' petrified trees in Arizona. The amazing thing is that evolutionists claim the wasps evolved about 100 million years *after*

the tree they were fossilized in was petrified.

Fossils have also been found in places and positions that are impossible according to evolutionary theory. For example, did you know that fossilized sea creatures can be found on nearly every mountaintop in the world, including Mt. Everest? One recent find included the excavation of about 500 gigantic, fossilized giant oysters that were buried 13,000 feet high in the Andes mountains, about 250 miles southeast of Lima, Peru. The obvious question is how this collection of 12 foot wide, 650 pound oysters ended up buried 13,000 feet above sea level. Evolutionists say that they got there when a massive tectonic plate under the Pacific Ocean collided with the South American plate, causing the Andes, and its fossils to uplift. They also claim that the oysters are from the Jurassic period, and are about 200 million years old. This presents a serious problem, since it is well known that the erosion rate outpaces uplift rates. In fact, the Andes range, as they stand now, will completely erode in 56 million years at the present rates. The 200 million year date for these giant oysters seems impossible. In addition to the oysters, evolutionists also have no logical answer for the presence of fossilized sea creatures on mountaintops around the world. It is very reasonable to think that sea creatures were deposited on mountaintops largely as a result of the worldwide flood, for this is what the evidence suggests.

Polystrate fossils, which include fossilized plants and animals extending through different 'evolutionary ages' in the geologic record, are another major problem for evolutionists, and is further evidence that their dating scheme is flawed. For example, did you know that many polystrate trees throughout the world have been found completely encased in rock, extending through several layers, with the top of the trees no further decayed than the bottom? This indicates that the trees were covered up quickly and completely, not over a long period of time. The evidence is better explained by a worldwide flood than evolution.

Also consider the example of an evolutionary professor who discovered a fossilized shellfish shaped like an ice-cream cone standing on its tip. The amazing thing about the location of this shellfish, as reported by the evolutionist, is that it spanned two different geologic layers that were separated by a supposed 20 million years. The evolutionist wondered, as I do, how the shellfish could have remained standing on its tip for 20 million years without falling over or being decayed as it was slowly buried. The fact is that it is impossible for a shellfish to stand on its tip for 20 million years without falling over or being decomposed. The only way for this shellfish and other fossils to be preserved is for the living organism to be rapidly buried under sediment and water, the exact conditions that would be caused by a flood. Even evolutionists have now conceded that fossil formation requires flood conditions on at least a localized scale. The massive, worldwide scale on which these fossils have been found demands more than a series of localized floods and absolutely requires a worldwide flood.

Another striking example of a polystrate fossil was a well preserved skeleton of an 80 foot long baleen whale discovered by miners in Lompoc, California in 1976. The most interesting thing about the whale is that it was found standing at a perfect 180 degree angle *on its tail.* According to the evolutionary geologic dating system, this whale died while standing on its tail and remained standing on the tail for many millions of years while it was slowly buried, remaining undecomposed throughout this vast period of time. This is obviously an impossible situation, but it is what evolutionists would like you to believe. In contrast, a very reasonable explanation for the whale's body being encased and preserved at a 180 degree angle through several rock layers is a worldwide flood, which would quickly cover the body in layers of sediment before scavengers and the ravages of weather could decompose its skeleton.

Population Dynamics and Genetic Evidence

Here's another good reason to believe the evolutionary age of the Earth must be incorrect . . . if humans have existed on this Earth for nearly one million years as evolutionists say, then why hasn't this planet experienced overpopulation issues long before now? The world's average population growth over the recorded centuries has been 2 percent per year. Beginning with one human couple, and conservatively figuring the average population growth over the years to be a mere 1/2 percent, it would only take 4,000 years to produce the world population we have today. If the Earth was really as old as evolutionists say, and humans have been around for about 1 million years, then there would be trillions upon trillions of people living on this planet. (At the very least, there would be trillions upon trillions of gravesites.) Certainly this has never happened, so this is another major strike against the evolutionary timetable.

In contrast, the fact that it would take about 4,000 years at a 1/2 percent growth rate to reach the world population of today fits perfectly with the Biblical timetable, which says that the worldwide flood wiped out nearly all humans around 4,000 years ago. From this point, according to the Bible, the 8 remaining individuals (Noah, his wife, his sons and their wives) propagated the Earth. The biblical timetable and the current world population mesh perfectly, while the evolutionary timetable doesn't even come close.

Interestingly, dramatic new mitochondrial DNA evidence (called the Noah's Ark hypothesis) strongly suggests that all humankind originated approximately 6,000 years ago from one single woman. Parallel research on the Y chromosome has revealed that all humans came from one single man, who also lived about 6,000 years ago. Even famous evolutionary paleontologist Roger Lewin admitted, "The mitochondrial DNA technique appears to support the Noah's Ark hypothesis."[58] This exciting new evidence provides further support for the original creation of Adam and Eve in the Garden of Eden about 6,000 years ago as presented in the book of Genesis.

Based on the evidence I've already shown, it should be clear that it's time for evolutionists to revise their timescale. Our earth is certainly not several billion years old, as evolutionists claim, but is very possibly only several thousand years old, corresponding exactly with the biblical timeline. I could provide much more evidence against the evolutionary time scale, including exciting new research that demonstrates the Grand Canyon was formed as a result of the worldwide flood several thousand years ago as described in the Bible, not over millions of years, plus other more technical arguments such as the decay rate of the Earth's magnetic field, amount of helium in the atmosphere, volume of salt in the sea, and the rate at which the moon is receding from the Earth, but I see no need to continue beating a dead horse. If you would like to further study all the various evidences against all aspects of the evolutionary theory, including the age of the Earth, I'd point you to several excellent sources that are listed in the "Recommended Reading" section near the end of this book.

EVIDENCE# 7- MUTATION AND NATURAL SELECTION AREN'T ENOUGH

In review, evolutionists believe that a tiny hot ball of non-intelligent matter which came from nothing and nowhere exploded violently, and ultimately created, among other things, a chaotic primordial soup of dead particles and energy on Earth. Then something miraculous happened to create the first intricately ordered cells of life, which, as we've seen before, is biologically and statistically impossible. But let's play along again and imagine for a second that matter created itself before it existed, that the "Big Bang" really did happen and that life somehow arose from the dead particles of a chaotic primordial soup.

Following from their impossibly monumental assumptions that all these events happened, evolutionists then suggest that mutations and natural selection ('survival of the fittest' genes in a population) are the main shaping factors that caused primitive life to evolve into the awesome diversity of intricately ordered living organisms we see today. Evolutionists declare that since we can observe species changing slightly through these mechanisms and with the passage of time we therefore have evidence for 'Molecules to Man' macroevolution.

Evolutionary Misconceptions

First, let me dispel a misconception that many evolutionists have long held against biblical creationists. Some argue that biblical creationists believe God made fixed, rigid, unchanging life forms, where each individual in a species is identical or nearly identical to all others. This **is not** what the Bible teaches . . . I would point you to Genesis 30:39 for just one example. The Bible does not teach uniformity, but diversity in genetics and phenotypes (outward display of inward genetics) among individuals of a species. I believe the Bible even allows the possibility for new species to form as part of an original kind (such as the dog kind, cat kind, cattle kind, frog kind, horse kind, etc . . .) with a large, original gene pool.

We can still see remnants of a large, diverse, original gene pool in humankind, for example. Scientists have estimated that if it were physically possible, just two human parents could produce far more children than all the atoms in the known Universe, without getting two exactly the same. (A combination of genetics with statistics reveals that up to 10^{2017} genetically distinct children could be produced from one single couple.) Humankind is a great example of the incredible genetic diversity God has built into each kind He created. He included such incredible genetic diversity in His creation so that each kind could successfully adapt to and exploit a variety of habitats on Earth by *losing* unsuitable genes and expressing suitable ones. This is a wonderful design that promotes the survival of each original created kind.

That being said, I will agree with the evolutionists that it is possible for species to change slightly with the passage of time, especially when they are geographically isolated into unique environments. I will also agree that natural selection is the chief shaping factor in the changing of species. Natural selection wonderfully explains the fact of adaptation (the shifting around of existing genetic information to allow creatures to adapt to long-term environmental changes.) Natural selection is a good explanation for how species adapt, but whether it is adequate to allow the formation of new species is a matter of strong debate. As professor Dean H. Kenyon stated in an affidavit presented to the U.S. Supreme Court, ". . . let us dispose of a common misconception. The complete transmutation of even one animal species into a different species has never been directly observed either in the laboratory or in the field."[59] Richard B. Goldschmidt admitted, "It is true that nobody thus far has produced a new species or genus, etc., by macromutation. It is equally true that nobody has produced even a species by the selection of micromutations."[60] Steven M. Stanley clearly supported these claims by saying, ". . . no human has ever seen a new species form in nature."[61]

Lane P. Lester and Raymond G. Bohlin have found that animals can only change to a certain extent. They said, "A rule that all breeders recognize is that there are fixed limits to the amount of change that can be produced."[62] But whether natural selection is capable of forming a new, reproductively isolated species or not, really makes no difference. Even if it could be demonstrated that entirely new species have formed, it does not provide any evidence for macroevolution. This is because every time a species changes, it *LOSES* genetic information.

The Theory of Evolution Crumbles into Ruin

Because of this loss, natural selection, often harmful mutations and geographic isolation, combined with other factors, are simply not enough to explain 'Molecules to Man' macroevolution. It is not enough to explain how you arose from a primordial soup of dead particles and energy. For an original unicellular life form with 'only' 100,000 base pairs of DNA in a primordial soup to ultimately become a fish, bird, or human with 3.2 billion base pairs per DNA molecule, or anything else, requires an immense addition of genetic information. Natural selection and mutation always cause *a loss of genetic information.* Therefore, natural selection, mutation, and thus evolution cannot explain how more complex, highly ordered organisms like humans or even simpler bacteria can arise from super primitive original life forms. To say that humans evolved from molecules is as ridiculous as saying that if a business loses a little money each year, the losses will ultimately add up to a profit.

Dr. Lee Spetner from John Hopkins University states in his scholarly and highly researched book, *Not by Chance* that, "The neo-Darwinian theory is supposed to explain how the information of life has been built up by evolution. The essential biological difference between a human and a bacterium is in the information they contain. All other biological differences follow from that. The human genome has much more information than the bacterial genome. *Information cannot be built up by mutations that lose it.*"[63] (Emphasis mine) He further explains following his studies that, "All point mutations that have been studied on the molecular level turn out to reduce the genetic information and not to increase it . . . Not even one mutation has been observed that adds a little information to the genome. That surely shows that there are not millions upon millions of potential mutations the theory demands. There may well not be any. The failure to observe even one mutation that adds information is more than just a failure to find support for the theory. It is evidence against the theory. We have here a serious challenge against the neo-Darwinist theory."[64] Mutations only work to cause changes within existing genetic information, and instead of creating new and improved information in the form of a new species, they always result in a loss or change of genetic information, and 99.9999 . . . % of the time those losses or changes are harmful and help lead to the destruction of the species. As Spetner said, this is "a serious challenge against the neo-Darwinist theory."

Harvard evolutionist Richard Lewontin recognized the limitations of natural selection by stating, "Natural selection operates essentially to enable organisms to maintain their state of adaptation rather than to improve it."[65] Alfred Russell Wallace, considered to be the co-inventor of the theory of natural selection with Charles Darwin, later abandoned the theory upon closer examination of the evidence. He concluded, "(I) found this argument (for natural selection) convincing until I attempted to explain the advanced state of human faculties."[66] He realized that a super complex human could not have arisen by chance from much simpler bacteria, and concluded that, "A superior intelligence has guided the development of man in a definite direction and for a special purpose."[67] Many former evolutionists have reached the same conclusion.

Roger Lewin, recounting the results of a conference including the world's leading evolutionists in Chicago, recorded that "The central question of the Chicago conference was whether the mechanisms (mutation and natural selection) underlying microevolution (adaptation) can be extrapolated to explain the phenomenon of macroevolution. At the risk of doing violence to the positions of some of the people at the meeting, the answer can be given as a clear, No!"[68] Even evolutionists are beginning to doubt that natural selection and mutation are the mechanisms that drive molecules to man macroevolution. Those still clinging to the hope that these mechanisms provide the answer are simply sweeping the facts under the rug.

Macroevolution through natural selection and mutation (or any other proposed mechanism) is a sophisticated sounding argument for those evolutionists who still accept it, but it is really a pointless one, since they must first answer unanswerable questions such as how matter can create itself before it exists, or how complex life can arise by pure chance from non-life? Only then can they even begin to think of discussing the evolution of all things through natural selection and mutation. And yet even here, we can see their argument fail. Evolution is a philosophy whose foundations are crumbling on all fronts.

EVIDENCE #8 - FAILURE ADMITTED

To conclude this chapter, I'd like to drive the final nail in the coffin of the evolutionary theory by further highlighting the admission of failure by many former and current evolutionists. These admissions, some by the most prominent past and present leaders of the theory, are perhaps the most powerful and condemning evidence against evolution . . . if evolutionists admit the failure of their own theory, then why should we believe it?

Following are just some of the additional quotes from former or current evolutionists that I've collected during my ten years of research on the subject. ALL additional quotes (to the best of my knowledge) are in context from former/current evolutionists or non-creationists. This is a fairly large collection of quotes, but I certainly could have added a lot more . . . this is how overwhelming the self-admitted evidence against evolution is. I would strongly encourage you to read them all, and use them in your own debates against evolutionists. I've broken the quotes into 5 subject areas which follow the evolutionary timeline from the supposed 'big-bang' origin of the Universe through the formation of all the species on Earth today. I hope this format will make for easier understanding and convenience.

Concerning the Origin of the Universe . . . The Big Bang Fizzles Out

1) "Despite the widespread acceptance of the Big Bang theory as the working model for interpreting new findings, not a single important prediction of the theory has yet been confirmed and substantial evidence has accumulated against it."[69]—Tom Van Flandern

2) "The evidence is accumulating that redshift (a major component of the evolutionary origin of the Universe) is a shaky measuring rod."[70]—Margaret Burbidge

3) Concerning 'dark matter' and 'dark energy,' the matter and energy that evolutionists say would exist if the Big Bang actually occurred, David B. Cline said that evolutionists, ". . . know little about that sea. The terms we use to describe its components, 'dark matter' and 'dark energy' serve mainly as expressions of our ignorance."[71] (I don't believe evolutionists are ignorant . . . many are brilliant, but misguided minds.)

4) ". . . most every prediction by theorists about planetary formation has been wrong."[72]—Scott Tremaine

5) "Yet non stop erosion poses a difficult problem for the very existence of Saturn's opaque rings—the expected bombardment rate would pulverize the entire system in only 10,000 years!"[73]—Jeffrey N. Cuzzi

6) "The whole subject of the origin of the moon must be regarded as highly speculative."[74]—Robert C. Haynes

7) "Even the most enthusiastic cosmologist will admit that current theories of the nature of the Universe have some big holes."[75]—Robert Matthews

8) "Nobody really understands how star formation proceeds. It's really remarkable."[76]—Rogier A. Windhorst

9) "There is much doubt, however, that galaxies evolve from one type to another at all."[77]—George Abell

10) "We cannot even show convincingly how galaxies, stars, planets and life arose in the present Universe."[78]—Michael Rowan

11) "Indeed big bang cosmology has become a bandwagon of thought that reflects faith as much as objective truth."[79]—G. Burbidge

12) "Nobody has the foggiest idea what happened the Tuesday before the Big Bang. In truth, we have no clue."[80]—Bob Berman

13) "No one knows where the material that formed the Universe came from."[81]—John Guest

14) (According to the "Big Bang" model), "There shouldn't be galaxies out there at all, and even if there are galaxies, they shouldn't be grouped together the way they are. The problem explaining the existence of the galaxies has proved to be one of the thorniest in cosmology. By all rights, they just shouldn't be there, yet there they sit. It's hard to convey the depth of the frustration that this simple fact induces among scientists."[82]—evolutionist Dr. James Trefil, professor of physics at George Mason University when asked to explain some of the fundamental problems of the "Big Bang" model

15) "When I began my career as a cosmologist some twenty years ago, I was a convinced atheist. I never in my wildest dreams imagined that one day I would be writing a book purporting to show that the central claims of Judeo-Christianity are in fact true, that these claims are straightforward deductions of the laws of physics as we now understand them. I have been forced into these conclusions by the inexorable logic of my own special branch of physics."[83]—former evolutionist, Dr. Frank Tipler

Concerning the Rise of Early Life . . . Primordial Soup Blues

1) "Little is known about what happened during the first 85 percent of Earth's history."[84]—John Guest

2) "One has only to contemplate the magnitude of this task to concede that the spontaneous generation of a living organism is impossible."[85]—George Wald, Professor of Biology at Harvard University

3) "All of these trees of life with their branches of our ancestors, that's a lot of nonsense."[86]—famous fossil hunter Mary Leakey said this 3 months before her death

4) "It is futile to pretend to the public that we understand how an amoeba evolved into a man, when we cannot tell our students how a human egg produces a skin cell or a brain cell."[87]—Dr. Jerome J. Lejeune, discoverer of the cause of Down's syndrome

5) "Gee is adamant that all the popular stories about how the first amphibians conquered the dry land, how the birds developed wings and feathers for flying, how the dinosaurs went extinct, and how humans evolved from apes are just products of our imagination, driven by prejudices and preconceptions."[88]—Peter Bowler

6) "The likelihood of the formation of life from inanimate matter is one to a number with 40 thousand naughts (zeros) after it. It is enough to bury Darwin and the whole theory of evolution. There was no primeval soup, neither on this planet nor on any other, and if the beginnings of life were not random, they therefore must have been the product of purposeful intelligence."[89]—Sir Frederick Hoyle, after mathematically analyzing just one small portion of the chirality problem

7) "More than 30 years of experimentation on the origin of life in the fields of chemical and molecular evolution have led to a better perception of the immensity of the problem of the origin of life on Earth rather than to its solution. At present, all discussions on principle theories and experiments in the

field either end in a stalemate or in a confession of ignorance."[90]—Klaus Dose

8) "Molecular evolution is not based on scientific authority . . . Since there is no authority on which to base claims of
knowledge, it can be truly said, the assertion of Darwinian
molecular evolution is merely bluster."[91]—Michael Behe

9) "If a theory claims to be able to explain some phenomenon
but does not generate even an attempt at an explanation, then
it should be banished. In effect, the theory of Darwinian
molecular evolution has not published (evidence) and so it
should perish."[92]—Michael Behe

10) "In the face of the enormous complexity that modern biochemistry has uncovered in the cell, the scientific community is paralyzed."[93]—Michael Behe

11) "The simplicity that was once expected to be the foundation
of life has proven to be a phantom; instead, systems of hor-
rendous, irreducible complexity inhabit the cell."[94]—Michael
Behe

12) "The result of these cumulative efforts to investigate the cell,
to investigate life at the molecular level, is a loud, clear, piercing cry of design! The result is so unambiguous and so significant that it must be ranked as one of the greatest
achievements in the history of science."[95]—Michael Behe

13) "If it could be demonstrated that any complex organ existed
which could not possibly have been formed by numerous,
successive, slight modifications, my theory would absolutely
break down."[96]—Charles Darwin (Many complex "organs"
have been uncovered by modern molecular biology.)

14) "The first appearance of new beings is a mystery of mysteries."[97]—Charles Darwin

15) "No prebiotic simulation experiments have been reported in
which polymers are formed directly from simple inorganic
and organic starting materials"[98]—James Ferris of the
Rensselar Polytechnic Institute Department of Chemistry

16) "A recent conference on 'The Origin of Homochirality and
Life' made it clear that the origin of this handedness (chirality)
is a complete mystery to evolutionists."[99]—J. Cohen

17) "The real trouble (in explaining the evolution of the first cell in a primordial soup) arises because too much of the complexity seems to be necessary to the whole way in which organisms work."[100]—A.G. Cairns-Smith, pro - natural selection

18) Brilliant chemist and physicist, Professor Ilya Prigogine, winner of two Nobel Prizes in chemistry, admitted, "The statistical probability that organic structures and the most precisely harmonized reactions that typify living organisms would be generated by accident, is zero."[101]

19) "We have seen that living things are too improbable and too beautifully 'designed' to have come into existence by chance."[102]—Dr. Richard Dawkins, one of the world's leading evolutionists

20) "The origin of life by chance in primordial soup is impossible . . . a practical person must conclude that life didn't happen by chance."[103]—Hubert Yockey

Concerning the Record of the Rocks . . . Fossil Flops

1) "Why is not every geologic formation and every stratum full of such intermediate links? Geology assuredly does not reveal any such finely graduated organic chain, and this is the most obvious and serious objection which can be urged against my theory."[104]—Charles Darwin, founder of the theory of evolution

2) "The absence of fossil evidence for intermediary stages between major transitions in organic design, indeed our inability, even in our imagination, to construct functional intermediates in many cases, has been a persistent and nagging problem for gradualistic accounts of evolution."[105]—the renowned evolutionist, Stephen Jay Gould

3) "The earliest and most primitive known members of every order already have the basic ordinal characters (are fully formed) . . ."[106]—George Gaylord Simpson

4) "The origins of most higher categories (of living organisms) are shrouded in mystery; commonly new higher categories appear abruptly in the fossil record without evidence of transitional forms."[107]—D.M Raup and S.M. Stanley

5) "No matter how far back we go in the fossil record of previous animal life upon earth, we find no trace of any animal forms which are intermediate between the various major groups or phyla . . . Since we have not the slightest evidence, either among the living or the fossil animals, or any intergrading types following the major groups, it is a fair supposition that there never have been any such intergrading types."[108]—A.H. Clark

6) "Practically all orders or families known appear suddenly and without any apparent transitions."[109]—R.B. Goldschmidt

7) "In the geologic sequence, the flowering plants (and other creatures) first appear suddenly and in great diversity in Cretaceous, 'upper dinosaur' rock."[110]—former evolutionist Dr. Gary Parker, whose findings provide evidence of an instantaneous creation of fully formed creatures and a life-burying worldwide flood, exactly as described in the Bible

8) "It is a simple ineluctable truth that virtually all members of a biota remain basically stable, with minor fluctuations, throughout their durations . . ."[111]—Paleontologist Niles Eldredge (If the fossil record has shown no change throughout the duration of time, then there has been no evolution . . . this fact alone destroys the theory.)

9) "We cannot identify ancestors or 'missing links,' and we cannot devise testable theories to explain how particular episodes of evolution came about."[112]—Peter J. Bowler

10) It is well known that the insects of today are strikingly similar to those insects that first appeared on the Earth. C.T. Brues said about the insects that, "Some of the specific types have persisted throughout the 70 million years since then with little or no change."[113]

11) "There is almost nothing to give any information about the history of the origin of flight in insects."[114]—E.C. Olson

12) "The (evolutionary) transition to the first mammal is still an enigma."[115]—Roger Lewin

13) "Not one change of species into another is on record . . . we cannot prove that a single species has been changed."[116]—Charles Darwin

14) "Contrary to what most scientists write, the fossil record does not support the Darwinian theory of evolution because it is this theory which we use to interpret the fossil record. By doing so, we are guilty of circular reasoning if we then say the fossil record supports the theory."[117]—Evolutionist Ronald West, Kansas State University (Evolutionists point to the fossil record as the strongest evidence for their theory, so this statement again highlights the weakness of their evidence and reasoning.)

15) "As our present information stands, however, the (fossil) gap remains unabridged, and the best place to start the evolution of the vertebrates is in the imagination."[118]—Homer W. Smith

Concerning the Philosophy Behind the Theory . . . Evolution is a Religion, not Science

1) ". . . I am quite conscious that my speculations run beyond the bounds of true science . . . It is a mere rag of an hypothesis with as many flaw[s] & holes as sound parts."[119]—Charles Darwin

2) "The more one studies paleontology, the more certain one becomes that evolution is based on faith alone."[120]—T.L. Moor

3) ". . . the philosophy of evolution is based on assumptions that cannot be scientifically verified . . . whatever evidence can be assembled for evolution is both limited and circumstantial in nature."[121]—G.A. Kerkut

4) "We evolutionists can only imagine what probably existed, and our imagination so far has not been very helpful."[122]—Richard Dickerson

5) "We (evolutionists) have been telling our students for years not to accept any statement on its face value, but to examine the evidence, and therefore, it is rather a shock to discover that we have failed to follow our own sound advice."[123]—John T. Bonner

6) "At this point, it is necessary to reveal a little inside information about how scientists work, something the textbooks don't usually tell you. The fact is that scientists are not really as

objective and dispassionate in their work as they would like you to think. Most scientists first get their ideas about how the world works not through rigorously logical processes but through hunches and wild guesses. As individuals, they often come to believe something to be true long before they assemble the hard evidence that will convince somebody else that it is. Motivated by faith in his own ideas and a desire for acceptance by his peers, a scientist will labor for years knowing in his heart that his theory is correct but devising experiment after experiment whose results he hopes will support his position."[124]—Anti-creationist science writer Boyce Rensberger. (Evolution certainly is based on faith alone . . . it has no foundation whatsoever in the facts of science.)

7) "The details (of how evolution could have taken place) are difficult and obscure."[125]—James Crow

8) "If a fundamental (Christian) ever got hold of this stuff (evidence against the evolutionary dating system), he could make havoc out of the radiometric dating system. So keep the faith."[126]—Dr. Gary Parker, recounting the words of one of his former evolutionary professors

9) "Virtually all the fundamentals of the orthodox evolutionary faith have shown themselves to be of either extremely doubtful validity or simply contrary to fact."[127]—Dr. Arthur C. Constance

10) "Evolution is a religion. This was true of evolution in the beginning and it is true of evolution still today."[128]—Michael Ruse

11) "Evolution is unproved and unprovable."[129]—Arthur Keith

12) "I have asked myself whether I may not have devoted my life to a fantasy. I am ready to cry with vexation at my blindness and presumption."[130]—Charles Darwin

13) "This situation, where men rally to the defense of a doctrine they are unable to defend scientifically, much less demonstrate with scientific rigor, attempting to maintain its credit with the public by the suppression of criticism and the elimination of difficulties, is abnormal and undesirable in science."[131]—W.R. Thompson

14) "My attempt to demonstrate evolution by an experiment carried on for more than forty years has completely failed . . . the
idea of evolution rests upon pure belief."[132]—Dr. N.
Heribert Nilsson, Director of the Botanical Institute at Lund
University Sweden

Concerning the Design Evident in Nature . . . There is a Creator

1) "We are left with no substantive defense against what appears
to be a strange conclusion—that life was designed by an intelligent agent."[133]—Michael Behe
2) "It is hard to believe that the vastness and grandeur of nature
is all a matter of chance."[134]—Robert Clark
3) "And when we examine the respective evidences still more
closely, we shall find that there are almost insuperable difficulties with the evolutionary explanation of each of the different evidences. They can all be understood much better in
terms of special creation than in terms of evolution."[135]—
former evolutionist Dr. Henry M. Morris
4) "Divine intervention was the only explanation for the origin
of the qualities that made *Homo sapiens* (humans) special."[136]—Alfred Russell Wallace, and famous evolutionist
Robert Broom
5) "The laws of science as we know them at present, contain
many fundamental numbers, like the size of the electrical
charge of the electron and the ratio of the masses of the proton and the electron. The remarkable fact is that the values of
these numbers seem to have been very finely adjusted to make
possible the development of life . . . it seems clear that there
are relatively few ranges of values for the numbers that would
allow the development of any form of intelligent life. This
means that the initial state of the Universe must have been
very carefully chosen indeed if the hot big bang model was
correct right back to the beginning of time. It would be very
difficult to explain why the Universe should have begun in
just this way, except as the act of a God who intended to

create beings like us."[137]—famous evolutionist, Stephen Hawking

6) After considering the incredible precision of the universe, a *Scientific American* article stated that one could reasonably conclude that "God is a mathematician of a very high order, and He used very advanced mathematics in constructing the universe."[138]

7) "So long as the universe had a beginning, we could suppose it had a creator."[139]—Stephen W. Hawking

8) "There are hundreds, perhaps thousands, of scientists (as of 1972) who once were evolutionists but have become creationists in recent years—I myself was one of these, having accepted the theory all through college. Since that time, however, as a result of considerable reading in all the various sciences which bear on the creation-evolution question, as well as in the Bible, I personally have become thoroughly convinced that the Biblical record, accepted in its natural and literal sense, gives the only scientific and satisfying account of the origin of all things. Many other scientists today can give a similar testimony."[140]—Former evolutionist, Henry Morris, Director of the Institute for Creation Research

A Personal Testimony

As a 1998 graduate of the Wildlife and Fisheries Science major at Penn State University, I had the privilege of listening to one lecture involving evolution after another. This was actually a good experience, since it confirmed my suspicion that evolution is a ridiculous theory and cemented my belief that the God of the Bible is the Designer of all that we see. Time and time again, while my professors described the theory of evolution, I could sense the doubt in their voices. Some sounded as if they were teaching it because they were forced to by the University administration. One seasoned professor, who was considered a leading authority on the theory, actually broke down in class and admitted that "evolution is pure fantasy and has absolutely no scientific evidence." I was pleasantly surprised that a staunch evolutionist would make such a dramatic statement and made sure that I jotted it down before he continued on to his next point.

As I read my evolution-biased textbooks outside of class, I discovered the same doubtful words. I recorded nearly all of the doubtful phrases dealing with evolutionary relationships among species. Here is a partial listing of the phrases I've recorded: "Relationships remain controversial," "Probably," "Suggest," "Ornithologists debate," "Maybe," "Traditional debate," "Contention," "May not all be related," "May be more closely related," "Usually considered," "Is still debated," "The taxonomic boundary is vague," "The relationships remain obscure," "It is now believed," "Debate continues," "Possibly related," "Tentatively included here," "Dispute this assignment," "Possibilities remain controversial," "Or," "But," "May be related . . . or perhaps instead," "The classification has a turbulent recent future," "Convergence in ecology and morphology has confused the family classifications."

The following are phrases I found when evolutionists were confronted with the ultimate question of 'What is the origin of life, and how did it evolve?': "Hypothetical," "Possible to imagine," "Could be," "Presumably," "Believed," "Debate abounds," "Consider speculations," "Uncertain," "Remains unclear," "Generally hazy," "Lively debate continues," "Very tentative," "Only suggesting," and "Imagine."

The last word, 'imagine,' sums up the evolutionary position on the origin of life, for that is really what they are doing. The theory of evolution remains alive in the minds of evolutionists, not because the theory is true, but only because they are either genuinely deluded into believing the lie or are unwilling to part with their pride and admit they were created by a Divine Designer far more intelligent than they are. I realize that this last statement probably stepped on some toes, but it needed to be said, nonetheless.

At the same time I observed these statements in my college textbooks, I found the same textbooks and some professors routinely using words such as 'design,' 'machine' and 'awesome' to describe the natural world. Along with the constant use of these words, the overwhelmingly intricate order that I discovered at all levels of nature jumped out at me every time I studied my notes.

The three most important lessons I've learned from my 10 years of research on the theory of evolution are that: 1) Evolution is a lie, promulgated mainly by the scientific community and biological professors, with aid from the media, to a largely unsuspecting public; 2) True science always confirms the creation stance; 3) God is my sole Designer, Creator, Sustainer and Savior. I hope you have already accepted at least the first two facts, and that by the end of this book, you will accept the last as well.

A Final Word

Hopefully, the evidence in this chapter has convinced you that evolution is a dying theory not worthy of your allegiance. However, if

you are continuing to embrace the theory, realize that at its philosophical foundation evolution secretly claims that since we are animals, we will live, we will die and our existence is essentially meaningless. A senior writer for *Scientific American* shared this 'inspiring' belief in a recent article, "Yes, we are all animals, descendants of a vast lineage of replicators sprung from primordial pond scum."[141] Do you really want to share such an unfounded, dismal and hopelessly depressing belief?

For the evolutionist, (or anyone else who rejects God as the Creator), there is no hope beyond death. I've experienced the claims of evolutionists long enough to know that an endless cycle of death and decay is the underlying theme of the theory. Even if it was true, which it certainly is not, why would anyone want to believe it? Do you really want to hold to this hopeless belief in spite of the facts? It can truly be said that evolution is a crumbling, dying theory which offers no greater hope for you than decay in the grave. Do you want a meaningful, joy-filled life and a greater hope than death and decay in the grave? If so, then read on till the end of this book, for you'll find that there are excellent reasons to believe hope beyond death and a brilliant eternal future in a perfect place can be a reality for you.

CHAPTER 2

Blast Off!

Now that we've laid the theory of evolution to rest, and shown the validity of the creation stance, we'll turn our eyes towards the heavens and begin to unmask the wonder of our Divine Designer. I for now will assume that this Designer is the God of the Bible . . . if you don't wish to make this assumption yet, that's OK, because in chapters 9 and 10 I will convincing prove that the God of the Bible is indeed the only possible Creator. Psalms 19:1 in the Bible speaks about this Creator, stating that, "The heavens declare the glory of God; and the firmament shows His handiwork."[1] Romans 1:20 proclaims, "For the invisible things of Him (God) from the creation of the world are clearly seen, being understood by the things that are made (humans), even His eternal power and Godhead, so that they (humans) are without excuse."[2]

The Bible is God's Word. The verses I've included are just two of many which declare that we can see the evidence of God in creation. So, according to God Himself, we will be able to prove His existence if we search for Him while examining creation. If you sincerely search for, yet fail to see God in creation, then either you are spiritually blind, or God is a liar, and you can't trust His Word. But, if God is right, then you will see His existence in creation, and the fact that He exists should change your life forever.

In the following chapters, we will tour the Universe in pursuit of our Creator. I believe the search will be short, since evidence for the existence of God surrounds us. Creation clearly bears the mark of its Creator . . . the fingerprints of God are everywhere. (It's alright if you don't understand all the astronomical, statistical and biological terms and concepts I'll be describing in the next few chapters . . . the key thing I'd like you to realize is that this Universe, from head to toe, is incredibly complex, yet intricately ordered. Such complexity and order demands a supremely intelligent Designer. So, don't get bogged down by the details, if you don't understand them . . . I simply challenge you to search for the signature of God in creation. I'll begin with convincing evidence of design . . . that which we can clearly see in nature, and conclude with the most convincing . . . cellular and sub-cellular design. So, if you aren't convinced that this world is designed by reading Chapters 2–7, although I believe it is still obvious to the sincere seeker, then hang on, because the evidence in Chapter 8 is sure to blow you away. And I promise that the evidence that lies beyond in the final three chapters is the most compelling and important of all. If you read nothing else, please at least read these final chapters.) For those who are already convinced that the God of the Bible is your Creator, sit back and enjoy the amazement of creation. For those who are still unsure, I challenge you to examine the evidence very closely. It's time to let the journey begin!

To begin our journey, imagine yourself jumping aboard the Creation-1 space shuttle and traveling to the extreme edges of our Universe. As you travel, I'd ask you to ponder the immensity, complexity and order in outer space. Just how immense, complex and ordered is the Universe? Astronomers have uncovered many stunning facts that help to answer this question. Following is a sampling of some of these facts:

The Milky Way

To begin with, let's consider the size of our own galaxy, the Milky Way, which is only one of an estimated 100 billion in the Universe. The Milky Way, which is shaped like a spinning fried egg, is estimated to contain 200 billion stars, be 100,000 light years wide and 1,000 light years thick. (As a disclaimer, be aware that trigonometric constraints in determining angles of greatly distant objects limit the accuracy of measurements to no more than 300 light years. Objects further away than 300 light years cannot be mathematically claimed as completely accurate distances . . . they are only our best estimation. Due to this, evolutionists who claim that certain objects are 15 billion light years away cannot use this as absolute 'proof' that the Universe is 15 billion years old. Even more importantly, if you understand that God created this world with the appearance of age, i.e. as in Adam and Eve, who were created as adults in the beginning, then there is no problem with stars or any other object existing 15 billion light years away. God's power should not be limited . . . He is certainly capable of creating a mature Universe. So please understand that I will be using the estimated distances from our limited technology to describe the vastness of our mature, powerfully formed Universe.)

Since light covers 186,282 miles per second (=16 billion miles/day = 5.87 trillion miles/year), the Milky Way is 5,870,000,000,000,000,000 (5.87 quintillion) miles thick and 5.87 quadrillion miles wide. The Milky Way rotates at a speed of 136 miles per second, yet its circumference is so large that it will take 225 million years to spin completely around just once! (One astronomer said that if our solar system, with the Sun and nine planets, was the size of a coffee cup, then the Milky Way galaxy in comparison would be the size of North America!)[3]

But the Milky Way, while massive, is relatively small on the galactic scale. For example, if you left the surface of Earth this instant, and traveled at the speed of light to the end of our neighboring galaxy, Andromeda, it would take approximately 2 million light years. (It has been estimated that one light year, 5.87 trillion miles, is the approximate total distance that all the motorized vehicles on Earth travel during the course of a year, combined.) Doing a little math, we'll discover that a trip from the surface of Earth to the end of Andromeda at the speed of light would cover about 1,180,000,000,000,000,000,000 (1.18 sextillion) miles. Put into perspective, consider that the United States from border to border is about 3,000 miles wide . . . to us, this seems like a large distance. But, in comparison, a trip to the end of Andromeda would be 393,000,000,000,000,000 (393 quadrillion) times longer than a road trip across America.

The Even Larger Universe

Yet, the Universe is far larger than this, since the Milky Way and Andromeda are only part of one galaxy cluster, and there are millions of known galaxy clusters. Who knows how many galaxies and galaxy clusters exist past this? With our improved technology, astronomers have recently discovered that there are at least 50 billion distinct galaxies and have estimated there may be a total of 100 billion galaxies in the Universe. 100 billion may or may not be a good estimate . . . I would suggest that only God knows for certain how many galaxies and galaxy clusters exist. While we don't understand everything, as even astronomers admit, what we do know about the immensity and complexity of the Universe simply boggles our finite minds. Consider the overwhelming thought, for example, that planet Earth is only a very small speck in a super-sized, incredibly detailed Universe, and you, in size, are only a very small speck on this planet. Thoughts like this stress our minds to the limit, but to imagine the grandeur and awesome power of the one Who designed everything in all its wonderful detail is unfathomable.

Star Power

The Universe is more than a collection of swirling galaxy clusters . . . it also includes stars, comets reaching speeds of 1.2 million MPH, moons, asteroids, planets and more . . . each is wonderful in their own way. For example, the few thousand stars you see twinkling in the night sky are just a tiny fraction of the estimated ten billion trillion scattered throughout the Universe. There are enough stars in the Universe for each of the 6 billion people on Earth to receive 1.5 trillion, if they were being handed out. Still, the Universe is so immense that if each star was a person, the nearest neighbor, on average, would be as far away as the Earth is from the Moon (about 250,000 miles).

An example of the many other interesting and incredible facts about stars is the discovery that gravity has squeezed some of them into such a dense material that a single handful would easily weigh more than all the buildings and vehicles in a large city combined! I would encourage you to do your own research to learn more about stars and other objects swirling around in our Universe . . . this book is not the place for a comprehensive study . . . my goal is to only whet your curious appetite. However, I would like to now focus our attention for a moment on our most important star, the Sun . . .

The Sun

The Sun is the star nearest to Earth, roughly 93 million miles away in a vast Universe. It is a massive, 865,000 mile wide fiery spinning ball of hot gases that is well over 1 million times the size of the Earth. This average sized star (some, like the red giant *Betelgeuse*, are 1,200 times larger) creates intense pressure in its core that is 2 trillion times the pressure of Earth's atmosphere. The currently accepted theory on the power source of the sun (which has been a "hot" debate for quite some time) is that its intense internal pressure constantly fuses hydrogen atoms together in a continual nuclear reaction that boosts core temperatures to 27 billion degrees Fahrenheit. The fusion of up to 4 million tons of hydrogen fuel per second is so violent and constant that it equals the force of 100 billion nuclear bombs going off each second! Estimates state that the amount of energy produced per second could keep the USA supplied with electricity for the next 50 million years.

The extreme inner temperature of the Sun creates a raging inferno, with each square inch of its surface area constantly flooding the Earth with an intensity of light equal to 300,000 candles. Yet, the Sun is considered a weak star in the Universe . . . some stars, such as Deneb, burn brighter than 60,000 Suns combined. But the Sun is a perfect partner for life on Earth, providing just the right amount of consistent light and heat. The brightness of some stars changes daily, as they expand and contract like a giant bubble. If the Sun did this, the Earth's temperature would fluctuate by hundreds of degrees each week. But since our Sun is a star with steady light, our temperatures remain within the range of tolerance. It appears that the Sun was designed specifically for life on planet Earth.

The Planets

During the next stop in our whirlwind tour of the Universe, I'd like to briefly describe some of the physical attributes of all 9 planets in our solar system, ending in Chapter 3 with the characteristics that make Earth the only planet designed for human life within the solar system and known Universe. We'll begin with the planet nearest the Sun, Mercury.

Mercury

Mercury is 28.5–43.2 million miles from the Sun, depending upon its orbital position, and its mass is 1/20th that of the Earth. Its atmosphere of sodium is so thin that there is nothing to stop meteors from smashing into its surface. All you would see on a voyage across Mercury would be a surface deeply pitted with the scars of multiple meteor collisions, vast, empty basins, cliffs and endless views of yellow dust. The thin atmosphere causes another problem as well, since it is unable to provide any insulation, resulting in extreme temperatures. Day temperatures on Mercury soar to 800°F, while night temperatures plunge to -300°F. Mercury is also devoid of water . . . it does appear to have small ice caps at each pole, but the caps are made of acid, not water.

Venus

Venus, at almost 67 million miles from the Sun, has a mass 4/5th that of Earth. It is the hottest planet in the solar system, and its surface is as barren as any desert on Earth. The buildup of deadly carbon dioxide gas in its atmosphere has created a runaway 'greenhouse effect,' trapping so much of the Sun's scorching heat that temperatures reach a blistering 900°F. The atmosphere of Venus would be lethal to humans. It is very deep and thick, creating enormous pressure on the surface. It is also made of poisonous carbon dioxide gas and filled with clouds of sulfuric acid gas belched out by volcanoes on its surface.

Mars . . . Does Life Exist There?

Now we'll skip to Mars, the 4th planet from the Sun. Mars is 141 million miles from the Sun, and 1/10 the mass of Earth. There has been much debate whether life existed on Mars or not, but the answer to this question is not nearly as important as evolutionists would like us to think it is. To date, it has not been conclusively proven that life existed or exists on Mars, and even if life did exist there at one time, it certainly was not intelligent life that in any way resembled human beings physically or mentally. Even making the monstrous, non-evidenced assumptions that life on Mars did exist and that some of the life seeds from this or any other planet were sown on Earth does not make the evolutionist's argument any easier. They still need to explain, among other things, the ultimate origin of matter without God, and how these 'life seeds' evolved into humans on Earth, both of which I've shown in Chapter 1 is utterly impossible. So, again, whether the Creator put life on other planets is really a meaningless question with respect to the Creation vs. Evolution 'debate.'

The bottom line is that with respect to human life, it is obvious that neither this planet nor any other planet (as I'll show in the next chapter) was created for humans to inhabit. Human life on Mars, even today, would have to be lived in a bubble, since the planet itself can't support humans. The surface of Mars contains a high proportion of iron dust, rusted red by its stifling, carbon-dioxide rich atmosphere. It also has no usable water, including only 2 small ice caps, and has no obvious vegetation to begin food production. In addition, evening temperatures drop below -100°F. Life on Mars would not be very pleasant. The evidence clearly shows that Earth alone was uniquely created for human life . . . we exist and have existed only here and in no other part of the known Universe.

Jupiter

Jupiter is the 5th planet from the Sun, close to 500 million miles away. It is twice as heavy as all other planets put together, with a mass 318 times and a volume 1,300 times greater than Earth. Jupiter also spins faster than any other planet. Despite its size, it spins around in only 9.8 hours, which means its surface is moving 27,900 miles per hour. If you think the spinning rides at an amusement park are exciting, just imagine living on Jupiter, swirling at 27,900 MPH! Your body would literally be flattened like a pancake to the surface of the planet. In fact, your body probably would be sucked into the surface, considering that the power of Jupiter's gravity is so great that it is able to suck volcanoes of sulfur from the surface of one of its fifty-two moons. The tremendous bulk and rapid spin of Jupiter churn up the metallic insides to such a degree that the planet is essentially a giant dynamo, possessing a magnetic field ten times as strong as that on Earth.

The weather report from this hostile planet is not very appealing, with magnetic storms, crushing air pressure and cosmic radiation showers. Jupiter is made mostly of hydrogen and helium gas, but this is squeezed so hard by gravity that it has turned to liquid. Beneath the thin atmosphere of ammonia, there is an ocean of liquid hydrogen 15,500 miles deep. The surface is covered with a thin layer of swirling clouds of ammonia, which indicates powerful storms. One storm, called the 'Great Red Spot,' is 25,000 miles in diameter, (which is several times the size of the Earth) and has lasted at least 330 years. The surface temperature is -238°F, which would turn our bodies to ice almost upon contact. Clearly, Jupiter is not a place for human life.

Saturn

Saturn, the 6th from the Sun, at about 885 million miles away, has a mass 95 times greater than Earth. Saturn features rings around the planet, which exist in definite bands labeled A-G. These bands are composed of countless billions of tiny chips of dust and ice, which are very thin . . . no more than 160 feet deep, but which stretch about 160,000 miles out into space. Concerning the rings of Saturn, astronomy and physics professor Donald DeYoung said, "Astronomers find it incredible that such intricate detail has remained in place for billions of years, although an evolutionary view of long ages leaves little choice."[4] Non-creationist Jeffrey N. Cuzzi admitted, "Yet non stop erosion poses a difficult problem for the very existence of Saturn's opaque rings—the expected bombardment rate would pulverize the entire system in only 10,000 years!"[5] (Since the rings of Saturn still exist, the logical conclusion is that they have existed for less than 10,000 years, which rejects the evolutionary age, and supports the biblical age of Saturn and the Universe.)

Saturn, while large, is relatively light for its size, weighing a "mere" 600,000,000,000,000,000,000,000 (600 sextillion) tons. It is so light, that if you filled a large enough bathtub with water, Saturn would float away like a rubber ducky. On a more serious note, the surface temperature of Saturn averages negative 290°F, far too cold for human life, and is composed of ammonia, not oxygen. Water is also non-existent and the surface winds on Saturn are even faster than those on Jupiter, roaring at 1,100 miles per hour. Just imagine trying to stand in those conditions . . . we have trouble with even a 'minor' 100 MPH hurricane.

Uranus

Uranus, 7th from the Sun at about 1.8 billion miles away, has a mass 14 times greater than Earth. It has an atmosphere of hydrogen and helium, but beneath are oceans of liquid methane. This planet does not contain water or oxygen. Uranus is also so far away from the Sun that temperatures drop to -340°F. Winds constantly whistle through the atmosphere, whipping up huge waves in the icy oceans of methane below. Again, as with the others we've discussed, Uranus is not a place for humans.

Neptune

Neptune, 8th from the Sun at 2.8 billion miles away, has a mass 17 times greater than Earth. It is so far away that it takes almost 165 years to orbit the Sun. Like Uranus, Neptune has a thin atmosphere of hydrogen and helium with a deep ocean of liquid methane below. This makes Neptune appear as a beautiful cobalt blue in our solar system. An interesting fact about Neptune's moon, Triton, is that it is the coldest known place in the solar system, plunging to temperatures of -390°F. The moon is so cold that its volcanoes erupt ice instead of lava. This moon is easily recognized by astronomers, since it resembles a green watermelon with pink ice cream on both ends. The "ice cream" caps are actually caps of frozen nitrogen.

Pluto

Pluto, the 9th and final known planet in our solar system, orbits between 2.92 and 4.57 billion miles from the Sun. It is the smallest planet, five times smaller than Earth, and has a mass only 1/50th of Earth. If you stood on distant Pluto, the Sun would appear to be only a tiny dot which shines as palely as the moon does toward the Earth. Due to this great distance, surface temperatures on Pluto average -365°F.

It should be obvious that no other planet in the solar system, except Earth, is designed to support human, or likely any other type of life. Again, whether life exists elsewhere in the Universe, is an irrelevant question in regard to the ideal design and creation of planet Earth.

One fact is certain . . . Earth was perfectly designed for us, and we were perfectly designed for it. This design is not an accident either . . . it is an intelligent design . . . an intelligent design demands an Intelligent Designer. This Designer, as I will demonstrate in Chapters 9–10, is the Almighty God of the Bible.

Order in the Universe

Before we end our brief tour of outer space and rocket back towards Earth, I ask you to consider the incredible order that exists in the cosmos. The Universe is not a chaotic collection of galaxies, galaxy clusters, stars, comets, asteroids, planets and moons, but is a precise system that works more efficiently than the best engineered human machines. DeYoung said, "Within the solar system, the planets circle the sun, and the moons in turn circle their respective planets. Gravitational attraction causes all the objects to move with clocklike perfection."[6] It is simply amazing that the 9 planets in our solar system have orbited in perfect precision, year after year, for thousands of years, without colliding.

Also, meditate on the fact that the movement of the approximately ten billion trillion stars in the Universe is so precise that atomic clocks have been set by them. The error factor of star movement is 1/1millionth of a second per 1000 years, and this error is admittedly human. The orderly movement of stars, planets and other heavenly bodies can't be explained without including God in the equation. DeYoung clearly stated that, "The exact motion of the sun, moon, comets and stars is proof of God's controlling presence."[7] As Sir Isaac Newton said, "This most beautiful system of the sun, planets, and comets could only proceed from the counsel and dominion of an intelligent and powerful Being."[8] The intricate order and precision that exists at the Universe level screams loud and clear that the Divine Designer is also the Sustainer of the Universe. But the evidence of Divine Design becomes even more compelling as we rocket towards home . . . I challenge you to read on!

CHAPTER 3

Home, Sweet Home

As we speed toward Earth on the next phase of our journey, I'd like to give you a few facts about our planet. The Earth, as we all know, is the 3rd planet from the Sun, which is about 93 million miles away. The circumference of the Earth is 24,815 miles, and its diameter is 7,910 miles at the Equator. The Earth weighs 6,000 trillion tons. This exact size is crucial . . . if the Earth were any smaller it would not have the gravitational pull to retain the water and atmosphere necessary for life. The thinner atmosphere would offer less protection from the thousands of meteors that assault our planet daily, and would be so greatly influenced by the heat of the Sun, that life would fail. A much larger planet would have a more powerful gravitational field that would greatly increase the weight of every creature on Earth. If the Earth were even twice as large, you and everything else would weigh 8 times more than you do now, which would obviously slow life to a crawl.

Our planet's axis tilts at a 23.45 degree angle toward the Sun, which is the perfect angle for the equal distribution of the Sun rays that power food production on Earth. This exact tilt provides the seasonal variation that allows a wide variety of crops to grow throughout the year. This tilt also prevents the North and South Poles from becoming too cold and moderates the high temperatures at the equator. Without the exact tilt, it has been said that half our Earth would be inhospitable, since there would be no chance for food production.

The orbit of Earth is also exact, and it must be, since our existence depends upon it. Our planet may seem still, but it is actually spinning like a top on its equatorial axis at 1002 miles per hour. At this speed, the Earth whirls completely around every 23 hours, 56 minutes, 4.09 seconds. This speedy spin contributes to the annually equal distribution of sun rays on the Earth. Earth is not only spinning, but is also hurtling precisely through the galaxy at about 66,000 MPH during its orbit around the Sun, which is roughly 30 times the speed of a rifle bullet. At this rate, the Earth covers 582,729,560 miles during its yearly orbit, which lasts exactly 365.42 days. (During an average lifetime, about 70 years, the Earth will travel approximately 41 billion miles. During the time it takes you to read this page, the Earth will travel more than 1,000 miles!) The exact orbital speed of Earth is vital, since an excess speed would cause the planet (and us) to rocket away from the life-preserving Sun, while a speed too slow would cause us to be drawn in by the gravitational pull of the Sun and be burned to a cinder. Obviously, an orbital speed either too fast or too slow would mean a disastrous death for us all. The exact orbital speed of Earth keeps us on a consistent path around the Sun. This speed is exact, not by chance, but because God designed it that way.

Our planet not only orbits in a precise path, but is also located the perfect distance from the Sun. If we were any closer, we'd figuratively become burnt French fries, and if farther away, we'd be frozen popsicles. 93 million miles from the Sun is the perfect and only location in the solar system that will support human life. The moon is also located in the perfect position for humans to thrive on this planet. Consider that if the moon were any closer, it would cause the strength of the tides to be greatly increased. This could cause ocean waves to sweep across the continents, killing nearly every living land creature, and it is possible that the oceans would heat to the boiling point from the resulting friction! In contrast, a more distant moon would reduce the strength of the tides. Marine life would certainly suffer as a result of the more stagnant water, and we would also be affected by the lessened productivity of the oceans. The moon is in the perfect location to nourish life on both land and sea. By

God's design, the Earth is located the perfect distance from both the sun and moon.

The Protective and Providing Atmosphere

The Sun, although it is the energy source for nearly all life on Earth, would also be deadly if the Earth were not so ingeniously designed. Streaming from the 4 billion °F corona of the Sun each second are 1 million tons of electrically charged particles that race directly toward Earth at 310 miles per second. This lethal stream, called the solar wind, would kill us all if it weren't for a unique property of the Earth that helps form one of the most important layers of the atmosphere. The Earth acts as a giant magnet, due to its core of iron and nickel. Since the outer core of the Earth is liquid, and the inner core solid, they rotate at different rates. This creates circulating currents, which effectively turns the Earth into a massive solenoid. The magnetic powers of the Earth are able to prevent the electrically charged particles of the solar wind from reaching the surface of Earth and decimating all its inhabitants. This magnetic war takes place 37,000 miles above the surface of Earth in the magnetosphere, which is the outermost layer of our atmosphere.

There is also another potentially deadly giant lurking just above the Earth . . . without a well designed atmosphere, we'd all be doomed. Planets and moons are not the only thing in the galaxy whizzing around the Sun. Thousands upon thousands of chunks of rock and ice of all shapes and sizes, from the size of a car, to several hundred miles across are hurtling through space. These lumps of space debris are called asteroids. It is estimated that each day a little over 100 tons (40,000 tons per year) of this space debris rains down upon Earth. Sometimes, this debris rains in such great concentrations that we see them as golden meteor showers in the night sky. Thanks again to a well designed atmosphere, a large percentage of asteroids burn up before reaching the surface of Earth. Only a very small number of meteors (asteroids that have entered the Earth's atmosphere) reach Earth to become meteorites. There are no documented human deaths due to a meteorite strike. The fact that we are not bombarded to death by meteorites is due to God's brilliant design of a protective atmospheric blanket.

This protective atmospheric blanket of gases provides Earth with many other benefits as well. Without it, this planet would be as lifeless as any other in the solar system. To begin with, it gives us the air we need to breathe. The atmospheric mix of 78% Nitrogen, 21% Oxygen and 1% of other elements is the exact mix required for human life . . . this perfect mix does not occur on any other planet. Our atmosphere also gives us clean water to drink by constantly purifying and recycling the water supply on Earth through a process called the water cycle.

The water vapor and limited carbon-dioxide in the atmosphere keeps us warm by trapping the Sun's heat during a process called the 'greenhouse effect.' The atmosphere also shields us from the potentially excessive ultraviolet sun rays through a special ozone layer. Without this layer, nearly every creature on Earth would be afflicted with cancer, and the quality of life would decrease dramatically. In addition, the atmosphere provides us with the weather we need to survive. (Everything we call weather involves the churning of the atmosphere's lowest layer as it is stirred by the warmth of the Sun.)

Lightning, for example, is just one of the weather phenomenon essential to our existence. For your information, meteorologists estimate that approximately 50,000 thunderstorms occur each day, sending about 8.5 million lightning bolts to Earth, which collectively generate about 4 billion kilowatts of energy. Lightning bolts, which are only inches across, can range from 200 feet to 20 miles long, reach temperatures of $50,000^{\circ}F$ (4 times hotter than the surface of the Sun), travel at 90,000 miles per second and carry over 125 million volts of electricity.

Why is lightning essential to our existence? Because nitrogen is necessary for plant growth, and although 22 million tons of it floats over every square mile of Earth, nitrogen in its atmospheric form is unusable to plants. Nitrogen must undergo a chemical change before plants can use it. Lightning is one of the primary agents responsible for this change. Lightning literally helps create plant fertilizer, and as we will see later, plants are vital to the survival of all life. Thus, without lightning, there would be little usable nitrogen for plants, which would lead to little or no plant growth, which ultimately would result in the death of humans and other life forms. Lightning is one of many essential weather elements formed in our well designed atmosphere.

As We Rocket Towards Earth . . .

Let's continue our journey to the surface of Earth by finally rocketing through the atmosphere. As we travel back through Earth's atmosphere, you will notice that even this has a distinct order. The uppermost layer, which we've already mentioned, is the magnetosphere, where the magnetic warfare that protects us from lethal solar wind and cosmic rays takes place. Below the magnetosphere is a skin of gas that surrounds the Earth. This gaseous skin occurs in 5 ordered layers. From top to bottom, you'll notice the ionosphere, thermosphere, mesosphere, stratosphere (which includes the ozone layer), and the troposphere (where most clouds and weather form). Order is a common theme throughout all of creation. Order demands design. And a design this intricate and precise demands a Divine Designer.

As we approach the surface of Earth, you'll see that it is not a uniform sphere, but includes unique landforms, such as mountains, hills and valleys, which both collect and shed water. Again, the shape of Earth is important to our survival, for if it were a uniform sphere, the immense volume of water in the oceans alone would cover the surface of Earth 800 feet deep. Thank God that our Earth is not a uniform sphere!

The force of gravity will become more evident as we crash through the atmosphere. Gravity, as with everything else we've discussed so far on our tour of Earth, is necessary for human life. Gravity is one of the glues that hold the Universe together . . . it is the force that keeps the Earth in one piece, keeps your feet on the ground, and keeps planets circling the Sun in precision. The force of gravity has been repeatedly tested with super sensitive torsion balances, each time showing that the gravity factor is exactly 2. Why is this important? Because a gravity factor that is not exactly 2 would lead to the eventual catastrophic decay of orbits in space, which would lead to the ultimate destruction of the Universe and all the life forms within it. The force of gravity displays elegant and essential design.

81

But the precision of gravity alone would be insufficient to support life if it were not perfectly related to other fundamental forces of the Universe like the strong nuclear force and electromagnetic force. The strong nuclear force expresses the strength of the electrical force that holds atoms together, and this force divided by the force of gravity between atoms always equals the number N, which is 1,000,000,000,000,000,000,000,000,000,000,000,000,000. If this number were any smaller, only a short-lived miniature Universe could exist and no creature could grow larger than a grasshopper. The extraordinarily precise balance between the gravitational and electromagnetic forces also allows life to exist. If this balance were even 1 part in 10^{40} different, the Sun would not radiate enough energy to sustain life on Earth. Precision on this scale demands the existence of a super-intelligent Designer and Sustainer.

The Unique Design of our Planet and Universe

Scientists throughout the centuries have understood that the finely-tuned order in the Universe and on our planet in particular point unmistakably to the existence of a Divine Designer. The brilliant scientist Sir Isaac Newton, who is most famous for discovering the law of gravity in 1687 said, "Our most beautiful system of the sun, planets and comets could only proceed from the dominion of an intelligent and powerful Being."[1] Nineteenth century physicist, Lord Kelvin, inventor of the Kelvin temperature scale, stated plainly, "Mathematics and dynamics fail us when we contemplate the earth, fitted for life but lifeless, and try to imagine the commencement of life upon it. This certainly did not take place by any action of chemistry, or electricity or crystalline grouping of molecules under the influence of force or by any possible kind of fortuitous concourse of atoms. We must pause, face to face with the mystery and miracle of the creation of living creatures."[2]

While the founding fathers of science understood the observable evidence of God surrounding them, God has been largely ignored by the scientific community until recently. A TIME magazine article declared, "In a quiet revolution in thought and argument that hardly anyone would have foreseen only two decades ago, God is making a comeback. Most intriguingly this is happening . . . in the crisp intellectual circles of academic philosophers."[3] A number of scientific breakthroughs in the astronomical and biological realms have revived the case for the Intelligent Design of the Universe. This case is called the 'Anthropic Principle,' and it is a very persuasive argument. Part of the argument includes the fact that the Earth and Universe are ruled by several fundamental laws and constants. The thought is that the precision of the equations for these laws and numbers is unexplainable without an Intelligent Designer.

Contemporary scientists, such as MIT physicist Dr. Vera Kistiakowsky and astronomers Sir Fredrick Hoyle and George Greenstein are among the growing group that has admitted the scientific validity of the Anthropic Principle. Dr. Kistiakowsky wrote, "The exquisite order displayed by our scientific understanding of the physical world calls for the divine."[4] Hoyle admitted, "A common sense interpretation of the facts suggests that a superintellect has monkeyed with physics, as well as with chemistry and biology, and that there are no blind forces worth speaking about in nature. The numbers one calculates from the facts seem to me so overwhelming as to put this conclusion almost beyond question."[5] Greenstein said, "As we survey all the evidence, the thought insistently arises that some supernatural agency—or rather, Agency—must be involved. Is it possible that suddenly, without intending to, we have stumbled upon scientific proof for the existence of a Supreme Being? Was it God who stepped in and so providentially crafted the cosmos for our benefit?"[6]

It seems that even such staunch evolutionists as Stephen Hawking are being swayed by this argument. After discovering that the proton must be exactly 1,836 times heavier than the electron for life to exist, he wrote, "The laws of science as we know them at present, contain many fundamental numbers, like the size of the electric charge of the electron and the ratio of the masses of the proton and the electron . . . The remarkable fact is that the values of these numbers seem to have been very finely adjusted to make possible the development of life."[7] It is clear to an increasing number of scientists that the governing rules of the Universe and Earth are far too exact and fine tuned to be the product of blind chance from non-intelligent, lifeless matter that came from nowhere and nothing. The following are 16 examples of the exact physical values that keep the Universe together and make life on Earth possible.[8] Hundreds of similar fundamental laws and constants exist, each of which must be exact to within thousandths of a percent to assure our existence.

Physical Law	Exact Value
speed of light in vacuum	299 792 458 m s^-1
magnetic constant	12.566 370 614 . . . e-7 N A^-2
electric constant	8.854 187 817 . . . e-12 F m^-1
characteristic impedance of vacuum	376.730 313 461 ohm
molar mass of carbon-12	12e-3 kg mol^-1
molar mass constant	1e-3 kg mol^-1
conventional value of Josephson constant	483 597.9e9 Hz V^-1
conventional value of von Klitzing constant	25 812.807 ohm
standard atmosphere	101 325 Pa
standard acceleration of gravity	9.806 65 m s^-2
natural unit of velocity	299 792 458 m s^-1
atomic unit of permittivity	1.112 650 056 . . . e-10
joule-kilogram relationship	1.112 650 056 . . . e-17 F m^-1
kilogram-joule relationship	8.987 551 787 . . . e16 J
inverse meter-hertz relationship	299 792 458 Hz
hertz-inverse meter relationship	3.335 640 951 . . . e-9 m^-1

In addition to these fundamental laws and constants of the Universe, astrophysicists, such as Dr. Hugh Ross have recently conducted detailed research on what factors are necessary for the existence of life on a planet. To date, they have identified 323 factors critical to life, ranging from the tilt of the planetary axis to the quantity, timing and placement of methanogens. Again, a variation in just one factor by as little as one-thousandth of a percent would make life impossible or at least much more difficult, depending on the factor. Earth, of all the planets in the Universe, is the only one to have met all 323 critical life requirements. Following is a small sampling of these 323 factors with a short description of what Dr. Ross has postulated would happen if these critical life factors were changed from the exact value needed for life:[9]

1. If distance from parent star

    1. farther: planet too cool for stable water cycle.
    2. closer: planet too warm for stable water cycle.

2. If oxygen to nitrogen ratio in atmosphere

    1. larger: advanced life functions would proceed too quickly.
    2. smaller: advanced life functions would proceed too slowly.

3. If carbon dioxide level in atmosphere

    1. greater: runaway greenhouse effect would develop.
    2. less: plants not able to maintain efficient photosynthesis.

4. If ozone level in atmosphere

    1. greater: surface temperatures too low.
    2. less: surface temperatures too high; too much uv . . . cancer

5. If oxygen quantity in atmosphere

    1. greater: plants/hydrocarbons would burn up too easily.
    2. less: advanced animals would have too little to breathe.

6. If parent star metallicity

    1. too small: life chemistry not possible
    2. too large: radioactivity too intense; life poisoned

7. If soil

    1. too nutrient poor: diversity, complexity of life-forms limited.

2. too nutrient rich: diversity, complexity of life-forms limited.

8. If atmospheric pressure

   1. too small: lungs won't function.
   2. too large: lungs won't function.

9. If quantity of soil sulfur

   1. smaller: plants deficient in certain proteins . . . . death
   2. larger: plants will die from sulfur toxins

Dr. Ross calculated the probability that Earth, with its unique life-providing characteristics, was a product of pure chance from a 'Big Bang' explosion. He concluded that there is a 1 in 10^{304} chance that all the critical life factors could arise randomly if all the factors were in existence. Since this number is far above the level of statistical impossibility (1 in 10^{50}), the only logical explanation for the existence of a planet as perfectly designed for human life as Earth is that an infinitely intelligent Designer made it that way. (Of course the probability that Earth arose by chance is even less if you take the evolutionists viewpoint, since they essentially believe that this intricately complex Earth came from nothing and nowhere.)

Interestingly, Dr. Ross also calculated the possibility that a planet similar to Earth exists in the Universe. Following the scientific estimate that there are a maximum of 10^{22} planets in the Universe, he found the chance is only 1 in 10^{282}. So, statistically speaking, the possibility that life exists on other planets is zero, considering the numerous and specific requirements needed for life. Dr. Ross explained the importance of his statistical findings in words by saying, "Astronomers have discovered that the characteristics of the Universe, of our galaxy and of our solar system are so finely tuned to support life that the only reasonable explanation for this is the forethought of a personal, intelligent Creator whose involvement explains the degree of finetunedness. It requires power and purpose."[10]

Many other contemporary scientists now share the view that this world must have been designed by an Intelligent Agent. NASA astronomer John O'Keefe wrote, "We are, by astronomical standards, a pampered, cosseted, cherished group of creatures . . . If the Universe had not been made with the most exacting precision we could never have come into existence. It is my view that these circumstances indicate the Universe was created for man to live in."[11] British astrophysicist Paul Davies agreed, "There is for me powerful evidence that something is going on behind it all . . . it seems as though somebody has fine-tuned nature's numbers to make the Universe . . . the impression of design is overwhelming."[12]

Order At and Below the Surface

Our tour of the Universe is complete . . . the Creation-1 spaceship has safely landed on the surface of Earth, and it is time to climb out. We will not set our feet on the surface yet, but will descend from our shuttle into a specially constructed spiral staircase that will carry us into the heart of the Earth. Imagine that the earth immediately outside the staircase is sealed off with a transparent, heat resistant casing. As we spiral down 3,956 miles to the center of the Earth, you will observe that the Earth, like the atmosphere, is divided into a number of ordered layers. It is certainly not a chaotic mess. Near the surface, you'll see the Continental Crust, which extends downward 5 miles. Next is the Oceanic Crust, which ends about 50 miles from the surface. Below this are the Lithospheric Mantle, Athenosphere, Upper Mantle, Lower Mantle, Outer Core, Inner Core, and finally the center of the Earth. The temperature here is estimated to be about $7,000°F$ (3,850 degrees Celsius). After ascending the spiral staircase, again noting the order of the Earth's layers, imagine that you emerge at the surface of Earth, and are standing on the Florida coastline, ready to dive into the Atlantic Ocean.

But before diving in, you look down at your feet. Once again, you notice something that is essential to life on Earth . . . soil. Plants require soil for growth, and we, along with nearly all other creatures on Earth, either directly or indirectly depend upon plant growth for survival. Plants need 16 essential chemical elements, along with air, water, proper temperatures and sunlight for growth. Soil can't provide sunlight, but it does provide everything else, since it has a uniquely designed structure to regulate root temperatures, trap the necessary air, water and nutrients. Soils come in all shapes and sizes, with each soil type a specific mixture of clay, silt and sand particles that support specific plant communities. Soil type influences plant types, which determines wildlife communities in that area. So, in reality, the diversity of soil types is largely responsible for the diversity and success of nearly every land creature.

Soil not only supports all land life, but also provides a home for many creatures. Beneath your feet lives a complex treasure chest of organisms, which again, are vital to our existence. One source estimates that more than 2 tons of living creatures inhabit a single acre of soil. Another states that in just a spoonful of soil there are more microorganisms than all the people on Earth. One spoonful of fertile soil is home to approximately 200 nematodes, 248,000 algae, 288,000 amoebae, 444,000 fungi, 11,680,000 actinomycetes and 101,120,000 bacteria! A diversity of arthropods, reptiles, amphibians and mammals join this impressive collection of microscopic creatures to form a living army of soil dwellers that aerate the soil as well as systematically decompose all the dead matter that falls to Earth.

Just consider a planet without this army of decomposers . . . everything that dies would simply pile upon each other. Dead plants and animals would be stacked literally miles into the air, eventually submerging even our highest skyscrapers. Without the behind the scenes work of soil dwelling decomposers, all land-bound life would ultimately be smothered to death, unable to move among the mountains of dead flesh. Soil and the decomposers in it are part of God's grand design to support life on Earth.

Soil also provides at least one other important benefit . . . it purifies water as it percolates through the ground to water-bearing aquifers that contain over one half of the world's drinking water supplies. Without the living filter of soil, we would be drinking or using contaminated water every time we turn on the faucet.

Water . . . the Lifeblood of Earth

This brings us to the next part of our tour. As we remain standing on the Florida coastline, gazing at the Atlantic Ocean, one thing dominates our view . . . water. This special liquid, as I'm sure you all know, is essential to life. What you may not realize is that water in a usable form is found *only* on planet Earth. Is this and all the other unique qualities of Earth an accident? No, these qualities, as I've already demonstrated, are impossible to get by chance from nothing. However, their coordinated existence is very reasonable when you accept them as part of the provision of a Wise Designer in creating an ideal environment for human life.

As we look at the vast Atlantic Ocean, you may wonder how much water there is on Earth. Well, 75% of the Earth's surface is covered with water, and there are 320,000,000 cubic miles of water in the oceans alone. The oceans comprise 97% of all water on Earth, 2% is frozen in ice caps, and only 1% is fresh and available for human use. Yet, this supply is large enough to meet all our needs if we use it wisely. 60% of our drinking water supply is found in groundwater aquifers, which contain an estimated 31 million cubic miles of water. Groundwater springs, purified river and stream water supply the other 40%. Certainly not all areas of the world are blessed with abundant amounts of water, but there is an adequate reservoir worldwide. This reservoir of water is purified and recycled for our continual use through a soil and rock filtration system as well as an ingenious water cycle, which I've already mentioned.

How important is water to our survival? To start with, consider that your body is 65–70% water by weight. 67% of this water is found in cells, 25% is located between cells, and the remaining 8% is in the blood. All other organisms, even those living in deserts, are composed of at least 50% water. If the human body loses over 8% of its water supply . . . in other words, if someone goes 3–4 days without drinking water, the body will die. You need to drink, on average, about 1 quart of water daily to maintain this healthy supply. Water, in some ways, is more important than food, since it is possible to survive up to a month without food.

Several characteristics of water make it a special substance. Each water molecule (which measures only 1/18 billionth of an inch), is made of 2 positive hydrogen atoms, and 1 negative oxygen atom. The shape of water molecules and the fact that one pole of the molecule is positive while the other is negatively charged, allows them to attract other molecules rapidly, just like a magnet. The shape, polarity and hydrogen bonding between water molecules combine to enable them to exhibit adhesion, cohesion, dissolve substances, evaporate, condense and be less dense as a solid. All these unique properties are necessary for life to exist on Earth.

For example, it is very important that the solid state of water (ice) is less dense than liquid water, because this means ice will float. What if ice didn't float? All creatures that live in water would die, since ice would form when the temperature plunges below 32°F, and would then sink to the bottom, literally crushing all life. The fact that ice floats is essential to the survival of all water-borne creatures. Floating ice also insulates the liquid water that lies below it, allowing fish and other creatures to survive the harsh winter. In addition, during the spring thaw, the ice will melt, and as a liquid, will sink to the bottom, stirring up nutrients and oxygen that will allow aquatic life to thrive just as the critical breeding season approaches in many species. This timing is no coincidence, but is by design.

The expanding abilities of ice also make it a powerful soil former. Liquid is able to seep into small rock cracks, where it will eventually freeze and thaw (up to 70 times a year in some regions). Freezing water is a mighty force, able to expand and exert a pressure equaling 30,000 pounds per square inch on surrounding rock, eventually breaking it apart and turning it into life supporting soil. Soil creation is just one of the ways in which water supports the vitality of life.

Water is also critical due to its unique characteristics of adhesion (attraction between water molecules and other surfaces), and cohesion (attraction between water molecules). Without these qualities, plants would not be able to extract water from the soil . . . without water, plants would die, and a world without plants would also perish. Also, without the adhesive and cohesive properties of water, our blood would be unable to flow through our bodies, which would again result in a rapid death for us.

The Specific Importance of Water to the Human Body

The following are just some of the vital functions of water within the human body:

1) *Water Dissolves a Variety of Substances*
   Water dissolves more substances than anything else because it is polar (magnetically charged). Due to this property, water is able to attract and dissolve other polar substances, such as sugar. These substances are then able to travel through the blood stream and nourish our body. Without the dissolving power of water in our blood, the substances we need would not be dissolved and carried to the cells that form the foundation of life. Certainly, without the dissolving power of water, we'd die.

   On the other hand, water is unable to dissolve non-polar substances in our body, such as oils and fats. This is an important feature of water, since these substances are a major component of the cells in our body. If water was designed to dissolve fatty substances, our cells, and ultimately our bodies would literally melt away into a big pile of mush.

2) *Water Cools as it Evaporates:*
   Water is continually evaporating from the surface of our skin through the approximately 2.5 million sweat glands on our body. Without the cooling effect of water, our body, which constantly produces energy, would overheat and die.

3) *Water has a High Heat Capacity:*
   Because water has a high heat capacity, this means it doesn't heat up or cool down too quickly. And since our bodies are made mostly of water, this means that we don't heat up or cool down too quickly. Either case could cause death . . . the high heat capacity of water keeps us alive.

4) *Water is a Great Transporter:*
   Water in our blood helps carry essential nutrients, hormones, enzymes, oxygen and other life sustaining materials to our cells. It also plays a crucial role in cleansing our bodies. Respiration, digestion and other various metabolic reactions produce waste materials such as carbon dioxide and uric acid which must be removed from the body, since

an excessive buildup of these wastes can be fatal. Water aids the kidneys and large intestines in transporting wastes out of the skin through sweating and carbon dioxide through respiration. Water acts as both a food delivery and garbage person in our bodies . . . again, without this quality of water, we would not last long.

5) *Water is a Lubricator:*
The mucous linings of various organs and the fluids between internal organs contain water. These linings and fluids ease movement and reduce friction between internal organs. In joints, for example, water helps bones slide back and forth more smoothly.

6) *Water is a Synthesizer:*
Water helps synthesize special hormones and enzymes that are used to control reactions in the body, such as those involved in the digestive process. (Hormones are chemical messengers produced in special organs like the adrenal gland, pituitary gland and pancreas, which affect the growth and behavior of various cells. Enzymes are special proteins that are designed to increase the speed and reduce the energy needed for chemical reactions to take place).

The importance of water within our bodies cannot be overstated. If water had not been designed with such unique dissolving, evaporating, temperature regulating, transporting, lubricating and synthesizing properties, humans, and likely no other life forms could exist on this planet. Besides aiding in nearly all the physical and metabolic reactions within our complex bodies, this amazing substance is also capable of, among many other things, cracking giant boulders, keeping massive elephants cool, supporting the weight of 6-legged creatures (such as water-striders) on its surface and making mountains of salt and sugar disappear. This unique and incredible substance is, in many ways, the lifeblood of planet Earth. Such a wisely designed substance didn't appear by chance from nothing and nowhere, as evolutionists claim . . . it was designed by a wise Designer who foresaw the needs of His creation.

CHAPTER 4

Design Patterns in Creation

We are still standing on the Florida coastline, prepared to take a swim. But the weather is great... sunny with blue skies, a pleasant temperature and slight breeze, so let's enjoy the beach a little longer while we consider

some general design patterns that encompass all of creation.

The most obvious pattern in nature is an incredible degree of *ORDER*. We can see this by simply looking at the multilayered levels of life. The lowest level, including quarks, leptons and bosons, are organized into specific atoms, atoms are organized into specific molecules, molecules are organized into specific nucleotides, nucleotides are organized into specific DNA, and so on until you have an organized organism. An organism is the sum of many smaller levels of super organized life. (I will further discuss the cellular-level organization of organisms in Chapter 8.)

Order and organization not only exists far below the organism level, but above it as well. For example, individual organisms are arranged as part of a species population, which join populations of other species to form specific communities, which are organized in specific habitats, which form at least 13 specific biomes that create 8 zoogeographical regions which lead to 5 major climatic regions that characterize planet Earth, which orbits in precision with other planets, moons, stars, galaxies and galaxy clusters to form an incredibly organized Universe. From head to toe . . . from the super-sized Universe, down to the submicroscopic quark, and at every level in between, the marvelous mind of the Master Designer takes center stage.

For the next several pages, we will focus our attention on just one of the many levels of life . . . the species level. A species is defined as a reproductively isolated group of organisms. In other words, a dog can successfully mate only with another dog, and it takes two cats to make another cat. A cat and dog can't cross species lines to produce a fertile animal.

Order Between Species

God has placed several ingenious systems into nature to maintain order both within and between species. First, we will examine a few of the systems God has placed between species. One of these systems deals with the dog and cat example mentioned above. Consider, for a moment, what would happen if there was no species distinction . . . if cats could mate with dogs, turkeys with elephants, salamanders with giraffes, and so on. Obviously, genetic chaos would rule in the natural world. We'd have chickens running around with drooping elephant trunks, cats with snouts like a crocodile and frogs with furry, clawed feet like lions. It certainly would be an interesting world, but not an efficient one, since nothing would be designed to do anything very well. Fortunately, God has put barriers between species to prevent them from mating and causing genetic chaos.

These barriers come in two forms: pre-zygotic (before a fertilized egg is formed) and post-zygotic (after a fertilized egg is formed). Pre-zygotic barriers prevent mating and fertilization in 5 ways:

1) *Habitat Isolation* - Different species live in different habitats and regions of the world . . . if species don't meet, they can't mate.
2) *Temporal Isolation* - Mating and flowering times occur at different times of the day or year for different species.
3) *Behavioral Isolation* - Mating behaviors, such as the distinct songs of birds, and unique courtship rituals further separate species. For example, the brilliant feather display of the peacock won't do anything to stimulate an American Robins' reproductive drive.
4) *Mechanical Isolation* - Structural differences in genitalia or flowers physically prevent copulation or pollen transfer between distinct species.
5) *Gametic Isolation* - Male and female gametes will often fail to attract each other if copulation somehow occurs.

Post-zygotic barriers are more complicated to understand, so I won't boggle your mind with the arduous biological details. But in a nutshell, these barriers are designed to prevent the development of a viable, fertile organism from the accidental mating of two different species. For example, this means that even if two separate species, such as a horse and donkey mate to form a living mule, the mule, or any other hybrid animal will be sterile, unable to reproduce itself. If a hybrid can't reproduce itself over the long term, then it's not a viable species. Pre and post-zygotic barriers form an effective system which prevents intraspecific breeding, efficiently separating and maintaining order between species.

Order and separation is maintained between species in other ways as well. First, each of the estimated 50–80 million species in the world possesses unique shapes, sizes and skills. These differences make different species perfectly designed for different niches within a community. A community of species works similarly to a community of people. Just as each person in a community has a specific address, each species has a specific location where it thrives, whether this in the upper branches of the canopy, below the ground, or somewhere in between. And just as each person is endowed with certain skills to perform a specific job within that community, each species is physically designed to skillfully perform a specific role within their community. This special role is called a niche.

If species weren't designed to be physically, physiologically and behaviorally different, then multiple species would be fighting for the same resources in the same ways at the same time in the same place. But, by God's design, species are different . . . these differences allow a community of species to orderly divide the same finite food, space, nesting and housing resources in different ways and places at different times. This wonderful system greatly reduces energy draining conflict between even tightly packed communities of species for similar resources and allows all to survive. In fact, in the average community, thousands of plants, animals and microorganisms work together as one fantastic organism, as each fulfills its unique, God-given role.

Order Within Species

I've just briefly discussed some of the ways in which order is maintained between species. Now we'll quickly consider how God maintains order within a species, where all individuals are virtually identical, and are competing for the same resources in the same way and place at the same time. This may seem impossible to do, but if you study nature, you'll see that God has done it. He has done it through installing communication and competitive dominance hierarchies into each species.

Each species has their own unique communication code and every individual within a species communicates with each other in some way, whether it is through vocalizations, special movements, smells or chemical cues. There is a communication signal to fit every situation an organism could face. If individuals could not communicate, chaos would rule creation. Consider the human race, for example . . . what would happen if each person were a bump on a log, not able to speak, move, write or use any other part of their body to communicate in any way? Obviously, this would be a very inefficient world. There would be no or little cooperation without communication, and a world without cooperation would be a sad one indeed. I believe God has implanted the ability to communicate within the genetic makeup of every organism. It is this communication that helps create a more orderly, efficient world.

Communication within a species is not always positive, and this is a good thing. For example, among birds, there is a universal 'Danger!' call that all bird species seem to be able to understand. Many mammals also seem to be able to pick up on the alarm call of birds. Studies have shown that even plants can communicate when danger is approaching, such as an infestation of gypsy moths. The infected plant is actually able to communicate with other plants that the gypsy moths are on the way by sending chemical cues through the air. These chemical cues stimulate the leaves of undisturbed plants to wither up slightly and become more bitter tasting to discourage pests from eating them.

Another negative form of communication is essential to the survival of species. Aggressive vocalizations, gestures, smells and/or chemical signals are given off by species that are competing for food and space resources, as well as mating privileges. This aggressive communication is good since it sets up something called a 'dominance hierarchy.' Dominance hierarchies use mainly physically non-violent forms of communication to assure that the genetically stronger individuals in a species obtain the best territories, best food within that territory and best mating privileges. Although it may seem cruel to exclude weaker individuals, from a species survival standpoint, this is a great design, since only the best genes will be passed on to the next generation. (Compassion for the poor and needy is one of many characteristics that separate humans from animal species.)

The territoriality instinct found in many species is a wonderful way to maintain order within a species. Every individual in a species requires individual space to meet their personal needs. You can see an example of this individual space by observing birds on a wire . . . if you do so, you will notice that each bird is almost an identical distance apart. This distance represents the bird's (or any other species) personal space. Territoriality can be seen on a grander scale when you examine the community level, in which each individual (usually males with the best genes), take their piece of the pie. After the initial competition to set up territories, order is reached within a species. The dominance hierarchies that have already been established will then maintain this order.

To illustrate why territoriality is important, just imagine what would happen if all the humans on Earth decided they wanted to move to Central Park in New York City. Undoubtedly, all the space resources would be taken up very quickly and tempers would start to flare as people fight for last few precious square inches of real estate. We could try, but it simply is not physically or emotionally possible for 6 billion+ people to all jam into Central Park. Clearly, we, as humans need territories to maintain order. Likewise, territories in nature are one of God's ways of maintaining order within species.

Order Beyond the Species, Community Levels

God has also built in several tremendous systems to maintain order beyond the species and community levels. Food webs, predator/prey relationships, nutrient cycling and biological clocks are just some of the ways in which God keeps the biosphere together. (The biosphere includes all life on Earth, from the lowest ocean depths to the highest point that birds can fly in the atmosphere.)

Spider webs, as intricate as they are, pale in comparison to the food web that connects all living things. The biospheric food web probably contains at least several billion simpler food chains. An example of a simple food chain would be: 1)The Sun, which is the foundation and power source of nearly all food chains on Earth >>>> 2)Plants, which through harnessing the power of the Sun, make all the food on Earth >>>> 3)An herbivore (plant eater), such as an insect >>>> 4)An insect eating carnivore (meat eater), such as a frog >>>> 5)A primary predator, like a snake >>>> 6)A secondary predator, such as a bird >>>> 7)A tertiary predator, such as a bird eating peregrine falcon >>>> 8)Decomposers, upon death of the falcon >>>> 9)Plants, which start the process all over again. This very simple food chain combines with many others to form an almost indescribably complex, yet well ordered food web. This well ordered system assures that every organism has something else to eat as food is recycled through the biosphere.

The predator/ prey relationship is at the heart of the food web that connects planet Earth. The epic battle between predator and prey involves several impressive tactics, such as camouflage, mimicry, warning coloration and a host of other strategies that I will touch upon in later chapters. Predators are perfectly designed to capture prey and prey is equally skillful at avoiding being eaten. This equal level of design maintains the balance of nature. If predators were too skillful at capturing prey, then prey species would soon become extinct, and predator species would quickly follow, since they would have little to eat besides themselves. On the other hand, if prey were too skillful at avoiding predators, predators would eventually become extinct, and prey would pay the price as well, since their populations would skyrocket, leading to the eating of nearly every scrap of food on Earth, which would be followed by painful population crashes involving much death due to starvation. (For example, it has been calculated that the bodies of single-celled paramecium would fill all known space in the Universe within 5 years if allowed to reproduce and feed unchecked by predators and other controls. Death due to massive starvation and possibly disease from contact with rotting carcasses would soon follow.) Certainly, a world without both skillful predators and prey paints a very dismal picture. Fortunately, God has made predators and prey equally adept at catching food and avoiding becoming food. The result we see is order and balance in nature.

Also tied in with the food web that maintains life on Earth is an ingenious series of nutrient cycles. Every organism is made of and requires certain nutrients for their existence. These nutrients, such as nitrogen, phosphorus and sulfur are constantly being passed through the food web back to decomposers and plants, which can again be eaten by herbivores. Life, in a biological sense, is really just one complex, simultaneous, cycling circle of nutrients. This simultaneous cycling of nutrients, which meets the needs of all organisms, is a wonderful part of God's grand design for life on Earth.

Biological Clocks - Part I

In nature, timing is everything. And although wild plants, animals and all other species aren't able to read a calendar, their complex behaviors are timed perfectly. How do they accomplish this? Science has shown that each cell in every organism includes a special, built-in biological clock. These biological clocks, as with every other aspect of creation, are essential for the existence of life. Biological clocks use the patterns of the Sun to perfectly coordinate daily and annual rhythms in every creature. Studies have proven that even those organisms which are in the dark for most or all of their lives exhibit rhythmic daily and annual behavior patterns that are set by internal biological clocks. But, for the majority of species, who are exposed to the Sun, changes in day length cause hormones to be released within the body, which triggers certain behaviors at precise times.

Why are biological clocks that are set mainly by the pattern of the Sun so important? Without daily rhythms, chaos would again be the rule. There would be no specific eating and sleeping patterns in nature, niches would be destroyed and communities would collapse. There would be days when every creature is trying to feed in the same area at the same time . . . it would be similar to the entire population of Los Angeles trying to make it through a single red light on a two lane road all at once. Obviously, it wouldn't work very well. Biological clocks work well to maintain daily order in nature, and assure that seasonal behaviors occur at just the right time. Without seasonal biological clocks, birds wouldn't migrate, animals wouldn't mate, flowers wouldn't bloom, pollination wouldn't occur, seeds wouldn't form to promote a new generation of plants and so on. Still, a clock without day length triggered hormones would fail. And if these behaviors don't occur at precisely the right time, as they do, then plants, animals, humans and all other organisms would suffer greatly and possibly become extinct.

Where do the internal biological clocks that regulate the lives of all species come from? Scientists admittedly have no answer, since there is no natural source they can point to. I would strongly suggest that the biological clocks that order all creation have a supernatural source . . . they must be God-powered, for there is no other plausible explanation.

This has been an extremely quick overview of just some of the ways in which God has established order between and within species in a community, as well as over the entire biosphere. I could certainly include many more examples that would take up many more pages, but I hope you've gotten the idea by now. *ORDER* is the main theme of planet Earth, as well as the Universe. The intricate order we see demands a design, and a design this complex demands a Divine Designer. This Divine Designer, as I will convincingly show in Chapters 9 and 10, is the Almighty God of the Bible.

Other Patterns in Creation

Besides order, there are several other patterns and lessons that emerge when we study nature. The following are just 5 of these:

1) *Life is Persistent*
   Life thrives everywhere, from the highest tip of Mt. Everest at 29,000+ feet above sea level to the lowest pit in the Mariana Trench, 36,198 feet below the surface of the Western Pacific Ocean. Life also exists in the brutal Arctic, where temperatures commonly plunge more than 100°F below freezing, as well as in the sultry Sahara, which, as the world's largest desert, is a vast, 3.5 million square mile ocean of sand.

   Fairy shrimp and bacteria are just two examples of species well designed to adapt to environmental stress. Fairy shrimp are hardy creatures, able to survive being deep frozen or even boiled in hot springs, where temperatures reach a scalding 160°F. Bacteria are among the most resistant life forms on the planet, thriving despite being boiled, dried out, frozen or even made into crystals in the laboratory. When conditions are right, bacteria can break out of their 'hibernation' and continue as if nothing happened. They also persist in extreme places, such as 15,000 feet under the ground, where they eat oil (which forms a byproduct that reacts with water to create hydro sulfuric acid that has contributed to the formation and enlargement of some caves). Bacteria also abound in the caves they help form, although some locations are more than 1000 feet below the surface and offer no light . . . only stark darkness. Despite these conditions, bacterial life thrives in amazingly diverse, incredibly ordered communities. Just

101

as above ground, each bacteria species fills a special niche in their community, which supports and sustains life. Even in forbidding underground habitats, life persists as a perfectly designed and well ordered community of creatures. No habitat on Earth is truly hostile to life . . . wherever you may search, you will find organisms that God has designed to not only survive, but thrive.

2) *We Need Other Life*

No species, including humans, can live alone. Despite our many technological advances, we still depend upon the orderly interactions of the millions of different animals, plants, fungi and microscopic creatures that share the planet with us. The species of the world supply basic necessities, such as food, clothing, breathable air, drinkable water, as well as fuels, fibers, building materials, medicines, natural areas for peace of mind and much more. Clearly, we need other life to sustain our own.

Consider, for example that **all** of our food comes from natural sources . . . it doesn't just magically appear on the supermarket shelves. To appreciate how much we need other species for food alone, imagine that you stopped at fast food restaurant for lunch and ordered a hamburger, fries, an apple pie for dessert and a carton of milk to wash it down. Where did your meal come from? The hamburger and milk are both cow products. Cows feed upon at least 17 species of pasture grasses, grains and legumes. Bacteria in the cow's stomach makes digestion of the plants possible, and bacteria in our stomachs allow us to digest milk and also provides us with several B vitamins and vitamin K. The bread in hamburger rolls includes, at a minimum, flour from wheat, sugar from sugar cane and yeast fungus. French fries are made from potatoes and one or more corn or soybean species are used to fry them. If you have lettuce, tomatoes, pickles and onions on the hamburger, then add four more species. The apple pie filling is made from one or more apple varieties, spices from several plant species, butter or margarine made from milk, vegetable oil and sugar. The crust contains flour from wheat and vegetable shortening from several plant species. The existence of all these food items also rely upon an immense number of pollinators, seed dispersers and decomposer species for the survival of the necessary plant species. So, when you add it all up, literally thousands of organisms are required for this one simple meal.

Every species is important . . . even tiny and often despised creatures, such as bacteria, algae, protozoa, fungi, slime molds, lichens, liverworts, mosses and insects are essential to human life. Bacteria, for instance, provide us with the following benefits: 1)Decomposition and recycling of dead material, 2)Protection from disease, 3)Aids in the production of antibiotics like Erythromycin, Streptomycin and Tetracycline, as well as other medicines to prevent the further spread of disease, 4)Promotion of food digestion in the intestines, 5)Makes basic elements like carbon and nitrogen available to plants, which feed us all, 6)Cleans oil and other pollutant spills and 7)Controls insect pests. Of the 1 million+ known bacteria, only a few are detrimental to humans. Bacteria are a great example of how God uses even the smallest creatures to make the world go around.

Overall, it is estimated that the annual benefits derived from natural ecosystems is $33 trillion. Obviously, we need other creatures. And just as He has done with our atmosphere, water, soil and the other elements that make Earth unique, God has provided other species for our survival. He knew we would need them, and as a wise Designer, He gave them to us.

3) *Creation is Beautiful*
If you've ever taken a moment to gaze upon a majestic mountain, glistening waterfall or golden sunset, you probably realize how beautiful our world is. The colorful canvas of creation also includes glowing autumn leaves, brilliant spring blossoms, pristine, crystal mountain streams, the fluttering streaks of color we call butterflies, multicolored, almost magical rainbows, the marvelous stars above, and occasional natural fireworks that light up the night sky . . . these and so many more,

are the artistic masterpieces of nature. Even non-living rocks can be full of beauty . . . water, ice, wind and the proper shade  of sunlight are some of the tools in God's paintbox, which He uses to transform life-less rocks into colorful forms more spectacular than anything achieved by a human sculptor. The beautiful earth was made for our enjoy-ment and is a breathtak-ing work of art that boldly bears and declares the signature of God.

4) *Creation is Imperfect*

You may have been wondering how I can proclaim that the world is so beautiful and full of order, when a lot of what we see around us is chaos, disease, death and destruction. This world is a place of moral decay where people cold heartedly run planes into skyscrapers and children murder other chil-dren at school without regrets. We certainly live in a cold, heartless, wicked and imperfect world.

Consider weeds as an example of imperfection from na-ture. These pests cost American farmers an estimated 5 bil-lion dollars annually in crop loss and control measures. This agricultural loss doesn't even consider the discomfort, lost time and expense experienced by the millions who suffer from hay fever and other respiratory ailments, either caused or ag-gravated by menacing weed pollen. Other costs that should be added include injury or poisoning of people or livestock by thorny or toxic weeds plus the unsightliness and fire haz-ard created by weeds along roadsides and in vacant lots. In addition, aquatic weeds choke waterways, interfere with navi-gation, conflict with fish, wildlife and recreational interests and impede malaria control. Weeds are a good example of just how imperfect our world is.

So, how could an all-wise and loving God create a world full of such imperfection, chaos, disease, death and destruction? As much as we may dislike it, the answer is that He didn't, but we did. If you read Genesis Chapter 1 of the Bible, you'll see that the world was 'very good' when it was created. It was perfect. Then a very powerful three letter word . . . sin . . . corrupted the perfect world that God created. When God created us, He gave us free will as any loving parent would . . . He gives us the freedom to make our own choices, then to reap and learn from the consequences. God does not rule over us with the iron fist of a dictator. He doesn't want to force us to love and respect Him as our Creator, since forced loved is not true love. God's greatest desire is for us to choose to love Him freely, and not by force.

But unfortunately, instead of choosing to love and respect their Creator, and using the free will given by God for good, mankind has ignored their Creator and used their freedom of choice for evil, sinful purposes. Because of the sinful choices of man, a perfect God had to punish mankind for their correction, like any good Father would do. Because man has messed up and sinned, "the whole creation groans and travails in pain together until now."[1] We live in a sin cursed world, and nature bears its scars. (I will further discuss the effects of sin and God's solution for that sin in chapter 11 . . . Also, if you'd like to read further on the question of why pain and suffering exists in God's world, there are several excellent books that deal more thoroughly with the subject . . . a few of these are listed in the recommended reading section near the end of this book.)

While man's choice to sin against God is the greatest reason for an imperfect world, I believe that human mismanagement is another reason. Again in Genesis 1, God called humans to be good stewards of the Earth and everything that dwells upon it. Unfortunately, we have not been the best stewards of the Earth. The following are just 3 ways in which we have collectively degraded our world:

Introduction of Alien Species:

Alien species are not designed to be where they are now, and it shows, since their presence can be devastating to native species. Aliens are so destructive because they have few or no natural predators in their new setting, allowing them to thrive and choke out the native species that preceded them. A few examples of aliens that have been either intentionally or accidentally introduced by humans and their destructive effects are the:

EUROPEAN STARLING - This bird has been a significant force in reducing populations of native cavity nesters such as woodpeckers, Eastern Bluebirds, Tree Swallows and others. A large number of other alien bird and mammal species are also wreaking havoc on our native animal populations.

GYPSY MOTH - Accidentally released in Eastern Massachusetts in the early 20th century, this insect pest has caused the cyclical destruction of oaks, pines and other tree species in the Northern and Central United States. Other non-native insect pests that are taking a bite out of our forests include the Elm Leaf Beetle (introduced to America in 1869), Larch Sawfly (1880), Larch Casebearer (1886), Beech Scale (1890), Pear Thrips (1904), Balsam Wooly Adelgid (1908), Smaller Elm Bark Beetle (1909), European Pine Sawfly (1914), Birch Leafminer (1925), Basswood Thrips (1925), Red Pine Scale (1946), Hemlock Wooly Adelgid (1953), Larger Pine Shoot Beetle (1992), European Spruce Bark Beetle (1993) and Emerald Ash Borer (2002).

CHESTNUT BLIGHT - This disease was introduced into the US and has selectively destroyed the American Chestnut, a formerly dominant tree species in Eastern forests. Other non-native diseases which are collectively degrading our forests include Beech Bark Disease (introduced to America in 1890), White Pine Blister Rust (1906), Larch Canker (1927), Dutch Elm Disease (1930), Sclerodermis Canker (1930), Butternut Canker (1960) and Dogwood Anthracnose (1976).

KUDZU -VINE - Brought from Japan to America in 1911, this plant species has since spread rapidly throughout the Southeast, destroying whole woodlots. Japanese Knotweed, Purple Loosestrife, Multiflora Rose, Garlic Mustard, Musk Thistle, Canada Thistle, Bull Thistle, Jimsonweed, Goatsrue, Giant Hogweed, Tartarian Honeysuckle, Autumn Olive, Mile-a-Minute vine and a host of other alien plant species are successfully dominating and eliminating our natural native vegetation. Alien species have undoubtedly had an adverse affect upon our native populations, and humans are the reason for it. We have no one to blame but ourselves.

Habitat Destruction:

In the last 200 years, the human population has grown six fold, from 1 billion in 1800 to over 6 billion today. This increase has led to the destruction of untold acres of forest and other habitats in an effort to expand and develop our world. The destruction of habitat is closely tied to the extinction of species. For example, tropical forests which contain 155,000 of the 250,000 known plants in the world and which are the source of half the medicines prescribed worldwide (the National Cancer Institute has identified 2,000+ tropical rainforest plants with the potential to fight cancer)[2], will be gone in 177 years at the present rate of deforestation.

As another example, in Pennsylvania, 56% of the original wetlands have been destroyed. 84% of the native amphibians, 46% of birds, 44% of reptiles and 37% of vascular plants depend heavily upon wetlands for their existence. If wetlands are totally destroyed, these species will be wiped out as well. Worldwide, we are destroying habitat so rapidly that about 3 species become extinct *every hour*. The loss of these species is a major loss for all, and upsets the balance in nature that God had created. You can only lose so many spokes (species) on a wheel (biosphere) before the wheel falls apart. We may be starting to approach that point.

Pollution

Since the start of the Industrial Revolution in the early 1900's, we've greatly polluted our world, more than ever before. One of the effects of this revolution includes the destruction of the ozone layer, which has contributed to increased cancer rates among humans and many animals. Acid rain is also a result of human industry, and has been shown to greatly reduce reproductive success in many animals, such as amphibians. The examples of ways in which we've polluted our world could go on and on.

Nature, left to itself, functions very efficiently and orderly, just as God designed it. But humans, mainly through sin, and partly through mismanagement, have dramatically and forever changed the landscape of nature, so that it no longer functions the way God had originally created it. While we currently live in a self-corrupted world, there is still obvious beauty and order surrounding us. Because we can still clearly see this beauty and order, we have no excuse for denying the existence of God.

5) *God has a Plan when Things Go Wrong*
Imagine a forest that has been charred to the ground by fire. Upon first inspection, it might seem like a total loss, but if you wait just a few weeks, you'll see that God has a CPR plan to bring seemingly dead forests back to life again. This resurrection plan is called 'old field succession' and involves the orderly, gradual and continuous replacement of one vegetative community with another.

The growing conditions immediately after a fire are severe, including low soil moisture, a desiccating wind and direct sunlight that would fry most plants to a crisp. But God has designed a special set of plants called 'pioneers,' which are able to not only withstand, but thrive under the intense conditions. Pioneers include several grass species, asters, gold-enrods, annual and biennial herbs, which dominate the bare field for 1–3 years. Pioneers are able to sprout quickly following a disaster since their seeds are numerous and long-lasting, as they wait buried beneath a mature forest floor. It has been estimated that as many as 100,000 dormant seeds per square meter exist beneath a mature forest floor. These seeds can remain dormant for a long time . . . archaeologists in Denmark were even able to successfully germinate pioneer seeds that were 1700 years old![3] Once the conditions are right, pioneers can grow quickly, photosynthesize efficiently (grasses have a special type called C-4 photosynthesis, that allows them to use less water to grow, which is ideal for a burned forest condition), and reproduce rapidly (biennial pioneers feature brightly colored flowers which attract a wide variety of pollinators).

After the pioneers stabilize the disturbed area, a perennial herbaceous plant community moves in during years 3–10 of the recovery plan. A more stable perennial herbaceous-woody plant community dominates in years 10–60, followed by a mature woody plant community, including large trees that become established after year 60.

Old field succession is just one of God's CPR plans . . . He has a plan that can handle any disaster in nature. He also has a CPR plan for you, which, among other things, can give you eternal life in a forever perfect place. I will discuss the possibilities that God has waiting for you in much greater detail in Chapter 11.

CHAPTER 5

A Swim in the Atlantic

We've been on the beach all morning, and are starting to get a suntan. We stick our toes in the salty water . . . it feels great . . . it's finally time to take a dive into the depths of the Atlantic Ocean. It's also around noon, so we'll gulp down some lunch first, grab our scuba gear and call on the S.S. Sustainer to ship us a few miles out into the Atlantic Ocean. As we jump in, we'll discover a world vastly different than the one we know on land.

The world's oceans contain a striking display of over 200,000 known plant and animal species spread over 5 distinct habitats . . . deep sea, polar, temperate sea, tropical coral reef and open water. We will soon visit each of these habitats as we continue our exploration of planet Earth. But, as we descend into this world of wonder, the first thing we notice is a sleek swordfish sailing past us at nearly 60 miles per hour. The swordfish is considered to be one of the swiftest swimmers in the sea, and is just one of a dazzling array of approximately 29,000 known fish species in the world.

Similarities in Fish Design

Fish dominate the waters of this world through a marvelous variety of morphological (outside features), physiological (inside features) and behavioral designs. They occupy an extraordinary diversity of habitats, thriving in vernal pools, intermittent streams, tiny desert springs, the seemingly measureless reaches of the open oceans, deep oceanic trenches, cold mountain streams, salty coastal bays and so on through a nearly endless list of aquatic environments.

Fish are perfectly designed to reside in the watery realm. To begin with, they have fins instead of legs to move around. Although the number, length, location and shape of the fins vary among species, fish in general feature the following fins: tail fins for fast, powerful swimming bursts; dorsal, anal and caudal fins, which act as rudders, providing balance; pelvic and pectoral fins for turning and banking (these fins act just like airplane wings, and are also the fins used when a fish wants to 'put on the brakes'). Fins are often supported by special filaments called rays and are put in motion by powerful W-shaped muscles running from head to tail. These W-shaped sheets of muscle (called myomeres) lock into one another like a series of orange road construction cones, allowing for a complex interacting system that works in perfect unison. Fish are designed with a variety of muscle types to fit different situations . . . red muscles enable endurance, white provides speed and pink offers a mixture of speed and endurance. Each species of fish has a unique mixture of muscle types perfectly suited for their lifestyle. The skeletal system of fish is well designed to withstand the heavy compression load placed upon it by the powerful contractions of the muscular system during swimming. Many fish also feature air bladders, which help them float and swim easier. (These air bladders also improve hearing by intensifying sound in a fish's body.)

Fish are remarkably able to breathe in the low oxygen conditions present in water. While the atmosphere of Earth contains about 20% oxygen, well oxygenated water has only .001–.0015% oxygen. Fish must, and can deal with this condition, because they are equipped with finely folded gills that efficiently extract oxygen from the water and release waste gases, like carbon dioxide and ammonia into the water.

Fish skin is protected by scales and lubricated by mucous glands that reduce water friction and help protect fish from diseases and cuts. Internally, many fish have a special countercurrent blood exchange system that allows them to stay warm, even in sometimes frigid water. Under this system, blood vessels run parallel to and actually touch each other. This allows warm blood coming from the heart to heat colder blood returning from the extremities, resulting in a nearly uniform temperature throughout the body. Some fish even have an extra layer of protection in cold situations, exhibiting special antifreeze in their veins to efficiently regulate body temperature.

Fish are also designed with a lateral line system that runs along the sides of their bodies, from head to tail. This line is a special touch sensory organ that is able to detect minute changes in water pressure, giving fish an accurate picture of the watery world surrounding them. Using this system, even blind cavefish are able to locate food with such great precision that it can ingest the food without sight. This dual system is also one of the three reasons why fish are able to pinpoint sounds with such great accuracy. The second is the air bladder, which was already mentioned. The third involves the two internal ears of fish, one positioned on each side of the brain to better interpret sounds and maintain balance.

Fish eyes were made to work well underwater. They are able to see color and can tell the difference between light and dark. Their eyes are both monocular and binocular, which enables them to see in nearly all directions at the same time as well as judge distances accurately.

Fish are also equipped with wonderful senses of smell and taste. They live in a world of dissolved chemicals, so they must be and are able to detect and interpret these chemicals well. Fish have more than 10,000 taste buds on their mouth, tongue and lips. Some, such as catfish, can even taste their environment through taste buds located on their skin and whisker-like barbels. Fish have nostrils that funnel scents to a specialized smelling (olfactory) organ. Some fish, such as Pacific salmon, are famous for their smelling, able to literally sniff their way back to the exact fresh water tributary in which they were born to produce the next generation. They can amazingly find their way 'home,' although they have wandered for several years and thousands of miles in the Pacific Ocean. (Other fish, such as yellow fin tuna, have a built in electromagnetic compass, due to magnetic crystals found in their head. This compass allows them to better orient themselves with the magnetic pull of the North and South poles.)

Differences in Fish Design

The many similarities between fish species make them collectively well designed to live in water, but there are many significant differences as well. These differences, as we will see, are also an example of great design that allows all species to coexist in the oceans with minimal conflict. The most obvious differences between fish are their shapes and sizes. Fish range in size from the 12-millimeter Marshall Island goby to the 40-foot long whale shark, which is the largest living, cold-blooded animal on Earth.

Fish also come in a wide variety of body shapes, which are well suited to their lifestyle. There are at least six categories of body forms in fish, including the:

1) *Rover-predator type* - This is the classic shape that most people think of when they describe a fish. These fish have streamlined (fusiform) bodies, pointed heads, forked tails and evenly distributed fins that provide stability, maneuverability and speed. This is the perfect body form for speedy predators, such as sharks, swordfish and bass, which actively chase down prey.

2) *Lie-in wait predators* - These torpedo-like, flat headed fish are equipped with a mouth full of sharp, pointed teeth, which make them well designed to capture fast swimming prey. Their fins are also placed far back on the body and are in line with each other, which give species such as pikes, barracudas and gars the super thrust they need to ambush prey. Many of these species are also cryptically colored and demonstrate secretive behavior to better hide from and ambush prey.

3) *Surface-oriented predators* - This type of fish, which includes mosquito fish and killifish, are normally smaller, with upturned pointing mouths, large eyes, a flattened head and fusiform body shape. This body form is perfectly designed for capturing plankton and small fish that live near or insects that land on the water surface.

4) *Bottom-feeding fish* - These fish, which include flounders, are designed for life on the bottom. They display a horizontal, pancake-flat shape, with both eyes set on top of the head to

see predators above, and a twisted mouth on the bottom to feed on prey below. Others in this group feature suction cups to cling to the bottom and barbels ('whiskers' equipped with taste buds) for finding food even at night on murky bottoms.

5) *Deep-bodied fish* - This group includes species such as butter-fly fish, which look like vertical pancakes, being much taller than they are wide. This unique shape enables them to maneuver in tight quarters such as coral reefs and rock crevices. This body form is also ideally suited for plucking small invertebrates from the bottom.

6) *Eel-like fish* - These snake-like predators are able to slither their way into small crevices to find food and to avoid becoming food.

The form of a fish's body, especially its mouth, is suited to capture the food it prefers. Some have toothless mouths, and literally vacuum food into their mouths with a special sucking tube. Some use their heavy snouts to turn over rocks and devour what is beneath them. Many have teeth that allow them to capture other fish and larger aquatic life. Some strain microscopic plants and animals, called plankton, from the water with hundreds of closely spaced gill rakers. Others have teeth in their throats, which they use to grind food against a special horn-like pad in their mouth.

Fish employ various methods while filling their stomachs, including chasing or stalking and attacking prey, or lying in wait and violently striking at passing prey. Some may float about in the current waiting for food to flow to them, root it out of bottom debris, or graze underwater plants. The feeding styles are many and varied.

Fish also feed at different times when situations are crowded, such as in a coral reef community. You can literally see different shifts in this community, as some feed during the day shift and "come home" to sleep, just as a separate set of day sleeping species emerge to begin the night feeding shift.

Fish feed at different levels in the water column as well. Some feed mainly at the bottom, some at the top, and others in between. Some like to feed by the shore near vegetation and others in more open water. Some feed near fast water riffles, others in slow moving pools.

Territorial behaviors also differ among species. Some fish prefer to wander as part of a school to feed and breed. (These schools are not random, chaotic masses of fish. If you watch, you'll notice that they have a definite order, moving in a coordinated fashion through complicated maneuvers, with its members precisely spaced.) Other fish do not school, but live separately and violently defend a well defined territory. The only time they allow other members of their species near is during mating season. Many fish fall somewhere between these two extremes.

Fish also utilize a rich variety of signals in their effort to communicate with one another. These signals include visual, auditory, chemical and electrical cues. Each species uses a unique set of stimuli that can be recognized in exact ways by specific individuals. This communication system is stunning in its complexity, and works perfectly to maintain order in aquatic life.

Mating and reproductive strategies likewise vary greatly among species, with the mating of each species governed by distinct courtship rituals. Some species mate and reproduce in the same waters they live in all year, while others, such as salmon, smelt and shad follow exact migratory paths at the same time each year to freshwater breeding areas. Some bear few live young and provide much parental protection, others release several million (the Louvar can produce up to 47 million eggs at a time!) tiny eggs, which are designed to cling to vegetation. Some fish release average numbers (several thousand) of quickly hatching eggs and provide moderate parental care in nests. Some, such as mouth brooders, even carry fertilized eggs in their mouths until they hatch and completely develop. There are many reproductive strategies not mentioned, but all are successful (barring negative human influences such as over fishing).

(One amazing aspect about reproduction in fish, and other life forms on Earth is that it occurs at just the right moment, as set by the Sun and built in biological clocks, so that young are born precisely when food supplies are at their peak levels. The fact that all 3 million+ known species on Earth reproduce and bear young during ideal environmental conditions is no mistake . . . it is by God's design.)

While fish are designed similarly in many ways, they are separated by important differences in body form; feeding, social and reproductive preferences, styles, times and locations, which reduces competition between species and allows all to survive. This system, where each species occupies a unique niche is clear evidence of wise design by a wise Designer.

Fish, as wonderful as they are, are only a small percentage of the 200,000+ species that flourish in the water habitats of the world. We will now continue on our oceanic escapade to the five major habitats and examine the design of at least one resident from each habitat. (Recognize that some of these species may live in more than one of these habitats over the course of a year.)

Deep Sea Habitat

We will begin by descending into the abysmal deep sea habitat, where some of the most bizarre creatures on Earth roam. For this part of the tour we will need to use the Deep Sea Designer submarine, since pressures at this depth in the ocean would crush a human body flatter than a dime. But in a great feat of engineering, God has amazingly succeeded in designing several creatures to withstand the crushing pressures, chilling temperatures and endless darkness of the ocean depths. Because of the rugged conditions of these ocean depths, little research has been done there, and thus we know little about the creatures that live there. For this reason, the following is only a brief listing of design features for just a few deep water creatures that we have limited knowledge about:

FANGTOOTH - This fearsome-looking predator has long, sharp jaws to seize any prey that wanders its way. It also is shielded from head to toe by a series of hard, bony plates, which protect it from larger predators, as well as the massive pressure of the deepest ocean abyss.

DEEP SEA ANGLERFISH - The most striking feature of this creature is its bioluminescent lure, which is attached on the end of a long "fishing line" that is connected to the forehead. This glowing, wriggling lure, which looks like a leafy frond of seaweed, confuses predators while attracting mates and prey. Other deep sea creatures have similar designs to capture food, since it is scarce at the bottom. When a meal passes by they must be quick to seize it. Deep sea predators are well designed to accomplish this.

GIANT SQUID - Not much is known about the mysterious and elusive giant squid. But what little has been uncovered is evidence of amazing design. The giant squid is thought to average 56 feet long, which makes it a formidable creature that few predators, except the mighty sperm whale, will tackle. They also possess the largest eyes in the animal kingdom, each spanning 16 inches across. These monstrous eyes enable them to see effectively, even in the dark ocean depths.

GIANT TUBE WORMS - Designed to live at the very bottom of the ocean, giant tube worms thrive near cracks or vents in the floor, which pour out a steady stream of scalding, sulfur rich water. Each worm is approximately 10 feet long and is about as thick as your arm. They are able to ingest the sulfur, and with the aid of over 100 billion symbiotic bacteria per square ounce of tissue, make food to eat. Giant tube worms are one of the few creatures on Earth designed to survive without the Sun.

DEEP-WATER BARNACLE - Many deep sea creatures don't require live food, but are instead decomposers of the food crumbs that fall from the water above. The deep-water barnacle and other decomposers remain attached to the ocean bottom, capture and strain food from the water using feather-like tentacles. Decomposers are a necessary part of every habitat on Earth, and it's not by accident that they exist there. Decomposers exist by the design of a wise Designer.

As we arise from the abyss, consider the fact that life in the sea is not ruled by chaos, but by an obvious order that allows each creature to coexist in the habitat they were perfected created for. Just as on land, order in aquatic life is maintained by an intricate food web powered mainly by the Sun, nutrient cycling systems enhanced by regular tides, predator/prey relationships, biological clocks, dominance hierarchies, reproductive separation between species and interspecific communication, among other things. As I've said several times before, intricate order demands a design and design demands a Designer. There is simply no other reasonable explanation for the complex and amazingly intricate order of life, both on land and in water. There must be a God Who created it all!

Polar Habitat

From the crushing, abysmal deep seas we have arrived at another intimidating habitat . . . the icy waters surrounding the North Pole. Some of the fiercest storms on Earth ravage the Polar Regions, with howling, 100 mile per hour frozen gales seemingly blowing in all directions at the same time, sending temperatures plummeting more than 100 degrees below freezing. This habitat is so harsh that even on the warmest of days the temperature barely approaches freezing (32°F). But despite the bleak and frigid conditions, polar seas are some of the most life filled ocean regions on Earth. Millions of tons of microscopic plants and animals, along with crabs, lobsters, sea stars, barnacles, squid, seals, sea lions, walruses, polar bears, whales and many other species have been designed to live there.

> *POLAR BEARS* - Polar bears are the largest bears in the world, reaching 10 feet in length and over 1,400 pounds in weight. They are solidly built mammals, with a strong skeleton including large molars to crush plants and canines to kill animal prey. Adding to their bulk are massive, muscular shoulders and front legs that provide great strength. Polar bears can move quickly when needed, able to outrun a horse over short distances (if a horse were on their menu, of course). The foot pads on a polar bear are rough, like sandpaper, which prevents them from slipping on ice. (The microscopic design of the pads is so effective that researchers at the Ford Motor Company copied it in making slip resistant footwear designed to reduce industrial accidents.)[1] The broad paws also act effectively as paddles and the hind legs work like a rudder on a ship to propel and guide the polar bear's streamlined body through icy waters in pursuit of prey. They also display an

excellent sense of smell, able to detect prey from over 1 mile away. Thick white fur almost entirely covers their heavily built body. The nose is the only part of the body where heat can escape. Each of the hollow hairs acts as a mini greenhouse, trapping the energy of the Sun. Their skin is black below the fur, which allows polar bears to absorb and retain the maximum amount of heat. A thick layer of fat lies below the skin to allow them to combat -120°F Arctic winters. Polar bears are well designed for life in the Arctic.

HOODED SEALS - Blubber, a thick layer of fat under the skin, is essential to Arctic marine mammals. Babies are able to quickly pack on this life preserving fat as they develop. Hooded seal pups are a great example of this. Pups nurse for only 4 days after birth, the shortest nursing period of any animal on Earth. In this short time, they gain 11 pounds per day, ballooning from a birth weight of 48 to 92 pounds. Put into perspective, for you to gain 44 pounds in only 4 days, you'd have to eat an extra 38,500 calories a day . . . to accomplish this feat, you must eat 17 hamburgers, 42 cheeseburgers, 25 regular orders of French fries, 12 thick, creamy chocolate milk shakes and 15 hot fudge sundaes every day for 4 days, and this is on top of your normal daily diet. The secret to the exceptionally rapid growth is the special milk of the mother seal, which is 50–70% fat. God has provided a great design for the survival of hooded seal pups, as well as other marine mammal young.

Temperate Seas Habitat

The temperate seas are a welcome sight following our trip to the brutal Arctic. The MVP (most valuable plant) in this habitat are kelp, which are able to individually grow over 200 feet long. Kelp have sturdy strands of plant material that firmly grip rock surfaces to anchor them on shallow ocean bottoms. They also feature gas-filled bulbs, which help them stay afloat, as well as wide, leafy fronds, which collect sunlight for plant growth at the water surface. Kelp are truly amazing plants and a forest of them provides a perfect home for a whole new community of creatures that are perfectly designed to live there. A healthy kelp forest can be home to more than 800 marine animals, and a single plant can support more than 1 million organisms. As with many habitats, kelp forests offer different zones for diverse assemblages of creatures to live in. At the base of the kelp, called the holdfast habitat, you'll find many microorganisms, as well as crustaceans, brittle stars, hydroids, bryozoans and sea cucumbers. In the mid water habitat, kelp bass, rockfish, clingfish and other invertebrates have found a perfect niche. A variety of fish, crabs, and mollusks call the upper portion of the kelp forest home. As with other habitats, each species has a God-given niche, a place where they can live, eat and reproduce with minimal competition.

Tropical Coral Reef Habitat

The stunningly beautiful coral reef communities host an extraordinarily diverse number of sea creatures. All shapes, sizes and colors of animals, ranging from sharks to snails, and everything in between, reside there. An astonishing variety of fish, including 30–40% of all fish species, are associated with tropical reefs. In fact, only tropical rain forests house more species than tropical reefs. Yet, even in this jam-packed, complex community, there is order, apparent by the fact that each creature has a specific address and job to perform.

OCTOPI - The mysterious octopi (plural for octopus) represents just a few of the 1/2 million species that inhabit the coral reef. As with all other residents of the reef, they are well de-signed to live there. The most obvious feature of octopi are their 8 sucker covered arms, which allow them to move eas-ily across the seafloor, or swim if necessary. Octopi have up to 1600 suction cup-like suckers on their arms, which act as accurate taste and touch sensors. But octopi are far more than arms . . . they also have sharp, parrot-like beaks which are strong enough to crush shells and inject venom into prey to immobilize it, making an easier meal.

They display a number of qualities that make them bet-ter hunters and better at avoiding hunters. One of these is their remarkable camouflage ability which allows them to quickly change the color and texture of their skin to create an amazing variety of patterns that match almost any background. For example, an octopus can be dark brown and smooth one minute, cherry red and knobby the next, and only a moment later be bright blue and ruffled. They also have the ability to change their body shape . . . even large octopi can slip into very small openings, such as a rock crevice. If all these fail to avoid predators, they can call upon a set of special glands to shoot an inky substance at them. The ink clouds the water and is designed to block the chemical receptors of would be predators, allowing the octopus to escape. Octopi are certainly well designed for ocean life.

More Amazing Design Features of Ocean Creatures

Octopi exemplify some of the brilliant defense strategies that God has given to salt water creatures. As another of many examples, lion fish display gaudy warning coloration to advertise the deadly poison in their spines, effectively discouraging potential predators. Warning coloration is a very effective predator deterrent throughout the entire animal kingdom. Camouflage is another technique that is common to most animals. For example, many fish are dark on top to match the dark seafloor below and light below to match the sunnier, lighter surface waters above. This design, called countershading, allows fish to blend into their surroundings and avoid predators that are trying to see them from above or below.

Some sea creatures are more extremely designed to avoid predation, physically resembling their surroundings. These include leafy sea dragons, which mimic floating seaweed, and stone fish which look like . . . you guessed it . . . stones. Many sea creatures, like the octopi, can change to match their surroundings. Flounders are famous for their ability to match their background. They've even been proven to make a good imitation of a checkerboard when placed on one in the laboratory.[2] The variety of defense and predatory designs is almost endless . . . here are just a few more examples:

- Electric eels can deliver jolts up to 600 volts . . . each jolt lasts about two- thousandth of a second, and is capable of knocking out an animal as large as a horse.

- Porcupine fish can swell up with water to three times their size, becoming a poisonous, spiny mass the size of a small basketball.
- Sea anemones exhibit one of the fastest known movements in the natural world when they discharge their stings into a victim. Each sting cell on a jellyfish contains a coiled, barbed thread, which shoots out at a speed of more than 6 feet per second, with an acceleration 40,000 times the force of gravity, which is about 10,000 times that experienced by astronauts at lift off!
- Pistol shrimp snap their claws shut to stun predators or prey. The water force caused by their closing is equal to a speeding bullet, and for just an instant, as the claws are snapped together, frictional forces cause them to have a temperature equal to the surface of the Sun.
- The most bizarre defense strategy of all may belong to the sea cucumber. When alarmed, it will eject a mass of toxic, sticky, spaghetti-like tubules which often ensnare and discourage potential predators. If severely threatened, they will even expel their internal organs, such as their stomach and intestines for predators to feed upon while they escape. They can do this since they've been given amazing regenerative abilities, quickly replacing lost organs.

Tropical reefs certainly include a vivid, vibrant and sometimes bizarre collection of well designed characters. We've only seen the tip of the iceberg . . . to document the fascinating abilities and behaviors of all these curious creatures would require at least several books. But now it's time to leave and move onto our 5th and final oceanic habitat . . . the open waters.

Open Waters Habitat

The spacious open waters are home to an amazing variety of creatures. Residing here are some of the largest creatures in the world, including the behemoth Blue Whale.

BLUE WHALE -Here are some interesting facts I've dug up on this mighty mammal . . . Blue whales, the largest creatures to ever live, can grow up to an incredible 110 feet in length and weigh as much as 120 tons, which is equal to 25 elephants, the largest creature on land. Blue whale babies weigh 2.7 tons . . . Mothers, imagine trying to have a child this size! The adults feature smooth, streamlined bodies, powerful, 15 foot wide tail fins and flippers to sail through the water like a massive submarine. Their other body parts are equally impressive. For instance, their heart is as large as a small car, tongue weighs as much as one African elephant, and mouth is 20 feet wide. Through this monstrous mouth, they can inhale over 2,000 pounds of krill in a single meal, which collects in a stomach large enough to hold over 2 tons of food at once. The massive Blue Whale is truly the behemoth of the sea. But it is just one of the many impressive species found there.

SHARKS - Sharks are another of the fantastic creatures that roam the open seas. Like them or not, sharks are an excellent example of the many well designed organisms that call the oceans their home. Let's swim with a hunting shark and observe how it is designed for the kill.

The first noticeable feature of a shark is that, like other fish, it displays countershading. This shading scheme makes sharks nearly invisible to their prey, allowing them to stealthily glide within striking range. Another important quality of sharks is their swimming efficiency, which allows them to slice through the water after their prey. Powerful muscles drive long heterocercal tails and pectoral fins through the water. These complex body parts are just right for propulsion, steering and stability in the water. Swimming efficiency is further increased by the tiny, overlapping placoid scales, which also act as a protective armor coat for the skin. Faster swimming shark species possess special channels between their scales which absorb turbulent flow, reducing the drag of passing water, maximizing speed and efficiency.

Internal characteristics also promote effective swimming. These include cartilaginous skeletons, which are lighter and more pliable than bone. This increased flexibility contributes to the shark's graceful, sinuous swimming motion. In addition, shark livers are filled with oil, which aids floating and swimming, since oil is lighter than water. Also, some sharks have a countercurrent exchange system installed in their bodies, which enable them to always be warm-blooded and sail more swiftly through cold water. Sharks are swimming machines, designed as well or better than our best engineered automobiles.

But there is far more to a shark than just its swimming ability. Everything about them makes them highly effective predators. We'll continue to tag along with this swimming machine as it tries to locate prey. Sharks use a variety of well designed senses to find a meal and analyze their surroundings. Among these are well developed olfactory sacs in their nostrils that can detect one part of blood in one million parts of water. (This is the equivalent to smelling one drop of blood diluted in a large swimming pool containing 1 million drops of water.) And like all fish, sharks are built with a special lateral line sensory system running along its sides. The lateral line system of sharks is so sensitive that it can detect the low frequency vibrations of a struggling animal from over 1 mile away. This is one of the reasons why sharks can swarm so quickly around a dying creature.

One of the most remarkable senses sharks have is their ability to detect minute electrical fields. They accomplish this with a specially designed organ called the Ampullae of Lorenzini, which are small, gel-filled pits in the snout and other parts of the body. This organ works exceptionally well since all living organisms create electrical fields around themselves. Sharks have the ability to detect these electrical fields almost anywhere, even if their prey is buried in the sand or hidden in a rock crevice. Excellent swimming and prey location abilities alone make sharks efficiently designed predators. But there is more . . .

Imagine that our shark . . . we'll call it Sammy . . . has found some prey, and is now zeroing in on the target. Sammy is well equipped to capture, kill, ingest and digest the prey. Only five feet away now, Sammy is ready to sink his teeth into his next victim. But first, a pair of specially created nictating membranes close over Sammy's eyes. These tough membranes will protect the eyes from injury that could be caused by the wild thrashing of prey that is captured in the shark's jaws.

Sammy has now seized his prey in a moment of violent, furious force. Once prey is caught in the jaws, it will not easily escape. Some sharks are equipped with up to 5,000 triangular, saw-blade teeth that are each up to 2 inches long. These teeth can exert biting pressures exceeding 2,000 pounds per cubic inch. They are also being continually shed and replaced. Some sharks may lose up to 30,000 teeth in a lifetime, but regardless of how many they lose, they always have a mouth full of ever-sharp teeth. In addition, shark jaws are loosely attached to the skull, and include special ligaments that can extend forward as the shark bites. In this way, the jaws can be made even larger to devour more sizeable prey.

Sammy has now ingested his prey, sending it on its way to a large stomach and remarkably efficient spiral valve intestine system. The spiral valve is a corkscrew shaped ridge in the intestine that greatly increases the surface area for food absorption, which in turn improves digestive speed. The spiral valve is also neatly packed so that it does not increase the length of the intestine and take up valuable internal space. Sharks may be considered 'primitive' to an evolutionist, but from the external scales to internal spiral valves, it is clear that the shark is a well designed predator created by an All-Wise Designer.

However, this design would not be that wise if all 350 shark species were the same. They would then be fighting each other for the same preferred food sources in the same way, location and time. Obviously, this system wouldn't work . . . but God has wisely separated shark species to avoid competition and allow for the survival of all. Sharks differ in their size, where they live and what they prefer to eat. Different species display different types of teeth to capture different types of prey. Some have long-spiked teeth to snag small, fast moving fish . . . others have serrated, triangular teeth to cut chunks of flesh from larger prey. Still others have broad, flat teeth to crush the outer covering of hard-shelled prey. As with all other groups of similar species, each shark species is designed to fill a unique niche in the ocean world.

Order and Provision in Watersheds

It is now time to leave this wondrous ocean world and swim upstream. We'll call upon the S.S. Sustainer again to carry us to the Chesapeake Bay, which borders Virginia. From the bay, we will enter the mouth of the freshwater Susquehanna River, and travel up its corridor to the mouth of Towanda Creek, located in Bradford County, Pennsylvania. We will then hike up Towanda Creek to the Schrader Creek tributary. We'll continue up this tributary to Carbon Run and follow its course up to the highest point on the highest visible peak. We've completed this whirlwind 1000 mile+ trip in less than 30 seconds, so let's take a moment to stand on the mountaintop, regain our breath and think about

what has just flashed before our eyes.

We've traveled up something called a watershed and are currently standing at the pinnacle of two watersheds. A watershed is a land mass that drains water in an orderly way. The world includes thousands, perhaps millions of smaller distinct watersheds, separated by mountains and hilltops. These smaller watersheds include even smaller 1st, 2nd, 3rd, etc . . . order streams, which flow toward valleys to form larger order streams (up to 10, like the mighty Mississippi River). All smaller ordered watersheds combine to form one huge watershed, where all water flows efficiently to a central point . . . the oceans that surround the continents.

What would happen if water did not flow in an orderly way off land during storm events? Property damage would possibly be even more widespread, and chaos might rule even during smaller storm events. But watersheds do much more than convey rainwater off the land in an orderly way. They also serve as a highway for nutrients and aquatic creatures who want to move, and are a major component of the water cycle that helps sustain us all. Watersheds are an effective water and nutrient conveyance system that help promote our survival. Once again, God has wisely given us what we need.

Before we move on, I'd like to take just a moment to consider some of the products that aquatic ecosystems (oceans, estuaries, marshes, lakes, rivers, etc . . .) provide to humans. For starters, they are the source of fish, shellfish, wild and domestic rice, soup stock, watercress, water chestnuts and ingredients for several vitamins. Seaweed is a source of algin, carrageenin and agar, which are used as stabilizers, thickeners and emulsifiers in hundreds of food products. These seaweed derivatives are used to make foods like ice cream smoother and creamier, and keep ingredients like chocolate suspended in chocolate milk. Algin alone is used in beverages, medicines, dairy products, processed foods, paper, cosmetics, ceramics, paint and insecticides. Certainly this list does not begin to describe the multitude of benefits we derive from aquatic ecosystems. The key point is that along with nearly everything else on Earth, we depend upon the well designed residents of the watery realm for our survival. Planet Earth is full of far too many ordered systems and uniquely sustained by too many essential elements to be a product of pure chance which suddenly appeared from nothing. Earth is God's grand design for the welfare of His most loved creature . . . humans.

Ordered Life in Freshwater Habitats

Freshwater rivers, streams, lakes, ponds, etc . . . host an amazing collection of creatures. Fish are the most obvious inhabitants of freshwater systems, and just as in saltwater, freshwater species are separated into niches by a variety of physical, chemical, biological and behavioral factors that allow all to thrive.

Following are some quotes I've gathered from evolutionary biased, college-level textbooks describing fish community structure . . . "Most temperate stream fishes have a considerable degree of behavioral plasticity that allows them to interact successfully with a variety of other species in a way that minimizes competition for food and space."[3]; ". . . the species found together in a fish community complement one another ecologically, thereby minimizing competition and maximizing the utilization of the resources present."[4]; "Despite the highly variable composition of lake fish communities, studies invariably indicate that they have a high degree of organization."[5]; "It is clear that many of the stream fish communities are highly structured. The specializations and interactions among the fishes and between the fishes and their environment can only be called awesome."[6] By their own admission, evolutionists proclaim a high degree of specific order in nature, which demands a design that requires a Divine Designer. Such intricate order does not arise from mindless chaos by chance, but can only be devised and created by an Intelligent Mind.

Freshwater habitats include much more than fish, also supporting intriguing organisms like hydroids that can be completely sliced in two or turned inside out and still recover to become a perfectly formed creature again. An impressive array of macroinvertebrates also live there. 'Macros' are large enough to be seen, and include streamlined animals with built in rock cling attachment devices designed to withstand turbulent water flow in riffle areas. Stoneflies, surface skating Water striders and Whirligig beetles, which swirl around like wind up toys on the surface of a pond are also examples of macros. Whirligig beetles are equipped with eyes divided into two parts . . . one part allows them to see predators in the air above, the other enables them to spot prey in the water below. 'Whirlies' are just one of the many well designed freshwater insects that are separated into specifically prepared niches within ordered communities. Unique feeding styles, such as shredding, predation, grazing and collecting are just one factor which assures that order exists within the macroinvertebrate community, as it does in all levels of life.

Order Comes in Small Packages Too

We can see a lot, but ordered life exists far beyond our finite vision. Anton Van Leeunhoek and Robert Hooke, the inventors of the first microscope, were also the first to discover the powerful vitality within a single drop of water, surprisingly finding thousands of tiny microorganisms. What they saw was impressive, but we now know that a billion bacteria, plus millions of protozoa and hundreds of thousands of diatoms occupy a square centimeter of a streambed, and that the collective efforts of these microscopic creatures provide and/or process most of the energy that supports the visible life within a stream system. Without microscopic life, the entire aquatic ecosystem would collapse. Microorganisms are vital links in the food supplies of fish, aquatic birds, reptiles, amphibians, mammals and even humans. Without them, we could not survive. God wisely provided them so that we could.

> BACTERIA - In nature, powerful designs often come in small packages. For proof of this, we need to look no further than simple bacteria, which are so small that 8 million could fit on the cross section of human hair. But bacteria are far from being simple creatures. For instance, did you know that bacteria have used wheels long before humans 'invented' them 5,000 years ago? Certain bacteria, for example, include intricately detailed rotary engines, including joints and drive shafts in their cell wall to propel 6 hair-like paddles (called flagella) in a circular motion at up to 100,000 revolutions per minute. These flagella, which are equally distributed around the sausage shaped body, propel the bacteria in any direction at speeds up to 15 body lengths per second, forward or backwards. (This is the equivalent of 150 miles per hour for us!) The flagella propelled rotary engine is itself powered by proton batteries within the bacteria. The fuel for this battery comes from the nuclei of hydrogen atoms that are moved around by electrical fields. So amazingly, just one tiny bacterium includes a

fuel source that powers a battery, which drives an engine that propels a series of paddles. Bacteria, although small, are incredibly complex machines, detailed by the infinite wisdom of a Divine Designer.

WHEEL ANIMALS - For further proof that the Creator is a God of details, consider the wheel animals (also called rotifers). Wheel animals are a small group of very small creatures (the largest are only 1/8 inch wide, although most are far tinier) that resemble miniature cups on a stalk. They feature beating tufts of cilia, which literally throw food into their mouth and allow them to move. They are also built with a head, jaw-like mouthparts, a discernible body, sex organs, brain, simple eye to detect light and dark, strong muscle strands to pull in the cilia during times of attack, a stomach, digestive glands, bladder for waste fluids, anus to outlet digestive wastes, a foot and pincer-like toes. They are amazingly hardy, able to survive being dried out, frozen or almost boiled by shriveling up into a tough-cased resting stage. When conditions are right, the animal quickly revives and goes on with life. All this amazement and intricacy is stuffed into an animal less than 1/8 inch wide . . . wheel animals are living proof that God has designed detailed living machines in small packages. But, as we'll see in Chapter 8, the level of design goes much deeper than this.

CHAPTER 6

It's a Green
World After All

I think we've finally caught our breath, so let's take the opportunity to absorb the majestic view from the top of Barclay Mountain. From this somewhat lofty mountain peak we can see two watersheds . . . one flowing down the left side of the mountain to a valley, and another flowing down the right side to a second valley. We also notice something surrounding these watersheds and dominating most of the landscape . . . trees.

Trees and other plants are some of the most recognizable things on Earth. The 250,000+ plant species in the world come in all shapes and sizes, ranging from those that are barely visible under a microscope to the mighty 'General Sherman' Sequoia in Central California, which is 272 feet tall, 82 feet around and estimated to weigh 2000 tons, making it the largest living organism. Plants also hold the record for age (one Bristlecone Pine in the White Mountains of California is 4,700 years old) and height (some Redwoods reach 400 feet). Additionally, some plants sport leaves up to 65 feet long (Raffia Palm), flowers over 3 feet wide (Rafflesia of Southeastern Asia), leaves that are strong enough to support the weight of a child (Great Water Lily of South America, with leaves 6 feet in diameter) and seeds that weigh 44 pounds and float thousands of miles before lodging in the soil of a foreign shore (Coco de mer coconut).

Photosynthesis

Plants certainly are amazing, but are also of great importance . . . without them, we truly could not survive. In fact, we need them more than any other living creature. Why are plants so essential to life on Earth? The answer lays in one word . . . photosynthesis. The Sun, even at 93 million miles away, is the powerful engine that drives life on our planet. Plants, mainly through their leaves, act as miniature solar collectors to harness the power of the Sun and convert it to a form of energy that life on Earth can use. Photosynthesis is the process that plants use to convert water and carbon dioxide in the presence of sunlight into food. So, without getting into a lengthy discussion of chemical processes, here is the foundational formula for the existence of life on Earth: Water + Carbon Dioxide +

Sunlight captured by the chlorophyll found in chloroplasts within leaves and other green plant parts = Food (in the form of carbohydrates) + Oxygen + Water. Scientists are admittedly mystified and are still searching for the cause of this "magical" formula. But in reality, all they must do is look towards God the Creator, since He is the ultimate cause.

Plants, through using this basic formula, are the food and oxygen factories on Earth. Without them, we could not eat or breathe. The food we eat and oxygen we breathe can be traced back to the chlorophyll within tiny leaf chloroplasts (there are about 1/2 million chloroplasts per square millimeter of leaf surface). On a global scale, the productivity of these chloroplasts is astounding . . . it is estimated that through photosynthesis, chloroplasts make about 176 billion tons of carbohydrates per year. No other chemical process on the planet can match this output . . . and no process is more important. Trees also provide countless tons of oxygen to breathe. One study showed that a single acre of trees provides enough oxygen daily to keep 18 people alive. In addition, trees remove billions of tons of potentially harmful pollutants from the atmosphere. The U.S. Forest Service estimates that trees annually save New York City $10 million and Chicago $9 million in air pollution services.[1]

The Provision of Plants

Besides acting as our lifeline, what other benefits do plants provide to us? The following is just a partial list:

1) *Water Purification* - Plants store, purify and slowly release water back into the atmosphere, making our water more usable.
2) *Soil Enhancement* - Plants provide a rich soil fertilizer when it drops its leaves, leaching important minerals like calcium, magnesium, nitrogen, potassium and phosphorus into the ground. These and other essential nutrients will eventually be recycled for reuse by plants as part of wonderfully designed nutrient cycles.
3) *Shelter and Food for Wildlife and Humans* - Animals nest and den in several areas of a tree, as well as feast upon plants throughout the year. There are about 30,000 edible plant species in the world . . . four of these . . . wheat, corn, rice and potatoes, provide 80% of the world's food supply. Lumber for homes, furniture and other needs are also provided by forests. It has been estimated that the average American home contains 50 different tree species and 10,000 board feet of lumber. Our forests have so far met this need.
4) *Watershed Protection* - Streamside forests provide many benefits, including: a)Habitat and travel corridors for fish and wildlife, b)Shading, which stabilizes water temperatures, further improving habitat, c)Food, which is provided to the aquatic food chain through fallen leaves, d)Reduced stream bank erosion through anchoring the soil with their roots, e)Filtering of harmful pollutants and sediment before they

enter and degrade the stream system, and f)Minimization of flood impacts by absorbing much rain water, lowering water levels and velocities.

5) *Medicine* - More than 40% of all prescription drugs in the U.S. come from plants and the medicinal value of plants is estimated to exceed $84 billion per year worldwide. Yet despite their incredible medicinal potential, only 5% of all plants have been tested for their usefulness. The following is just a partial list of plant provided medicines:

Medicine	Use	Source
Aspirin	Painkiller	Willow bark
Vincristine	Child cancer treatment	Periwinkle
Vinblastine	Cancer treatment	Periwinkle
Digitalis	Heart stimulant	Foxglove
Quinine	Anti- Malarial	Cinchona
Morphine	Painkiller	Opium Poppy
Codeine	Painkiller	Opium Poppy
Taxol	Ovarian and Breast cancer	Pacific Yew

Besides these needs, it has been estimated that trees alone provide at least 5,000 other products and services beneficial to humans. Among these are fuel and heat provision during cold winter months; help in settling out and holding small particles and pollutants (i.e. dust, ash, sulfur dioxide, smoke) which could damage lungs; service as a windbreak in winter, keeping buildings warmer; muffling of traffic and other noises, as well as adding beauty to the world.

I'm sure you're familiar with some of the useful products of trees, such as paper and food (fruits, nuts, etc . . .). But plants offer us so much more, including: furniture, doors, toothpicks, picture frames, paintbrush handles, cereal boxes, candy bars with almonds, synthetic sponges, baseball cores, wooden chopsticks, vanilla flavoring, paint thinner, turpentine, chewing gum, paint, bottle corks, rubber gloves, plastic combs/brushes, baseball bats, boats, plastic eyeglass frames, maple syrup, carpeting, cellophane, rayon and other fabrics, thickening agents in shampoos, suntan lotion, shatterproof glass, cosmetics, fiber board, imitation leather, various dyes, drugs, oils, perfumes, soaps, varnishes, waxes, printing ink, shoe polish, crayons, cleaning fluids, electrical insulation, jams, jellies, cooking spices, tennis rackets, musical instruments, sewing shuttles, bobbins, candles, piano keys, ship models, bacteria fighting toothpaste, cameras, cough syrup, astringents, insect repellents, wound plaster, waterproof cement and more. Needless to say, trees are valuable for more than one reason. The presence of trees and other plants on Earth is no fluke . . . they are the wise provision of a wise Designer Who knew that we would need them.

The Ordered Layers of Plant Life

It's time to leave our mountain peak and saunter back through the forest toward civilization. But as we stroll back, we'll be on the lookout for design patterns that point us to the Master Designer.

As we begin our walk, it will become obvious that several layers of forest life exist simultaneously. In fact, there are at least 5 distinct layers in a forest, including the:

1) *Soil Layer* - Soil, as I've already discussed, is home to billions of organisms, both large and small. Soil is the foundation of any land habitat.
2) *Forest Floor (Herbaceous Layer)* - Building upon the foundation of soil, the forest floor is often carpeted with herbaceous plants, such as ferns, and by masses of wildflowers that grow from a rich nutrient source of decaying leaves, needles, feathers, feces and other organic remains. Certain animals, such as many species of small mammals, reptiles, amphibians and birds like Bobwhites and Ovenbirds live almost exclusively on the forest floor.
3) *Shrub Layer* - In this layer, shrubs such as rhododendron, spicebush and huckleberry provide homes that are perfectly designed for many types of birds and mammals.
4) *Understory (Small Tree Layer)* - Small trees, such as Flowering Dogwood, Redbud and Witch Hazel create a niche for many other species, including warblers and woodpeckers.
5) *Canopy Layer* - This layer is dominated by larger trees and a whole new set of species that is well designed to live there.

137

Similarly stratified order in plant life exists in all other habitats worldwide as well. Consider, for example, just one more habitat . . . . the rocky seacoasts that extend from Labrador to Southern Maine. Twice per day, the tide ebbs and flows, bringing essential nutrients ashore. In places where the water rises especially high (such as the Bay of Fundy, where the world's highest tides rise over 50 feet,) vertical zones of life are conspicuous. High on the shore, in the splash zone, you will find blue-green algae and certain lichens. These plants are designed to survive saltwater spray and near drought conditions. Just below, in the mid shore zone, are yellow-brown rockweeds, which are exposed to air for a good part of the day. Irish moss and red seaweed thrive in the lower shore zone. Leathery brown kelp lives in the shore-sea interface zone and into the waters beyond. Vertical zones of vegetative life are also common on other seacoasts around the world.

The forest, seacoast or any other habitat type displays distinctly ordered layers of plant life, each layer offering specific animal species a perfect place to live. Animals fill these ordered plant layers in an orderly way, each claiming a niche that works perfectly for them. This ordered plant and animal layering system, which occurs on both vertical and horizontal scales, is a great design that promotes the mostly non-competitive survival of all species involved. Such a great design must come from the mind of a Great Designer.

The Specific Timing of Plant Reproduction

You might wonder how all these distinct plant layers can exist simultaneously, appearing to work as a unified whole to collectively support the needs of its residents. Why don't some plants simply dominate an area, excluding the seemingly weaker, more fragile plants? For example, why doesn't a forest of mighty canopy trees shade out and eliminate all the other forest layers?

The secret lies in the timing of plant reproductive cycles. Different plants produce flowers or other reproductive structures at different times throughout the year, based on their unique responses to day length. These diverse reactions allow all species to be pollinated and pass their genes unto the next generation. If all plants tried to reproduce at the same time, pollinators would be overwhelmed, and overall plant survival would suffer. In a forest setting, the best design would be for herbaceous plants on the floor to leaf out and reproduce first before they are shaded out by the plants that are above. It would be best for each layer from the forest floor up to reproduce in succession . . . with the herbaceous layer reproducing first, then the shrub layer, followed by the understory layer and finally the canopy layer.

Not surprisingly, this is exactly what we see in nature . . . herbaceous plants are first and canopy plants are last. Some herbaceous plants, such as Skunk Cabbage, bloom as early as February, well before any of the plants above it begin sprouting leaves to shade them out. They can bloom this early since they are physically equipped to produce substantial heat . . . up to $70°F$, which melts nearby snow. This heat also helps release special odor chemicals that attract early season pollinators. Other herbaceous plants also complete their reproductive cycles by early spring before leaves from above rob life giving sunlight. Early reproductive schedules are a wonderful design that enables tiny wildflowers and herbs to coexist with mighty canopy giants.

Moving one and two layers up in a forest, we discover that understory shrubs and small trees, which bloom after herbs, are built to be hardy, able to withstand long periods in low light conditions as the canopy trees above shade them out. Eastern Hemlocks (which, by the way, are the Pennsylvania state tree), can survive for over 60 years in low light understories, waiting for the moment when a towering canopy giant crashes to the ground. When a gap is created by the death of a canopy tree, hemlocks and many other species seemingly spring to life as they quickly shoot up towards the light above.

Pollination

Pollination is a process as essential to human life as photosynthesis. Photosynthesis without pollination wouldn't do us much good, since plants that can't reproduce will eventually become extinct. As plants become extinct, so would nearly all other life forms. Pollination is one of the foundational processes of life, involving the transfer of male pollen to female ovaries, where it develops into seeds.

139

Plants are well equipped with a variety of ingenious strategies to attract equally well designed pollinators to assure that pollination occurs. Pollination can occur without the aid of pollinators, utilizing the forces of wind and water to transfer pollen. But most plants produce flowers to capture the attention of pollinators, who are mainly insects. Flowers entice pollinators to draw near by their petal arrangement (many plants have petal arrangements that perfectly fit the shape of specific pollinators), and fragrance (either good . . . some actually resemble the shape and smell of female insects to attract male pollinators, or bad, such as in Rafflesia flowers, which smell like rotting meat to attract flies).

Many flowers also entice insects with attractive coloration. Although most flowers appear only white or yellow to us, insect  pollinators, such as bees, can see the ultraviolet colors that flowers give off. These colors often appear as converging stripes or some other pattern to guide insects directly to the nectar inside, much as runway lights help guide airplanes safely to the ground. Insects and other pollinators are coated with sticky pollen from male anthers in the process. Plants have several methods to assure that this happens. For example, Mountain Laurel (the official Pennsylvania state flower), features flowers with 10 pollen bearing anthers tucked away in specially made pockets within the flower. These anthers are spring loaded, and when an insect walks on them, the pollen is released, pelting the insect's body with pollen. Some flowers even trap insects once they've entered the flower to assure they pick up pollen as they thrash about. (Don't feel too sorry for the insects, since they outnumber us 12 million to 1.)

The pollen that is picked up will be carried to the next flower, where it is transferred to the sticky female stigma. Plants also have intriguing methods to assure that this exchange happens. For example, Beach Peavine plants have a special structure, called a keel, which, when an insect of the exact right size lands upon it, drops down, causing the female pistil to poke the insect, picking up any pollen it is carrying. In a flash, before the insect knows what hit it, the male anthers are then thrust forward to dust the insect with a fresh load of pollen to carry to the next Beach Peavine flower.

Pollinators are just as well designed to pick up pollen as plants are to coat them with it. To start with, an orderly division of labor assures that nearly all flowers are pollinated. For example, Bumble bees, being larger, hairier and warmer, pollinate blue, violet, yellow and white flowers that reflect UV light during cooler mornings, while smaller and cooler honey bees take over the warmer afternoon shift to pollinate the same type of flowers just as Bumble bees "go home" during the heat of the day to stay cool. Moths and butterflies also demonstrate this well orchestrated division of labor. Butterflies pollinate flowers that are upright, fragrant, tubular, red, yellow and orange during the day, while moths pollinate white and yellow tubular flowers at night. As another example, birds, such as hummingbirds, are efficient pollinators during the day, while certain bat species pollinate similar flowers at night.

All pollinators are wisely designed for efficient pollen transferal. Moths and butterflies, for example, carry long, coiled tongues to reach nectar at the bottom of tubular flowers, picking up and unloading pollen in the process. The long, tubular bill of the hummingbird is ideal for pollination of long, tubular flowers. Bees are equipped with stiff body hairs that form 'pollen baskets' that are perfect for picking up a fresh load of pollen and depositing it on the stigma of the next flower. Bees also have an elaborate communication system designed for more efficient nectar retrieval and pollen transfer. They perform complicated 'waggle dances' to let other bees know the precise location of major food sources. Studies have shown that this form of communication is very accurate.

It is no mistake that flowers feature attractive petals and luring nectar to entice pollinators who are well designed to spread pollen from flower to flower. This basic relationship benefits both pollinators, since they do receive a food reward in the form of nectar, and plants, since the pollen has been spread to begin the next generation. As stated before, this well designed relationship assures the survival of all life on Earth. God is the Orchestrator of the great symphony we call pollination.

Amazing Designs in Seed Dispersal

Just as photosynthesis is worthless without pollination, pollination is of no value without pollen fertilization, seed production and dispersal. The journey of a single pollen grain continues from the sticky female stigma, down a long tube called a style, into an ovary, where it is fertilized and eventually develops into a seed. Yet, even at this point the seed is of little worth unless it is dispersed.

But God has given plants several ingenious strategies to distribute seeds throughout the planet. One method is for the plant to physically propel the seeds off into the wild blue yonder. These plants feature trigger mechanisms, which are set off when an animal brushes lightly against the seed bearing fruit. An explosive reaction then occurs, hurling entire fruits up to 50 feet away from the parent plant. (If the seed landed under a parent plant, the seedling would eventually compete with its parent, which would be counterproductive to the success of both . . . thus it is imperative that seeds are thrust from their parents . . . the fact that they are is clear evidence of a wise design.) For its size, the Starred Spearthrower may hold the world record for seed (spore, in this case) throwing. The tiny, yellowish-orange, star-shaped fungi cups convulse violently to propel egg shaped spores more than 13 feet high and out up to 18 feet when rain hits the cup. How amazing is this? Proportionally, this is the equivalent of a human kicking a football well over a mile high and nearly 2 miles in distance!

Several plant and fungi species rely upon the wind for dispersal. Some produce tremendous numbers of ultra light seeds that can easily blow with the slightest breeze. Aspens, for example, send super light seeds (there are over 3 million seeds per pound) blowing miles from the parent plant with the first stiff wind. I'm sure that many of you as children, (or maybe even as adults) have stepped on a puffball (a tiny round brown or tan fungi ball) and watched over 1 trillion spores explode and disperse into the air. Wind dispersal is certainly an effective strategy for scattering seeds or spores . . . yellow birch trees, for example, can sow over 1 million seeds per acre with the aid of the wind.

Maples, with light, papery propeller-like blades, use the power of wind to helicopter seeds far away from the parent plant. Milkweed and dandelions use feathery parachute structures to drift for miles in the wind current before striking ground. (Interestingly, studies have shown that dandelion seeds contain 'moisture reactors' that close the feathery parachutes during moist or rainy conditions to prevent a short trip below the parent plant. When the conditions are just right, these feathery parachutes will open and fly with the wind. If these seeds should happen to fall into water instead of fertile soil, the parachutes will convert the seed into a mini sailboat by curling its bristles above the surface of the water to catch the wind that so often flows across the surface of a water body.) Dandelion seeds are well designed to fly or sail to fertile soil.

Water is a major dispersal force as well, transporting seeds, such as those of a Sycamore tree, several miles from its parent to germinate on mudflats, sand and gravel bars. (Coconut seeds are the water dispersal champion of the world, physically designed to float over 1000 miles and survive more than 1 year in salt water to reach distant shores.) Water-borne species, such as Coconut and Sycamore trees, grow quickly and will help stabilize beaches and stream banks, helping protect our properties in the process.

Fire, as destructive as it can be, is also a creative force in nature, dispersing seeds of several pine tree species. Plants, such as Jack Pine, require fire to open their serotinous, tightly packed, seed containing cones. Fire is the only force that can release these seeds, which represent some of the only tree species created to stabilize areas with dry, infertile soil.

Plant Seed/Animal Relationships

Besides water, wind and fire, God has also designed a unique relationship between plants and animals to promote efficient seed dispersal. Many seeds are coated with glue-like substances and/or are equipped with spines, cleavers, hooks, barbs or burs that attach to animals (and human clothing) as they pass by. Anyone who has walked through a thicket of cockleburs knows just how well these seeds can hold on. (The sticking power of this seed type is so great that it inspired the inventor of Velcro.)[2] These seeds will cling to human clothing or animal fur for up to hundreds of miles before they are eventually shaken off. And if the seeds happen to fall upon unsuitable soil, they can remain dormant for 40 years or more until suitable conditions return. Sticky seeds, as much as we may hate them, are well designed for dispersal and rapid growth at a moments notice.

Most seeds have more desirable coverings than the "weed seeds" we've just considered. Many plants produce seeds that are engulfed by fleshy, fragrant and colorful fruit. Fruit is very well designed to

attract seed dispersers. Not only are they often fleshy and fragrant, but they also give off vibrantly colored "foliar flags" to signal that they are ripe and ready to be eaten. Furthermore, these foliar flags are flown at just the time when animals need to see them the most. Fruits become ripe and brightly colored at the exact time that waves of migrant birds are headed south and desperately require fuel for their journey. Vividly colored autumn fruits allow migrants to quickly identify and consume food before they travel south for the winter. Migrants will then disperse these seeds hundreds or thousands of miles from their parents. (Seeds

144

are not consumed with their fleshy coats, since they are designed with tough outer linings to safely pass through the digestive systems of birds and other animals, and are planted in the ground with rich fertilizer as the animals defecate.)

Both plants and animals benefit from this seed dispersal relationship. Plants benefit since seeds are safely spread far from their parents, (some animals, such as gray squirrels and blue jays will even plant seeds into the ground) while animals benefit from a quick, convenient and plentiful food source before the harsh winter. Fall fruit, which is high in fat content, is designed to provide the ideal food for migrants, hibernators and active winter residents since fat provides twice the energy per weight that sugar supplies.

The plant fruit and animal relationship does not end just before winter, but continues throughout most of the year. During autumn, as low sugar/high fat fruits wave their foliar flags and are quickly consumed, other low sugar/low fat fruits are produced. These fruits are slow to rot due to their special chemical makeup. And although they are not as appealing as the other type of autumn fruit, they do provide a long-lasting, dependable food source that aids active residents in resisting the stresses of winter. High sugar/low fat fruit is also produced in mid to late summer. These fruits arrive just as the abundant spring flush of insect food wanes. This provides a constant food source well into the autumn season. Through fruit, and other aspects of the planetary food web, God has wisely provided a constant and ideal food source to feed His creatures throughout the year. The seed dispersal system is too well designed to be a product of chance from nothing.

Complex Horizontal and Vertical Order in Trees

Before continuing on our stroll, we'll take a moment to consider the complex, systematic design that can be found in what appears to be a simple tree. From the outside, a tree may appear to be just a huge hunk of wood with leaves that stretches toward the sky. But as we look inside to the heart of a tree, we'll discover unimaginably intricate detail. As we begin to consider these intricacies, let's first imagine that we are camping below a mighty white oak that is 150

145

feet tall, 8 feet in diameter and about 800 years old. Below this oak are scattered several acorns that are not much larger than our thumbs. As we look at the acorns in our hands and then compare them to the towering oak, we are struck by the fact that a small seed such as this has the potential to become a massive forest giant someday. Even more amazing is the microscopic detail within this forest behemoth . . . it is simply astounding to think that all the genetic information required for this minute design is housed within a single seed the size of your thumb. (As impressive as this is, we shall see even more mind boggling things in Chapter 8.)

From the tiniest root hairs buried deep in the ground to the highest leaves in the canopy, each part plays a crucial role in helping the tree "factory" to function. Following is a brief rundown of some of those parts and their roles:

1) *Seeds* - All trees begin as tiny seeds . . . when this seed is planted in suitable soil, it will sprout. Seeds do have a definite up and down side, and it is interesting that even if the down side of a seed is pointed up, the seed will still grow in the right direction. Regardless of how the seed is planted, roots will always grow downward and shoots or stems will always grow upward. Seeds obviously don't have a brain . . . they don't "know" if they are growing in the right direction . . . yet they do grow the right way every time because they are designed to do so by the Master Designer.

2) *Roots* - As the roots sprout from the seed and begin to probe through the soil, they are protected by special root caps. In time, these meager pioneer roots can grow into an impressive system that can stretch to include 7,000 miles of interconnected roots in just one large chunk of soil (such as in some rye grasses). Roots can also grow 400 feet deep into the soil to anchor a tree to the ground. (The 400 feet deep roots were found in a wild fig tree in Transvaal, South Africa.) Certainly, most tree root systems are shorter and shallower, but each is a well ordered system containing lateral roots (which grow outward), and taproots (which grow downward) that branch

into finer roots called rootlets, which further divide into many, extremely thin root hairs that greatly increase the surface area for absorption of water, oxygen and essential nutrients. Also, over 95% of vascular plants have symbiotic fungi called mycorrizhae that are incorporated into their root systems to further increase surface area and improve absorption. Roots are an intricately ordered anchorage, water, oxygen and nutrient uptake system.

3) *Bark* - As we travel above ground, the first layer we will see is the bark. Bark acts as a suit of armor against the outside world, effectively protecting the tree from harmful insects, animals, other plants, disease and severe weather. If this defense system is damaged, the tree is remarkably able to heal itself by covering over the wound, just as we would by putting a bandage over a minor cut or scrape.

4) *Phloem* - Trees include a highly efficient water and nutrient transportation system that works as well or better than our own highway food delivery systems. Through root pressure, (pushing of water and nutrients from the roots to the trunk) transpiration, (the evaporation of water from special pores on trunk and leaf surfaces that "pulls" water and nutrients upward), gravity (which pulls water and nutrients down) and the special adhesive and cohesive properties of water that I've already described, water and dissolved nutrients are able to move up and down through two specially designed parallel highways to nourish all parts of the tree. Phloem (also called the inner bark) is one of these parallel highway networks. This system employs a series of specially interconnected, microscopic sieve tubes to effectively deliver sap (sugar and nutrients dissolved in water) from the leaves downward to its roots.

5) *Cambium* - Just inside the phloem is a very thin layer of growing tissue called the cambium. Within this layer, cells are created to form new cambium, phloem and xylem.

6) *Xylem* - This layer (also called sapwood) is inside the cambium and like the phloem, is part of a tree's ingeniously designed sap delivery system. Xylem uses special microscopic

tubes called tracheids and vessel elements to carry sap from the roots up to the leaves.

7) *Heartwood* - This is the innermost layer in a tree, and is composed of dense, dead wood. In many ways, this is the central core and heart of a tree, providing the strength necessary for a tree to stand.

Extending above ground from the roots again, we will discover vertical order to join the horizontal order we've just discussed. Root hairs lead to rootlets . . . roots then lead to the trunk, which support the branches that support leaves and buds.

8) *Leaves* - Leaves are the solar panels of a tree, acting as the food factory for both the tree and ultimately all life on Earth. For this reason the leaf may be the most important structure on the planet. The importance of the leaf and the photosynthetic process that occurs in its chloroplasts can't be overstated. Besides being extremely important, a leaf is also a well designed, complex, highly ordered structure including veins that support and create a transportation network for nourishing sap to course through. They also have tiny holes called stomata on the underside that allows purified water to escape back into the atmosphere for living creatures to use. This transpiration process, as stated before, is necessary to help pull water from the roots to nourish all parts of the tree, including leaves. Stomata also enable the tree to 'breathe' by creating an entry and exit point for the gases necessary for and generated by photosynthesis.

Designed Growth Patterns in Trees

If you study the structure of trees, you will learn that God has designed tree species to adapt their leaf arrangement, size and shape for maximum photosynthetic efficiency under different environmental conditions. For example, in studying a Sugar Maple growing in the open, we'll see that it exhibits a multilayered pattern, while one growing in the forest will display monolayering. I'd like us to briefly consider the design characteristics of each pattern.

Multilayered Pattern - A Sugar Maple showing this pattern will have multiple layers of smaller, deeply notched leaves. This is an efficient design in the open for several reasons. First, this pattern allows leaves to absorb sunlight most efficiently. Open area trees receive more and brighter sunlight at all angles throughout the course of the day. The best design would be to expose the maximum leaf surface at all angles, from the uppermost to the lower branches . . . this is exactly what we see in multilayered, open area trees. Multilayered trees expose a leaf area 2–3 times greater than the ground area below it, allowing it to capture nearly all the available sunlight. But this exceptional leaf area would be a poor design if only some of the leaves could capture sunlight . . . however, the leaves are shaped and sized so this does not happen. Smaller deeply notched or lobed leaves allow 15–45% of the sunlight to filter past the first exposed branch, which continues to diffuse until the branch farthest from the sun is reached. All leaves are reached, resulting in the maximum amount of sunlight being collected. If you would stand under a multilayered Sugar Maple on a summer day, you would experience dense shade . . . this is due to the fact that the tree has captured the maximum possible sunlight. Under this system, you can be assured that the photosynthetic factories within leaf chloroplasts are kicked into high gear on a sunny day. Multilayering provides an additional benefit in open areas. Wind blows more fiercely at all levels in an open area . . . the smaller, more deeply notched or lobed leaves expose less surface area to be blown, making it harder to extract the leaves than if they were larger. If the wind does succeed in removing some leaves, the loss of a few smaller leaves will have less photosynthetic impact than a tree losing a few larger leaves. In more ways than one, multilayering is the ideal pattern for open areas.

Monolayered Pattern - A Sugar Maple tree found in the forest will display an entirely different pattern than those in the open. Instead of many smaller, deeply notched or lobed, multilayered leaves, a forest Sugar Maple will have fewer and larger, shallow notched or lobed leaves arranged precisely in only one or two non-overlapping layers. This design is ideal for a forest setting, since there are many trees competing for the same sunlight resource. Forest trees tend to grow taller and straighter than well branched, wider open area trees in an effort to outcompete their neighbors as they all reach for the light. It would make sense to design a forest tree with only large, non-overlapping leaves at the top, since the leaves below would be shaded out anyway, and would be a waste of energy to produce. Monolayered trees, despite having fewer leaves than multilayered trees, are just as well designed. The single or few layers of leaves in the canopy are able to capture over 90% of the sunlight that strikes them, making forest trees efficient photosynthetic machines.

You may have also noticed that leaves are generally angled slightly toward the Sun rather than facing it directly. This wonderful design assures that leaves receive less concentrated sunlight per unit area, reducing heat stress and water loss. At the same time, the angled leaf allows sunlight to diffuse over a greater surface area, exposing more tiny chloroplasts for greater photosynthetic production.

Leaves are also amazing for at least one other reason . . . they are the channels through which chemical messages can be sent. Research has shown that trees (especially proven in Sugar Maples and Oaks) are able to communicate with others of the same species to warn of an impending insect attack or disease. An infested tree can actually release chemical messages into the air through their leaves, 'warning' trees of the same species up to 200 feet away. The captured chemical message will then induce the uninfected tree to alter their leaves so they taste less desirable to insects.

The above sections have been an extremely quick overview of some of the more basic parts of a tree, their functions, order and growth patterns. But the microscopic design goes even further than I've discussed . . . miniscule elements, such as parenchyma, collenchyma and schlerenchyma cells are vital to the survival of trees since they collectively make up the larger, more recognizable parts of a tree. If you pick up a good biology textbook, I'm sure you'll agree that the deeper you look at any part of a tree, the more intricate the design. If you were to dissect a tree, piece by piece and study it under a microscope, you would discover several layers of design, with each layer joining others to form a more visible, equally well organized layer. Trees contain design upon design upon design. While brief, I hope this description of a generalized tree has given you an idea of the vertical (roots to canopy) and horizontal (bark to heartwood) order and adaptable growth patterns that exist in trees. A tree is a microcosm of the larger Earth and Universe that God has created.

Tree Design for Winter Survival

As one last diversion before we descend towards the valley, just imagine that the clock has been turned ahead 6 months, and that we are standing in the midst of a frigid Barclay Mountain winter where temperatures may drop below $0°F$. How do trees withstand such bitter winter weather . . . furthermore, how do plants survive brutal Arctic winters that can make the average Pennsylvania winter feel like a warm, sunny shore side vacation?

The two major groups of trees, evergreen and deciduous, can survive because they are designed to do so. We will consider evergreen design first. Evergreens are a group of trees that don't lose their needles during the winter. They can survive frigid winters since their needles are small and wax coated to reduce water loss. Also, the needles, buds, roots and stems contain very little moisture and are filled with a resinous botanical "antifreeze" that prevents them from freezing. (Studies have shown that Hemlocks, just one type of evergreen, are able to endure winter temperatures that plunge to $-112°F$.) Also, some evergreens are triangle shaped, allowing them to shed and withstand the weight of a heavy snowfall. Pine trees feature pointy, thin needles and flexible branches to prevent snow collection and branch breakage. Leaves of Alpine evergreens possess tightly clustered, thick, waxy and often hair covered needles to maintain warmth and reduce evaporation. The fact that evergreens can hold onto their leaves throughout winter also means that they can begin photosynthesis as soon as the ground thaws and liquid water is available.

Broad-leaved deciduous trees, unlike evergreens, drop their leaves during autumn to reduce the possibility of damage through collecting heavy snowfall during winter. As the leaves drop during autumn, seals are forming to prevent water and air from entering where the leaf left a scar and freezing the inside of the tree. By the time the leaves have all dropped, the precious leaves, stems and flowers that represent next year's growth have already been formed and are stuffed into tiny packages called buds, which are located at the end of twigs. Buds are well designed to protect these valuable miniature tree parts, since they are covered with tough, waxy and sometimes hairy scales that provide a warm and waterproof winter coat. At just the right time, as temperatures warm and days become longer, sap rises from the roots to the buds. The protective winter scales then fall off the buds, and the tree leaves, stems and flowers unfurl to create a brilliant springtime display. As the leaves enlarge, broad-leaved trees quickly make up the photosynthetic time they've lost to evergreens during early spring and autumn, due to their wider solar panels. Both evergreen and broad-leaved trees are well equipped for winter survival and prosperous growth throughout the year.

Spatial Patterns in Plant Placement

You can now throw off the winter jacket, gloves, hat and turn the clock back 6 months to the middle of summer. Revived by the warmth, we are now trekking towards the valley, and notice another level of organization along the way. This organization deals with the fact that plant life is changing systematically with each drop in elevation. At the highest peaks of the mountain, hardy lichens dominated . . . below them shrubs were in charge . . . then we finally came to the tree line, below which trees and well structured, mature forests were the rule . . . now, at around 7:30 P.M, we've finally arrived at the base of Barclay Mountain, which is in the Towanda Creek valley. Here, there is a mixture of everything we've seen before, along with several open, rural fields. This vertical

152

vegetative zonation can be seen even more distinctly on higher mountaintops all around the world and exists on a horizontal scale as well. The pattern of plant and wildlife species from mountain valley to mountain top is the same pattern that exists from South to North. In fact, studies have shown that if someone would travel 100 miles north, they would encounter the same collection of species as they would by hiking 400 feet up a mountainside. The stratification is just more spread out if you choose to travel north, but it still is there. The key point is this . . . biological order exists on both horizontal and vertical scales in more than one way. This order is not by chance, but is instead a product of a wise design.

We are now standing in a special habitat called an ecotone, which serves as a transition zone between two different habitats. In this case, we are stationed in an ecotone between field and forest, which is one of the most dynamic and lively wildlife zones in the world. It appears that we have arrived at just the right time . . . it is dusk now and both the forest and field are coming alive. It's a perfect summer evening . . . about 70°F, with a light breeze, and a golden sun setting over the shimmering waters of Towanda Creek. Let's take a seat and enjoy the show as we search for more evidence of God's existence through studying creation.

CHAPTER 7

Order in the Wild Kingdom

W HITE-TAILED DEER - Again, as in all other realms of creation, we will see ample evidence in the animal kingdom that God is the Creator. As we lift our eyes, we spy one of the Creator's most graceful creatures . . . a White-tailed deer, which is silhouetted in the fading sunlight. White-tailed deer are

the state mammal in Pennsylvania, and are one of the most sought after and successful big game animals in the world, built to thrive in almost any conceivable habitat on Earth. They can run up to 40 miles per hour, leap 9+ feet high and over 30 feet in a single bound. Deer are powerful swimmers as well, buoyed up in water by

their hollow hairs, which help them swim several miles at a time. They have great eyes, including a wide field of view to detect the slightest motion during day or night. A pair of large, cup-like ears swivel independently to capture and funnel the smallest sounds gathered from every direction. Their tremendous sense of smell allows them to locate food, detect danger and identify the social status of other deer through chemical messages.

White-tails communicate through a complex collection of chemical, vocal and visual cues. They communicate vocally by using about 12 different sounds, including a variety of snorts, grunts, wheezes, bleats and bawls. Fawns will mew and whine to attract their mother's attention. Their famous white tails are also used for communication . . . a wagging tail means they are unalarmed, a flicking tail signals others to be alert, a horizontally raised tail means the deer has sensed danger and is ready to run . . . (stomping feet are usually accompanied with this behavior) . . . finally, when the tail is upright, you'd better shoot quickly if you're a hunter, because the white flag will soon be running rapidly in the other direction. Buck rubs and scrapes are visual and chemical "bulletin boards" where males leave their individual scent using a series of scent glands, including tarsals at the rear, interdigital glands between their hooves and forehead glands. These scents announce territorial rights, especially during the breeding season, and basically tell other bucks to "Get away!" and female does to "Come closer!" During fights for mating rights, male antlers serve as dominance symbols to help avoid fatal confrontations.

The white-tail's body is covered mainly with short, thinner reddish-brown hair during the summer to aid in temperature control, and with hollow gray-brown hair during winter to efficiently trap heat and remain insulated against the cold. Deer, along with nearly every other mammal, and most animals in general, have a light colored belly. This 'countershading' system, with darker tops and lighter bottoms, allow many animals to avoid predation. This system works well, since sunlight from above lightens the top portion of the body, while the bottom becomes darker as a shadow is cast. This optical illusion allows deer, and others to somewhat lose their 3-D form, flatten out and seemingly vanish into the background as they remain motionless. Countershading is just one of the effective camouflage techniques God has installed into His animal designs to enable them to remain elusive.

Another characteristic that White-tailed deer share with most mammals is their parental skill. Does are excellent mothers, providing great care for their few fawns, greatly increasing their survival rates. Fawns are also designed to be well camouflaged at birth, sporting over 300 white spots that are dappled randomly over their bodies to break up their outline and closely match the sun speckled forest floor. Fawns also emit little or no scent and instinctively remain motionless in the presence of danger. As these fawns eat and rapidly gain weight during the lush spring and summer months, they, along with their parents, utilize a complex digestive system, including a five chambered stomach housing dense populations of bacteria that help them easily break down the tough cellulose and lignin elements in plants. Other herbivores have equally well designed digestive systems. And White-tailed deer are just one of the 4,060 known mammals worldwide that are intricately designed from head to toe. Hair, elusive, low-light behavior, excellent camouflage, keen senses and exceptional parental care are just some of the qualities that make mammals one of the best built groups of creatures in the world.

BATS - While meditating on mammal design, we notice several dark brown streaks whizzing past our heads. These brown streaks are bats and they aren't diving at our heads, as myths proclaim . . . they are simply trying to catch dinner. Dusk is when bats begin to shine . . . evening after evening, these tiny mammals prove that they are the insect-eating champions of the world. Seventy percent of bats rely on insects as their primary food source . . . others eat fruit, nectar, fish and one species, the Vampire Bat, eats blood. (Vampire bats often do little harm to their victims, contrary to popular belief . . . in fact, the component of Vampire bat saliva that prevents blood from clotting in a wound, holds promise as a drug to effectively prevent heart attacks in humans.)

Most bats are voracious, flying insectivores, able to eat half their weight in insects every night. One Little Brown bat was observed catching an average of 1,200 fruit flies per hour, which equals one every three seconds. A colony of Mexican Free-tailed bats is able to consume 1/2 million pounds of insects per night! Just consider what our world would be like without bats and other insectivores . . . insects, which reproduce rapidly, would soon be creeping, crawling and flying up to and above our eyeballs. Thank God for bats!

He has designed 70% of bat species to be ideal insect catching machines. To begin with, their wings, although they appear fragile, are more tear resistant than a good pair of rubber gloves. The thin, streamlined wings are designed to provide both thrust and lift at the same time, producing more efficient flight. The position of flight muscles in the chest, back and shoulder areas allows bats to expend less energy (than if the muscles were in the wings) while they pursue prey. Many bats also feature tail flaps (a membrane between their legs), which they use as an air brake and/or insect trap. I'm sure that many would recognize enormous ears as the most distinguishing characteristic of a bat. These ears are built to funnel and help analyze high frequency sounds that bounce back after being echolocated from the mouth. Through echolocation, bats are able to determine the exact size, shape, texture, distance, speed and the direction their prey is moving. Using this system, bats can precisely locate objects as small as a human hair. The bat's radar system, which utilizes ultra-high frequency sound waves at more than 20 thousand cycles per second, equals or exceeds anything that man has invented . . . in fact, it was the bat that inspired the radar systems we use today. Michael Pitman said that "Ounce for ounce, watt for watt, it (the bat) is millions of times more efficient than the radars and sonars contrived by man."[1]

After filling their stomachs using their highly sophisticated prey location machinery, bats return to their roosts to sleep until the next evening. Most bats hang upside down while they roost . . . this presents a problem, since most creatures that are hung this way will soon die as the blood rushes to their heads. But bats are designed differently. God has installed special valves in their veins that prevent blood from rushing to their heads. God did not overlook any details when He made bats.

Bats are just one example of the many marvelous creatures He has created. And although small (Bumblebee bats are reputed to be the smallest mammal at only 1.25 inches wide, and equaling the weight of a penny), their importance is mighty, not only for controlling insect populations, but also as the sole pollinators and seed dispersers of several essential night blooming plants. (As an example of the orderly division of labor that permeates nature, bats are one of the chief pollinators, seed dispersers and insect eaters of the night, while birds accomplish these tasks during the day.) Whether you like them or not, we need bats. God knew we would need them, as well as many other creatures . . . as a Wise and Loving Designer, He has provided them all.

OWLS - Night is descending upon us quickly now . . . the air is slightly cooling and a brilliant crescent moon is settling an illuminating glow over the still lively forest. If we listen closely, we'll hear the wind whistling through the trees . . . yet it's not the wind at all . . . it's the nearly silent sound of wings piercing the night air. These wings belong to one of the most intimidating predators of the moonlit field and forest . . . the owl. Just as hawks rule the day sky, owls dominate the sky at night.

Owls are well equipped to thrive as hunters of the dark. They rely upon amazing twilight vision and even more astonishing hearing abilities to precisely locate prey at night. Their enormous eyes, which take up over half their skull capacity, contain an extra supply of rods that allow them to see almost 100 times better than humans in the dark. Their eyes are also placed close together, giving them excellent 3-D vision. Remarkable necks, which can rotate 270 degrees, provide all around vision. This neck design allows them to sit quietly on a perch and stare directly behind them without disturbing prey. The owl's incredible hearing ability is enhanced by a dish shaped face that funnels sound to ears that are 4 times more sensitive than cat ears. Both ears are large, but each has a differently shaped opening, and one is higher on the head than the other. This asymmetry causes sound to register sooner and louder in one ear than the other. By taking these two 'readings' and triangulating them, the owl is able to precisely pinpoint the distance and direction of even the smallest sound. Studies have shown that owls can hear a small mouse scurrying in leaves over 150 feet away, and identify its location within 1–2 degrees.

Once the prey is located, owls are well built to capture it. In flight, they feature feathers with soft edges that effectively muffle the sound of beating and swooping wings. This allows owls to silently descend upon their prey. As they move in for the kill, strong, sharp talons are the ideal tool for seizing and carrying prey. Sharp, hooked beaks then enable the owls to tear into and devour their meal. Owls are a mysterious and marvelous part of God's grand design.

CATS - As we continue to enjoy this summer evening, we notice a sleek form slicing across the moonlit field. We can't be certain, but it appears to be a mountain lion (also known as a puma or cougar). This elusive predator is just one of the many cats that are on the prowl throughout the world at this moment. Cats are perhaps the supreme predators of the world, equipped with a myriad of design features, including super-acute senses. Large eyes provide excellent binocular vision and depth perception along with a wide field of view to more efficiently stalk and seize prey. Cats have great day vision and superior night vision. They are able to see in the dark 6 times better than humans due to a specially designed reflecting area called the tapetum lucidum, which absorbs extra light and allows night hunting. When struggling to subdue prey, cats utilize a protective membrane which can be pulled over their eyes to keep dust out.

Cats are also well equipped to pick up sounds and scents. Large, rounded ears can rotate to draw in sounds from any direction and a special scent center on the roof of its mouth (called the Jacobson organ) can detect a wide variety of scents. Their sense of touch is also well developed, including long, stiff and sensitive whiskers that enable them to feel their way through tall grass or darkness, as well as judge distances more accurately.

Besides possessing acute senses, cat bodies are physically designed to perform when they pursue prey. For starters, most cats are well furred for warmth and camouflaged to deceive prey. Rapid acceleration, impressive running speeds, incredible jumping ability and brute strength combine in allowing cats to capture and cut down prey. Cheetahs are the fastest land animal in the world, able to accelerate from 0–45 miles per hour in just 2 seconds, and can exceed 70 MPH during quick bursts to tackle prey. Cheetahs are the quickest, but other cats aren't too far behind. Their speed is due to several design factors, including short necks that help streamline the body while promoting balance, fairly long legs constructed with quick, powerful muscles, a great heart and lung system to deliver a plentiful supply of oxygen to muscles and strong, flexible spines that provide an extra burst like a spring while running and jumping. As they pound the turf in pursuit of a meal, strong front leg bones and soft paw pads act as shock absorbers to cushion the impact. Most cats also have long tails that improve agility and balance which aids them when chasing swift, zigzagging prey. The same qualities that allow cats to run quickly also enable them to leap to amazing heights and distances. For instance, the mountain lion we are looking at can leap 16 feet high into a tree and some cats can easily cover 20 feet in a single bound. Exceptional jumpers, such as the snow leopard, have been observed to cover gaps of 49 feet with one leap! (If cats could learn to dribble and dunk, they would make an unstoppable basketball team.)

As a cat closes in for the kill, it can use its brute strength to tackle prey that is twice its size. It also unleashes a set of claws, which have been wisely designed to retract into special grooves in the paw while running to maintain their length and sharpness. (Only cheetahs have non-retractable claws . . . yet for them this is a great design, since they are a smaller cat that relies more on speed than power. The claws act as spikes, giving cheetahs a set of track shoes with exceptional traction and even greater speed.) All cats are built with a special dew claw, which they use to slash at and knock their victims to the ground. This uniquely shaped dew claw then holds struggling prey to the ground while the cat delivers a lethal bite with a pair of sharp, long curved canines that have proven to fit perfectly between the neck bones of prey. The powerful bite quickly breaks the spinal cord, reducing pain for the victim and energy wasting struggle for the cat. The canines are attached to a strong, short jaw that is part of a well designed skull including a high crowned back that provides greater space for the attachment of the massive muscles that power the mighty bite.

Once the victim has died, cats unveil an impressive set of utensils, including razor sharp claws that carve their meal and strong carnassial teeth for cutting, shearing, tearing and chewing meat. In addition to these utensils, cats have tongues which are covered with backward pointing spikes called papillae. This sandpaper-like tongue enables cats to literally lick meat off the bones of their prey. At this point, their well developed digestive system quickly processes their meal, which means that the cat will be on the prowl again soon. Cats are designed by God to be a superior predator.

But cats, while appearing to be vicious killers, can be incredibly gentle as well. Lionesses have a special gap behind their canines, with which they carefully pick up their cubs. Baby cats also feature loose flaps of skin on the back of their necks that perfectly fit the gap in their mother's mouth. Cubs are clearly designed to be picked up, and their mothers are designed to gently hoist them.

As we watch the sleek silhouette of the cougar fade into the forest, we look at our watch and notice that the night has suddenly slipped away. We'd better get plenty of sleep tonight, since tomorrow will be the busy final day during our tour of planet Earth.

WOODPECKERS - The following morning we are greeted by the sweet symphony of singing birds. But as we listen, we notice one sound that rises above this melody. This unique noise sounds somewhat like a jackhammer. To get a closer look at the source of this sound, we whip out our binoculars and zero them in on what appears to be a woodpecker. At first, we're a little annoyed by its 'jack hammering' as we try to wake up, but as we study a bit closer, we realize that it, like all others, is a well designed creature. With the aid of a field guide, we can see that it has exceptionally strong neck muscles and a reinforced skull to withstand the constant pounding of its strong, chisel-shaped bill against the tree trunk. During a strike, the head shoots forward literally quicker than a speeding bullet and exerts a force 1,000 times that of gravity upon contact. Woodpeckers are able to bash their bills into wood at up to 16 times per second, exceeding the rate of fire from a submachine gun. Special sponge-like tissue between the cranium and beak are able to withstand these powerful and sustained shocks. Woodpeckers are also equipped with well coordinated neck muscles that pull the braincase away from the beak with every blow and keep the head perfectly straight. Just a slight twist of the head combined with the force of a single hammer would tear the brain from its case. Scientists have admitted that the shock absorbing system in woodpeckers is superior to anything man has invented.

As it hammers up to 960 times per minute, miniscule sawdust is filling the air . . . but this is not a problem for the woodpecker, since it is built with a special tuft of feathers around its nostrils to prevent sawdust from entering. We also observe a stiff tail, which is used as a '3rd leg' to anchor the bird on the trunk. Strong, short legs, sharp claws, well coordinated tendons and zygodactyl toes (2 forward and 2 back on each foot) give woodpeckers' excellent grip on tree trunks. As the bird finally uncovers an insect, which it can literally hear under the bark with its exceptional hearing, it uncoils its 5 inch long, sticky barbed tongue from around its brain cavity to easily extract its meal. Woodpeckers are well designed to catch prey in this unique under the bark location.

THE BALD EAGLE - As we study the woodpecker, we sense a broad shadow crossing over our heads. Pointing our binoculars in that direction, we are thrilled to see the symbol of America gliding gracefully in the sky above us. The mighty and majestic Bald Eagle, with a wingspan up to 10 feet, is well designed to float on the wind currents as it looks and listens for prey below. Their hearing is acute, and their eyesight is even more amazing, at least 8 times more powerful than our vision. With their dual monocular and binocular vision system, they can see sharp images of small objects up to several miles away, in color. Eagles also are endowed with two special sets of eyelids, the first of which is used when in flight or observation from their nests located several thousand feet in the air. The second set is used when flying directly into the Sun, effectively shielding and allowing them to stare intently at the brilliant, blinding light. The eyes of eagles also include a series of tissues folded into pleats called pectens. Each pecten contains a fine network of lymph tubes, which act as fluid filled electrolytes, making them sensitive to the magnetic pull of the Earth. In young eagles, the tubes are pliable and adjust themselves to the lines of magnetic intensity from the North Pole just like an arrow on a compass. As the young eagle ages, the tube becomes rigid and permanently fixed in a position that coordinates precisely with their place of birth. When the eagle migrates from home, the pectens cause minor pressure and pain behind the eyes. This pressure will persist until the eagle returns home. Pectens are built in gyroscopes that allow eagles to accurately fly home from thousands of miles away. This infallible sense of direction is God directed.

But eagles are certainly more than wings and eyes. After spotting prey, they are able to dive-bomb at up to 200 miles per hour. They can then seize prey in powerful talons that are larger than the canine teeth of an adult lion. Finally, they can tear apart and consume prey on the spot with their sharply hooked beaks or can employ their strong flight muscles to carry prey larger and heavier than itself to a more secluded spot.

HUMMINGBIRDS - Turning our eyes back toward the ground, we spot a radiant ruby-throated hummingbird whirring past us in a blur of beauty. The intriguing hummingbird is one of the more colorful members of the bird community. They are also one of the more amazing . . . here are some facts to consider:

The hummingbird heart beats up to 1,250 times, lungs expand and contract 250 times and wings beat 2000–3000 times per minute! This energy output is equal to 10 times that of a person running 9 miles per hour. Imagine for a moment what it would feel like to be a hummingbird . . . If you were a 170 pound 'hummer,' you'd burn 155,000 calories per day and evaporate 100 pounds of perspiration per hour. You'd have to eat 1,300 hamburgers and drink 60 liters of water per day to stay alive. If you ran out of water, your skin temperature would soon reach the melting point of lead, and you'd eventually ignite! Now imagine migrating 600 miles across the Gulf of Mexico without stopping . . . hummingbirds do it with only 2.1 grams of food inside them. How do such tiny birds accomplish these great feats? The secret is their fuel source and excellent body design.

The fuel that keeps their super fast engines humming comes from the nectar of at least 1,000 flower blossoms per day. They are designed to efficiently extract this nectar for at least three reasons . . . their flight, bills and tongues. Hummingbirds are the only creatures that can hover in place, fly straight up and down or backwards. They can accomplish this since they are able to flap their wings in a back and forth figure eight motion. Powerful flight muscles that compose up to 30% of their body weight and a unique ball and socket joint in the shoulder allow the wings to move in a rowing figure eight motion. The shoulder joint is so flexible that the wing can swivel almost 180 degrees on the backstroke, enabling the bird to remain motionless. Also, the wing feathers are linked together by tiny hooklets that hold the barbules firmly, so that regardless of the direction in which the wings are moving, they always act as a smooth airfoil. Their uniquely designed flight abilities allow hummers to retrieve nectar (and pollinate) without taking the time to find a perch.

Special long, curving bills also aid hummingbirds in maintaining their active lifestyles. Different hummingbirds have different bill shapes, each of which perfectly fits a particular flower type(s). As amazing as the bills are, they would be of little worth without their tongues, which are extremely long, semi-tubular and split at the tip. The tongue can be extended well beyond the tip of their bills to feed on the nectar deep within the blossom. The tongue then acts as a piston, literally pumping nectar into their bodies at over 13 sips per second. Hummingbirds and long tubular flowers are an example of a well designed relationship between a flower and its pollinator, where both species benefit.

Bird Design

Birds are one of the most visible and vibrantly colored creatures God has made, and as evidenced by owls, woodpeckers, eagles and hummingbirds, they are a well designed part of this planet. But certainly not all birds are the same . . . the separation of bird species to maintain order is by God's infinite wisdom. If we study any bird community on Earth, we will notice many ways in which they are separated. For example, we will see many different types of birds feeding in unique locations (ex . . . ground, lower, middle and upper trunk, inner and outer branches, lower and upper canopy), at unique times (ex . . . early, late morning, afternoon, evening, night) in unique ways (ex . . . hawking, gleaning, probing, chiseling, leaf-tossing, sweeping, diving, stooping, dabbling, stalking, scavenging, etc . . .) on unique food items (ex . . . insects, amphibians, reptiles, small mammals, plant products).

These unique feeding strategies are due to unique body designs, especially in the beak, feet, wings and tongue. A bird's beak is, in many ways, the primary tool of its trade, as each is sculpted to consume certain types of food. As an example of beak diversity, consider that raptor beaks are sharp and hooked for tearing flesh, while parrot beaks are thick and massive for cracking nuts. A pelican's beak includes a stretchy throat pouch, which it uses as a fishing bag, while a curlew beak acts as a long, slim pair of tweezers perfect for probing in the mud. Tongue lengths also vary in birds to further avoid competition. For example, there are the tubular, fringed nectar feeding tongues of Bananaquits, the long, coiled, barbed probing tongue of a woodpecker, the short, broad, fruit eating tongue of a Trogon, the flesh eating tongue of a Sooty shearwater, and the food straining tongue of the Northern shoveler. Other examples abound.

Wing types also vary to influence lifestyle. Some, such as hawks, sport broad soaring wings, while others, such as the Peregrine falcon, have muscular, powerful wings built for speed (the Peregrine can exceed speeds of 200 MPH in a dive, during which they slam into their victims, literally tearing them in half). Others, such as swifts, display wings constructed for maneuverability through tight spaces, while other birds have a different design. Feet types also vary . . . some feature feet designed for perching, some for swimming, others for killing, while some possess another type. The key point is that each bird, ranging from the 9 foot tall Ostrich to the 2 inch long Cuban bee hummingbird, has been built with a unique body design which allows them to thrive where they live.

As we survey the field and forest, we observe many other types of creatures besides birds that are ideally designed to fill unique niches with minimal competition. The separation system found in each natural community on Earth works better than a well oiled machine, lasting longer and having fewer breakdowns along the way. But while there are well designed differences between and within bird and other species, there are important similarities that make them well designed as a group. Birds, for example, exhibit design similarities (and differences) even before they are born.

Bird Birth and Reproduction

The eggs in which baby birds develop are unique in size, shape, color and texture to often match the background of the uniquely placed nest of each species. And although different, each egg is a masterpiece of design. Eggs contain 3 main components . . . the yolk, albumen and shell. The yolk is an energy rich food supply and cradle for the embryo while it grows. The embryo within the yolk is surrounded by 3 membranes that support its life and growth . . . the amnion, chorion and allantoic sac. The amnion surrounds the embryo in a nourishing environment of water and salt. The chorion is a protective membrane that surrounds all embryonic structures. The allantoic sac enables the embryo to breathe oxygen from the outside and exhale potentially deadly carbon dioxide to the outside. This sac also acts as a sewer for the embryo, storing poisonous nitrogenous wastes while it develops. Finally, the allantoic sac includes a growing network of fine capillaries to keep the embryo well supplied with blood.

The second component of an egg, the albumen (or egg white) is composed of 90% water and 10% protein. It provides life preserving water to the embryo, acts as an elastic shock absorbing cushion when the egg is moved or jolted, and insulates the embryo from sudden changes in air temperature. The third component, the shell, along with conserving food and water, is permeated by thousands of microscopic pores that allow gases to pass through it. Yet, the shell is still strong enough to withstand the weight of an incubating adult. While tough, the shell is still delicate enough to allow a tiny chick to break out when the time is right. The egg, while appearing simple, is certainly a masterpiece that is designed to improve the reproductive success of birds.

Even before a chick breaks out of its egg, it is designed to communicate with appropriate behaviors. Special clicks tell parents when they are too cold or hot. Other clicks cause parents to switch from incubating to brooding behavior, which occurs just before hatching. Chicks also are equipped with an egg tooth and hatching muscles on the neck to break through the shell. After hatching, nestlings again exhibit appropriate behaviors in an effort to be fed and brooded. Some hatchlings have brightly colored and specially patterned feeding targets that help the parents direct food to their mouths.

Insects are the favored food of nestlings, since they are rich in protein, and they just happen to emerge during spring when hungry migrant birds are returning to build nests, reproduce and feed voracious youngsters. It is no surprise that insects emerge at the exact time when birds need them the most . . . it is by God's sovereign timing. (This timing is also a great design for insects since an incredible flush of them overwhelms predators, allowing many insects to survive to reproductive age.)

Also, the excrement of many baby birds come out packaged in a neatly sealed membrane called the fecal sac. Parents can easily deposit these baby diapers outside the nest to help avoid smell and possible predation of the nestlings. Birds are certainly well designed with God-given behaviors and physical characteristics before and shortly after birth.

While we're on the subject of new birth, let's briefly discuss how reproduction occurs in birds. First, remember that all reproductive and nesting activities are governed by internal biological clocks that work in precise coordination with the sun. In birds, increasing day length in late winter causes the anterior pituitary gland to produce hormones that trigger the gonads to produce sex hormones . . . androgens in males and estrogen in females. Without the sun and internal biological clocks, there would be no baby birds on Earth.

The breeding season begins as migratory male birds arrive first on the breeding grounds to establish dominance hierarchies and territories, which greatly reduces chaos when the females finally arrive. These hierarchies are established through often non violent "fights" involving colorful displays and species specific songs, some of which can be quite fascinating to listen to. For example, Nightjar

168

songs sound like the rumble of a distant motorcycle . . . Superb lyrebirds from Southeast Australia can mimic car sirens, telephones, a chainsaw, car engine and burglar alarms (wouldn't it be nice to have one of these around the house?). Other interesting songs include Red-winged blackbirds, which sound like a flute, Mockingbirds, which mimic human laughter, American redstarts, which sound like a rattly ticking clock and American bitterns, nicknamed the "Thunder Pumper" and "Stake driver" since its song sounds like a sledgehammer striking a stake.

Once the females have arrived, males again resort to often melodic and sometimes comical song, colorful plumage and elaborate display rituals to impress a prospective mate. Once mates are chosen and young conceived, nests are established. Each species has a unique nesting location and type. Nests can be located almost anywhere, from the ground to a craggy cliffside, made of almost anything, including mostly sticks, bark, mud and plant fiber, but also involving hair, large leafy lichens, seaweed, snake skins, cellophane, candy wrappers, and hairpins, among many other things. Nests can range in size from a simple scrape a few inches off the ground to the massive Bald eagle nest that can weigh over 2 tons. In these uniquely placed nests are species specific eggs featuring unique shapes, sizes, colors and textures to match the background of the nest, greatly increasing survival rates. (White eggs are laid only by those species that begin incubation immediately after the eggs are laid or who cover them with downy feathers each time they leave the nest.)

The females that incubate and brood the eggs feature a specially designed brood patch, which is a relatively bare area of skin containing a high mass of blood vessels that keep baby birds warm. Females are often less colorful than males, and for good reason, since their drabness camouflages them from potential predators, increasing the chances of successful brooding, birth and growth of her young.

Flight Design

Flight, along with reproductive and feeding activities, is one of the most noticeable characteristic of birds. They are the masters of the air just as fish rule the waters. Birds can hover in one place, fly backwards (hummingbirds), upside down, very high (a Ruppells

Vulture actually hit a plane at 37,000 feet high), very fast (Peregrine falcons exceed 200 MPH during steep dives) and can soar for long periods of time (no bird spends more time in the air than the Sooty tern, which can remain in the air for 3–10 years . . . they even eat, reproduce and sleep in the air . . . once young leave the nest, they may not touch the Earth again until they die). Sustained and often graceful flight sets birds apart from all other organisms. Experiments have shown that the ability to fly is not learned from parents, but is a skill that is unleashed from a baby bird's well designed genetic makeup. From head to toe, and even before birth, God has built most birds to be feathered flying machines. They are so well designed that we have copied birds to invent human flight. Birds are wonderfully designed to fly for several reasons.

Among those reasons are a light, yet strong skeleton, including a backbone and pelvis that functions as shock absorbers during landing, and a wishbone that compresses and powerfully springs out in perfect rhythm with beating wings to give an extra kick during flight. The bones, including a broad, flat breastbone, are strategically placed throughout the body to provide ideal attachment sites for the super strong flight muscles. Birds have combinations of red muscle fibers for sustained flight or swimming, white fibers for quick, powerful bursts while capturing prey or avoiding predators and pink muscle fibers for both endurance and speed.

Birds also have well designed circulatory and respiratory systems featuring a powerful, four-chambered heart and efficient, flow through lungs, which deliver fuel and remove both waste and excessive heat produced by intense flight. The legs of birds are often exposed during flight and swimming . . . this could present a serious problem in frigid air or water. But the countercurrent exchange system that has been installed in their bodies solves this problem. Functioning the same way as in fish, this system involves the contact of warm arteries streaming from the heart and cooler veins returning to the heart. This touching prevents freezing and maintains a constant temperature in exposed areas such as legs and feet. This allows birds to fly and swim even on the coldest days.

The legs of birds are often strong and springy at the joints to provide an extra burst into the air during takeoff. And while resting on a perch, the feet of flying birds feature special flexor tendons that automatically lock around a branch to anchor the bird to its perch. These tendons remain locked even during sleep to prevent the bird from falling to the ground. The tendons are released only when the bird is ready to fly again.

Feathers are perhaps the most obvious design feature of birds that propel flight. Small birds may have 2,000 and larger birds display up to 25,000 individual feathers. Soft and flexible primary, secondary and tertial contour flight feathers are light and hollow inside, yet very strong, and the individual feather bristles are intricately interconnected with barbules, which essentially act like Velcro to zip feathers together, providing a smooth, streamlined airfoil that reduces drag and turbulence, and increases thrust and lift. Within the wings are powerful tendons and compact packages of tiny muscles that control the subtle details of wing and feather position.

Birds are covered with more than flight feathers . . . down feathers provide insulation, semiplumes are responsible for insulation and buoyancy, especially in water birds, filoplumes transfer sound vibrations to the skin and sensitive bristles help detect the presence of flying insects. To maintain their feathers, birds are built with special uropygial glands which produce an oil that extends feather life and provides waterproofing.

Obviously, not all birds can fly. Those that can't are equipped with other design features to compensate for the lack of flight. For example, Ostriches, at 9 feet are the world's tallest bird. And although they can't fly, they are able to run up to 35 MPH on their long legs, outpacing a racehorse and most predators. Yet, even as a predator like a lion draws near, these vulnerable looking birds can use their strong leg muscles to literally kick like a mule. This kick becomes a slashing whip when super sharp toe claws are unleashed. These weapons are why Ostriches rarely fall prey to predators like lions. The idea that Ostriches bury their head in the sand when threatened is a myth.

Some birds, such as the Common loon can't run or fly well. But again, God has installed designs in their bodies to more than compensate. For example, loons have heavier bones, are able to empty their air sacs and can push all the air from their feathers (which keep them afloat) to sink straight down like a submarine. They can then remain underwater for long periods of time by shuttling oxygen to important organs while pursuing prey as they are propelled by webbed feet that are wisely placed far back on the body for extra paddling power. Once their prey is in sight, they are able to seize it securely in a spear shaped bill. Neither the ostrich, loon or other ground and water-borne birds can fly well, yet they are well designed to thrive in their special niche.

Migration

For those birds (including most) given the ability, flight is just one of a combination of design features that contribute to one of the most spectacular events in the life of many birds . . . migration. Some, such as the Arctic tern, fly 25,000 miles round trip during their annual migration. Migrants in general can fly 80–90 hours nonstop . . . on a human scale, this is equivalent to someone running consistent 4 minute miles for 90 hours straight, stopping for a quick meal and rest, then doing it all over again. If a migratory bird, such as a Blackpoll warbler burnt gasoline instead of body fat, it would be getting 720,000 miles per gallon! Birds are well designed migratory machines far more efficient than our best built automobiles.

Not only are migratory birds incredibly efficient, but they also follow remarkably precise migratory paths. One study involving a Gray-cheeked thrush made this fact overwhelmingly clear.[2] A team of scientists attached a radio transmitter to the leg of the thrush as it rested in central Illinois one afternoon before its take off at dusk. When the thrush took off, the ornithologists (bird scientists) followed it in a small plane. A severe thunderstorm and shortage of fuel forced their plane down during the night while the thrush flew on. After refueling, the ornithologist's plane took off again, and amazingly spotted the same thrush in the vast night sky. The thrush finally landed in Wisconsin after flying 650 kilometers on a firm compass bearing all night, without refueling. The migratory thrush clearly outperformed the ornithologist's man-made plane, but how did it fly so accurately through the storm? How do migrants in general travel with such precision?

Birds rely on at least 5 built in qualities as they migrate. First, they spot and follow visual landmarks with excellent eyesight. High soaring birds are believed to have the keenest vision of all, able to resolve details at distances 2.5–3 times greater than humans due to the large number of cones (daylight color receptors) in their retinas. Birds have anywhere from 400,000 cones per square millimeter (ex. House finches) to 1 million per square millimeter (ex. Common buzzard), compared to about 200,000 cones per millimeter in humans. Exceptional eyesight is why Northern Gannets can see schools of fish swimming below water from 100 feet above the surface before they plunge into the water with their missile shaped bodies to capture prey more than 100 feet below the surface. This is also how keen-eyed Peregrine falcons can spot prey over 5 miles away before dive bombing both air and water-borne birds.

Some migrants also use their amazing senses to literally hear and smell their way to wintering and breeding grounds. Experiments with Leach's storm petrels have shown that they can smell their migratory islands from several miles away. Tests on pigeons indicated that their hearing is far superior to ours as they are able to hear the sound of ocean surf and wind striking mountain ranges from hundreds of miles away. (Pigeons, along with most birds, can also 'hear' through their body as well as their ears since they are endowed with sensitive feathers on their face, body, wings and legs to detect small sound vibrations, which are useful in locating prey and avoiding predators. These sound detectors are always turned on, even in sleeping birds.)

Besides their spectacular senses of sight, smell and sound detection, migratory birds are built to be tuned into the frequencies of several cues given off by planet Earth. The Sun is one of these cues, acting as a reliable compass due its rhythmic regularity of rising in the East and setting in the West. It also moves through the sky at a predictable 15 degrees per hour. Birds are equipped with sensitive biological clocks that are synchronized with this precise movement, making the sun an effective migratory compass.

Predictable star patterns are another cue that migrants use . . . experiments in planetariums have proven that birds can accurately identify star patterns during different times of the year, and can use these patterns to fly on the appropriate migratory path. Research has also shown that migrants are sensitive to the Earth's magnetic field, and can use it as an aid to travel, even on cloudy or foggy nights. Studies have proven that at least some birds, such as Homing pigeons, have tiny magnetite crystals embedded between their skull and brain, which, along with special photo receptors, seem to give these migrants a magnetic compass as well. (It is now known that several 'primitive' species of algae, insects, slugs and bacteria are also equipped with sophisticated magnetic compasses.)

One of the truly amazing aspects of migration is that young, first time migrants are able to perform their initial migration without assistance from their parents. How can these young birds travel thousands of miles on a course they've never traveled to a place they've never been, without any help? Research has shown that they can accurately 'read' the sun, star and magnetic compasses to reach migratory destinations on their own. How can they do this . . . no one has taught them how to read these compasses . . . where, then did this knowledge come from? I would suggest that God has implanted a genetic map within each migrant which allows them to migrate with precision between breeding and wintering grounds. There is really no other explanation, unless you'd prefer to believe that complex behaviors and abilities like this came from a chaotic primordial soup of dead particles that came from a primeval explosion composed of non-intelligent matter which admittedly came from nothing and nowhere.

Biological Clocks - Part II

Precise arrival and departure dates are another impressive aspect of migration. Without fail, migrants seem to arrive at their wintering and breeding grounds with great predictability. Again, how do they 'know' when to leave and when to return? The answer lies in an elaborate system of internal biological clocks which they share with every other creature on the planet. Studies have shown that biological clocks are located in the cells of all creatures to precisely regulate basic daily and annual activity patterns. Circadian rhythms are the name of the biological clock that controls daily activity patterns by exactly matching the daily 24-hour cycle of the Earth's rotation on its axis.

The other biological clock, called a circannual clock, involves circannual rhythms which are synchronized to the annual cycle of the Earth's revolution around the sun. Circannual rhythms use the predictable patterns of the Sun to trigger a complex, yet orderly cascade of physiological reactions which set off an integrated network of behaviors that govern reproduction, molt, migration and other activities in birds. In migration, for example, increasing day length triggers increasing hormone levels that lead to premigratory fattening, which provides the energy migrants will need to complete the arduous journey. These hormones also stimulate the urge to migrate (this migratory restlessness is called 'zugunrhue'). Without these biological clocks and the Sun to govern both daily and annual activities, death and chaos would rule on planet Earth. God has wisely installed them as part of the design package of each creature to allow them to flourish on the planet He has created.

Insect Design

As the morning heats up we are confronted with one of the results of sin on Earth (which we'll discuss in more detail later). Pesky swarms of gnats are humming around our heads, into our ears and eyes and up our noses. It doesn't matter where we move . . . the menacing mob always seems to follow us. At times like this I'm thankful that God has placed birds, bats and other insect eaters on Earth. If He hadn't, the situation would be much worse . . . consider the following: If a single mating pair of house flies with an unlimited food supply began reproducing in April and all their offspring survived and mated, by August of that year there would be 191,000,000,000,000,000,000 flies resulting from the original mated pair. To picture how many flies this is, if you allow 1/8 inch of space per fly, the offspring from this one mated pair would cover the entire surface of the Earth 47 feet deep! Thank God for insectivores and other biological controls . . . without them, insects would soon overwhelm us.

Still, despite the predators and other controls, insects, in some ways, still dominate the world. Approximately 99 out of every 100 known animal species is an insect. About 1 million insect species are known to exist today, yet experts estimate that perhaps only 3% of the actually existing insect species have been discovered. Another estimate states that for every human being alive on Earth today, there are about 12 million individual insects. They certainly are abundant, and can be a major pest. Besides annoying us by buzzing around our heads or biting us, they destroy about 10 percent of our crops, causing billions of dollars in damage yearly. (The adverse effect of insects, as I've already mentioned, is ultimately a result of man's sin, and is not by God's original design.) Yet, despite their detractions, I think you will agree that they are well designed as a group, intriguing as individuals, and ultimately necessary for our survival.

Insects and other arthropods (including crustaceans and arachnids) have been built to conquer nearly all the habitats on Earth, from the highest mountains to the hottest springs, saltiest lakes, darkest caves and deepest seas. Three key design features have made arthropods so successful and widespread . . . 1)Hard outer body casings, called exoskeletons, which provide an effective body armor, 2)Wings, which are used to pursue prey and avoid predators and 3)Legs with flexible joints for efficient movement. Arthropods also have excellent senses of sight, smell and touch. Compound eyes provide exceptional detection of small movements from potential predators or prey. As part of this design, each eye is composed of a cluster of up to 30,000 lenses. Feelers and antennae are used to smell and even taste the smallest scent particles in the air around them. The antennae and tiny hair-like bristles on their body and legs can detect the slightest touch as well as the minute movements in wind and water currents.

Arthropods, while possessing many shared designs that allow them to thrive as a group, also have many differences which enable them to inhabit nearly all corners of the Earth. Insects alone range in size from tiny gnats and fairy flies (10 would fit on a pinhead) to fist sized beetles and moths with wingspans wider than your hand (exceeding 12 inches). Insects possess a seemingly endless variety of body designs, each of which is perfectly suited for a particular habitat and lifestyle.

As an example of the differences, consider that an array of digestive systems allow them to eat all types of plant and animal food, gorging on everything from wood to blood. Their mouthparts are designed for chewing, sucking, piercing and lapping food. Insects also display a variety of amazing designs for wings, body coverings, reproductive organs and other body parts. For example, consider the variety in leg designs . . . grasshoppers have powerful hind legs specialized for jumping, house flies feature adhesive pads on their legs which allow them to cling to almost any surface, honeybees have hind legs ideal for the collection, storage and transfer of pollen, and diving beetles have hind legs perfectly suited for swimming. The diversity of designs is almost endless for each body part . . . it would be very difficult to describe them all in detail. Yet, as in all other communities of creatures, this diversity is designed to reduce competition and conflict, which improves the survival rates of all community members. As in all realms of nature, God has successfully created niches to allow insects to survive on this planet.

Insects, arachnids and other arthropods, although generally small, are some of the most interesting animals on Earth. Consider the following:

BEES - As stated in an earlier chapter, bees are well designed food gatherers and pollinators, featuring elongated mouthparts to collect nectar, stiff hairs on their bodies that act as pollen baskets and elaborate 'Waggle dances' that communicate the exact distance and direction of major nectar (and indirectly pollen) sources, based on the position of the Sun. (There would be a major flaw to the Waggle dance if the eyes of bees weren't so well designed. The problem lies in the fact that the position of the Sun moves one degree of longitude for every four minutes that passes. But the remarkable compound eyes of the bee are composed of thousands of microscopic, hexagonal lenses that are able to identify the exact position of the Sun, regardless of its own position. The waggling bee is then able to alter its dance to be precisely in tune with the position of the Sun.) With a complete set of flight instructions, a bee is then able to use its high tech airspeed gauge, built in gyroscope and directional compass to precisely hit its pollination target. The sophisticated design and fantastic pollination services of bees are essential to our existence . . . without them, we'd all be in trouble.

But bees are far more than superbly designed, flying, food gathering and pollinating machines. Their social structure is also exceptional for such a small creature. The hive contains a highly efficient, well organized group of individuals, not a mass of confusion as it may seem. Hive members include scouts to locate nectar, collectors to fly and gather nectar, cell cleaners, nurses to feed the larvae (unhatched baby bees), a hive construction crew, garbage crew, guards to deter intruders and an air conditioning crew (includes those that flap wings, and those that gather water for the hive . . . the combined effect of water and flapping wings cools the hive, keeping larvae and other hive inhabitants moist and cool). The hive also includes one queen bee, which can lay up to 100 eggs per day, and drones, which mate with the queen. The cooperation of all individuals assures that life in the hive runs smoothly. Bees are physically and socially well designed by the Master Designer.

ANTS - Like bees, ants exhibit a highly organized social structure, with one or more queens laying eggs, soldiers to guard eggs, tunnelers which create hallways in the soil and collectors to gather food. They communicate very effectively with scent, able to identify each other and follow scented food trails to increase efficiency. They are built like super strong bulldozers, able to carry loads 50 times their own weight . . . this is the equivalent of you lifting a truck above your head by yourself! Although they only weigh a fraction of an ounce and look fragile with narrow waists and spindly legs, they are champion weightlifters. In fact, it has been calculated that they are mass for mass, 30–40 times stronger than a horse. With such astounding strength and powerful jaws, ants are easily able to kill, carve, and carry their food back to the nest. In addition, they help to create better soil by tunneling through it and are important to us as scavengers who clean up dead insect bodies.

HOUSE FLIES - These common insects are one of the most skillful aerial acrobats in the world, able to fly along at full speed with their feet facing the floor, and then suddenly reach their front feet over their rear to land firmly on the ceiling. Their feet are equipped to attach to almost any surface, including glass. Claws on the feet are used to grip rough surfaces, while pads including hundreds of tiny hairs that secrete a sticky substance are used when landing on smooth surfaces. Flies also feature taste buds on their feet, saliva chemically designed to quickly digest and liquefy food, and a raspy tongue to slurp up the liquefied food.

FLEAS - Fleas escape danger by leaping with a pair of long, powerful back legs. These legs are home to a special click mechanism that stores energy and then releases it suddenly when needed, like a spring loaded revolver. When they shoot upward, fleas achieve a speed around 50 miles per hour . . . the rapid rate of acceleration would easily break human legs, but flea legs are well designed to absorb this acceleration. The average flea measures just a few pinheads across (about 1/8 inch), but can leap up to 150 times their own length. To accomplish an equal feat, a human would have to leap over the length of 2 football fields (about 700 feet) or the height of a 100 story building in a single bound! For its size, fleas are probably the world's greatest animal athlete.

BEETLES - The over 1/2 million known beetle species account for 1/3 of all the animals that have been discovered on the planet. Literally hundreds of new species are being found each year. This group includes some of the largest, strongest and best protected species in the world. Some are as large as your fist, while others are incredibly strong. The Rhinoceros beetle, nicknamed the 'Hercules Beetle,' is the weightlifting champion of the world, able to support and carry over 800 times its weight. Beetles are also well designed to defend themselves against attack. Bombardier beetles, for example, escape predators by shooting a pulsing, toxic chemical stream from its rear, much like a machine gun shoots bullets. The irritating spray can exceed temperatures of 100°C (212°F), and when shot, also releases puffs of smoke which help the beetle escape while the would-be predator is momentarily confused. This short account doesn't even begin to touch the tip of magnificent beetle design worldwide.

BUTTERFLIES AND MOTHS - Butterflies display some of the best defense strategies in nature. Some species, such as Monarch butterflies, are poisonous and advertise their toxicity with bright warning coloration. Brilliant warning coloration is shared by many animals, ranging from fish to insects and is a powerful defense strategy, warning predators that eating them could be hazardous to their health. Studies have proven that these bold warning colors do indeed deter predators, just as they are designed to do. Butterflies, along with bees, ants and others also demonstrate mimicry. For example, Viceroy butterflies, through natural selection (God's design for species adaptability) look very similar to poisonous Monarchs, providing protection to the Viceroy. Insects in general exhibit some of the most creative mimicry in the animal world, resembling sticks, leaves, bark, flowers and other items to provide effective and ingenious camouflage protection.

Moths and butterflies throughout the world are equipped with colorful false eyes, wing border spots and lining, which they flash at potential predators. This defense design often scares or confuses predators long enough for the insect to escape. If not scared or confused, studies have shown that

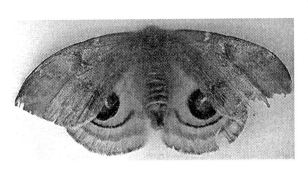

predator attacks are often misdirected toward false eyes, resulting in only minor damage to the outer wings, while the more vulnerable and vital body parts remain unharmed. Some species, such as the caterpillar stage of the Madagascan butterfly, have been even more extremely designed, using masterfully detailed markings, including huge eyes and fang marks to closely resemble snakes. These species even wriggle in the presence of would be predators to look more like a slithering reptile. While neither this tactic, nor any tactic deters all predators all the time, it has proven to be effective in many cases. Warning, flash and scare coloration, mimicry and camouflage are all great predator avoidance designs which point to the Supreme Designer.

SPIDERS - Spiders strike arachniphobic fear in the hearts of many who see them. The fact that 36,000 species have been identified and that each square acre of forest holds about 2 million individual spiders is not a comforting thought to those who fear them. Yet, despite their fearsome appearance, only a few spiders are harmful to humans. Collectively and as individuals, they are actually intriguing and well designed creatures . . . consider the following example:

The Samurai from the Philippines is only 1/5 inch long, yet it can spin enough silk in a year to circle the equator, and in 5 years, enough to reach the moon. Spider silk, which is only 1/5000 inch thick (some species silk is so thin that 18,000 strands would be needed to equal the width of a human hair), is literally stronger than steel. It has been calculated that a one inch strand of spider silk, which is 3 times stronger than a one inch rope of iron, can hold a weight of 74 tons. Besides its great strength, spider silk is incredibly elastic, able to stretch up to 1/3 its length. If it were possible for a spider to build a large enough web with super thick strands, it could literally catch a moving passenger airplane and shoot it back in the direction it came from like a rubber ball hitting a cement wall! The silk is so strong that scientists are actively harvesting it to make parachutes and bulletproof vests. (Also, spider venom has shown promise in preventing brain damage in stroke victims.)

Spiders are amazing for more than their silk. Some species can leap several feet in the air to grab flying insects, which they see with excellent eyesight. The Dancing White Lady spider of the desert can fold its legs to form a wheel when danger is near and speed away at more than 30 MPH. Spiders, in general, are super strong . . . pound for pound, they are 10,000 times stronger than we are. And for their size, their appetite is unparalleled, allowing spiders to annually

181

consume a weight of insects equaling half the weight of the human population. Without bats, birds, spiders and other insectivores (such as anteaters, which are built with 2 foot long tongues that swipe hundreds of termites with a single lick and up to 20,000 per day), the insect population would be out of control and this planet would be inhospitable. Fortunately for us, God didn't overlook any details when He created this world, including installing insect controls.

Insects, although sometimes troublesome (only 1% have actually been deemed as pests), have an important role to play on this planet. Insects are the primary pollinators of plants, which form the foundation of our food web. Without insects, many plant species would become extinct, and we, along with all other creatures, would struggle to exist. Insects also aid in the process of decay . . . as stated before, without decomposers, life in this world would eventually choke in the towering heights of endless dead organisms. In addition, insects provide a food base for many species of fish, amphibians, birds and mammals. Without insects, many other life forms could not exist either. So whether you love, hate or have neutral feelings towards insects, you must agree that they are well designed creatures that are essential to our survival. Insects, although marred by sin on Earth, are part of God's grand design for the survival of humanity.

Amphibian Design - Frogs

It is nearing noon now, and the day is really heating up, so let's have a picnic lunch on the cooler banks of Towanda Creek. As we camp under a large, shady Sugar maple tree, a few frogs jump into the water. Frogs, along with toads and salamanders, belong to a class of animals known as amphibians, which are designed to live both in water and on land. All frogs are tailless with strong back legs that can launch their streamlined bodies at least 10 times their length. They also have smaller front legs, a strong backbone and short, stout bodies to cope with and cushion the physical stresses of jumping and the impact of landing. Frogs feature large eyes on top of a wide-mouthed head, which allows them to see predators and prey while their bodies are almost totally submerged in water. When they spot prey, they can flip out long, sticky tongues with lightning speed to snag a meal. When mating season hits, both male frogs and toads are able to make loud, species distinct calls by inflating their flexible chins like balloons to resonate sound over greater distances.

Wood frogs and spring peeper frogs are two of the amazing amphibians that can be frozen alive to survive winter. Samuel Hearne, an 18th century Arctic explorer wrote the following upon discovering a frozen wood frog: "I have frequently seen them dug up with the moss, frozen as hard as ice, in which state the legs are easily broken off as a pipe stem. If you examined the frog more closely, you would notice that its eyes were cloudy, it wasn't breathing, it had no heartbeat and it would not bleed if any of its major organs were cut. Also, you could readily feel ice under the skin . . . all the animal's internal organs would be surrounded by a mass of ice. But upon wrapping them in warm skins and exposing them to a slow fire, they soon recover life."[3]

Spring peeper frogs undergo similar changes during the winter, with almost 1/2 their blood and other body fluids frozen solid. How can these animals, as well as others, survive such tortuous conditions? The secrete lies in their uniquely designed body chemistry. These species manufacture extra glucose sugar, which functions like biological antifreeze, concentrating their body fluids and reducing the amount of ice that forms, especially within cells and around vital organs like the heart and brain. In this way, these frogs can survive winter in a greatly reduced metabolic state, and simply hop away when warmer weather melts their icy bodies.

Reptile Design - Snakes, Turtles and Lizards

As we think about icy toads on a hot summer day, we are startled to our feet by a rattling noise coming from underneath a nearby log. It is a rattlesnake that has surprisingly ventured from Barclay Mountain to the Towanda Creek Valley. The snake does not appear to be a threat though . . . it is a safe 25 feet away, and is now slithering in the opposite direction. Snakes, along with turtles, lizards and a few other scaly creatures, belong to the reptile family, which is designed to live mainly on land.

Whether you like them or not, the rattlesnake we've just seen is a well designed specimen. Pit-vipers feature the most complicated killing equipment of any snake. Their large, thin fangs can be folded back against the upper jaw, but when they are needed, they can be quickly swung forward like a pair of hypodermic needles at almost 50 miles per second (180,000 miles per hour) to inject lethal venom from poison glands located behind the eyes. The highly potent venom, which is able to kill a quarter million rats with only a fraction of an ounce, will begin immediately digesting the internal organs of the prey, which greatly reduces struggle for the snake. Vipers also have special pits on each side of its head which detect infrared heat from warm blooded prey. These infrared 'binoculars' can provide an accurate heat picture of the surroundings and pinpoint prey location even in pitch darkness. The pits are so sensitive that they can recognize variations in temperature as little as 1/100th$^{\circ}$C. Vipers also feature a forked tongue, which enables them to accurately smell and taste the environment, including any prey in the area. Upon catching larger prey that has been immobilized with venom, the snake is able to open its jaws a full 180 degrees, and can unhinge them if necessary to swallow its meal. Snakes, while mysterious, sin cursed and sometimes frightening, are still a well designed part of God's creation.

As our heartbeat finally slows down following our encounter with the rattlesnake, we notice a huge, bowl-shaped rock lying in the water. But as we watch the 'rock,' we see it move and suddenly realize that it's not a rock at all . . . it is a turtle. Turtles and tortoises are constructed with nearly impenetrable shells, which provide great protection. The shells of some of these species also feature hinges, which can be used to entirely shield the soft body parts inside from outside predators. Shells are one of the main reasons why these reptiles live such long lives.

But not all turtles are confined to their shells when danger strikes . . . some, like the Alligator snapping turtle are designed to fight back. These behemoth turtles look like 200+ pound armored tanks and can unleash jaws powerful enough to bite through a rubber tire (and certainly a human finger) when provoked. But a suit of armor and mighty bite are just part of this animal's arsenal. They also have a special pink, wormlike projection on their tongue which they wriggle like bait to effectively lure fish into their bone crunching jaws. Not too many animals can resist the lure or escape the grasp of this well designed armored tank.

Lizards are another marvelous group of reptiles, endowed with some amazing abilities. For example, in an effort to escape predators, lizards (and some amphibious salamanders) can literally lose their tails. The tails have special break off points, and when a predator attacks, the tail can be broken and then wriggle vigorously to divert the attention of the predator while the lizard makes a speedy exit. The tail will soon grow back. Another escape artist, the Imperial flat lizard, has a flattened head and body to slide into narrow rock crevices that few predators can enter. It is then able to greatly expand its body size by puffing up with air, and wedges itself between the rocks, making it nearly impossible for predators to extricate them. Geckos are another fascinating lizard, able to climb straight up glass walls and even run across ceilings, since they were built with feet like suction cups. Their great grip is further enhanced by their pad covered toes, which together contain millions of microscopic hairs called setae. These setae contain such a strong adhesive force that the gecko can hold its entire body weight with only one toe touching a surface. It has been calculated that if the all the adhesive power of all the setae were used at one time, they could support the weight of a 280 pound man! The Basilisk lizard can actually run on water . . . using their long, scaly toes as a hydrofoil to skim the film-like 'skin' on the water surface, they have been observed covering distances exceeding 1300 feet. (This ability has earned them the title 'Jesus Christ lizard,' referring to the time that Jesus walked upon the waters of the Sea of Galilee.)

Chameleons are perhaps the best known and most intriguing lizards of all. They hunt insects in trees and are well designed to do so. Their feet are specially arranged to provide a strong grip on branches, with 3 toes wrapped firmly around one side, and 2 toes around the other. A strong prehensile tail can also be curled around branches to provide an extra anchor. With these gripping aids, the chameleon can remain motionless for long periods of time. It can also change its body color to perfectly match the background. While

185

waiting in camouflaged silence, the chameleon uses one of its independently revolving eyes to watch for prey, while the other scans the area for predators. When prey finally comes into range, it focuses both eyes squarely on its potential meal. Excellent eyesight allows them to accurately aim and shoot a long, sticky tongue with lightning speed, striking their victims in less than 1/100th of a second. Chameleons are certainly a well designed predator.

More Great Designs from the Animal Kingdom

BEAVERS - As we continue to enjoy the shade tree, we notice a medium-sized mammal toting an aspen branch downstream to repair its dam. The Beaver, which can sometimes cause problems by building dams in the wrong places by human estimation, is nonetheless an efficient engineer designed by the Master Designer. Newborn beavers are about the size of a walnut, but grow to become the 2nd largest rodent in the world, behind the Capybara of South America. Many design features make them well suited for their semi-aquatic lifestyle. Among these is a broad, flat, rubbery black tail that is important in temperature regulation, fat storage and as a powerful swimming rudder. It's also used in communication, as it slaps loudly against the water surface, effectively warning Beavers and other animals of approaching danger. Beavers are clothed with a dense, waterproof outer fur layer and an equally dense inner fur layer. These layers provide insulation and allow beavers to slice through water without being soaked and weighed down. This waterproofed condition is maintained by specialized double claws on the hind feet which extract oil from two abdominal glands and then apply this oil to the fur. The double claws act as a comb to effectively work the waterproofing oil into the fur.

The feet, eyes, nose and mouth of the beaver are also designed for semi-aquatic life. Their webbed feet partner with the tail to provide superb paddling power. The eyes are equipped with a special pair of underwater 'goggles,' which include a transparent, nictating membrane that covers the eyes and protects them from injury as well as providing a clear field of vision below the water surface. Their ears, nose and mouth all feature valves which can be closed to prevent water from rushing in. The lips close behind their teeth, enabling them to eat and gnaw underwater vegetation without drowning. The skull is broad and flat, with high crowned cheek teeth and a pair of large, strong, always-growing, chisel-like, razor sharp incisors that are perfectly designed for an herbivorous diet of bark, twigs and leaves. Beavers also display a special air passage to breathe oxygen while toting twigs underwater and possess large lungs and a liver that can store enough air and oxygenated blood to remain totally submerged for up to 15 minutes. The Beaver is just one of the many well equipped semi-aquatic creatures in this world.

OTTER - The otter is another, designed with a torpedo shaped, muscular body, stocky legs and long, tapered tail. Otters, which can be observed sledding down snowy hills on their stomachs apparently just for fun, use the same sleek form to slice through the water. Otter coats are composed of thick, oily underfur overlaid by long, glistening waterproofed fur. Its muscular tail provides propulsion, while webbed paws act as paddles. Like the beaver, it has valvular ears and nose, which can be closed underwater. Everything about an otter is designed for aquatic life . . . even the placement of its eyes is ideal, appearing near the top of the head, enabling it to still see above water, even as its body skims kayak style below the water surface.

PORCUPINE - Glancing to the right, about 50 feet downstream, we spot a stout, brown ball of spikes moving toward us. Whipping out our binoculars, we confirm that a porcupine is approaching. While looking like an animal having a very bad hair day, porcupines rely upon this wacky "hairdo" as the secret of their success. Their spiky appearance is due to a collection of over 30,000 quills that cover their bodies. The quills feature small, inward pointing barbs that can pierce skin upon contact. Once embedded, the quills then slowly slice their way through body tissue with each muscle pulse.

As anyone who has tried can tell you, these quills are nearly impossible to pull out . . . you sometimes must wait until they come out the other side. Porcupines are equipped with one of the better designed defenses in nature . . . with a system like this it's understandable why few animals will mess with it. 'Porkies' are loaded with other design features as well, including massive skulls that support large jaw muscles and razor sharp, ever-growing teeth that are characteristic of all rodents. Although they appear cumbersome, they are agile and superbly balanced in trees due to large, broad-soled feet that include many small tubercles, a large, movable, pad-like big toe (called a hallux) and other toes with long, curved claws to dig into and easily ascend tree trunks. Porcupines feature an interesting vocal repertoire, including grunts, coughs, moans, whines, snorts, screeches and chatters. When hurt or frightened, they can cry like a child and are capable of emitting a loud and penetrating scream similar to that of a mountain lion, which can be heard a mile away. The porcupine, despite its fantastic defense system, is still wary of humans. Our specimen has finally noticed us, and is now ambling in the opposite direction, up the nearest tree.

EARTHWORMS - After looking up as the porky climbs a tree, we look down to see a slithering form at our feet. It's not a snake, but rather an earthworm seeking some wetness on this sweltering summer day. The world's largest earthworm, the Giant Gippsland from South Africa, exceeds 20 feet in length, while the largest worms in the world can grow more than 100 feet long inside the stomach of a Blue whale! Our new found friend is not nearly that large, but it, along with other earthworms, is one of the most important creatures on the planet. Research has shown that in just 100 square feet of garden soil, earthworms alone bring 4–8 pounds of mineral rich soil to the surface every year. The 200–1,000 earthworms found in each acre enrich the soil as they till it, converting nitrogen, phosphorus, potassium and many micro nutrients into a form that plants can use. They also add calcium carbonate to the soil, which neutralizes soil acidity and improves plant growing conditions. Additionally, they aerate the soil and open pore spaces for water and oxygen movement, increasing plant growth and improving living conditions for other beneficial soil organisms, such as plant promoting mychorrizhal fungi. Earthworms prove that even the simplest of God's creations play a crucial role in the preservation of planet Earth.

ELEPHANTS - As we remain on the banks of Towanda Creek, sheltered by our shade tree, close your eyes and imagine sailing across the sea to a place where the largest beast on land roams. These beasts, the mighty elephants of Asia and Africa, are a breathtaking signature from the Master's hand. African bull elephants approach 7 tons, which equals the weight of 80 people, 6 cars, 12 large horses or 1,500 domestic cats. They reach heights of 13 feet, second only to giraffes, and live over 70 years, again second only to humans. These super-sized beasts are powered by impressively sized inner organs as well . . . such as a heart 5 times larger than ours and weighing 44 pounds, which is about the same weight as a small child.

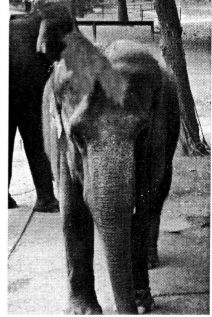

With such great inner and outer stature, elephants require a firm foundation. God has wisely placed legs directly under elephants, very much like the legs on a coffee table. This design, along with their strong, yet flexible skeleton, easily supports their great weight, even allowing them to kneel and squat. Elephant feet, which measure up to 5 feet around, are also designed to help support the massive frame above. Featuring a thick, fatty cushion on its heel, the feet act as giant shock absorbers, effectively spreading the weight. Their feet were made to move as well, since the skin on the soles are thick and cracked, giving them traction like grooved rubber tires, even in rugged mountain terrain.

Moving from the ground up we notice wrinkled skin, which is not a sign of age, but is instead an intelligent design for cooling their large surface area through the collection of mud and water. The large ears, although they flap, weren't made for flying. Instead, they serve as efficient air conditioners, as well as great hearing tools. The enormous ears are capable of funneling sound from as far away as 5 miles.

Their ivory tusks are designed well for lifting objects, digging up food such as edible roots or as a weapon for protection from predators. Trunks are certainly one of the most unique and versatile tools in nature. With their trunks, elephants can breathe, smell objects over 1 mile away, drink over 50 gallons of water per day, communicate, spray soothing dust and water over their bodies, fight, play and swim up to 6 miles without a break by using their trunks as a periscope to breathe above water. They can also feel and pick up objects as small as a coin or leaf with their fine tipped trunks, or utilize their 100,000+ individually moving trunk muscles to power objects as large as tree trunks off the ground.

The trunks also aid in consuming up to 440 pounds of food daily from more than 100 different species of plants. Food is passed like a relay baton to a set of 4 molars, each of which weighs about 9 pounds and is approximately 1 foot long (each molar is as large as and equal to the weight of a brick). Elephants receive six sets of molar teeth throughout their lifetime, using their scissor-like ridges to easily chop through tough plant fiber. Also aiding in the digestion process are an intestinal system weighing about 1 ton and a stomach containing billions of microscopic protists.

PROTISTS - Protists not only aid digestion in elephants and other plant eating herbivores, but also are essential to the survival of many other species. Numbering untold trillions, plant-like protists form the foundation of the oceanic food chain. It's incredible that even the mighty Blue whale depends upon a creature so small that 20 would fit within the period at the end of this sentence. The thousands of protists found in a single drop of seawater trap sunlight energy to live, grow and multiply into an abundant food source that all the creatures in the sea depend upon. Protists are a powerful reminder that God has packed important things in small packages. Importance and power in small packages will be one of the main themes in the next chapter, as we embark on an eye-opening journey into the human body.

CHAPTER 8

God's Greatest Masterpiece

We have seen many design masterpieces on our brief journey of the Earth, with each species and each process honed to perfection as it performs its unique, God-given role within the biosphere. But as we approach civilization, we spy God's greatest and most cherished masterpiece . . . humans. Leonardo da Vinci put it this way . . . "A work of art . . . that is a man . . . crafted and shaped by the hand of the Supreme Master."[1] Leonardo made this statement with authority, since he was the first to deeply study and reveal the stunning complexity of the human body through detailed anatomical drawings.

Da Vinci certainly hit the nail on the head, but modern science has proven that the human body is far more detailed than what he observed. The human body is a startling display of design and order at all levels of its organization, and each of these organized levels work together in harmony to allow human life to exist. I'd like to slowly peel away the different layers of human design, beginning with the largest building blocks . . . the systems.

Your body is composed of several wonderfully sophisticated systems, such as a skeletal system so well built that it puts skyscrapers to shame, a nervous system that works faster and more effectively than the Internet and a circulatory system that is a far better delivery system than all the planes, trains and automobiles in the world combined. Depending on who you talk to, our bodies include at least 12 systems: 1)Digestive, 2)Respiratory, 3)Circulatory (Cardiovascular), 4)Blood (according to some), 5)Urinary, 6)Reproductive, 7)Nervous, 8)Skin, 9)Immune, 10)Muscular, 11)Skeletal and 12)Endocrine. Certainly we could not live as we do without any of them . . . as a wise Designer, God has given us what we need. I will take the next few pages to briefly discuss the wise design that God has implanted in our systems.

NERVOUS SYSTEM

The nervous system, as with all other body systems, is composed of several ingenious organs, including the brain, spinal cord and the nerves that connect them. The brain, weighing about 3 pounds, appearing as a soggy, wrinkly gray walnut and feeling like mushy cheese, certainly isn't spectacular from the outside. But looks are definitely deceiving in this case, since the human brain is considered the most mysterious and marvelous object on Earth. Nobel Prize winner, Dr. Roger Sperry, stated, "Inside our heads work forces upon forces upon forces, unlike any other cubic 1/2 foot in the Universe."[2]

The brain, like all other organs in the human body, is made of tissue. The nervous tissue within our brains contains billions of neurons organized into a communication network of spectacular complexity. The 100 billion+ neurons each contain a certain bit of information, and each is tied to at least thousands of other neurons, creating over 100 trillion connections that permit us to combine smaller bits of information to create complex thoughts. Every cubic inch of the human brain contains at least 100 million nerve cells interconnected by 10 thousand miles of fibers, allowing the brain to store an equivalent of 25 million encyclopedia volumes at one time, which exceeds the information stored in the largest library in the world, the Library of Congress. To use the entire storage capacity of the brain, it has been estimated that something new must be learned every second for the next 10 million years!

The brain is not only a great storage closet, but is also the super efficient command center of the body. The chemical and electrical impulses constantly shooting through your brain cells produce all your thoughts, most of your actions and record every sensation via signals sent to and fro along the remarkable network of nerves that link your body to the brain like the wires in a computer. It has been noted that "The human brain consists of about ten thousand million nerve cells. Each nerve cell puts out somewhere in the region of between ten thousand and one hundred thousand connecting fibers by which it makes contact with other nerve cells in the brain. Altogether, the total number of connections in the human brain approaches 10^{15} or a thousand million million . . . a much greater number of specific connections than in the entire communications network on Earth."[3]

Despite its many connections the brain is not a mass of confusion, but is a well organized organ, divided into different areas, each with a different task that is essential to our survival. The core of the brain includes the thalamus, which controls your emotions. The midbrain, along with the medulla and pons (part of the brainstem) controls your breathing and heart rate, without your awareness, even during sleep. The hypothalamus controls your hunger, thirst and sleeping patterns. The cerebrum is responsible for our thinking, memory, speech, eyesight, hearing, control of movement and more. (The cerebrum includes the 'wrinkles,' which wrap around the core of the brain, and wisely expose a larger surface area to allow more nerve cells to be squeezed inside our skulls, and greatly increase our mental capacities.)

The brain is able to process up to 1 quadrillion (1,000,000,000,000,000) messages per second received from nerve cells that range from .04 to 40 inches in length, and which are linked together like beads on a string. These strands of nerve cells are strategically placed to serve every area of our bodies, and are capable of relaying messages at up to 300 miles per second, which is vital during dangerous situations. For example, due to our lightning quick nervous system, signals can travel from the brain to hands in a few milliseconds, allowing us to turn the wheel to avoid a car wreck or remove our hand from a hot stove. Without such a well designed system, those situations could result in injury or death.

Our brain, and nervous system in general, is unparalleled . . . it presents a vast gulf between humans and animals, making evolution incredulous. Evolution cannot explain the origin of the remarkable human nervous system. It is a masterpiece of organized design from the uppermost point of the brain to the lowest level in our toes . . . and we've barely scratched the surface. The intricacies lie far below the surface . . . I will deal with these details soon.

CIRCULATORY SYSTEM
(CARDIOVASCULAR SYSTEM)

The circulatory system, including the heart and an incredible system of blood vessels, rivals the nervous system in both complexity and order. The heart, like the brain, is one of the marvels of the human body, endlessly pumping blood through an intricate network of blood vessels that reach each of the 100 trillion cells in the body. Without this pump and the blood vessel network we'd die almost instantly. The blood coursing through the vessels is also essential, carrying the oxygen, nutrients and chemicals that every body cell needs to survive. It also washes away waste products like carbon dioxide (CO_2) which, in excess, would kill us. This system is not only crucial to our existence, but is also remarkable as well. The feats of the circulatory system are astounding . . . consider the following facts:

The fist-sized heart, weighing less than 1 pound, is an incredibly durable pump, including 4 paper-thin, one way valves that are literally tougher than iron. These valves open and close in precision to allow just the right amount of blood to flow through the heart to the rest of the body. The cells in the heart throb in exact unison due to a special SA (sinoatrial) node, which, as the 'pacemaker' of the heart, controls contraction speeds even while you're sleeping. (Thank God for that.) The incredible human heart pumps an average of 80 times per minute, and circulates about 5 quarts of blood through the body each minute. It pumps about 2,500 gallons daily, and in 85 years, will ceaselessly beat about 3 billion times and send over 60 million gallons of blood through the body . . . put into perspective, this is enough blood to completely fill a line of train tanker cars 50 miles long!

Blood, which is a mixture of platelets, red and white blood cells within a clear yellowish fluid called plasma, is pumped through over 75,000 miles of blood vessels at about 1 meter per second. This 75,000 mile blood circulation system begins in the heart, travels to the arteries, then smaller arterioles and even tinier capillaries, which fuse into venules that join into veins that return to the heart. This great system, which would circle the globe 2.5 times, allows us to perform our daily activities.

Red blood cells (RBC's), so numerous in the body that if laid end to end would circle the Earth 4 times, may be the unsung heroes of the circulatory system, for without them, the amazing feats of the heart would mean little. When needed, up to 140,000 concave shaped RBC's can be produced in the bone marrow every minute, and each cell will travel throughout the circulatory highway of the body about 200,000 times during its 120 day lifespan. Their shape has been proven mathematically and scientifically to be perfect for the maximum absorption of its precious cargo, including oxygen. Oxygen is held on board the RBC raft by a special protein called hemoglobin, which, with a chemical formula of $C_{3032}H_{4812}N_{780}Fe_4O_{872}S_{12}$, is one of the most complex molecules in existence. The circulatory system, with its incredible pump and piping network is intricately and ideally designed to the smallest detail, and is certainly a product of Intelligent Design, not a chaotic explosion of non-intelligent matter that came from nothing and nowhere several billion years ago.

RESPIRATORY SYSTEM

The circulatory (cardiovascular) system, as great as it is, would be ineffective at conveying oxygen unless there was a system to deliver this precious gas to it. The respiratory system serves as the vital link between the oxygen in the external atmosphere and the blood flowing ceaselessly throughout our bodies.

How important is oxygen? A lack of oxygen for even a few seconds can cause a loss of consciousness, and if cut off any longer, brain cells will begin to die, damaging the brain and killing us in extreme cases. Just as a fire requires oxygen to burn, body cells require oxygen to break down the food they receive from passing blood. Obviously, without the coordination of the circulatory and respiratory systems to convey oxygen, our bodies would collapse. But thankfully, God has wisely designed both systems to work together better than a well lubricated machine. The heart constantly pumps deoxygenated blood to the lungs, where it picks up a fresh supply of oxygen to carry throughout the body. Lungs are structured to effectively disseminate oxygen to the blood and extract carbon dioxide wastes from the blood.

But first, oxygen must be breathed through the nose or mouth, where it is humidified for easier gas exchange. From there, it travels through the throat, pharynx, larynx and trachea to the lungs. The lungs contain hundreds of airways, each called a bronchial tube, to create a 'bronchial tree.' At the end of each bronchial branch are grape like clusters of tiny alveoli, which exceed 300 million to greatly increase the surface area for gas exchange in the lungs. Including the alveoli, our lungs contain about 1,500 miles of airways, and if laid flat, would cover a surface area the size of a tennis court! Using a coordinating set of muscles to expand and contract a pair of lungs, the average person will breathe about 23,000 times per day, and over a lifetime will take about 600 million breaths and draw in over 75 million gallons of air. Breathing, along with our heartbeat and several other essential body functions occur simultaneously and continuously without our thought, even while we're sleeping. Again, thank God for such wonderfully designed bodies.

IMMUNE SYSTEM

The Immune System works in concert with the circulatory system and others to provide our body with an effective and elaborate arsenal of weapons to combat and destroy the sicknesses that invade our bodies. But before infection can invade, it must bypass several external guards, including the skin and bacteria. The human body is home to many kinds of bacteria, most of which are beneficial. They act as the first line of defense, often out competing and eliminating pathogens on the skin and in the mouth. (Often despised bacteria also help us digest our food, and produce substances such as Vitamin K, which helps blood clot following a cut.) The mouth, nose and cuts are concentration points for pathogens as they attempt to enter the body. But many of those trying to enter through the nose and mouth are trapped by tiny hairs in the nasal passages and trachea before being expelled. Platelets, part of the second line of defense, are tiny cell fragments whose main purpose is to quickly plug cuts to minimize blood loss and pathogen entry.

If successful in piercing the outer defenses, pathogens are attacked with a host of lethal agents. An army of over 35 billion white blood cells seek out and destroy invaders upon contact. This army fires a wide array of chemical and biological weapons at its enemies, including 'Killer T' cells. Macrophages, also called 'giant eaters,' are a type of Killer T cell, and just one can engulf and devour up to 100 harmful invaders at a time. B lymphocytes are another powerful weapon in this extensive arsenal, able to identify and make thousands of different antibodies, each of which are targeted to perfectly fit the active site of an invader, just like a puzzle piece. The antibody then acts as a neon sign to attract Killer T cells, which destroy the enemy. If it weren't for our incredibly and intricately designed immune system, we would all soon succumb to such 'minor' illnesses as the common cold.

MUSCULAR SYSTEM

Muscles are essential . . . every move you make . . . running, dancing, smiling and more depend upon them. We even need muscles to sit still . . . without them, we'd slump unto the floor like lifeless rag dolls. The muscles, which account for about 40% of our body weight, come in two types . . . voluntary and involuntary. Volunteers move when you want them to . . . if they moved involuntarily, you'd twitch and thrash around wildly, never able to accomplish anything. At the other extreme are involuntary muscles, like the heart and other vital organs, which work automatically and simultaneously . . . if they didn't, the consequences would be fatal.

Our bodies contain an amazing array of over 600 muscles, each with a specific shape and size perfectly suited to perform precise functions. Each of these muscles is composed of bundles of muscle fibers . . . some of the larger muscles contain a quarter million or more individual fibers. Each fiber is composed of hundreds of thin myofibrils, which are made of two alternating substances called actin and myosin, giving our muscles a striped appearance. When the brain sends a signal for a muscle to contract, myosin filaments are specially built with tiny hooks like Velcro that pull the actin filaments, causing muscle contraction as the two filaments slide past each other. Muscles are just one example of design upon design upon design in the human body. Our bodies are the sum of many intricately ordered biological layers that work together in unparalleled harmony. A body this wondrous cannot be the product of chance from nothing, but screams loud and clear for the existence of a Divine Composer.

SKELETAL SYSTEM

The skeleton acts as a strong, supporting scaffold and a remarkably dynamic framework that allows our bodies to move. It provides an anchor for our muscles, a mount for the skin and protects the heart, brain and other vital organs . . . without a skeleton, our bodies would fall to the floor as a massive, mushy lump of flesh. Obviously, we need a skeleton . . . as a wise Designer Who didn't overlook any details, God gave it to us.

Human skeletons include nearly 200 bones, each of which is 5 times stronger than a piece of steel with an equal weight. When you add this to the fact that these bones are strategically placed to support the mass and movement of the body, we can literally say that our frame is better designed than a human skyscraper.

The strength of a bone comes from their surprisingly complex internal structure. A fat storage layer, called the yellow marrow, lies in the center of the bone. This layer is engulfed by a spongy red blood cell factory called the red marrow, which is covered by another layer of spongy bone. To its outside is a strong casing layer of compact bone that houses many tiny tubes called osteons, which collectively are covered by a membrane called periosteum. Fresh bone material is constantly being created in cells called osteoblasts, while older bone is broken down by osteoclasts. This simultaneous system ensures that our complex bones remain relatively young and vibrant, even in old age. (Human bodies were built to live forever as a part of God's original design, but breakdown due to the effects of sin, which I'll further discuss in Chapter 11.)

Bones certainly don't stand alone in the skeletal system . . . a rubbery substance called cartilage combines with an intricate network of joints to connect the bones in our skeletal system. Our joint network employs many engineering marvels, including a shoulder joint that works like a ball and socket, knee and elbow joints which act like door hinges and a neck featuring a special swiveling joint that moves our head. These joints take a tremendous amount of stress as we perform our daily duties, but as with all other body parts, they are designed to endure. Joints are protected by a sleeve of tough, wear resistant collagen fiber and lubricated by incredibly efficient capsules containing special oil called synovial fluid.

DIGESTIVE SYSTEM

If we lost our digestive system, we'd be in big trouble, since a body without it is like a gas-powered car that won't break down gasoline . . . both would be inanimate objects. Our digestive system is basically a long tube through which food passes as it is broken down in an orderly fashion and absorbed into our bodies. How does this system work? First, our teeth and saliva are designed to turn solid food into mush, which is pushed down by powerful muscles in the esophagus to the stomach, where rippling muscles and powerful gastric juices, including hydrochloric acid, stand ready to attack. Partially digested food then moves to the intestines, which are folded over so often that, if unfurled, would stand 33 feet tall, equaling 5–6 times the height of the average person. The intestines also possess an impressive surface area. The small intestine alone exposes an area of 600 square meters . . . approximately the same size as a major league baseball diamond. Thousands of villi and perhaps millions of microscopic microvilli are the reason for such a massive surface area, which provides super efficient digestion and rapid food absorption by the blood. The small and large intestines function with machine-like precision, combining their large digestion areas with a battery of enzymes to quickly convert food into body energy.

HUMAN SENSES

As we've just seen, body systems are composed of interworking organs such as the heart and lungs. Several other fantastic organs power the perceptions of each person. The eyes allow us to see, ears to hear, skin to touch and feel, nose to smell and tongue to taste. All these are wonderful and important senses, but we will focus on just two . . . sight and sound, as well as the incredible organs that make these perceptions possible.

Eyes

Eyes are a miniature masterpiece, functioning better than the complex video cameras that were based upon their design. To begin with, the clear cornea focuses the picture you see in reality onto a lens, which changes shape automatically to maintain the sharpness

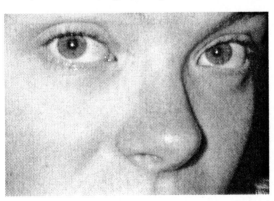

of the picture as it projects unto the paper thin retina in the back of the eye, where millions of light sensitive cells (called rods and cones) detect the picture, distinguishing literally millions of shades of color. (Each eye contains about 126 million rods for night vision and 7 million cones for day vision.) The retina far outperforms the best film products we have today . . . the most advanced film available can differentiate between a light range of 1000:1, while recent experiments have confirmed that the retina can easily differentiate and analyze a range of ten billion to one. Retina cells are capable of performing up to 10 billion calculations per second while determining the nature of the image transmitted to the eye by light photons. Even more impressively is the fact that the retina fills only 0.0003 inches of space, weighs less than a gram, and operates with less than 0.0001 watts of electrical charge. No supercomputer on Earth can match this output or efficiency. These special retinal cells then transmit the image to the brain via a special optic nerve. The optic nerve then analyzes more than one million messages per second while flashing signals to the brain at about 300 miles per hour! For protection, each eye is also designed with an iris, which controls the size of the pupil, and hence the amount of light. The iris assures that just the right amount of light reaches the sophisticated visual machinery within the eye.

This has been a very simple overview of the complex processes that occur in our eyes. (I would point you to Michael Behe's landmark book, *Darwin's Black Box*, for his description of the incredibly involved 21 step molecular process that occurs in our eyes each picosecond to allow us to see.) In an outdated, but still impressive 1985 article, Dr. John Stevens tried to express the complexity of the human eye. In this article he stated, "To simulate 10 milliseconds of the complete processing of even a single nerve cell from the retina would require the solution of about 500 simultaneous non-linear differential equations one hundred times and would take at least several minutes of processing time on a Cray Supercomputer. Keeping in mind that there are 10 million or more such cells interacting with each other in complex ways, it would take a minimum of 100 years of Cray time to simulate what takes place in your eye many times every second!"[4]

Ears

The ear is another of God's marvelous inventions, including at least one million moving parts. These parts are found in three areas . . . the outer, middle and inner ear. The outer ear is a tube that effectively funnels sound to the middle ear, which amplifies the sounds as it hits a tight wall of skin called the eardrum. The eardrum vibrates the sound rapidly, and rattles 3 tiny ossicle bones called the malleus (hammer), incus (anvil) and stapes (stirrup), which have been scientifically proven to be the perfect shape for transmitting sound to the cochlea within the inner ear. The cochlea is a curly, fluid filled tube that contains more than 100,000 motion-detector hairs that work more proficiently than a complicated keyboard. As the three ossicles rattle, they knock against the cochlea, making waves in the fluid. The minute detector hairs then wriggle in perfect harmony with the waves, each sending a unique tune directly to the brain along individually connected nerve hotlines. The brain then organizes these tunes into a musical composition of sound or just plain noise, depending on what you're listening to.

We've failed to come even close to touching the highest tip of the tallest iceberg with regard to body system, sense and organ design. Yet, I hope that this brief glimpse into the amazing abilities of these 7 systems, 2 senses and several organs has served to display the fact that we are not creatures of pure evolutionary chance, but are 'wonderfully made' by an Almighty God, just as the Bible says in Psalms 139:14.

If you are not convinced of this fact yet, I'd ask you to imagine for a moment that you are walking along a forest path and stumble across a fully functioning computer system. Without knowing where it came from, you must reasonably conclude that it was designed by an intelligent being, since its many intricate parts are ordered and organized far too well to be the product of chance. If you can believe this, then it is logically impossible to think that any of the human systems, senses or organs, which are far more complex, ordered and enduring than any computer, are the products of chance from nothing. Instead, just as the intricately ordered computer system is clearly a product of an intelligent designer, we must logically conclude that the far more intricately ordered human systems are the product of an even more Intelligent Designer.

The systems, senses and organs we've quickly considered are powerful proof that we were designed by an all-wise Creator. But while impressively persuasive, the evidence for the divine design of the human body only begins with its larger parts. The evidence for design and the existence of the Designer becomes more obvious as we delve even deeper into the microscopic and sub-microscopic mysteries of the masterfully sculpted human body. These mysteries are the subject of the remainder of this chapter.

The Incredible Human Cell

We've already seen that the human body is composed of ordered systems, each well designed to perform certain jobs. Further, we've found that systems contain organized organs, designed for a certain purpose. Organs are made of tissues, each performing their role to perfection. While exceptionally well designed, for the sake of time, we will bypass tissues to explore the next level of biological order . . . tissue creating cells.

Believe it or not, each human begins life as a single ovum cell (female egg cell fertilized by a male sperm cell) that is smaller than a pinhead. (In fact, about 1000 typical cells would be needed to cover the period at the end of this sentence.) More than 3 times a second, a human ovum cell is conceived on Earth . . . within this cell is all the information needed to construct a unique individual.

I ask you to stand in awe and carefully consider the fact that all our wonderful systems, senses and much more originate as a powerful, sub pinhead-sized package . . . the wonder of life almost exceeds comprehension. Yet, the same God Who was awesome enough to create the vast reaches of our Universe is almighty enough to stuff a human being into a space smaller than a tiny grain of rice. The humble beginnings of human life are a triumph of God's engineering greatness.

How marvelous is God's cellular design? How much power has he packed into a sub pinhead-sized human ovum cell? To answer these questions, we will walk down the ladder of biological order, beginning with organelles and ending with the most basic substance, the sub-subatomic building blocks of life. But before we observe the organelles, we must pierce the cell membrane. To accomplish this, first imagine that you are a microscopic sugar molecule floating in the bloodstream surrounding the cell. As we approach the membrane, we notice that cells vary widely in size, shape and specific structural features, but all are highly ordered structures that carry out the complicated processes necessary to maintain life.

As we dwell on this fact, we are instantly drawn inside a human cell . . . but not all molecules are so privileged. The cellular plasma membrane is a remarkable film only 8 nanometers thick . . . put into perspective, you'd have to stack them 8000 high to equal the thickness of a single sheet of paper. While minuscule, its fast and frantic traffic control duties are of major importance. The specific architecture of cellular membranes allows them to selectively control the passage of molecules between the cell and its external environment. This selective permeability is paramount, for if the cell could not physically admit essential elements and ward off unneeded or unwanted substances, the cell, and ultimately the body would die.

Now inside a cell, we can see that it is not a chaotic collection of chemicals. Semi-permeable membranes cover approximately 15 well structured organelles, each of which is a unique metabolic factory. Metabolism is the orderly sum of all the chemical reactions that occur in the cells and maintains the life of an organism. These reactions involve the concerted, organized interplay of thousands of different kinds of molecules within and outside organelles. While overwhelmingly complex, each chemical reaction proceeds in highly ordered, stepwise sequences which are catalyzed by specific enzymes.

Enzymes

Each organelle has its own special blend of enzymes and other molecules to carry out its specific functions. For example, the enzymes needed for cellular respiration (breathing) reside largely within the 1–10,000 mitochondria housed within each individual cell. If the cell was designed with the same number of respiration enzymes in each organelle, instead of being concentrated in mitochondria, then breathing would be very inefficient and our fast paced lifestyles would crash to a crawling halt. The fact that each organelle is endowed with a specific team of enzymes is essential to human life.

Enzymes themselves are necessary agents of life as we know it. The operation of each of the many specific metabolic pathways that sustain life are tightly regulated, switched on and off with precise timing by a team of enzymes. Chemical chaos would result without enzymes, since all the cell's metabolic pathways would be open at the same time. Imagine, for example, a substance synthesized by one pathway, but simultaneously destroyed by another. If this were the case, then our cells would be spinning their metabolic wheels, which would translate to a premature visit to the grave for us.

Enzymes not only govern metabolic reactions, but are designed to speed them up between one thousand and one million times as well. Each enzyme is equipped with a specific shape to perfectly fit the active site of a reacting substrate molecule. This lock and key fit greatly increases the rate of such complex reactions as respiration, electron transport, oxidative phosphorylation and hundreds of other intricately ordered chemical cascades. Without God's exemplary enzyme design, we'd be forced to live life at a snail's pace.

ATP Motors and Nanotechnology

Clearly, the cell is not just a disorganized bag of chemicals with thousands of randomly wandering enzymes and molecular substrates . . . it is rather a stirring cast of microscopic partners that collectively cause life to thrive. As an example of these impressive cellular components, consider ATP motors, which are found by the trillion in the human body and humble even the most sophisticated man-made machinery. Each human cell includes hundreds of these mitochondria-bound, minuscule motors, which are 200,000 times smaller than a pinhead, and employ a central wheel mechanism that efficiently cycles at about 100 revolutions per second to help keep life-giving energy flowing throughout our bodies. (ATP, adenosine triphosphate, is the body's main energy source at the cellular level, and these motors are capable of producing 300 ATP molecules per second.) We could not survive without these miniature motors that drive life.

The science of nanotechnology (the study of things less than one-billionth of a meter in size) is currently being used by at least 15 federal government agencies to research the possibility of using the microscopic designs of life, such as those found in ATP motors, to further the efficiency of life on a larger scale. The sciences of nanotechnology and molecular biology are continually providing the world with similar examples of amazingly ordered, efficient and precise cellular design, which makes denying the existence of an intelligent Designer possible to only the willingly blind.

While some still remain willingly blind, many evolutionists are beginning to buckle under the severe weight of evidence for intelligent design that is being discovered at the cellular level. Evolutionist Dr. Michael Gross admitted, "(With nanotechnology), we are talking about complicated and highly efficient machines having a size of only a few millionths of a millimeter. Nothing ever produced by human engineering efforts comes anywhere near the performance of these biological systems. It has become clear that nature's superiority is much more obvious on the nanoscale than in large-scale engineering."[5] If even evolutionists can recognize the design in submicroscopic cellular machines, shouldn't we? Further, shouldn't this fact drive us to logically conclude that an infinitely intelligent Designer is needed for nanoscale design? Those who sincerely wish to seek out the truth must logically conclude that God is the ultimate cause for this Universe and everything in it.

Proteins

As we rest just inside the mitochondrial membrane, let's slide down the next rung of the biological ladder to consider one of the most important building blocks of all cellular parts. Proteins and other molecules, such as lipids and carbohydrates form the raw materials God has used in the construction of all cells. For the sake of time, I will only discuss the design of proteins, which account for more than 50% of the dry weight of most cells.

Proteins are instrumental in almost everything the cell (and body) does, being involved in structural support, storage, substrate transport, cellular movement and intracellular communication. They are also a key defense against disease, and as enzymes, selectively accelerate metabolic reactions, among many other functions. A human body has tens of thousands of different protein types, each among the most structurally sophisticated molecules in nature, and each physically designed to proficiently perform unique roles within cells. There are 4 superimposed levels of architecture involved in the complex conformations of proteins . . . primary, secondary, tertiary and quaternary structure. The primary structure of protein is composed of unique sequences of 20 different amino acids, which join into precisely replicated chains including up to 100 amino acids.

These precisely replicated chains are being constantly created to renew the vitality of our bodies. Gerald Schroeder, a molecular biologist holding a Ph.D. from MIT described the amazingly precise and productive protein factories in each human cell this way, "Other than sex cells and blood cells, every cell in your body is making approximately two thousand proteins every second! A protein is a combination of three hundred to over one thousand amino acids. An adult human body is made of approximately seventy five trillion cells. Every second of every minute of every day, your body and every body is organizing on the order of 150,000,000,000,000,000,000 amino acids into carefully constructed chains of proteins. Every second; every minute; every day. The fabric from which we, and all life is built, is being continuously rewoven at a most astoundingly rapid rate."[6] It's simply illogical to believe that such a complex and precise renewal system is the product of the intelligence of dead primordial particles that came from nothing and nowhere. A system this amazing clearly demands a higher Intelligence . . . it demands the existence of God, the grand Orchestrator of the symphony of creation.

DNA . . . God's Language for Life

As we drop to another biological level, we find that chromosomes are a special type of protein. Each species of life displays a characteristic number of chromosomes within each cell . . . for humans, this number is 46. Within each chromosome is one giant, highly structured and information packed DNA molecule.

DNA (Deoxyribonucleic acid) is designed with a double helix shape, which enables a structure thousands of times longer than the diameter of a cell nucleus to be tightly stuffed into its sub cellular chromosome package. If the DNA in a single human cell were stretched out and laid end to end, it would measure about 9 feet. Even more striking is the fact that the average human body contains 10–20 billion miles of DNA distributed throughout about 75 trillion cells! (This distance is roughly the distance from the surface of Earth to beyond the edge of our solar system.) Another estimate states that if all the DNA in a single adult human were stretched end to end, it would reach from the moon to the Earth and back about 5,000 times! Still another calculation states that if someone collected one copy of DNA from each of the about 50 billion people that have lived on Earth, and put it in a pile, it would equal the size and weight of an aspirin! And yet this aspirin-sized pile would contain all the information needed to create all the characteristics of all the humans in history. The highly elaborate, double helical, multilevel DNA packing system is certainly the best in nature, and provides strong evidence for an Intelligent Designer.

DNA is a truly incredible molecule that holds all the information required to create a unique human, as well as all other living things. The many diverse forms of life are simply different arrangements and expressions of a common DNA language (God's language) for programming biological order. Shaped like a twisted ladder with precisely patterned rungs, DNA is perfectly designed to carry a complete and complicated code that orders all aspects of life, from the growth of a plant to the color of your eyes. DNA is composed of precise sequences of 4 nucleotide building blocks, just as words are made of specific combinations of letters. The precise arrangement of nucleotides enables DNA to convey specific information to program cellular activity.

The nucleotides are also made of smaller, intricately ordered building blocks, including a nitrogenous base joined to a pentose (5-carbon) sugar, which is bonded to a phosphate. The nitrogenous bases are the key to the incredible order in nucleotides, which leads to incredible order in DNA. Nitrogenous bases occur in 2 'families'— pyrimidines, which include cytosine (C) and thymine (T), and purines, which include adenine (A) and guanine (G). These bases always combine in the same pairs . . . cytosine with guanine and adenine with thymine to create the rungs of the DNA ladder.

A very conservative past estimate stated that the 46 DNA molecules in the nucleus of a single human cell contains about 6 billion base pairs . . . put into perspective, printing the one letter symbols for the 12 billion individual bases (A, G, C and T) the size of the letters you are reading now would fill about 20,000 books as thick as this one. Another estimate states that there is enough information capacity in a cell full of DNA to store 3–4 complete sets of the Encyclopedia Britannica, which includes 30 comprehensive volumes. In a more recent study, another researcher found that a single DNA molecule is capable of storing the information equivalent of 100 million 40 gigabyte hard drives, all within the space of one-thousandth of a millimeter. Another estimate states that if all the information in the DNA found in a single body were compiled, it would create enough books to fill the entire Grand Canyon to the top 78 times! Still another study concluded that 46 DNA molecules hold the information equivalent of the content of a pile of paperback books 500 times greater than the distance from the Earth to the moon! Whichever estimate you choose, it is clear that the amount of information that can be stored in a pinhead's volume of DNA is simply staggering.

The specific sequences of nitrogenous bases along the DNA ladder create 50–100,000 specific genes, each of which is always located in an exact spot (called a locus) on the DNA molecule found within chromosomes. The gene's unique sequence of DNA nucleotides provides a template for assembling a precise sequence of RNA nucleotides, which create amino acids that build proteins which direct a cell (and ultimately the body) to express certain phenotypes (physical characteristics such as skin, eye and hair color).

RNA is the molecule that links the information in DNA to protein information. RNA is vital, since DNA (with precise nucleotide sequences) and protein (with specific amino acid sequences), have different 'languages.' Without RNA we would not exist, since there would be no agent to transcribe and translate DNA language into protein language. Through RNA, each cell can translate the enormous amount of information stored in DNA to protein with remarkable accuracy in just a few hours. In total, the RNA of the average adult body, *every second* of every day, actively organizes about 150 quintillion (150,000,000,000,000,000,000) amino acids into carefully constructed protein chains, which perform a vast array of bodily functions, many of which we don't even have to think about, since our body is designed to perform them automatically.

In Review . . .

This have been a quick windshield survey of sub-cellular biological design to this point . . . believe me, we haven't even scratched the surface of the surface yet, for the design goes much deeper still and becomes much more mind boggling at all levels. (If you don't believe this, then try taking an advanced, college-level physiology course.) But even if you haven't been able to follow the biological lingo, I hope you've at least recognized two things: 1) life at the microscopic level is incredibly complex but is also 2) intricately ordered, which demands a design from a Divine Designer.

In review, we've seen in this Chapter that phosphate+ sugar+ ordered nitrogenous bases = ordered DNA, which includes ordered genes that = ordered RNA molecules = ordered amino acids = ordered proteins = ordered organelles = ordered cells = ordered tissues = ordered organs = ordered systems = an ordered body. Not only is every level of life individually ordered, but it's also essential and intricately designed to perform its harmonious and well coordinated role within the body. To see the evidence of God's existence, we need to look no farther than our own bodies.

The Chemical Ladder Leading to Life

We have finally descended to the bottom of the biological ladder, only to find ourselves standing at the top of a chemical ladder. Without the chemical ladder, there would be no biological ladder of life. As we carefully tread the rungs of the chemical ladder, we will discover the most basic foundation and origin of life.

Molecules and Elements

Balancing on the highest rung of this ladder, we encounter many elements that are essential to life. Each of these elements is engineered to be physically unique to fill a certain niche within living organisms. Collectively, the 109 discovered elements of Earth, along with environmental factors such as sunlight, atmosphere and land, give us everything we need to thrive. No other planet is endowed with such ideal conditions . . . Earth is not an accident that somehow appeared from a colossal cosmic explosion that came from nowhere. This planet is not the product of pure chance from nothing, but clearly must be the handiwork of a Divine Designer.

Carbon is a very special element, with a unique architecture that allows it to create 4 classes of large, complex and highly ordered diverse macromolecules . . . proteins, nucleic acids (DNA and RNA), lipids and carbohydrates. These 4 molecular classes separate life from non-life and include thousands of macro (large) molecules, each with a unique carbon-based conformation that allows them to perfectly perform their role in the cell and to interact in specific and predictable ways with other macromolecules to assure proper cell functioning. In molecular biology, as in the study of life at all levels, physical form and function are inseparable. This is an obvious example of design . . . just as in a machine shop, each part is physically created to perform a certain job.

Atoms

If the molecules of life were simply a chaotic mess of atoms that reacted in unpredictable ways, life would not be intricately ordered, as it so evidently is, and all life would break down into an unorganized mush (similar to the evolutionists hypothetical 'primordial soup.') The smallest cell in the human body is composed of over 50 billion atoms arranged into more than 100 different proteins, together with the staggering amount of genetic information encoded in DNA and RNA. The inescapable problem for evolutionists is the fact that each of these 50 billion+ parts must be present in its proper place at the beginning for a cell to function. The intricate levels of life must have been ordered from the very beginning, since no level is a solo act . . . all rely upon each other for proper body function . . . the removal of just one vital level would destroy life. Simply put, no order in the beginning = no life.

God has implanted safeguards at the transition of each level to assure that life remains ordered. For example, He has provided a special 'glue' to hold atoms together as they combine to form molecules. Covalent, ionic and hydrogen bonds are 3 of the most recognizable 'glues' that hold atoms together in a precise and predictable order. Without these special transitional bonds, molecules, and ultimately life could not exist. Every detail of life is crucial . . . it takes a Wise Creator to design and order all these intricate details . . . it is simply not possible for all these details to be created and ordered simultaneously (which they must be, since no detail is a solo act) by a primeval explosion that admittedly came from nowhere to produce a chaotic, unorganized primordial soup on Earth.

Atoms are so small that it would take 2 billion to equal the size of the period at the end of this sentence. The average human cell contains about one trillion atoms . . . in total, your body is made of 10^{28} atoms, which is more than all the stars in the Universe. (As part of the amazing renewal system that God has installed in your body, approximately 1,000,000,000,000, 000,000,000,000 of your atoms are replaced hourly, 90 percent are replaced annually, and 100 percent are replaced every five years. So, you literally become a new person every 5 years. If it weren't for the deadly effects of sin, your body would live forever.)

Sub-atomic Particles

Atoms, with their submicroscopic size, are considered to be the building blocks of all matter (everything that exists), but molecular biologists have confirmed that atoms are made of even smaller, well ordered parts. The basic building blocks of atoms are protons, neutrons and electrons. Do you realize how important the qualities of these submicroscopic particles are? For example, did you know that if protons were even the slightest bit heavier, this Universe would quickly collapse? If just a tad heavier, all the protons in existence would become unstable particles that would be destroyed in only a few minutes! The destruction of protons would lead to the destruction of atoms and essential life elements like carbon and hydrogen, which would lead to the destruction of you.

As further evidence of intelligent design at the smallest levels of matter, consider that neutral neutrons and positively charged protons are packed together to form a tight core at the center of the atom. Negatively charged electrons whiz around this nucleus at nearly the speed of light (about 186,000 miles per second). This means that electrons orbit around the nucleus billions of times in only millionths of a second! What holds together the atoms that form your body? Again, the secret is God's glue, which involves the electrical attraction between protons and electrons, and special nuclear forces that bind together the particles of the nucleus. These forces, along with gravity, are some of the basic forces that hold the Universe together. I would suggest that these foundational forces are God-designed glue as described in Colossians 1:16–17 of the Bible.

Sub-subatomic Particles

But the design and order goes deeper still. By smashing atoms together at extremely high speeds, scientists have discovered more than 200 sub-subatomic particles that form or include subatomic electrons, protons and neutrons. Quarks, leptons and bosons are the 3 basic units of sub-subatomic particles. Quarks, which form protons and neutrons, are so tiny that billions of them would fit inside a single atom, which, if you remember, is so small that 2 billion are needed to fill the space in the period at the end of this sentence.

Research has shown that there are 6 'flavors' (kinds) of quarks . . . 1)Up, 2)Down, 3)Strange, 4)Charm, 5)Bottom and 6)Top. In addition, each flavor has 3 varieties (colors) . . . 1) Red, 2) Blue and 3) Green, making a total of 18 different known sub-subatomic quarks. Bosons include photons, gluons (protons are made from clusters of 3 quarks held together by gluons), and weakons. Leptons include electrons, muons, taus and 3 kinds of neutrinos. (Interestingly, molecular biologists have recently discovered a new sub-subatomic particle, called *xi*, which has a lifespan of only a ten-billionth of a second. This means that in the course of one second, billions of *xi* particles have died and been created as part of God's wonderful life renewal system. Essentially, our body is being renewed at a rate close to the speed of light, although sin is constantly breaking it down, as I'll discuss in Chapter 11.) Science is constantly revealing that intricately ordered design and complex diversity exists at even the most foundational levels of creation.

We can now breathe a sigh of relief since we've finally reached the bottom rung of the incredibly tall, multilayered ladder of life. As we stand at the bottom, let's briefly review where we've been, again scaling the ladder in our minds.

THE LADDER OF LIFE

Incredibly Complex and Intricately Ordered (ICIO)

(ICIO)Universe . . . . .>>>
ICIO Galaxy clusters . . . .>>>
ICIO Milky Way Galaxy .>>>
ICIO Earth, including all
unique, life sustaining
features . . . . .>>>
ICIO Biomes . . . .>>>
ICIO Habitats . . . . .>>>
ICIO Communities . .>>>
ICIO Species . . . .>>>
ICIO Individual Organism .>>>   *GOD*
ICIO Systems . . . .>>>   *IS*
ICIO Organs . . . .>>>   *THE*
ICIO Tissues . . . .>>> *CREATOR!*
ICIO Cells . . . .>>>
ICIO Organelles . . . .>>>
ICIO Proteins . . . .>>>
ICIO Amino Acids . . . .>>>
ICIO RNA . . . .>>>
ICIO DNA (including genes in chromosomes).>>>
ICIO Nucleotides . . . .>>>
ICIO Molecules . . . .>>>
ICIO Elements (all 109 on Earth) . . . .>>>
ICIO Atoms . . . .>>>
ICIO Subatomic protons, neutrons, and electrons . . . >>>
ICIO Sub-subatomic quarks, leptons and bosons . . . .>>>

The Key Message:

Creation is incredibly complex at every level, from the 18 quark types to the 100 billion estimated galaxies forming millions of immensely sized galaxy clusters in an even larger Universe. But instead of chaos, this incredibly complex creation displays vitally intricate order and coordination, which can only be logically explained by the existence of a Supremely Intelligent Designer Who created it all.

PART II

The Bible Can Be Trusted

CHAPTER 9

Unmasking the Divine Designer

To any reasonable and unbiased mind, the evidence given in the first 8 chapters must lead overwhelmingly to the conclusion that we are not the highly evolved products of non-intelligent matter that came from nothing and nowhere, but were made by an intelligent Divine Designer. In these last 3 chapters, which are by far the most important, it is finally time to convincingly reveal the identity of the Divine Designer and then consider His plans for your life. I've alluded several times throughout this book to the fact that the God of the Bible is the sole Creator of this Universe, but have never supported that assumption with evidence. It is now time to provide this evidence.

You may be wondering how I can be bold enough to declare one God among many in this postmodern world which denies absolute truth. How can I be absolutely confident that the God of the Bible is the only true Creator, since this world worships many gods? Actually, there are several excellent reasons for this confidence . . . the first of these is the fact that the Bible has proven to be the only completely reliable and God-written 'religious' book in the world. The evidence clearly reveals that it is superior over all others.

REASON#1-THE BIBLE ALONE IS COMPLETELY ACCURATE

Any discussion dealing with the existence of the God of the Bible and all that He claims to be must begin with the Bible, which He declares as His word to man. If the Bible is just a mythical collection of fairy tales written by men to make us feel good, then God is a cruel hoax. God would be dead, Jesus would be a mere mortal at best, and you could basically throw Christianity in the trash.

So, how do I know without a reasonable doubt that the Bible can be trusted? Here's partly how . . . earlier criticism of the historical validity of the Bible has been decisively overturned by recent archaeological discoveries. Approximately 25,000 Old and New Testament sites had been excavated as of 1998. There are likely more today.

The great historian Philip Schaff laid the most important ground rule for historical/archaeological studies (or any other type of study) by stating, "The purpose of the historian is not to construct a history from preconceived notions and to adjust it to his own liking, but to reproduce it from the best evidence and to let it speak for itself."[1] Where does the evidence lead us in relation to the historical truth of the Bible?

Following are typical responses from those who have honestly studied the historical/archaeological issues related to the Bible . . . archaeologist Dr. Clifford Wilson said, "I know of no finding in archaeology that's properly confirmed which is in opposition to the Scriptures."[2] Millar Burrows from Yale has found that, "The Bible is supported by archaeological evidence again and again. On the whole, there can be no question that the results of excavation have increased the respect of scholars for the Bible as a collection of historical documents."[3] A.H. Sayce said, "Time after time the most positive assertions of skeptical criticism have been disproved by archaeological discovery; events and personages that were confidently pronounced to be mythical have been shown to be historical, and the older writers have turned out to be better acquainted with what they were describing than the modern critic who has flouted them."[4] Today, it's not just Christians who accept the historical truth of the

Bible, but even secular (non-Christian) historians/archaeologists have been forced based on the facts to accept Biblical accounts as historical, since nothing has been found to conflict the Bible, and everything found confirms it.

Following is a very small portion of what has been found by historical/archaeological work mainly within the last century. If you carefully consider the evidence, I think you'll agree that the Bible is filled with real people, places and events . . . it certainly is not a fairy tale.

The Bible . . . Real People

They've been labeled the 'Super Skeptics,' literary scholars who doubt that the characters in the Bible were actual living people. According to them, the Bible is just a fable composed of the life events of mythical people. But, in the last 100 years or so, since Biblical archaeology has kicked into high gear, these same skeptics have been forced to admit the fact that the Bible includes real human beings. A small sampling of the individuals concretely proven to have really lived and their related Bible references include:

- Jehu (II Kings 9:1–10:36)
- Shishak (I Kings 14: 25–26),
- Nebuchadnezzar (Daniel 1:1)
- Omri (I Kings 16:24)
- Belshazzar (Daniel 5)
- Sargon II (Isaiah 20:1)
- Joshua (Joshua 1:1)
- Jaazaniah (Jeremiah 40:8)
- Sennacherib (II Kings 18:13–19:37)
- Gedaliah (Jeremiah 40:5)
- Esarhaddon (II Kings 19:37)
- Jothan (II Chronicles 27)
- Uzziah (II Chronicles 26)
- Merodach-Baladan (II Kings 20:12–19)
- Manasseh (II Chronicles 33)
- Ahaz (II Chronicles 28)
- Jehoichin (II Kings 24:6–17)

- Menahem (II Kings 15:19,20)
- Xerxes I (Esther; Ezra 4:6)
- Augustus, Roman emperor at Jesus' birth and during His childhood (Luke 2:1)
- Tiberius, Roman emperor during Jesus' adulthood and crucifixion (Luke 3:1)
- Herod Antipas, political ruler during Jesus' life (Luke 23:7)
- Pontius Pilate, procurator of Judea during Jesus trial, crucifixion and resurrection (Matt 27)
- Emperor Claudius during the early church age (Acts 11:28; 17:7; 18:2)
- Herod Agrippa I, persecutor of the early church (Acts 12:1-23; 23:35)
- Nero, also a persecutor of the early church (Acts 25:11, 12,21; 26:32; 28:19; Philippians 4:22)
- Key Old Testament figures such as Moses, Abraham, King David, Isaac and Jacob
- Key New Testament figures like Matthew, Mark, Luke, John, Peter, Paul, and James
- Most importantly, the existence of Jesus is not only recorded in the Bible, but further confirmed by ancient historians who lived during Jesus' time

Certainly, the Bible is not a mythical tale documenting the lives of phony individuals. It includes the real lives of real people, as confirmed by secular history and archaeological studies. The Bible has proven to be an accurate historical text on at least two other fronts as well, since it includes real places and events.

The Bible . . . Real Places

Skeptical scholars have long scoffed at the notion that many biblical places actually existed and that the details given by the Bible about those places are accurate. But the following archaeological discoveries (along with many that aren't listed), provide overwhelming evidence that even the most contested infrastructural details of biblical places were a reality. Here are a few of the thousands of places that have proven to be real:

- Antioch of Syria (Acts 11:26)
- Athens (Acts 17:15)
- Babylon (II Kings 25)
- Caesarea (Acts 8:40)
- Corinth (Acts 19:1)
- Ephesus (Acts 18:19)
- Ezion-geber (Numbers 33:35)
- Hazor (Joshua 11:10)
- Jericho (Joshua 6:20)
- Jerusalem (Matthew 21:1)
- Megiddo (Armageddon) (Joshua 12:21)
- Ninevah (Jonah 3:2)
- Philippi (Acts 16:12)
- Rome (Acts 28)
- Samaria (I Kings 16:24)
- Shechem (Joshua 17:7)
- Ur (Genesis 11:28)
- The base of the Tower of Babel (Genesis 11:1–9).
- The royal palace in Babylon (Daniel 5)
- Joseph's palace in On (Genesis 41:45)
- Esther's palace (Esther 1:2)
- Solomon's horse stables (I Kings 9:19; 10:26–29)
- Solomon's navy (I Kings 9:26)
- Hezekiah's tunnel (II Kings 20:20)
- Bethlehem, where Jesus was born (Luke 2:4–7)
- Nazareth, where Jesus grew up (Matthew 2:23)
- The Garden of Gethsemane, where Jesus prayed and was arrested (Interestingly, trees dating from the time of Jesus' arrest remain standing in the garden today) (Matthew 26:36)
- The foundation of the synagogue at Capernaum (John 6:25–59)
- The house of Peter at Capernaum (Matthew 8:14–16)
- Jacob's well (John 4)
- The tribunal at Corinth (Acts 18:12–17)
- The theater of Ephesus Acts 19:29)
- Herod's palace at Caesarea (Acts 23:33–35)

- The Mount of Olives (II Samuel 15:30) where Jesus was arrested (the Garden of Gethsemane is located on this mountain) and where Jesus will return during His second coming

I could go on and on with examples of biblical people and places that have been found, but I guess I'll stop here. The point should be clear by now. The spade of archaeology has confirmed over and over again that even the most obscure individuals and minute infrastructural details belong in the realm of reality. The Bible has stood the test of time and proven to be an accurate history book. There is no longer any reason to doubt the accuracy of the Bible, even in the most remarkable cases, such as the recording of fantastic events, including the following:

The Bible . . . Real Events[5]

- The worldwide flood is confirmed by several secular sources written after the biblical account and many scientific facts from the geologic record (Genesis 6–9)
- Long life before the flood and much shorter lives following the flood is documented on "The Sumerian King List" tablet (Genesis 5,11)
- Adam's original sin in the Garden of Eden is supported by the later Story of Adapa and the effects of that sin as evident in the existing world (Genesis 3)
- The division of one language into many at the Tower of Babel is supported by later ancient Sumerian and Babylonian documents (Genesis 11:1–9)
- Pharaoh Shishak's invasion of Judah is recorded on the walls of the Temple of Amun in Thebes, Egypt (II Chronicles 12:9,10)
- Moab's rebellion against Israel is recorded on the Mesha Inscription (II Kings 3:4,5)
- The siege of Sargon II on Samaria is recorded on his palace walls (II Kings 17:3–6, 24; 18:9–11)
- Sennacherib's invasion of Judah, is recorded on the Taylor Prism (II Chronicles 32:1)

- Sennacherib's assassination by his sons is documented in the annals of Esarhaddon (II Kings 19:37)
- Ninevah's fall, which occurred exactly as predicted by God's prophets Nahum and Zephaniah, is recorded on the Tablet of Nabopolassar (Zephaniah 2:13–15)
- Nebuchadnezzar's conquering of Jerusalem is recorded in the Babylonian Chronicles (II Kings 24:1–14)
- Jehoiachin's captivity in Babylon is recorded on the Babylonian Ration Records (II Kings 24:15–16)
- Babylon's fall to the Medes and Persians is recorded on the Cyrus Cylinder (Daniel 5:30–31)

Other events proven by archaeology include:

- Hezekiah paying tribute to Senacherib as recorded in II Kings 18:14–16
- King Jehu paying tribute to King Shalmaneser III of Assyria as mentioned in II Kings 9–10
- Egypt's victory over Judah in 925 B.C. as described in I Kings 14; II Chronicles 12
- Nebuchadnezzar's attack on Lachish as found in Jeremiah 34:7
- The destruction of Ai and Bethel as detailed in Joshua 8
- Canaanite oppression in Israel as mentioned in Judges 4:3
- Captivity of Israel as recorded in II Kings 17:5,6,24
- The Exodus of Israel out of Egypt has long been laughed off by liberal scholars. These scholars insist that Israelites weren't even living in Egypt at the time of the Exodus, but relatively recent archaeological discoveries have proven otherwise. For example, archaeologists working in the Nile Delta have unearthed the remains of houses that are completely different than the Egyptian houses surrounding them. Further excavation demonstrated that these houses fit the exact pattern of Israelite houses later built in Canaan. Even more convincing is the fact that these houses were found in Tell el Dab'a, which is the location of the biblical city Ra'amses, where the Bible says the Israelites lived in slavery to the Egyptian pharaoh.

Also, the pathway that Israel traveled on their journey to Canaan has been well documented.

The Battle of Jericho

One of the seemingly most unbelievable events in the Bible concerns the destruction of Jericho. Skeptics have long believed that Jericho never existed, and definitely not during the time of Joshua, so this battle, they've said, is a myth and the Bible recording it is unreliable. But Jericho has been found and shown to be in existence at the time of Joshua, proving the skeptics wrong and the Bible right. Concerning the battle, God said in Joshua 6 that the Israelites marched around the heavily fortified city walls (the 2 adjacent walls protecting the city were 6 and 12 feet thick and both were 30 feet high) for seven days, and blew their trumpets, causing most of the inner wall to fall inward, upon the wicked inhabitants of the city, while most of the outer wall fell out flat, away from the city, forming a perfect ramp for Israel to invade. This is a remarkable event that skeptics had said was impossible, since city walls have never been known to fall in this way . . . yet this is exactly what archaeological study has proven. (Garstang found during his excavations at Jericho that the walls really did fall outwards, creating a perfect invading ramp for Israel to take the city. The archaeological proof matches perfectly with the biblical description in Joshua 6:20.)

In addition, God said the city would be destroyed by fire. A British archaeologist, Kathleen Kenyon, wrote in her excavation report of the Jericho site that "The destruction was complete. Walls and floors were blackened or reddened by fire, and every room was filled with fallen bricks, timbers and household utensils; in most rooms the fallen debris was heavily burnt."[6] God also said that no food would be taken, but that every bit of silver, gold, iron and brass was to be taken. Fossilized remains of food supplies indicate that no food was taken . . . precious grain-filled jars collectively containing enough food for several months were still filled to the brim. Food supplies were always taken during a siege, except in this case. Archaeology confirms that this seemingly unlikely circumstance occurred exactly as described in the Bible. With regard to the precious metals, excavations have shown that every scrap of it had been taken, just as

God said. Maybe even more amazingly, God promised that he would protect Rahab and all that is in her house during the siege, since she had recently helped hide Israeli spies. Archaeologists have found evidence showing that Rahab's house, which was located on the city wall (Joshua 2:15), was indeed miraculously spared.

The ancient city of Jericho was located near a major watercourse. Since the annals of history indicate that cities lying near major watercourses are never abandoned forever, secular archaeologists have been shocked to discover that Jericho, with its prime location, had lain barren since the day of its destruction by Israel. The findings of archaeology confirm the amazing biblical narrative. Also, God warned that anyone who tried to rebuild Jericho on its actual site would lose their firstborn and youngest son. A man named Hiel from Bethel tested God 550 years later to see if His promise was true (I Kings 16:34). Not surprisingly, historical records and archaeological remains indicate that his firstborn and youngest sons both died as a result of his efforts to rebuild the city, just as God had promised.

There are many more examples I could give to provide historical support for biblical events, such as further evidence for the worldwide flood described in Genesis. But these various events have been evidenced in great detail by many other books, so I see no need to provide even more examples. Still, I hope that you've gotten the point with the short list I've given . . . the Bible is not a fairy tale, but is instead a reliable recording of real people, places and events.

Skepticism of the historical accuracy of the Bible was strongest in the eighteenth and nineteenth centuries, but each claim has been discredited with the passing of time. The great archaeological discoveries of past decades have now forced even radical critics to admit that the Bible is a reliable historical source. Dr. William F. Albright, widely regarded as one of the world's greatest archaeologists, wrote that "The excessive skepticism shown toward the Bible has been progressively discredited. Discovery after discovery has established the accuracy of numerous details."[7] Scholar Norman Geisler said, "Examination of the evidence suggests that the Bible is extremely reliable in historical and scientific matters, and its critics have been proven wrong over and over again."[8] He continued, "While many have doubted the accuracy of the Bible, time and continued research have consistently demonstrated that the Word of God is better informed than its critics."[9]

So, the next time someone casts doubt upon the historicity of the Bible, share with them the concrete archaeological examples I've shared with you. Christians no longer need to take a backseat to 'Super Skeptics,' who profess to know it all. The spade of archaeology has proven God's Word, the Bible, to be historically trustworthy time and time again. And since His Word has proven historically trustworthy, even in the seemingly most unbelievable cases, we would be wise to soak in the more important spiritual truths that this wonderful book contains, especially since no other 'religious' book in the world can claim equal accuracy. The Bible stands alone in its reliability.

The Reliability of the Bible is Confirmed by the Science of Textual Criticism

While archaeological studies have shown that the Bible is historically reliable, the science of textual criticism has confirmed that the Bible we hold in our hands today includes the same words that God spoke through men several hundred and thousands of years ago during the recording of the original autographs. The science of textual criticism has proven over and over again the reliability of our Old and New Testament records. Because the Old and New Testaments were not handed down in a single manuscript, but through thousands of copies circulated throughout the known world, manuscript families can be compared against other manuscript families to determine where, when and if copyist errors or scribal explanations entered into the text. That is how we can ensure the accuracy of what we call the Bible. And it is very accurate.

Accuracy of the Old Testament

We have good reasons to believe that the Old Testament texts we have today are extremely accurate copies of the original text. Flavius Josephus, a first century Jewish historian said, concerning the importance put on preserving the original words of the Old Testament that, "We have given practical proof of our reverence for our own

Scriptures. For although such long ages have now passed, no one has ventured either to add, or to remove, or to alter a syllable; and it is an instinct with every Jew, from the day of his birth, to regard them as the decrees of God, to abide by them, and, if need be, cheerfully to die for them. Time and again ere now the sight has been witnessed of prisoners enduring tortures and death in every form in the theatres, rather than utter a single word against the laws and the allied documents."[10]

Other historical records also state that the reverence of the scribes, and Jewish people in general was so great that they would willingly endure a tortuous death rather than to have the slightest portion of scripture altered. Historical accounts like these strongly argue the case that nearly every letter and accent from the original Old Testament autographs has been carefully preserved for us today. Jewish scribes (who copied the Bible) had meticulous copying methods to check everything that was checkable, including individual letters. Whole manuscripts were destroyed if an error was detected.

The historical accuracy of biblical transmission (copying) is very impressive. It began with a class of Jewish scholars called the Sopherim, who dedicated their lives to the guarding and accurate transmission of original Old Testament autographs starting in the 5th century B.C. until A.D 100. Groups called the Zugoth and Tannaim also guarded and transmitted the autographs during this time period.

From A.D 100–500, a group of people called the Talmudists were responsible for copying the Bible. According to Samuel Davidson, who has thoroughly studied their methods, Talmudists strictly used the following minute regulations while copying the Biblical text from original manuscripts: "1) A synagogue roll must be written on the skins of clean animals, 2) prepared for the particular use of the synagogue by a Jew. 3) These must be fastened together with strings taken from clean animals. 4) Each skin must contain a certain number of columns, equal throughout the entire codex. 5) The length of each column must not extend over less than 48 or more than 60 lines; and the breadth of each column must consist of 30 letters. 6) The whole copy must be first-lined; and if three words be written without a line, it is worthless. 7) The ink should be black, neither red, green, nor any other colour, and be prepared according to a definite recipe. 8) An authentic copy must be the exemplar, from which the transcriber must not in the least deviate. 9) No word or letter, not even a yod, must be written from memory, the scribe not having looked at the codex before him . . . 10) Between every consonant, the space of a hair or thread must intervene; 11) between every new parashah, or section, the breadth of nine consonants; 12) between every book, 3 lines. 13) The fifth book of Moses must terminate exactly with a line; but the rest need not do so. 14) Besides this, the copyist must sit in full Jewish dress, 15) wash his whole body, 16) not begin to write the name of God with a pen newly dipped in ink, 17) and should a king address him while writing that name he must take no notice of him."[11]

Davidson further explained that "the rolls in which these regulations are not observed are condemned to be buried in the ground or burned . . ."[12] The work of the Talmudists was precise and can be highly trusted. What they handed down to the next generation was an exact copy of the original manuscripts which they transcribed.

During A.D 500–900, a group called the Massorites accepted the task of copying the original Biblical text. Bible scholar Sir Frederick Kenyon stated that "The Massorites numbered the verses, words and letters of every book. They calculated the middle word and letter of each book. They numbered verses which contained all the letters of the alphabet. These trivialities had the effect of securing minute attention to the precise transmission of the text. The Massorites were indeed anxious that not one jot nor tittle, not one smallest letter nor one tiny part of a letter should pass away or be lost."[13] F.F. Bruce concurred that "The Massorites were well disciplined and treated the text with the greatest imaginable reverence, and devised a complicated system of safeguards against scribal slips. They counted, for example, the number of times each letter of the alphabet occurs in each book; they pointed out the middle letter of the Pentateuch and the middle letter of the whole Hebrew Bible, and made even more detailed calculations than these. 'Everything countable seems to be counted,' says Wheeler Robinson, and they made up mnemonics by which the various totals might be readily remembered."[14] The intricately accurate Massoretic copies are the standard Hebrew text used today.

Scholar Robert Wilson has found evidence for the accuracy of the Old Testament through his study of the comparative chronologies of the almost 40 kings living between 2000 B.C. to 400 B.C., as described in the Old Testament and secular history. After finding an impressive parallel of the Old Testament with secular history, he stated, "With reference to the kings of the same country and with respect to the kings of other countries . . . no stronger evidence for the substantial accuracy of the Old Testament records could possibly be imagined, than this collection of kings."[15] He later explained the possibility that the biblical record would match exactly with the known chronology of kings, saying "Mathematically, it is one chance in 750,000,000,000,000,000,000,000,000 that this accuracy is mere circumstance."[16]

Wilson said that, "The Hebrew Bible (Old Testament) has been transmitted with the most minute accuracy."[17] Norman Geisler further explained, "The thousands of Hebrew manuscripts, with their confirmation by the Septuagint and the Samaritan Pentateuch, and the numerous other cross-checks from outside and inside the text provide overwhelming support for the reliability of the Old Testament text . . ."[18] William Henry Green concluded, ". . . it may safely be said that no other work of antiquity has been so accurately transmitted."[19]

The Dead Sea Scrolls

Despite the strong historical and textual evidence, skeptics still denied the accuracy of the Old Testament. But the finding of the Dead Sea Scrolls in 1947 decisively overturned their weak denials. The Dead Sea Scrolls are considered one of the most important archaeological discoveries of all time, since it gave the world a copy of the Old Testament that predated all other existing Hebrew manuscripts by 1,000 years. The really important thing to understand is that the scrolls are nearly identical with copies made 1,000 years later, and with those that we have today, confirming accurate copying throughout the ages. Gleason L. Archer Jr. said, "Even though the two copies of Isaiah discovered in Qumran Cave 1 near the Dead Sea in 1947 were a thousand years earlier than the oldest dated manuscript previously known, they proved to be word for word identical with our standard Hebrew Bible in more than 95 percent of the text. The 5 percent of variation consisted chiefly of obvious slips of the pen and variations in spelling. They do not affect the message of the revelation in the slightest."[20]

Based on the evidence, Robert Wilson has concluded that "The proof that the copies of the original documents have been handed down with substantial correctness for more than 2,000 years cannot be denied."[21] (The Dead Sea Scrolls were written in 125 B.C., the Masoretic Text of the Old Testament in A.D 916, and this year is A.D 2004 . . . since the Dead Sea Scrolls are essentially identical with the Old Testament we have today, we can conclusively say that the Old Testament has been accurately copied for over 2,100 years. Further, when considering the painstaking accuracy of the earliest Jewish scribes, we can take this date back to the 5th century B.C., when the original papyrus autographs were probably disintegrating due to their age. So, we can say with a great deal of confidence that the Old Testament we have today includes the exact message God wanted us to hear in His words.)

Scholars Critique the Accuracy of the New Testament

Concerning the New Testament, Australian archaeologist Clifford Wilson wrote, "Those who know the facts now recognize that the New Testament must be accepted as a remarkably accurate source book."[22] Scholar J.P. Moreland said, ". . . the text we currently possess is an accurate representation of the original New Testament documents."[23] Scholar Norman Geisler said, "There is more abundant and accurate manuscript evidence for the New Testament than for any other book from the ancient world. There are more manuscripts copied with greater accuracy and earlier dating than for any secular classic from antiquity."[24] Geisler continued, "It is also safe to say that the New Testament is the most accurately copied book from the ancient world."[25] Geisler further said that "The fact that there is outstanding manuscript evidence for the New Testament documents is even *admitted by critical scholars*."[26] Dr. Benjamin Warfield, late professor at Princeton Theological Seminary, who held 4 doctorate degrees, stated, "If we compare the present state of the New Testament text with that of any other ancient writing, we must declare it to be marvelously correct. Such has been the case with which the New Testament has been copied—a care which has doubtless grown out of a true reverence for its holy words . . . the New Testament is unrivaled among ancient writings in the purity of its text as actually transmitted and kept in use."[27]

Bible scholars Norman Geisler and William Nix have observed that, "The New Testament, then, has not only survived in more manuscripts than any other book from antiquity, but it has survived in a purer form than any other great book—a form that is 99.5% pure."[28] The .5% discrepancy between copies includes a handful of minor spelling errors and switched words that in no way affect the teachings of the Bible. When eliminating the minor spelling errors and switched words, Geisler said, "The resulting text is 99.99 percent accurate, and the remaining questions do not affect any area of cardinal Christian doctrine."[29] As Sir Fredrick Kenyon, the famous archaeologist and Bible scholar has found, "Both the authenticity and the general integrity of the books of the New Testament may be regarded as finally established . . ."[30] Kenyon continued, "No other ancient book has anything like such early and plentiful testimony to its text, and no unbiased scholar would deny that the text that has come down to us is substantially sound."[31] (I'll give much more evidence for the accuracy of the New Testament in Chapter 10.)

The Verdict is In . . .

Concerning the entire Bible, Kenyon summarized the evidence when he said, "The last foundation for any doubt that the scriptures have come down to us substantially as they were written has now been removed . . . the Christian can take the whole Bible in his hand and say without fear or hesitation that he holds the true Word of God, handed down without essential loss from generation to generation throughout the centuries."[32]

REASON #2 - THE FULFILLMENT OF OLD TESTAMENT PROPHECY IS UNEXPLAINABLE WITHOUT THE EXISTENCE OF GOD

We've established the fact that the Bible is an accurate history book, and that the text we hold today is an essentially errorless copy of the original manuscript. But this doesn't prove that it was written by God, since even men are capable of recording history accurately. To prove that God wrote the Bible, I will turn to perhaps the most powerful evidence of all . . . Old and New Testament prophecy. This evidence makes the fact that God wrote the Bible simply undeniable.

Fulfillment of Old Testament Prophecies

Many Old Testament prophecies record God's decisive intervention in human history. The following is a very small sampling of the hundreds of already fulfilled Old Testament prophecies, as proven by the record of history. My purpose is not to provide a comprehensive list, but rather to introduce you to the fact that fulfillment of detailed and often age-distant prophecy is proof of God's inspiration. Old Testament examples include:

- In Nahum, the destruction of Ninevah is predicted. According to Diodorus Siculus (a historian), the city was destroyed nearly a century later, by the exact method predicted.
- Daniel 2:40 accurately predicts the characteristics of the Roman Empire several hundred years before it even existed.
- In II Kings 20:16–17, the siege on Jerusalem by Babylon is predicted more than 100 years before it happened, as recorded in Jeremiah 52:17.
- Jeremiah 25:11–13 predicts the 70 year reign of Babylon years before they took control. Babylon reigned exactly 70 years, and was destroyed, just as predicted.

- In Isaiah 13:17–20, the destruction of Babylon was predicted more than 200 years before it happened. As verse 20 predicts, it also has never been reestablished throughout all the years of human history.
- In Isaiah 44:28 and 45:1, Cyrus is named and his position as King of Persia is predicted 180 years before his reign (Ezra 1:1). It is remarkable that it says Jerusalem and the temple will be rebuilt, since it was still more than 100 years before Babylon destroyed it! Also, concerning Cyrus, his decree was predicted in II Chronicles 36:22–23 almost 60 years before he gave it in Ezra 1:3.
- In Genesis 50:25, Joseph's bones were transported 262 years after he predicted it. This happened in Joshua 24:32.
- In I Kings 13:2, Josiah's exact name and position were predicted almost 300 years before his birth, as recorded in II Kings 22:1 and II Kings 23:16.

Some skeptics have claimed that the accuracy of modern 'prophets' rivals the prophetic accuracy of the Bible, reducing the amazement of biblical prophecy. The truth is that, although the prophecies of modern 'prophets' are often vague and related to current events that are easily foreseeable within the 'prophet's' lifetime, the best still managed to be correct only 6 percent of the time.[33] In sharp contrast, biblical prophecies are detailed, specific, and sometimes given hundreds of years before they actually happened by men that had no cultural or political knowledge of the age they were prophesying about. Yet, the Bible has proven to be correct 100% of the time. If men and women are unable to accurately predict vague events in the age they live in, they certainly cannot prophesy detailed events hundreds of years in the future without supernatural guidance. It seems very clear that the prophecies contained in the Bible must have been made by God.

Dr. Bernard Ramm observed that, "Prophecy in many cases is very minute in its specifications. It is not only a matter of vague generalization or happy guesses. People are named before birth; kingdoms are outlined before their historical existence; battles are described before occurring; and personal destinies are delineated before the persons themselves are born."[34] Ramm concluded that prophecy ". . . is the seal of divine omniscience upon the pages of the Holy Bible."[35] He also contends that the phenomenology (study of things beyond human reason, including prophetic fulfillment) of the Bible can be explained only by God's intervention. He said that *"The sum total of the phenomenology of the Bible is a witness to the divine breath in the Bible . . . Christianity stands verified by a supernatural Book."*[36]

Ramm is only one of many who has reached these conclusions. Rev. C.I., Scofield D.D. observed during his lifetime of intensive study that "Fulfilled prophecy is a proof of inspiration because the Scripture predictions of future events were uttered so long before the events transpired that no merely human sagacity or foresight could have anticipated them, and these predictions are so detailed, minute and specific as to exclude the possibility that they were mere fortunate guesses. Hundreds of predictions concerning Israel, the land of Canaan, Babylon, Assyria, Egypt and numerous personages—so ancient, so singular, so seemingly improbable, as well as so detailed and definite that no mortal could have anticipated them—have been fulfilled by the elements, and by men who were ignorant of them, or who utterly disbelieved them, or who struggled with frantic desperation to avoid their fulfillment. It is certain, therefore, that the Scriptures which contain them are inspired"[37] by God. As Norman Geisler said, "The Bible is the only book that both claims and proves to be the Word of God."[38]

If God is responsible for the prophecies, as the evidence overwhelmingly demonstrates, then He exists. The fact that He exists should certainly change our lives forever . . . we must conclude that we are not wandering alone in a chaotic universe, but are under the watchful eye of a personal, transcendent God, who has a designed purpose for each human life. I'll explain the wonderful plan God has waiting for those who trust in Him in the final chapter.

REASON #3 - MESSIANIC PROPHECIES INDICATE
THAT GOD WROTE THE BIBLE AND JESUS IS GOD

Messianic prophecy is a special branch of Old Testament prophecy. At least 61 distinct Old Testament Messianic prophecies (some scholars have placed this number near 300) have been fulfilled in exact detail by Jesus Christ alone through His birth, life, death and resurrection. The truly amazing thing about Old Testament prophecy is that each prediction was given more than 400 years before it actually happened, as admitted by even the most radical critics of the Bible. {The Hebrew Scriptures were translated into Greek during the reign of Ptolemy Philadelphius, (285–246 B.C.) . . . to make a copy, a complete version of the Old Testament must have been in existence. The significance of this is that the Messianic prophecies of Christ must have been made at least 250 years before Christ came to earth, a time span too great for any man or collection of men to predict 61 prophecies accurately. The Old Testament was likely complete far before the reign of Ptolemy Philadelphius, but it had to be complete no later than 250 B.C.} Whether you choose the 450 B.C. date accepted by most scholars or 250 B.C. makes no difference, for man could not have accurately predicted all these prophecies from this far out . . . this means that God must have.

According to statistical research performed by Peter Stoner[39] there is a 1 in 10^{17} (1 in one hundred million billion) chance for just eight detailed messianic prophecies to be accurately written by men several hundred years before they occurred. To help you visualize the immense impossibility, consider the fact that if the state of Texas were covered 2 feet deep in

silver dollars (or a similar depth of quarters) with only one marked, the pile was mixed up, and a volunteer was blindfolded prior to the mixing, that person would also have a 1 in 10^{17} chance of jumping into the pile and randomly selecting the one marked silver dollar. These certainly aren't very good odds.

It has further been determined using the science of probability that the odds of men accurately nailing 48 of these prophecies on the head are only 1 chance in 10^{157}. (Remember that any event with odds of more than 1 chance in 10^{50} is considered statistically impossible.) To help understand the impossibly small odds of this happening, consider that a person would also have a 1 in 10^{157} (1 in a trillion, trillion, trillion, trillion, trillion, trillion, trillion, trillion, trillion, trillion, trillion, trillion, trillion) chance of picking one marked electron in a solid cubic inch of electrons while blindfolded. How small is an electron? It would take 2.5×10^{15} of them laid side by side, single file in a line to stretch one inch across the page you are now reading. There would be so many electrons in this one inch line that counting them at a rate of 250 per minute, 24 hours per day, 7 days a week would take 19,000,000 years to reach the end of the line. Counting a solid cubic meter at the same pace would require 1.18×10^{38} years! (In his book, *Science Speaks*, Peter Stoner had originally calculated that this would take 'only' 6.9×10^{21} years, but this is an error . . . it actually would take 17,000,000,000,000,000 times longer to count every electron in a cubic inch of electrons.) For the atheist, the discovery of this error makes their case against the existence of God even more incredulous.

Based on these statistics alone, we can safely say that no man or collection of men could have made these predictions . . . it's statistically impossible. The odds are even greater when we consider that the specific details of all 61 distinct prophecies were precisely fulfilled by Christ. If man did not make these predictions, then God must have. This is the only reasonable explanation.

Did the Apostles Alter the New Testament to Make Jesus Look Like the Messiah?

Some critics have suggested that the apostles altered the New Testament so that the life of Jesus would coincide with Old Testament prophecies. Louis S. Lapides, who was born a Jew (and who, disillusioned with the dissatisfaction he found while experimenting with Buddhism, Hinduism, Scientology and Satanism), finally found true satisfaction as a Christian. He is now a Pastor, after having been captivated by the power of biblical prophecy. Pastor Lapides, who has spent many hours researching the subject, explained that it is not possible that the apostles falsified Jesus' life to coincide with Old Testament prophecies due to the system of checks and balances that existed within both the Christian and non-Christian communities at the time when the New Testament was written. Within the Christian community, Lapides said, "When the gospels were being circulated, there were people living who had been around when these things happened. Someone would have said, 'You know it didn't happen this way. We're trying to communicate a life of righteousness and truth, so don't taint it with a lie."[40] Lapides further questioned why the apostles would have knowingly fabricated prophecies that Christ fulfilled and then willingly die for someone that they secretly knew was not the Messiah, but who was lying, dead and decaying in a grave. Good question. It makes no sense why the apostles would have done this . . . clearly they had no motivation to lie about the life of Christ.

Lapides added that the enemies of Christ, such as the Jewish religious leaders who were alive during Christ's life, and also when the New Testament was being written and preached to the world, would have gladly pounced on any opportunity to expose the lies being taught by early Christians. Lapides has observed, "Even though the Jewish Talmud refers to Jesus in derogatory ways (because He had exposed their hypocritical lifestyle), it never once makes the claim that the fulfillment of prophecies was falsified. Not one time."[41] Why is this important? It means that if even the enemies of Christ don't deny that He fulfilled all the Old Testament prophecies, such as His predicted resurrection from the dead, especially when they so easily could have, then Jesus really must have fulfilled these prophecies in exact detail.

Did Jesus Purposely Fulfill the Prophecies to Fool the World?

Some critics argue that Jesus deliberately fulfilled these prophecies to make Himself appear to be the coming Savior predicted in the Old Testament. But this argument holds no water when you realize that if Jesus was just a human, there is no way that He could have fulfilled prophecies that were outside of human control, such as His place of birth, time of birth, manner of birth, exact price that Judas was paid to betray Him, manner of death, reaction of the people at His crucifixion, piercing following death, manner of burial, and so on. However, if He was and is God, then there is no problem with Him fulfilling prophecies that were beyond human control. The fulfillment of humanly uncontrollable prophecies is powerful proof that Jesus is God, as He claimed. As Lee Strobel, author of *The Case for Christ*, has written, Jesus is "the sole individual in history who has matched the prophetic fingerprint"[42] of God.

Sampling of Fulfilled Old Testament Messianic Prophecies

The following is a small sampling of Old Testament Messianic Prophecies fulfilled by Jesus Christ . . . (For a somewhat more extensive listing of fulfilled Messianic prophecies, please refer to Appendix 1 near the end of this book.)

Psalms 22 is a graphic, prophetic picture of death by crucifixion. The bones (of the hands, arms, shoulders and pelvis) out of joint; the profuse perspiration caused by intense suffering; the action of the heart affected (v.14); strength exhausted and extreme thirst (v.15); the hands and feet pierced (v.16); and partial nudity (v.17) are all involved in crucifixion. All these circumstances were fulfilled precisely in the death of Christ. The desolate cry of verse 1 (Matthew 27:46); the periods of light and darkness of verse 2 (Matthew 27:45);

the mocking of verses 6–8, 12, 13 (Matthew 27:39–43); and the casting of lots in verse 18 (Matthew 27:35) were also literally fulfilled.

Crucifixion was invented as a Roman form of execution. Considering that Psalms 22 was written about 800 years before the Roman Empire and crucifixion even existed, the proof of God's inspiration is irresistible. No man or collection of men could have seen this event 800 years in the future and described it so accurately, especially when there was nothing in his culture to relate to crucifixion.

Daniel 9:24–26, written about 570 years before the birth of Christ, predicts that Jerusalem would be rebuilt 49 years (1 week = 7 years in ancient terms) from the decree of Artaxerxes in 444 B.C. It was, as Ezra and Nehemiah record. But most importantly, it says that the Messiah would be "cut off" 434 years after this. Amazingly, Christ was cut off 483 years (49+ 434) after the decree, just as the Bible said. In fact, if you do a little math, you will discover that the prophecy was exact to the day. March 5, 444 B.C is the date of the Decree of Artaxerxes to Nehemiah (Nehemiah 2:1–8). 69 (7+62) weeks from this date is equal to 483 years (69 weeks x 7 years per week). 483 years multiplied by 360 days (the number of days in the Jewish prophetic calendar) equals 173,880 days. 173,880 days from March 5th, 444 B.C brings us to March 30th, A.D 33, which is the exact day when Jesus entered Jerusalem to be killed ("cut off"). Daniel's God-given prophecy is exact to the day!

Christ is also referred to in I Chronicles 17:11, Psalms 16:10 (prediction of resurrection), 41:9 (fulfilled in John 13:18), 69:9 (fulfilled in John 2:17), 69:21 (fulfilled in Matthew 27:34), 110:4 (fulfilled in Hebrews 6:20), Proverbs 8:22–36, Isaiah 9:6–7, 11:1, 11:10, 25:8, 41:27, 42:1, 49:6, *chapter 53*, which is another amazingly accurate and vivid description of Christ's suffering prior to His death, agonizing crucifixion and burial given over 700 years before it happened, 60:3, and Jeremiah 33:14–15. I invite you again to refer to Appendix 1 near the back of this book for further examples. Still, even this is not a complete list.

Christ and His disciples explained the significance of Old Testament prophecies in Luke 24:25, 27, 44–45, John 1:45, 5:39, Acts 3:18 and 10:39, II Peter 1:19–21, and Revelation 22:7. Please take the time to read all the verses listed and consider the evidence I've just presented. I'm confident you will discover the powerful fact that God must have written the Bible and that Jesus must be God.

REASON #4 - THE WORLD STAGE IS NOW BEING SET FOR THE FULFILLMENT OF NEW AND OLD TESTAMENT PROPHECY

New Testament (and Old Testament) prophecy presents a powerful case that God is in control of this world and should compel you to take the Bible very seriously. If the Bible is not God's Word, then try to explain why the world stage is seemingly being set for the fulfillment of each prophecy, given at least 2,000 years ago. There is no reasonable explanation for the fact that the course of this world is going exactly as the Bible said it would, unless you accept the truth that the Bible was indeed written by an omniscient God Who knows the future before it happens.

To begin, I'd ask you to take a close look at world events in the past several years, and consider the direction this world is taking. Watch the news, pick up a newspaper, and then dive into several prophetic passages that predict events that will occur during the end of this age. I think you will discover that everyday more of the prophecies concerning the end times are becoming closer to reality. If you don't believe that the Bible is an accurate predictor of the future, I'd invite you to study Matthew 24, Luke 21, 17:26–30, Mark 13, Revelation and others to witness how the stage is being set today. (Since I will only be briefly touching upon the subject here, I would encourage you to supplement your study with several excellent texts dedicated to end time prophecy, some of which I've mentioned in the Recommended Reading section near the end of this book.)

Using the Matthew passage as an example, consider that God said He will judge the world again when the morality of society is ". . . like it was in the days of Noah"[43] (Matt.24:37). The moral condition of society is undeniably similar to the way it was in Noah's days

244

(Genesis 6). The stage is clearly being set for prophecies concerning increased disease, hunger, severe weather (Matt.24:7) and wars (Matt.24:6) to be literally fulfilled during a 7 year period called the 'Tribulation,' which will be the worst period in human history. Who can deny that hunger is perhaps one of the biggest problems in the world today, with current starvation statistics overwhelming any other period in human history? Previously unheard of diseases seem to be popping up all the time . . . first there was AIDS, then the West Nile Virus, more recently the SARS and Monkey pox Viruses . . . what will be next?

Concerning wars, did you realize that at least 50 simultaneous conflicts are occurring throughout the world today—we only hear about US related wars. Also, despite the arms treaties in place, there is at least 1 military weapon and 4 thousand pounds of explosives for every man, woman and child on Earth. As part of the severe weather prophecy, consider that during the years 1900–1969, there was an average of 6 earthquakes every 10 years; during 1970–1995, there were 17 quakes per 10 years, and since 1996, there have been 10–20 major quakes per year for an average of 100–200 every 10 years. Is this a coincidence? I don't think so . . . I believe these statistics fall perfectly in line with what God predicted would happen as this age draws to a close.

There have been many false christs; David Koresh in Waco and the Heaven's Gate cult are just two fairly recent examples (Matt.24:5, 11, 24–26). In the case of the Heaven's Gate cult, they said that salvation was in a spaceship (desert). Cults are on the rise—some estimate there are over 10,000 today, and some of the leaders proclaim to be Christ.

The love of many (Matt.24:12) has waxed cold. We must look no farther than the recent rash of cold, heartless school shootings and the attack on the World Trade Center in New York City on 9/11/01, which has spawned our attack on worldwide terrorism. Violence also runs rampant on TV, in books, magazines, video games, music and many other modern entertainment sources. This increase in violence certainly describes the Bible prophecy that love will grow colder.

Revelation 13, 17 and 18 predicts that conditions in Europe will resemble those in the ancient Roman Empire during the last days. Not surprisingly, Europe is beginning to unite with a common parliament and currency (the 'Euro'), just like ancient Rome. They have even been heard to describe themselves as 'the revived Roman empire.' The technological revolution, and unifying of the world (through the Internet, worldwide economy, UN) was predicted in Daniel 2, 7 and 8, and is beginning to happen. A serious study of prophecy will make it obvious that the predicted political conditions are beginning to fall in place . . . the world stage is being set for the events of the Tribulation period as described in the Bible.

The '666' prophecy in Revelation 13:16–18 says that the economy and trade would be regulated by numbers in the last days, and that people will "receive a mark in their right hand and foreheads"[44] which will contain their identification number. There is no doubt this is very possible today. Did you realize that we now have the technology to, and have experimented with implanting computer chips containing vital personal information into the right hands of consenting people?

Jesus predicted chaos and confusion (Luke 21:25) on earth before His return. I believe that we are living in an increasingly confused and chaotic world, especially following the traumatic events of September 11, 2001 in America. It was predicted (Luke 21:25) that we would see amazing things in outer space. Astronomers have fairly recently discovered such things as solar tornadoes, which reach wind speeds of 310,000 MPH and are at least 1,000 times larger than any hurricane on Earth. More amazing things will be seen during the Tribulation.

The Old Testament also contains several end time prophecies. Proverbs 30:11–13 describes the moral condition of this world so well. Daniel has several prophecies that were promised to be "sealed unto the end,"[45] and their fulfillment would be obvious to those who can understand what has been predicted. Daniel 12:4 is a prime example, stating that in the end times, "many shall run to and fro and knowledge shall increase."[46] Knowledge is increasing at an astounding rate today . . . the sum total of scientific knowledge is doubling every 2 years. This staggering increase is unprecedented in human history. But there are many other verses besides this that appear to be very realistic possibilities in the near future. For example, Isaiah 51:6 says, "the earth will wax old as a garment."[47] It is beginning to. Experts predict that oil reserves will last for only

50 years, natural gas for another 60 and coal resources are estimated to be gone by 2225. Other natural resources are also being polluted and destroyed by our industrial world. Ezekiel predicts a rebuilt 3rd temple in Jerusalem during the last days. (The 2nd temple was destroyed in A.D 70 by Rome, and still awaits rebuilding). Interestingly, serious and detailed plans for construction of the 3rd temple are already underway.

II Peter 3:3–6 predicts an increase in scoffers, especially regarding the fact of creation, the worldwide flood and second coming of Jesus Christ. This is certainly the case today, with postmodernism and the theory of evolution running rampant in our society. Matthew 24:9 foreshadows an increase in persecution of Christians during the last days. Persecution is at an all time high in our modern world—160,000 Christians were killed for their faith in foreign countries last year alone. The Bible predicts an increase in false prophets (Matthew 24:11)—you can visit the magazine rack of almost any supermarket checkout line to see that this is becoming a reality. Also, as predicted, "The gospel of the kingdom shall be preached in all the world for a witness unto the nations; and then shall the end come" (Matt.24:14)[48]. With the mass media of today, all nations will soon be reached with the gospel message. It is promised that the end will come soon and Jesus Christ will return to earth.

I don't know exactly when Jesus will return (Matt.25:13), but I do know that His Word is true, and that He has remained faithful to it throughout the ages. All that He said He would do, He has done (Joshua 21:45, I Kings 8:56). If He said He will return, then He will return . . . we can count on it, and must be prepared when He does.

Although I don't know when He'll return, I believe that based on the current course of this world, it appears that His return may be very near. It's impossible to reasonably deny what you can clearly see. What we can clearly see is that the fulfillment of prophetic signs is becoming a more reasonable reality every day. The stage is seemingly being set . . . Christ could return at any second. If He returned with your next breath, would you be ready?

REASON #5 - ISRAEL AND THE BIBLE STILL EXIST

The fact that Israel and the Bible even exist is a testament to the powerful, guiding hand of God. Israel should have been annihilated several times, but this tiny nation has survived, while great empires like Babylon, Persia and ancient Rome have all fallen. God said He would preserve them throughout history, and He has done it.

The Bible has survived wars, persecution, and massive campaigns to eradicate it throughout thousands of years of human history. This is not surprising, since Jesus said in Matthew 24:35 that "heaven and earth will pass away, but my words will never pass away."[49] God's Word has proven to be indestructible.

As an example of miraculous Bible survivability, consider that only 25 years after the Roman emperor Diocletian ordered that all churches be destroyed and all Bibles be eliminated by fire, Constantine, a succeeding Roman emperor ordered that 50 copies of the Scriptures (which was a lot of copies at that time) be prepared at the government's expense.[50]

Sidney Collette, citing another example, said, "Many centuries later, Voltaire, the noted French infidel who died in 1778, said that in one hundred years from his time Christianity would be swept from existence and passed into history. But what has happened? Voltaire has passed into history, while the circulation of the Bible continues to increase in almost all parts of the world, carrying blessings wherever it goes . . . As one truly said, "We might as well put our shoulder to the burning wheel of the sun, and try to stop it in its flaming course, as attempt to stop the circulation of the Bible."[51] Ironically, in 1828, about 50 years after Voltaire's death, the Geneva Bible Society moved their operations into his house and used his personal printing press to produce thousands of Bibles for worldwide distribution.[52]

H.L. Hastings added this tribute to the survivability of the Bible and futility of the enemies trying to destroy it: "Enemies for eighteen hundred years have been trying to refute and overthrow this book, and yet it stands today as solid as a rock. Its circulation increases, and it is more loved, cherished and read today than ever before. Critics, with all their assaults, make about as much impression on this book as a man with a tack hammer would on the Pyramid of Egypt. The hammers of the critics have been pecking away at this book for ages, but the hammers are worn out and the anvil (Bible) still endures. If this book had not been the Book of God, men would have destroyed it long ago. Emperors, and popes, kings and priests, princes and rulers have all tried their hand at eliminating it . . . they die and the Book still lives."[53]

Bible scholar Bernard Ramm said that the Bible has been ". . . banned, burned and outlawed from the days of the Roman empire to present-day . . . But here again, all efforts to stamp out the Bible have been unsuccessful. No other book has been so persecuted; no other book has been so victorious over its persecution. It is the martyr among books, and always rises from the pool of its own blood to live on."[54] Later, Ramm wrote, "A thousand times over, the death knell of the Bible has been sounded, the funeral procession formed, the inscription cut on the tombstone, and committal read. But somehow the corpse never stays put. No other book has been so chopped, knived, sifted, scrutinized and vilified . . . (despite this,) the Bible is still loved by millions, read by millions, and studied by millions."[55]

As Ramm's quote states, God's Word has not only survived, but it has thrived, and is by far the best selling and most widely read and spread written work of all time—nothing else is even remotely close. During the 1990's, the top 5 selling authors were John Gresham, Stephen King, Danielle Steel, Michael Crichton and Tom Clancy, who collectively sold 190 million books during this ten year period. This number sounds impressive until you compare it to the Bible, which sold well over 5 billion copies during this same time period. Today, with advances in media and the dedicated labor of missionaries, the

Bible is currently available and read in at least 2,287 languages, making it by far the most popular book in the world.

This book, God's Word, has influenced countless numbers of people, from paupers to princes, since it was written. Here are some quotes by past US Presidents regarding God's book; our first President, George Washington, stated, "It is impossible to rightly govern the world without God and the Bible."[56] Andrew Jackson unashamedly admitted, "That Book (the Bible), sir, is the rock on which our republic rests."[57] Woodrow Wilson was clear about the source of his wisdom when he said, "There are a good many problems before the American people today, and before me as President, but I expect to find the solution to those problems just in the proportion that I am faithful in the study of the Word of God."[58] Theodore Roosevelt said, "A thorough knowledge of the Bible is worth more than a college education."[59] Dwight D. Eisenhower praised the Bible with these words, "The Bible is endorsed by the ages. Our civilization is built upon its words. In no other book is there such a collection of inspired wisdom, reality and hope."[60] Ronald Reagan summed up the Bible in 16 succinct words, "Within the covers of the Bible are all the answers for all the problems men face."[61] Of all these, Abraham Lincoln may have summed up the Bible the best by stating, "In regard to this great book, I have but to say, I believe the Bible is the best gift God has given to man."[62]

Far from waning in the 4,000 years since its God-breathed words were first recorded, the Bible's influence and power continues to grow. Have you experienced the power of the Bible in your daily life? If you haven't, I would strongly encourage you to follow the example of past US leaders. If you allow God to work in your life through the study of His Word, your life will be changed in a positive way forever. Are you willing to experience God's power through one of His greatest gifts to you?

REASON #6 - Christianity is a unique faith
POINTING TOWARDS A UNIQUE GOD

How can I definitely say that the God of the Bible is the only true God and Creator? How can I discount the ancient gods and beliefs of the many world religions? Here are just a few reasons:

1) Christianity is Based on the Concrete Facts of Proven History . . . Other Faiths are Based More on Feeling than Fact

Christianity is not a man-made religious philosophy . . . it is not a blind leap of faith into the dark. Norman Geisler said, "Unlike many other religions today that appeal to mystical feeling or blind faith, Christianity says, 'Look before you leap . . . He added that we should *think* about what we believe. God places no premium on ignorance, nor does He reward those who refuse to look at the evidence. On the contrary, He will condemn those who refuse the plain evidence He has revealed (Rom. 1:18–20).'"[63] Unlike other faiths, Christianity is loaded with 'plain evidence' for its truth. While other religions may have small elements of historical fact, the Christian faith is based entirely on verifiable historical facts, including the death, burial and resurrection of Jesus Christ (which I will provide evidence for in the next chapter). The Bible is not only historically accurate, but is scientifically accurate as well . . . as Donald DeYoung, and many others have learned, "When the Bible touches on scientific subjects, it is entirely accurate."[64]

The archaeological evidence for the historical truth of the Bible compares very favorably to the archaeological evidence for other religions. For example, although Joseph Smith, the founder of Mormonism, claimed that the Book of Mormon is "the most correct of any book upon the earth,"[65] archaeologists have thoroughly disregarded this claim. Smithsonian Institute archaeologists have found "no direct connection between the archaeology of the New World and the subject matter of the book (of Mormon)."[66] Authors John Ankerberg and John Weldon elaborated on this fact following

251

intensive research, by stating, "In other words, no Book of Mormon cities have ever been located, no Book of Mormon person, place, nation or name has ever been found, no Book of Mormon artifacts, no Book of Mormon scriptures, no Book of Mormon inscriptions . . . nothing which demonstrates the Book of Mormon is anything other than myth or invention has ever been found."[67] If the Book of Mormon is not even historically reliable, as Joseph Smith said it would be, then its spiritual teachings certainly can't be trusted either.

But the Book of Mormon does not stand alone in its inadequacy, for no other religious book can claim the historical accuracy of the Bible, as proven through archaeology. Dr. Gleason Archer, who in his quest to validate the truths of the Bible became an expert in Bible customs, mastered over 30 Middle Eastern languages from Old Testament times, and researched the subject of biblical criticism for over 30 years. As a result of his quest, Archer wrote the *Encyclopedia of Bible Difficulties*. In this book, he said, "As I have dealt with one apparent discrepancy after another and have studied the alleged contradictions between the biblical record and the evidence of linguistics, archaeology or science, my confidence in the trustworthiness of Scripture has been repeatedly verified and strengthened by the discovery that almost every problem in Scripture that has ever been discovered by man, from ancient times until now, has been dealt with in a completely satisfactory manner by the biblical text itself—or else by objective archaeological information . . . no properly trained evangelical scholar has anything to fear from the hostile arguments and challenges of humanistic rationalists or detractors of any and every persuasion. There is a good and sufficient answer in Scripture itself to refute every charge that has ever been leveled against it."[68]

While Christianity is a reasonable faith, including verified historical facts and exceptional textual and prophetic accuracy, Norman Geisler has observed during his 40 years of research that those involved in cults and false religions must believe despite the facts against their faith. He stated that "Cultists often accept teachings by a kind of blind faith that is impervious to sound reasoning."[69] For example, he related that "One educated Mormon we encountered said he did not care if it could be proved that Joseph Smith was a false prophet; he still would remain a Mormon."[70] As another example, he said that "One Mormon missionary said he would believe the Book of Mormon even if it said there were square circles!"[71]

While cults and religions freely ignore the facts about their faith, Christians need to do no such thing, for the facts are on our side. The overwhelming scriptural and confirming archaeological evidence makes Christianity unique—it is a faith not based mainly on feelings, but entirely on facts. The truth of Christianity can be checked out, and it has passed the test, while others have not. The superior historical accuracy of the Bible should compel us to study it as the sole source of spiritual truth.

2) The Bible is Textually Superior to the books of All Other Faiths

The Bible is not only factually superior over the books of all other faiths, it is also textually superior. Concerning the alleged errors in the Bible, prodigious scholar Norman Geisler said, "Islamic (and other) critics have long contended that there are numerous errors in the Bible. However, they are long on criticism and short on proof. In fact, they have not discovered a single error in the Bible. Rather, the only errors to be found are in their criticisms. Indeed, we have carefully examined every error in the Bible alleged over the past forty years and have not found a single one! Eight hundred of these alleged errors are discussed in our book, When Critics Ask. We have found that . . . there are no demonstrable biblical errors. Other scholars have come to the same conclusion."[72] Later, Geisler reaffirmed that, "Critics claim the Bible is filled with errors. Some even speak of thousands of mistakes. The truth is there is not even one demonstrated error in the original text of the Bible . . . After forty years of continual and careful study of the Bible, one can only conclude that those who think they have discovered a mistake in the Bible do not know too much about the Bible—they know too little about it!"[73] He then confidently asserted, "The Bible has withstood the criticisms of the greatest skeptics, agnostics, and atheists down through the centuries, and it is able to withstand the feeble efforts of unbelieving critics today."[74]

The lack of errors, massive number of existing manuscripts and the early dating of those manuscripts in relation to the events described are some of the factors making the Bible a superior book. How well does the textual reliability of the Bible compare with that of other world religions? Very well.

For example, while the New Testament we have today has been demonstrated to be over 99% identical to the earliest manuscripts copied about 1800 years ago, informed Mormon and non-Mormon historians both admit that the present form of *The Book of Mormon* is quite different from the existing form. There are known to be at least 3,913 differences, as the current book has been revised by Joseph Smith and his successors over only the last 150 years. (The *Book of Mormon* is only one of many religious books having such a sorry record of inconsistency.) Why would you trust in the teachings of a book that has changed so much and which contains such a large number of concretely proven historical errors?

Dr. Edwin Yamauchi, an expert in ancient history, in comparing the date religious books were written in relation to the date their founders lived and taught, said, "For example . . . most of the Zoroastrian scriptures were not put into writing until after the 3rd century A.D. The most popular Parsi biography of Zoroaster was written in A.D. 1278. The scriptures of Buddha, who lived in the 6th century B.C., were not put into writing until after the Christian era, and the first biography of Buddha was written in the 1st century A.D. Although we have the sayings of Muhammed, who lived from A.D. 570 to 632 in the Koran, his biography was not written until 767, more than a full century after his death."[75]

Based on these dates, most of the Zoroastrian scriptures were written about 1300 years after the unconfirmed existence of Zoroaster. The most popular Parsi biography was written 2,278 years after his supposed birth. The scriptures of Buddha were written 700 years after he was thought to have been born. Even Buddhist scholars admit that there is little historical evidence for the life of Buddha, making it impossible to reconstruct an accurate record of his life. Muhammed's biography was written 135 years after his death. In sharp contrast, there is strong evidence that the gospel of Mark, documenting the birth, life, teachings, miracles, death, burial and resurrection of Christ was written within only five years after His resurrection. Unlike other religious books, the Bible is saturated with concrete, proven historical facts.

We also have approximately 25,000 nearly identical ancient copies of the New Testament, compared to only a handful of copies for most religious books. Even more importantly, the original copies of the New Testament were written within only years after Jesus' resurrection by eyewitnesses who knew Him personally, while the original copies of other religious books were often written hundreds of years after the death of the founder by men who did not know the founder personally, leaving much room for legend to develop. Dr. Yamauchi concluded, "The fact is that we have better historical documentation for Jesus than for the founder of any other ancient religion."[76] This fact means that we can have greater trust in the teachings and reality of Jesus than for any other major religious founder in the world.

No other religion in the history of mankind can claim the textual accuracy that we find in the Bible. The fact that it is the most textually accurate religious book in the world should make any reasonable person trust its teachings above the teachings of all other error-laden and textually suspect books.

3) The Prophetic Accuracy of the Bible is Superior to the books of All Other Faiths

The Bible has shown to be prophetically superior to those relatively few religious books and publications that claim prophetic truth. While no prophecy in the Bible has been incorrect, prophecies such as those from the Jehovah's Witnesses concerning the second coming of Christ have obviously been incorrect. They've erroneously predicted His return in 1799, 1874, 1914, shortly after 1914, around 1925, within the generation beginning 1914, and so on. They and apocalyptic cults have clearly not learned to stop trying to predict a date that no man can know, for their predictions continue even today. With each false prediction, the reputation of their religion is greatly tarnished. But while they are tarnished with time, the reliability of the Bible and Christianity has been strengthened with time.

From Norman Geisler we learn that, "Many cult leaders claim to have a direct pipeline to God. The teachings of the cult often change and, hence, they need new "revelations" to justify such changes. Mormons, for example, once excluded African Americans from the priesthood. When social pressure was exerted against the Mormon church for this blatant form of racism, the Mormon president received a new "revelation" reversing the previous decree. Jehovah's Witnesses engaged in the same kind of change regarding the earlier Watchtower teaching that vaccinations and organ transplants were prohibited by Jehovah."[77]

In contrast, Christianity is set apart by changeless prophecies from the Bible that were fulfilled in exact detail hundreds or thousands of years after they were given. No mere religion, past or present (which themselves were prophesied), has predicted the future so accurately. There are other books which claim that they are divinely inspired, such as the Islamic Koran and the Hindu Veda. But these books do not contain any predictive prophecy to demonstrate that they were written by a god. The failure of the prophetic track record of other books contrasted with the verified fulfilled prophecy of the Bible is a strong indicator that the Bible is the only God-written book in the world.

Sidney Collette relayed the following . . . "Former Boden professor of Sanskrit, M. Montiero-Williams, made this comparison after forty-two years of studying the intricacies of the books of Eastern religions: 'Pile them, if you will, on the left side of your study table; but place your own Holy Bible on the right side—all by itself, all alone—and with a wide gap between them. For . . . there is a gulf between it and the so-called sacred books of the East which severs the one from the other utterly, hopelessly, and forever . . . a veritable gulf which cannot be bridged over by any science of religious thought.'"[78]

4) The Bible is Unique in its Formation and Harmonious Teaching

The unique formation and harmonious teachings of the Bible provides further evidence for its' Divine Authorship. Concerning the unique formation, F.F. Bruce has found that, "If we enquire into the circumstances under which the various Bible documents were written, we find that they were written at intervals over a space of nearly 1400 years. The writers wrote in various lands, from Italy in the west to Mesopotamia and possibly Persia in the east. The writers themselves were a heterogeneous number of people, not only separated from each other by hundreds of years and hundreds of miles, but belonging to the most diverse walks of life. In their ranks we have kings, herdsmen, soldiers, legislators, fishermen, statesmen, courtiers, priests and prophets, a tentmaking Rabbi and a Gentile physician . . . For all that, the Bible is not simply an anthology; there is a unity which binds the whole together."[79]

The fact that the Bible is harmonious in its' teaching is amazing considering the fact that the nearly 40 human writers who came from such diverse cultures and time periods, wrote under different circumstances (from war to peace) in different places (from dungeons to palaces) about hundreds of the most controversial topics imaginable, yet never once do they disagree. It would not be possible to take any 40 men in even a 100 year period and have them agree on every point of every controversial topic as the Bible does. The harmonious unity of the Bible is positive evidence that calls for the existence of a single Divine Author who inspired men to write His words.

5) The Bible is Unique in its Requirements for Eternal Salvation

All other religions of the world are fundamentally one religion— one of salvation by works. Each of these religions sets up a particular series of religious rites, commands, restrictions and ethical principles to follow, and then teaches that if a person does these things they will be given eternal salvation or some other reward. Christianity is unique—it proclaims that man can't save himself by works, but that God has already done the work necessary for us to have eternal life in a perfect place . . . to receive this free gift, we simply need to trust in Him as our Savior.

Jesus Christ has provided a wonderful way which no cult or world religion offers. All others require that you follow the teachings of a dead man or woman and do good works to save yourself . . . the living Christ has done all the work necessary for our salvation . . . we simply need to believe that He died on the cross for our sins. Salvation through Christ is simple by design . . . it is God reaching down to man, as opposed to all other beliefs that have man reaching up to a superior being or force.

The Bible is also unique in its honesty, dealing openly with the sinful imperfections of many of its most prominent people, making them look very bad in the eyes of the reader. For example, the sins of the patriarchs are mentioned (Genesis 12:11–13;49:5–7); King David's adultery with Bathsheba and his attempted cover up is revealed (II Samuel 11–12); and the faults of Jesus' disciples were exposed (Matt 8:10–26;26:31–56; Mark 6:52; 8:18; Luke 8:24,25,9:40–45; John 10:6;16:32).

It is apparent that no man or collection of men would have written a book that included such a scolding condemnation of mankind, giving no hope of salvation through ourselves. The salvation standard of the Bible cannot be attained by man. This makes the Bible a unique book. The uniqueness of the Bible provides more positive evidence that God is its' Author.

6) Jesus' Sinless life is Unmatched by any Cult/ Religion Founder

Norman Geisler wrote concerning the comparison between Christianity and competing cults and religions that, "There are also some moral dimensions to be considered. Among those that crop up most often (in cults and religions) are legalism, sexual perversion, intolerance, and psychological or even physical abuse. Again, though, not every cult manifests every one of these traits."[80] In this section we will consider some of these 'moral dimensions' that separate Christianity from most if not all cults and religions.

Volumes could be written about the individual and collective moral failures, historically, scientifically and theologically contradictory, self-defeating and proven false teachings and predictions of the founders of cults and world religions, so obviously this short section of the book does not provide a comprehensive treatment of the subject. (Several excellent books, such as *The Kingdom of the Cults,* by Walter Martin and *When Cultists Ask* by Norman Geisler and Ron Rhodes provide more details if you are interested.) Here, I will briefly expose some of the often hidden or ignored moral failures and doubtful actions of the founders of just 5 of the cults and religions.

The reason for exposing some of these moral failures and questionable acts is not to poke fun at these 5 founders, but to show that they were far from perfect. I don't take pleasure in exposing the faults of another person, but in this case, when the eternal future of mankind is at stake, I believe it is necessary to tell the truth even when it hurts. I realize that some of those who hold strongly to their beliefs in spite of the historical evidence will be offended by these descriptions of their founders, but I must speak the honest facts about these individuals and just hope that most of those reading this book will be open-minded enough to make a decision based on the facts, wherever they may lead, instead of making a biased and emotional decision based upon preconceived ideas that they are unwilling to change.

For the open minded, I believe that this simple, historically supported comparison of the morality of Jesus with the founders of these 5 cults and religions will help you to make a better informed decision about whose teachings you will choose to follow and place your eternal trust in. I remind you again that the facts I am presenting are not based on bias, but on history. Unfounded bias has no place in discussions concerning such important issues as the eternal future of the human soul. That being said, I can confidently say following my research that from an historical standpoint Jesus wins hands down in the morality comparison.

My plea is that you will carefully consider the following facts if you have thought about becoming a part of or are already involved in one of these (or any other) cult or religion. Please ask yourself if you are willing to trust your eternal future to the teachings of these fallen teachers. It is certainly true that a cult or religion rises and falls with its founder, for the founder formed the foundation with his/her teachings . . . without him/her, the cult or religion would not even exist. My argument is that if the founder can be shown to be untrustworthy, then their teachings are also unreliable . . . the teachings of a fallen founder do not provide a good foundation for earthly or eternal life. The following are a few proven details on the imperfect immoral lives of just 5 fallen founders compared with the proven perfect morality of Christ:

CHARLES TAZE RUSSELL

Jehovah's Witnesses and the Watchtower Bible and Tract Society

It is a well documented fact that Charles Taze Russell, founder of the Jehovah's Witnesses, was involved in several greed-driven scandals such as the "Miracle Wheat Scandal," and used his powerful claim to 99% of the cult's income to bolster his personal finances. A 1913 edition of the *Brooklyn Daily Eagle* said that "Pastor Russell's religious cult is nothing more than a money-making scheme."[81] He was also proven to be a liar on the witness stand and in his ministry dealings, fraudulently making promises that he never carried through on.

With a moral record like this, it is no surprise that Jehovah's Witnesses of today have tried to forget their faulty founder, but his teachings are still an integral part of the belief system of Jehovah's Witnesses. If you're a current or prospective Jehovah's Witness, are you willing to stake your eternal future on the foundational words of a proven greedy, liar?

Further, concerning the New World Bible translation, did you know that *none* of the members of the translation team had any formal training in translating the original Greek and Hebrew found in the Bible? Since none of them had training, their translation is full of errors, and it can be easily picked apart by a competent Bible translator. So, not only are the foundational beliefs of Jehovah's Witnesses from a faulty founder, but their 'Bible' is also a proven faulty translation. Are you willing to place your eternal trust on such a faulty foundation?

JOSEPH SMITH JR.

Church of Jesus Christ of Latter-day Saints (Mormonism)

It is well known by historians that Joseph Smith Jr. spent large amounts of his time digging for imaginary buried treasure with his father and brother. As reported by his own mother and father, he sought this treasure through the use of supernaturally empowered seer-stones, divining rods, talismans and tools of ritual and occultic magic.

Smith's mystical background explains the story of how Mormonism began. Supposedly, an angel called Moroni (whom he later contradictorily called Nephi) presented to Smith a series of "golden plates," which he said contained the *Book of Mormon* in "reformed Egyptian" hieroglyphics (a language which Egyptologists freely admit never existed). With the plates, Smith said Moroni gave him a special pair of miraculous, super-sized golden spectacles which were used to translate the hieroglyphics. He also claimed that on May 15, 1829, John the Baptist was sent in person by Peter, James and John to Pennsylvania to personally anoint him as an Aaronic priest.

Among other outlandish and unfounded claims, Smith declared that "the Book of Mormon is the most correct of any book on earth."[82] This claim has been utterly destroyed by the concrete findings of archaeology, which prove beyond a shadow of a doubt that the book of Mormon is likely the most historically inaccurate religious book on earth. Even Mormon scholars have admitted that Smith's claim about the *Book of Mormon* is hopelessly false. In addition to the historical inaccuracies, the book includes plagiarisms and false prophecies. The abundant inaccuracies in the book make its theology extremely questionable . . . why would anyone put their eternal trust in the words of a book which is full of proven errors?

Scholars also admit that Smith was morally corrupt. Sixty-two residents of Palmyra, New York who were intimately familiar with the lifestyle of the Smith family signed a statement saying, "We the undersigned, have been acquainted with the Smith family for a number of years while they resided near this place, and we have no hesitation in saying that we consider them destitute of that moral character which ought to entitle them to the confidence of any community. They were particularly famous for visionary projects, spent much of their time in diggings for money, which they pretended was hid in the earth: and to this day, large excavations may be seen in the earth, not far from their residence, where they used to spend their time digging for hidden treasures. Joseph Smith Sr., and his son Joseph, were in particular considered entirely destitute of moral character and addicted to vicious habits."[83] This statement was made while Smith was still living in the community, and was never refuted by him. Are you, as a Mormon, willing to follow the foundational teachings of a morally corrupt, mystical man who dabbled with the occult and wrote a hopelessly false book by the admission of Mormon scholars?

MARY BAKER EDDY

Christian Science

Mary Baker Eddy was hypocritical in the fact that she spoke passionately against the use of doctors and drugs, but she frequently used a doctor in her final years and repeatedly used morphine to alleviate pain. She also denied the reality of pain, suffering and disease, yet she herself wore glasses, used morphine for her pain, and had her diseased teeth removed. Eddy did not practice what she preached, and her own body condemned her teachings about pain, suffering and disease, which most certainly do exist. She also claimed that the Bible was her only authority and guide in determining the truth (as stated in *Science and Health*, pg 126), yet she and her followers have clearly contradicted this claim numerous times in speeches and writings.

Besides being a hypocrite, she was also a plagiarist. While she strongly condemned the practice of plagiarism in her writings, she hypocritically plagiarized many different texts, quoting these sources word for word in some cases, and then called them her own. Even worse, she claimed that these clearly plagiarized words were spoken to her by God Almighty.

Eddy was more than a hypocritical plagiarist, however. She was a very greedy hypocritical plagiarist. It is incontestable that she used such money-making schemes as the infamous "Tea Jacket Swindle" to amass a personal fortune of more than 3 million dollars at her death. She even threatened that those who did not sell her books and contribute money to her bank account would be removed from the membership of the First Church of Christ (name of the Christian Science headquarters).

Horace T. Wentworth, who knew Eddy quite well since his mother lived with her in Stoughton, gave this warning near the year 1870, "As I have seen the amazing spread of this delusion and the way in which men and women are offering up money and the lives of their children to it, I have felt it is a duty I owe to the public to make it known. I have no hard feelings against Eddy, no ax to grind, no interest to serve; I simply feel that it is due to the thousands of good people who have made Christian Science the anchorage of their souls and its founder the infallible guide of their daily life, to keep this no longer to myself. I desire only that people who take themselves and their helpless children into Christian Science shall do so with the full knowledge that this is not divine revelation but simply the idea of an old-time Maine healer."[84] No Christian Scientist has ever been able to refute the above statements.

If you are involved with or interested in Christian Science, are you still willing to place your eternal trust in the words of a proven greedy, hypocritical plagiarist like Mrs. Eddy?

SUN MYUNG MOON

The Unification Church

According to Moon, the high point of his spiritual quest was a vision of Jesus which supposedly matched the images on his "holy cards." This experience is claimed to have occurred on April 17th, 1936, which all Unification writings record was Easter Sunday. The devastating fact for the Unification Church is that April 17th, 1936 is a Friday, not a Sunday, as any calendar from 1936 will show. If Unification writings cannot get the day of their most significant event right, this sheds doubt on the accuracy of their other writings.

The faulty morality of Moon also casts much doubt on the validity of his beliefs . . . while he claims to be the perfect "Lord of the Second

Advent," his imperfect actions certainly don't back up this claim. Moon has a proven track record as a sex offender. His teachings required that a married woman have sex with him to "cleanse" her before she had sex with her husband. He has been arrested/jailed three times for his sexual crimes . . . he was arrested on August 10, 1948 at the Bo An Police Department in North Korea on charges of "irresponsible sexual activity," sentenced to 5 years in Hung Nan prison for bigamy and again arrested for irresponsible sexual activity on July 4, 1955.

Additionally, Moon has spent 13 months at a federal prison in Danbury, Connecticut on tax evasion and perjury charges. He also was caught red-handed using church funds to purchase expensive gold watches, stock and to pay college tuition for his children. Moon believes that "heavenly deception" is acceptable . . . this is something he has practiced often throughout his lifetime.

Moon is a lying, greedy, tax-evading sex offender . . . are you willing to stake your eternal future on the teachings of this man?

SIDDHARTHA GUATAMA

Buddhism

Certainly not all religious founders were/are as immoral as the four mentioned above, but the actions of some are so questionable that it is incredible to think that anyone would want to follow their example. The actions of Siddhartha Guatama (better known as the Buddha) during his spiritual quest for truth fit into this category. As part of his quest, he constricted his diet to grass and seeds, and in one experiment, ate dung. He also experimented with lying on thorns, refusing to sit, never taking a bath, holding his breath until his head screamed in pain and sleeping in the middle of rotting human corpses. Are you willing to follow the teachings of a man who tried to find spiritual truth in these ways? The questionable actions of the Buddha should make you consider the rationale behind his teachings.

JESUS CHRIST

Christianity

In issues of morality, the annals of history have proven Jesus Christ to be exemplary. Those who speak otherwise simply don't know the facts. His matchless character and perfect life is equaled by no other person in human history. The following is a short list of the many tributes given by men to the matchless, moral perfection of Jesus Christ . . .

William Lecky said, "It was reserved for Christianity to present to the world an ideal character which through all the changes of eighteen centuries has inspired the hearts of men with an impassioned love; has shown itself capable of acting on all ages, nations, temperaments and conditions, has been not only the highest pattern of virtue, but the strongest incentive to its practice . . . The simple record of (Jesus') these three short years of active life has done more to regenerate and soften mankind than all the disquisitions of philosophers and all the exhortations of moralists."[85]

The great military general Napoleon Bonaparte observed, "I know men and I tell you that Jesus Christ is no mere man. Between Him and every other person in the world there is no possible term of comparison. Alexander, Caesar, Charlemagne, and I have founded empires. But on what did we rest the creations of our genius? Upon force. Jesus Christ founded His empire upon love; and at this hour millions of men would die for Him."[86]

Napoleon continued, saying, "Superficial minds see a resemblance between Christ and the founders of empires, and the gods of other religions. That resemblance does not exist. There is between Christianity and whatever other religions the distance of infinity . . . Everything in Christ astonishes me. His spirit overawes me, and His will confounds me. Between Him and whoever else in the world, there is no possible term of comparison. He is truly a being by Himself. His ideas and sentiments, the truth which He announces, His manner of convincing, are not explained either by human organization or by the nature of things . . . The nearer I approach, the more carefully I examine, everything is above me—everything remains grand, of a grandeur which overpowers. His religion is a revelation from an intelligence which certainly is not that of man . . . One can absolutely find nowhere, but in Him alone, the imitation or the example of His life . . . I search in vain in history to find the similar to Jesus Christ, or anything which can approach the gospel. Neither history, nor humanity, nor the ages, nor nature, offer me anything with which I am able to compare it or to explain it. Here everything is extraordinary."[87]

The great historian Philip Schaff remarked, "This Jesus of Nazareth, without money and arms, conquered more millions than Alexander, Caesar, Mohammed, and Napoleon; without science and learning, He shed more light on things human and divine than all philosophers and scholars combined; without the eloquence of schools, He spoke such words of life as were never spoken before or since and produced effects which lie beyond the reach of orator or poet; without writing a single line, He set more pens in motion, and furnished themes for more sermons, orations, discussions, learned volumes, works of art, and songs of praise, than the whole army of great men of ancient and modern times."[88]

Sholem Ash declared, "Jesus Christ is the outstanding personality of all time . . . No other teacher—Jewish, Christian, Buddhist, Mohammedan—is still a teacher whose teaching is such a guidepost for the world we live in. Other teachers may have something basic for an Oriental, an Arab, or an Occidental; but every act and word of Jesus has value for all of us."[89]

Mark Hopkins said, "No revolution that has ever taken place in society can be compared to that which has been produced by the words of Jesus Christ."[90]

Bernard Ramm said, ". . . it is true that historical record bears witness to the conviction that Jesus Christ is the greatest man that ever lived."[91]

As William E. Channing observed, "The sages and heroes of history are receding from us, and history contracts the record of their deeds into a narrower and narrower page. But time has no power over the name and deeds and words of Jesus Christ."[92]

Frank Mead said, "Jesus is in every respect unique, and nothing can be compared with Him."[93]

Even the skeptic David Strauss was forced to admit about Jesus that, "He remains the highest model of religion within the reach of our thought; and no perfect piety is possible without His presence in the heart."[94]

As proclaimed by Christians and admitted by skeptics, Jesus is the most perfect man who ever lived. This is not an emotional conclusion, but is based on the evidence from history. Since Jesus is the most perfect, morally matchless man who ever lived, and since no other founder of a cult or religion has even come close to equaling Him, isn't it reasonable to follow His words over the words of any other? But there is something else about Christ that forever sets Him apart from any other man . . .

7) Jesus' Miraculous Acts are Unmatched by Anyone

Verified miracles that lie outside the bounds of human magic and trickery can powerfully authenticate the teachings of a teacher. The founders of world religions and cults don't rely heavily upon miracles to authenticate their teachings. The relatively few they say they've performed have not been proven genuine in any way. In sharp contrast, Jesus often used miracles to prove beyond doubt that He was God in the flesh. And unlike the few supposed miracles performed by others, we have excellent reasons to believe that Jesus' miracles were not a result of human trickery or magic, but were genuine. If they were truly supernatural miracles, then we have every reason to believe that He was God in the flesh, just as He claimed, since He has accomplished something that no other man or woman in human history has been able to do.

Dr. Bernard Ramm provided the following evidences for belief in the unique, supernatural reality of Jesus' miracles:

1) *"There were many miracles performed before the public eye.* Jesus healed in the cities, at the busy corners, when surrounded by a mob, when speaking before multitudes in the open or in a house. They were not for the most part done in secret or seclusion or before a select few. Most of them were

public property, as it were. There was every occasion and opportunity to investigate the miracles right there. No effort is made to suppress the investigation. Such clear, open, above-board activity is good evidence of actual occurrence."[95] As Paul reminded Festus, the miracles and acts of Christ were not "done in a corner" (Acts 26:26). They were public miracles for all to see and refute if they were false.

2) "*Some miracles were performed in the company of unbelievers.* Miracles are always popping up in cults that believe in miracles. But when the critic is present the miracle does not seem to want to occur. But the presence of opposition or of critics had no influence on Jesus' power to perform miracles. More than once, right before the very eyes of His severest critics Jesus performed miracles. Now certainly, to be able to do the miraculous when surrounded by critics is a substantial token of their actual occurrence."[96]

3) "*Jesus performed His miracles over a period of time and in great variety.* The imposter always has a limited repertory and his miracles are sporadic in occurrence. Not so with Jesus. His miracles were performed all the time of His public ministry from the turning of water to wine in Cana to the rising of Lazarus. Further, He was not limited to any special type of miracle. Sometimes He showed supernatural powers of knowledge, such as knowing that Nathanael was hid in a fig tree; or he showed power over a great host of physical diseases—blindness, leprosy, palsy, fever, insanity and death itself; or He was able to quell the elements as He did in stilling the waves and the wind; or He could perform acts of sheer creation as when he fed thousands of people from very meager resources."[97]

Ramm continued, saying that "Imposture on this scale is impossible. The more times He healed, the more impossible it would be if He were an imposter. Further, it is incredible to think that for three and one-half years he maintained one consistent imposture. The number of miracles, their great variety, and their occurrence during all His public ministry are excellent evidence that Jesus actually performed the miracles the Gospel writers record."[98]

4) *"The evidence from the Gospels cannot be undone by appeal to the pagan miracles.* Pagan miracles lack the dignity of the Biblical miracles. They are frequently grotesque and done for very selfish reasons. They are seldom ethical or redemptive and stand in marked contrast to the chaste, ethical, and redemptive nature of the miracles of Christ. Nor do they have the genuine attestation that Biblical miracles have. Therefore, to examine some pagan miracles and show their great improbability, and then to reject all miracles on that ground is not fair to Biblical miracles."[99] The miracles of Christ are uniquely genuine and well evidenced . . . they truly belong in a category separate from the supposed miracles of cultists and founders of religions.

5) *The reality of Christ's miracles is affirmed by His followers.* As Ramm stated, "The Christians were soon persecuted, and underwent trial by fire, sword and dungeon. At such occasions the possibility of recanting or exposing something as fake are at a maximum. But there is no record of any Christian ever renouncing Christianity, when so persecuted, on the grounds that the miracles claimed by Christianity are fake."[100]

6) *The enemies of Christ have never denied, and have actually confirmed the reality of His miracles.* Ramm said, "That Jesus was hated by many of His fellow countrymen is a matter of Gospel record. Yet the inhabitants of Palestine who had sufficient motive in their hatred and sufficient proximity to the life of Christ have never written a line in denial of a single miracle. On the other hand, some of the very opponents of the Christian faith admitted that Christ performed miracles, e.g., Celsus, Hierocles, and Julian the emperor."[101]

This last point may be the most powerful evidence that Jesus really performed the miracles He claimed. It is incredible that even the enemies of Christ admitted the reality of the miracles, since they desperately did not want the miracles to be genuine, and had every opportunity to disprove them before large masses of people. If they were simply magic or trickery, they would have exposed the fraud in a heartbeat. But they could not, for the miracles were real. For them to deny the miracles would have made them proven liars before the multitudes . . . they were not willing to risk their reputation by promoting a known lie. They were forced to accept the reality of Christ's supernatural miracles against their will.

Based on the above facts, it should be clear that there are excellent reasons to believe the miracles of Christ stand supernaturally and uniquely above the supposed miracles of all others. As Ramm has discovered, "The miracles of Christ have adequate and sufficient testimony to establish them as historically real."[102] All His miracles are amazingly realistic, but there is one miracle of Christ that stands far above all others . . . the resurrection.

The well documented Resurrection of Jesus Christ is perhaps the most powerful evidence that Jesus is God and Christianity is a superior faith. Of all the founders of cults and world religions, only Jesus Christ has risen from the grave, as I will prove in the next chapter. The bones of all other cult and world religion founders are still securely within their tombs, but the evidence overwhelmingly declares that Jesus is still alive. While a good number of cults and religions will admit that Jesus was a virtuous man and a great teacher, none accept Him as the only God and Savior of the Universe and most also reject the historical reality of His resurrection.

So, in deciding which religion to choose, the truth or non-truth of the unique bodily resurrection of Christ is of unspeakable importance. If it didn't happen, then Christianity is a lie and should die . . . but if the resurrection really happened, then it is devastating for all the cults and religions that deny it, as well as for those few who don't deny it. If it can be shown that Jesus did indeed rise from the grave that would make Him who He said He was . . . the *one* and *only* God and Savior of mankind . . . it would make all the cults and world religions wrong and Christ the only way. If He is the only God and Savior, as He claimed to be and as evidenced by His unique prophetic fulfillment, sinless, miraculous life and resurrection, then He is the only one worthy to be followed . . . it would mean that those caught up in cults and religions are truly wasting their time by following the teachings of mere dead and soon to die men and women.

In comparing Christ with the founders of cults and world religions, Norman Geisler explained, "And, regardless of what they claimed for themselves, no other world religious leader ever proved his claims by fulfilling numerous prophecies made hundreds of years in advance, living a miraculous and sinless life, and predicting and accomplishing his own resurrection from the dead. Thus, Jesus alone deserves to be recognized as the Son of God, God incarnated in human flesh."[103] In another book, Geisler said, "Christianity has better evidence and more witnesses writing closer to the time of the events than any other religion. Besides this, no religion offers the kind of miracles that Christianity can claim. No other religion has the record of specific prophecy or divine deliverance that the Bible gives. And no other religion has any miracle that can be compared to the resurrection of Jesus Christ in its grandeur or its testimony."[104]

Christ is superior to all others because He has done something that no other man or woman has done . . . He has risen from death and the grave. The final record from a few past founders is very clear:

Charles Taze Russell   *Died* January 8, 1942
    (Jehovah's Witnesses)

Joseph Smith Jr.   *Died* June 27, 1844
    (Mormonism aka
    "Church of Jesus Christ of
    Latter-Day-Saints)

Mary Baker Eddy   *Died* in 1910
    (Christian Science)

Siddhartha Gautama   *Died* in 483 B.C.
    (aka 'Buddha' . . . Buddhism)

Mizra' Alli Muhammed   *Died* July 8, 1850
    (aka 'The Bab' . . . Baha'i)

Lafayette Ronald Hubbard   *Died* January 24, 1986
    (Scientology)

Bhagwan Shree Rajneesh   *Died* January 19, 1990
    (Rajneeshism, one of
    hundreds of Hindu sects)

Abhay Charan De Bhaktivedanta Swami Prabhupada (ISKCON, another major Hindu sect; aka International Society for Krishna Consciousness aka Hare Krishnas)	*Died* in 1977
Vernon Howell (aka David Koresh . . . Branch Davidians)	*Died* April 19, 1993
Muhammed (Islam)	*Died* June 8, A.D. 632
Zoroaster (Zoroastrianism)	*Died* in 583 B.C.
Confucius (Confucianism)	*Died* in 479 B.C.
All other past, present, future cult, religion founders.	Have *Died* or will die
All other men and women	Have *Died* or will die
Jesus Christ (Christianity)	***STILL ALIVE!!!***

The record of history is very clear that Jesus alone has risen from the grave. If Jesus has indeed risen from the grave, then that substantiates everything He said about Himself . . . it means that He alone is the God and Savior of mankind, and His words, encompassing the entire Bible, are of unparalleled reliability. The reality of the Resurrection is the ultimate event in human history thus far . . . if it really happened, then it changes everything. Evidence for the reality of this Resurrection is the all-important subject of the next chapter.

PART III

Jesus is Alive!

CHAPTER 10

The Reality of the Resurrection of Christ

As I said in Chapter 9, the reality of the Resurrection is the ultimate event in the history of humanity so far . . . if it really happened, then it literally changes everything related to life on Earth. It would clearly define who God is, and what His purposes for mankind are. It would give meaning to life and would make eternal life in a perfect place a concrete hope instead of wishful thinking for those who trust in God. If the Resurrection happened, then Christianity is the only way to go both now and forever, since the God of Christianity is the only God and Savior of the Universe. By God's divine wisdom, the most important event in human history thus far, the Resurrection of Christ, is also one of the most verifiable facts in history.

Evidence for the resurrection is overwhelming. Dr. Thomas Arnold, author of the famous *History of Rome*, said, "Thousands and tens of thousands have gone through it (evidence for the resurrection) piece by piece, as carefully as every judge summing up on a most important case. I have myself done it many times over, not to persuade others but to satisfy myself. I have been used for many years to study the histories of other times, and to examine and weigh the evidence of those who have written about them, and I know of no one fact in the history of mankind which is proved by better and fuller evidence of every sort, to the understanding of a fair inquirer, than the great sign which God has given us that Christ died and rose again from the dead."[10] After examining the evidence from a judicial perspective, Lord Darling, former Chief Justice of England, concluded that, "There exists such overwhelming evidence, positive and negative, factual and circumstantial, that no intelligent jury in the world could fail to bring in a verdict that the resurrection story is true."[2] English scholar B.F. Westcott stated, "Indeed, taking all the evidence together, it is not too much to say that there is no historic incident better or more variously supported than the resurrection of Christ."[3] There are indeed some very good reasons to believe that Jesus really lived, died, was buried and rose again three days later, just as He said. Among those are . . .

REASON #1 - THE NEW TESTAMENT IS
TRUSTWORTHY

The New Testament is one of the main sources documenting the life, death, burial and resurrection of Christ . . . if it is unreliable, then Christianity falls apart, but if it can be proven trustworthy, then there is good reason to believe that the events it reports really happened. As the following will show, the New Testament is the most trustworthy book in the ancient world . . . if we dismiss it as inaccurate, then we must throw out every other work from ancient times. Here's why the New Testament is the most trustworthy book from ancient times . . .

The New Testament has Greater Numbers

Combining the 5,686 existing Greek copies with the 19,284 from other languages gives us nearly 25,000 known complete and partial copies of New Testament autographs recounting the birth, life, death, burial and resurrection of Christ, making it by far the most numerous and best-attested document of all ancient writings. In comparison to the abundance of New Testament copies, consider that ancient historical classics like Caesar's *Gallic War* survive with only nine or ten copies, Livy's *Roman History* has twenty copies, Tacitus's *Annals* has two and Thucydides' *History* has only eight. Twenty partial or complete copies of any ancient writing is considered excellent, and very few writings have that many copies. Homer's *Iliad* is a distant second to the New Testament with only 643 copies. The overwhelming textual evidence has caused scholar John Warwick Montgomery to state, "To be skeptical of the resultant text of the New Testament is to allow all of classical antiquity to slip into obscurity, for no documents of the ancient period are as well attested bibliographically as the New Testament."[4]

The New Testament has Better Accuracy

Also, while other ancient works were rarely translated into other languages, the Bible was, increasing the strength of the argument for the historical and textual accuracy of the New Testament. With the Bible we can not only compare Greek copies to other Greek copies, but can compare the original Greek to manuscripts from other languages to determine if errors entered the text during translation. Research has shown that not only are Greek copies virtually identical, but the comparative accuracy of Greek copies with copies from other languages is equally stunning. No other ancient writing can even come close to matching this claim.

The accuracy of the Bible is also superior to many more modern writings. For example, did you know that the New Testament is more accurate than the writings of Shakespeare? Shakespeare's writings, which have existed for less than 300 years, should seemingly have more accurate and identical copies than the New Testament, which was first written over 1900 years ago, but this is not the case. Except for a handful of phrases, every verse in the New Testament has been accepted by scholars as part of the original text . . . in contrast, within each of Shakespeare's 37 plays, there are about 100 readings that are disputed.[5] While none of the disputed passages in the Bible affects any doctrine, many of the disputed readings in Shakespeare's plays drastically change the meaning of the passages in which they occur. The New Testament is not only a clearly more reliable document than any other ancient work, but it has also proven to be more trustworthy than writings that are less than 300 years old. Those who deny that the New Testament is an accurate and reliable document simply don't know the facts.

The New Testament was Written and Copied Sooner

Perhaps even more convincing is that archaeologists, historical and literary scholars have proven that some New Testament books were written within years and most of the New Testament was written within 20 to 30 years after Jesus' death and resurrection. Copying was begun shortly thereafter . . . we now have the John Rylands fragments of the New Testament dating from 25 years after the completion of the gospel of John. We also have almost entirely complete copies (Chester Beatty and Bodmer Papyri) within 100–150 years of the original. An entire copy (Codex Vaticanus) exists from only 250 years after the original autographs. In stark contrast, the average ancient writing has no complete copies . . . these incomplete copies were written on average between 700–1400 years after the original. Geisler truly said that, "No other book from the ancient world has as small a time gap (between original composition and the earliest manuscript copies) as the New Testament."[6] Sir Frederick Kenyon has discovered that ". . . in no other case is the interval of time between the composition of the book and the date of the earliest manuscripts so short as that of the New Testament."[7] The short time gap is impressive evidence that the New Testament is more reliable than any other book from ancient history.

Even shorter is the time gap between the claimed occurrence of the events and when they were recorded as part of the New Testament. Just how short is this time gap? I Corinthians 15:3–8 in the New Testament is considered to be one of the earliest creeds of the church, boldly proclaiming the reality of the Resurrection. (There are at least 19 such early creeds whose main message is the fact that Jesus rose from the grave 3 days after being buried.) Dr. Gary Habermas, a world-renowned defender of the truth of the Resurrection, stated concerning the early dating of the I Corinthians creed, "It's not just conservative Christians who are convinced. This is an assessment that's shared by a wide range of scholars from across a broad theological spectrum. The eminent scholar Joachim Jeremias refers to this creed as 'the earliest tradition of all,' and Ulrich Wilckens says it 'indubitably goes back to the oldest phase of all in the history of primitive Christianity."[8] Habermas continued, following his own research, "I'd agree with the various scholars who trace it back even further, to within two to eight years of the Resurrection . . . this is incredibly early material— primitive, unadorned testimony to the fact that Jesus appeared alive to skeptics like Paul and James, as well as to Peter and the rest of the disciples."[9] He concluded, concerning this eyewitness account, "it just so happens to be the earliest and best-authenticated passage of all!"[10] German historian Hans von Campenhausen concurs that "This account meets all the demands of historical reliability that could possibly be made of such a text."[11] Dr. Habermas summed up the importance of this passage and others when he said, "The key is that a number of the accounts in Acts 1–5, 10 and 13 also include some creeds, like the one in I Corinthians 15, that report some very early data concerning the death and resurrection of Christ."[12]

Dr. William Lane Craig, widely recognized as one of the foremost authorities in the world on the subject of the Resurrection of Christ, stated concerning the gospel of Mark and the importance of its early writing that, "In fact, there's evidence it was written before A.D. 37, which is much too early for legend to have seriously corrupted it. A.N. Sherman-White, the respected Greco-Roman classical historian from Oxford University, said it would have been without precedent anywhere in history for legend to have grown up that fast and distorted the gospels."[13] A.D. 37 is a mere 4 years after Christ's Resurrection, which is far less than the several generations needed for a legend to arise. Bible scholar, Dr. Gregory Boyd further explained the importance of the short time gap by saying, "The gospels were written within a generation of Jesus (compared to as many as hundreds or thousands of years in other ancient and religious books). The closer the proximity to the event, the less chance there is for legendary development, for error or memories to get confused."[14]

Geisler continued, "Given that significant parts of the Gospels and other crucial New Testament books were written before (A.D) 70, there is no time or way for a legend to develop while the eyewitnesses were still alive to refute the story. A legend takes time and/or remoteness to develop, neither of which were available."[15] Studies by historians have shown that, based on the evidence of history, even two generations is not a sufficient period of time for a legend to form. The resurrection news, in sharp contrast, was being spread only *weeks* after it occurred in the very city where it was said to happen. Again, if the reports were false, they would have easily and gladly been refuted by the enemies of Christ. Geisler further explained, "The New Testament records show no signs of mythological development. Indeed, the miracle events are surrounded by historical references to real people, places, and times. The New Testament documents and witnesses are too early, too numerous, and too accurate to be charged with writing myths. Only an unjustified antisupernatural bias could ground any conclusion to the contrary."[16] The early writing of the Resurrection account is extremely important since it dismisses the legendary lie hypothesis proposed by critics.

The short time gap between the events described and their original recording and also between their original recording and copying leaves no room for the resurrection facts in the New Testament to be distorted . . . there was simply no time for a legendary lie to arise, especially in the presence of enemy eyewitnesses who knew the facts, and who would have certainly denounced and disproven the claims of the New Testament if they weren't true. In contrast, the large time gap between the actual events and the first known recording of other ancient writings and religious books leaves plenty of time for a legendary lie to arise outside of the presence of living eyewitnesses. The New Testament is more historically reliable than any other ancient writing or religious book in the history of humanity.

The New Testament was Written Earlier by Eyewitnesses

Unlike many ancient works, the New Testament accounts were written by the same people who were eyewitnesses to the events they wrote about. The writers of the New Testament actually observed the life, death and resurrection of Jesus first hand (II Peter 1:16). As respected scholar Norman Geisler explained, ". . . the New Testament records are authentic first century and firsthand information about the life, teachings, death, and resurrection of Christ."[17] Geisler continued, "Both the *authenticity* and the historicity of the New Testament documents are firmly established today. The authentic nature and vast amount of the manuscript evidence is overwhelming compared to the classical texts from antiquity. Furthermore, many of the original manuscripts date from within twenty to thirty years of the events in Jesus' life, that is, from contemporaries and eyewitnesses."[18] He concluded that, "No event in the ancient world has more eyewitness verification than does the resurrection of Jesus."[19]

Since most of the enemy eye-witnesses were still alive when the New Testament was being written and preached, making a false claim in their presence would have been fatal to Christianity . . . if the claims weren't true, at least some of these enemies would have shot down these claims. If the resurrection really didn't happen, then there would be at least one report to conflict the nearly 25,000 gospel sources, numerous secular sources, and archaeological evidence, but there are *none*. F.F. Bruce, Rylands professor of Biblical Criticism and Exegesis at the University of Manchester in England, observed, "The disciples could not have afforded to risk inaccuracies which would at once be exposed by those who would only be too glad to do so. On the contrary, one of the strong points in the original apostolic preaching is the confident appeal to the knowledge of the hearers; they not only said, 'We are witnesses of these things,' but also, 'As you yourselves also know' (Acts 2:22). Had there been any tendency to depart from the facts in any material respect, the presence of hostile witnesses in the audience would have served as a further corrective."[20] (Acts 2:32, 3:15, 13:30–31, 26:26 and I Corinthians 15:3–8 are other examples of passages where the apostles boldly appealed to the widespread knowledge of the public concerning the Resurrection.)

New Testament scholar Robert Grant of the University of Chicago concluded, "At the time they (the gospels) were written, there were eyewitnesses and their testimony was not disregarded . . . this means that the gospels must be regarded as largely reliable witnesses to the life, death and resurrection of Jesus."[21] If the Resurrection news was really a legendary lie, then the enemies of Christ would have gladly pounced at the chance to prove that it was a lie. But impressively, *none* of the bold proclamations of the disciples were ever disputed in the historical records. The only explanation for this is that the Resurrection of Christ really occurred.

The Historicity of the New Testament is Admitted by Modern Skeptics

Following 30 years of research on the historical accuracy of the gospel of Luke, 15 of which were spent attempting to undermine Luke's credentials as a historian, and to refute the reliability of the New Testament including the accounts of the life, teachings, death, burial and resurrection of Christ, Sir William Ramsay, one of the greatest archaeologists and historians in human history concluded, "Luke is a historian of the first rank; not merely are his statements of fact trustworthy . . . this author should be placed along with the very greatest of historians."[22] Ramsay also added that, "Luke's history is unsurpassed in respect of its trustworthiness."[23]

Geisler noted that part of Ramsay's historical evaluation of the book of Luke found that in "Luke's references to thirty-two countries, fifty-four cities, and nine islands there are no errors!"[24] Since there are no errors in the seemingly insignificant details, Geisler concluded that "Luke's narration of the life and miracles (including the resurrection) of Christ must likewise be accepted as authentic."[25]

Concerning the historicity of Acts, Ramsay, the former skeptic, recounted how his lifetime of research led him to accept Acts as historical, "I began with a mind unfavourable to it (Acts) . . . It did not then lie in my line of life to investigate the subject minutely; but more recently I found myself brought into contact with the Book of Acts as an authority for the topography, antiquities and society of Asia Minor. It was gradually borne upon me that in various details the narrative showed marvelous truth."[26] During his research, prominent historian A.N. Sherman-White found that, "For Acts the confirmation of historicity is overwhelming . . . Any attempt to reject its basic historicity even in matters of detail must now appear absurd. Roman historians have long taken it for granted."[27]

The book of Acts documents the history of the early years of the church and its proclamation of the resurrection. The first chapter of the book of Acts includes a record of the risen Christ, and the second unashamedly proclaims it as a fact. Impressively, none of the enemies of Christ denied what was being declared in these chapters, which they certainly would have if it weren't true. As Ramsay, Sherman-

White and many other former skeptics admit, Acts has now proven to be an historically accurate text written by the trustworthy historian Luke. If the early church history in Acts is accurate, as the evidence overwhelmingly suggests, then we have no reason to doubt that the details of the life, death, burial and resurrection of Christ given by the trustworthy Luke happened just as he said.

The Verdict of Scholars Who have Researched the Subject

F.F. Bruce, an expert historian, concluded that, ". . . there is no body of ancient literature in the world which enjoys such a wealth of good textual attestation as the New Testament. If the New Testament were a collection of secular writings, their authenticity would be regarded as beyond all doubt."[28] Bernard Ramm has found that "The Bible has survived the ravages of time in all its manifold means of destruction with a numerical and textual attestation that is many furlongs beyond even the closest competion."[29] Simon Greenleaf, one of the most prominent legal experts in human history concluded following an intimate examination of the New Testament by the standard of the law that, "copies which had been as universally received and acted upon as the Four Gospels, would have been received as evidence in any court of justice, without the slightest hesitation."[30] Geisler said, "In brief, from a strictly historical point of view, we could not have better evidence for the authenticity of events than we possess for the events in the life of Christ recorded in the New Testament."[31]

What is your verdict? Will you accept the New Testament as historically accurate in all accounts, including the life, death, burial and resurrection of Christ? Will you base your decision on the undeniable evidence or on unfounded bias? All who have seriously studied the subject, skeptical or not, have reached the conclusion that it is a highly reliable historical text. Again, what is your verdict?

REASON #2 - NEW TESTAMENT HISTORICAL FACTS ARE NOT DENIED, BUT ACTUALLY CONFIRMED BY ANCIENT CRITICS OF CHRIST

A survey of just 45 extra-biblical sources written at or near the time of Christ report at least 129 distinct facts about Christ that demonstrate, among other things, that He really existed, lived a virtuous, miraculous life, was crucified, was buried in a tomb that was empty 3 days later and reportedly rose again. Of this number, 17 are non-Christian sources including records from ancient historians Tacitus, Suetonius, Josephus, Thallus, government officials Pliny the Younger, Emperor Trajan, Emperor Hadrian, Jewish sources such as the Talmud, Toledoth Jesu, and non-Jewish sources like Lucian and Mara-Bar Serapion.[32]

Examples of non-Christian sources which support facts surrounding the crucifixion of Christ as described in the gospels include the Talmud, which says, "On the eve of the Passover, they hanged Yeshu (Jewish for Jesus)."[33] Mara Bar-Serapion asked, "What advantage did the Jews gain from executing their wise King?"[34] Tacitus said, "Christus, the founder of the name, was put to death by Pontius Pilate, procurator of Judea in the reign of Tiberius."[35]

Because of these admissions from ancient critics of Christ, "All efforts to prove that Jesus never lived simply do not gain any real hearing . . . some of the most radical and skeptical historians will admit the historicity of Jesus. The radicals among the form-critics grant that Jesus actually lived . . ."[36]

One of the most interesting aspects of Christ's life is His miracles, which are amazingly not denied and are actually admitted by ancient critics. As stated before, the various miracles of Christ were performed over a substantial period of time in public before large multitudes of people, some of whom were undoubtedly skeptics or enemies who would have gladly denied the occurrence of the miracles if they could. Paul informs Festus that the miracles of Christ were not "done in a corner," (Acts 26:26). The miracles were done before all, friend and foe, and news of the miracles doubtlessly spread throughout the region. Despite their hatred for Christ and jealousy that He was stealing their thunder, *never once* did an enemy living at the time of Christ write a single line denying that He performed these miracles. They did not deny them, since they knew they were true.

Impressively, some of the opponents of Christ, such as Celsus, Hierocles and Julian the Emperor, actually admitted in writing that He did indeed perform the miracles detailed in the New Testament. The admission of these facts must have been painful, but they are highly significant. Dr. Paul Maier noted that, "Positive evidence from a hostile, secular source, is the strongest kind of historical evidence. In essence, this means that if a source admits a fact decidedly not in its favor, then that fact is genuine."[37] The positive written admission of Christ's enemies regarding His miracles is powerful proof that He really performed them.

The fact of Christ's existence, His life, miracles and teachings, death by crucifixion, and burial in Joseph of Arimathea's tomb was admitted by ancient critics and is now also admitted by even the most radical contemporary scholars. The historical records also demonstrate that the ancient enemies of Christ never denied His most astounding miracle . . . the resurrection, which they had strong motivation and every opportunity to do. If Christ had not risen from the tomb, His enemies would have most certainly denied it . . . yet impressively, there are absolutely no denials of the resurrection message that the apostles were proclaiming within Jerusalem, and across the entire region. The silence of Christ's enemies regarding the resurrection is an eloquent admission of the embarrassing fact that Jesus really did rise from the dead.

I must state this powerful fact again . . . The enemies of Christ *never once denied* the fact of the resurrection of Christ. E. Hermitage Day said, "The simple disproof, the effective challenging, of the fact of the Resurrection would have dealt a death-blow to Christianity. And they had every opportunity of disproof, if it were possible."[38] While they resisted the truth of the Resurrection out of jealousy that Christ's message was becoming more popular than their own, they never once denied it. Geisler explained the importance of this, saying, "The fact that the consistent attitude of authorities toward the disciples was one of *resistance* not refutation is a strong indication of the reality of the resurrection of Christ."[39]

The Encyclopedia Britannica, in describing the life, death and resurrection of Christ observed, "These independent accounts prove that in ancient times even the opponents of Christianity never doubted the historicity of Jesus, which was disputed for the first time, and on inadequate grounds by several authors at the end of the 18th, during the 19th, and at the beginning of the 20th centuries."[40] F.F. Bruce has rightly said, "Some writers may toy with the fancy of a 'Christ-myth,' but they do not do so based on the historical evidence. It is not historians who propagate the 'Christ-myth' theories."[41] Otto Betz said "No serious scholar has ventured to postulate the non-historicity of Jesus."[42] No serious, truth-seeking scholar can deny that Christ was a real person who died on a cross, was buried and left an empty tomb during the first century A.D.

REASON #3 - THE FACT OF THE EMPTY TOMB IS
UNDENIED AND UNDENIABLE

The Resurrection news of Christ was not a minor event to be forgotten . . . if it was a lie, it would have been dealt with quickly and efficiently by those who would have had major motivation to do so. Both the Romans and Jewish religious authorities would have certainly corrected the apostles if they could prove they were lying. If Christ did not rise from the tomb, there would be at least a few documents or letters from the Jewish authorities, who hated Christ, the Roman government or other eyewitnesses to deny the resurrection news that was sweeping the region. But there are *none*. This is because the fact of the empty tomb was not an issue for either the early Christians or their enemies . . . . all involved knew that it was true.

The Romans were always quick to stamp out any uproar that threatened their peace and power . . . the resurrection news of Christ definitely caused an uproar. What appeared to be an upstart religion would eventually bring the Roman government to its knees. The Romans were embarrassed by the empty tomb, which they had sealed and guarded. If they or the Jewish religious authorities could have, they would have quickly produced the dead body, and spread abroad the news that the resurrection of Christ was a hoax, crushing Christianity forever. The same crowd that shouted, "Crucify Him!" certainly would have denied His resurrection if it really didn't happen.

Producing the dead body of Christ and carting it around Jerusalem would have killed the resurrection claims of early Christians quickly and completely. But their declaration could not be silenced, because everyone knew that it was true. They could see with their own eyes that the tomb was empty, and there was no body to be found.

Bernard Ramm explained that, ". . . all along the disciples taught and preached the resurrection, *right in the city of the death and resurrection of Christ,* and surrounded by the same people who put Jesus to death, who could wish for *no greater thing than to be able to substantially deny His resurrection.* This could have been done if Christ were not risen."[43] Paul Althaus states that the resurrection news "could not have been maintained in Jerusalem for a single day, for a single hour, if the emptiness of the tomb had not been established as a fact for all concerned."[44] A.M. Ramsey adds that the empty tomb was "too notorious to be denied."[45] Dr. William Craig said, "The site of Jesus tomb was known to Christians and Jews alike. So if it weren't empty, it would be impossible for a movement founded on belief in the Resurrection to have come into existence in the same city where this man had been publicly executed and buried."[46] Dr. Craig continued, "The earliest Jewish polemic (teaching) presupposes the historicity of the empty tomb. In other words, there was nobody who was still claiming that the tomb still contained Jesus' body."[47] J.P. Moreland observed, ". . . the Jewish polemic does not dispute that the tomb was empty . . . this is strong evidence that the tomb was in fact empty."[48]

Norman Geisler observed, ". . . the fact that neither he (Josephus) nor any other contemporary of the apostles make any attempt to refute the Resurrection is significant. If the tomb was still sealed or the body had been found, it seems that they would have mentioned it."[49] As John R.W. Stott said, the silence of Christ's enemies "is as eloquent a proof of the Resurrection as the apostles' witness."[50] Paul L. Maier discovered, "If all the evidence is weighed carefully and fairly, it is indeed justifiable, according to the canons of historical research to conclude that the tomb in which Jesus was buried was actually empty on the morning of the first Easter. And no shred of evidence has yet been discovered in literary sources, epigraphy or archaeology that would disprove this statement."[51] Michael Green concluded, "There can be no doubt that the tomb of Jesus was, in fact, empty on the first Easter day."[52]

Lee Strobel, a former skeptic of the Resurrection and hard-nosed journalist for the *Chicago Tribune,* recently wrote a book called *The Case for Christ,* which, in part, documents his personal investigation into the evidence for Christ's Resurrection. Strobel became thoroughly convinced of the truth of Christianity through his research, and during the preparation for his interview with Dr. William Craig, Strobel noted, "In preparing for my interview with Craig, I had gone to the Internet sites of several atheist organizations to see the kinds of arguments they were raising against the Resurrection. For some reason, few atheists deal with this topic (the reality of the empty tomb)."[53]

In summing up his detailed research on evidence for the empty tomb, Strobel wrote, "In the face of the facts, they (past and present critics) have been impotent to put Jesus' body back in the tomb. They flounder, they struggle, they snatch at straws, they contradict themselves, they pursue desperate and extraordinary theories to try to account for the evidence. Yet each time, in the end, the tomb remains vacant."[54] Just as the early skeptics of Christianity, modern critics can't reasonably dispute the empty tomb or the reality of the Resurrection, for this is where the evidence leads us.

REASON #4 - NATURALISTIC THEORIES HAVE FAILED TO EXPLAIN HOW THE TOMB BECAME EMPTY

As stated in Evidence #3, the tomb of Jesus was undeniably empty three days after his body was buried, as admitted by even ancient and modern skeptics. The question has never been *if* the tomb is empty, but *how* the tomb became empty. Those who have a bias towards supernatural events have tried to explain how the tomb became empty through human influence. But as this section demonstrates, so many exceptional circumstances and extraordinary security precautions existed during Christ's crucifixion, burial, entombment, sealing and guarding of His tomb that it becomes impossible for critics to defend their position that Christ did not rise from the dead by supernatural power. Before I begin to break down the best naturalistic theories that critics have, I'd like to briefly emphasize the fact that Jesus was really dead and really buried.

Jesus was Definitely Dead

As freely admitted by critics, Jesus Christ was definitely dead. Crucifixion was a public execution, and since Jesus' crucifixion occurred in Jerusalem just prior to a huge Jewish festival called Passover, it is likely that thousands would have witnessed and assured his death, especially since He received considerably more attention than most, if not all other crucified people of the past. Roman soldiers were familiar with the sight of death, and they thrust a spear in his side to prove that He was dead. Ancient non-Christian historians also gave witness to his death. As Norman Geisler explained, "In fact, there is more evidence that Jesus died than there is that most important people from the ancient world ever lived."[55] Wilbur M. Smith said concerning the death of Christ, "Let it simply be said that we know more about the details of the hours immediately before and the actual death of Jesus, in and near Jerusalem, than we know about the death of any other one man in all the ancient world."[56]

Jesus was Definitely Buried

In a similar statement about Jesus' burial, Smith said, "We know more about the burial of the Lord Jesus than we know of the burial of any single character in all of ancient history."[57] Concerning the burial account of Jesus in the New Testament, JP Moreland says, "No conflicting account is found anywhere, even among Jewish writings."[58] Based on his extensive research on the subject, Dr. William Craig concluded, "As a result, the majority of New Testament scholars today agree that the burial account of Jesus is fundamentally reliable. John A.T. Robinson, the late Cambridge University New Testament scholar, said that the honorable burial of Jesus is one of the earliest and best-attested facts that we have about the historical Jesus."[59]

Jesus lived, died, was buried and His grave is empty—about that there is no doubt; even the ancient and contemporary critics of Christ don't deny these facts of history. The only question remaining is how it became empty—was it by man or God? A number of theories have been proposed by skeptics to avoid the conclusion that the tomb became empty through the power of God. I will deal with and destroy the most popular theories of the past and present in this section. You will discover that the critics have run out of ammunition in their attempt to deny the Resurrection . . . they've given it their best shot with these theories, but have failed.

THEORY #1 - THE ROMAN SOLDIERS FAILED TO GUARD THE TOMB ADEQUATELY, ALLOWING THE BODY TO BE STOLEN

Before making the argument for the superior guarding of the tomb, let me downplay its significance first. Dr. Craig, stated, "Frankly, the guard story may have been important in the eighteenth century, when critics were suggesting that the disciples stole Jesus' body, but nobody espouses that theory today. The idea that the empty tomb is the result of a hoax, conspiracy or theft is simply dismissed today. So the guard story has become sort of incidental."[60] But while even the critics of the Resurrection don't believe Christ's body was stolen from the grave, and thus the guard story is not needed as evidence, many still aren't aware of this fact. Since the guarding of the tomb is an important fact of history that many people don't know about, and since it provides further assurance that the Resurrection was a supernatural event, I will take the time to discuss it here.

William Smith defined the size and behavior of the Roman guard posted at Christ's tomb by saying, "We may remark in passing, that four was the number for a Roman guard . . . of these one always acted as a sentinel, while the others enjoyed a certain degree of repose, ready, however to start up at the first alarm."[61]

Armed Roman soldiers were superior to any other in human history. T.G. Tucker gave the following description of the intimidating weaponry carried by a typical Roman soldier, "In his right hand he will carry the famous Roman pike. This is a stout weapon, over 6 feet in length, consisting of a sharp iron head fixed in a wooden shaft, and the soldier may either charge with it as with a bayonet, or he may hurl it like a javelin and then fight at close quarters with his sword. On the left arm is a large shield, which may be of various shapes. One common form is curved inward at the sides like a portion of a cylinder some 4 feet in length by 2.5 feet in width; another is six-sided—a diamond pattern, but with the points of the diamond squared away. Sometimes it is oval. In construction it is of wickerwork or wood, covered with leather, and embossed with a blazon in metalwork, one particularly well known being that of a thunderbolt. The shield is not only carried by means of a handle, but may be supported by a belt over the right shoulder. In order to be out of the way of the shield, the sword—a thrusting rather than a slashing weapon approaching three in length—is hung at the right side by a belt passing over the left shoulder. Though this arrangement may seem awkward to us, it is to be remembered that the sword is not required until the right hand is free of the pike, and that then, before drawing, the weapon can easily be swung around to the left by means of the suspending belt. On the left side the soldier wears a dagger at his girdle."[62]

There is nothing human which could have removed such a formidable guard of 4 armed Roman soldiers from their posts at the entrance to Christ's tomb, especially considering the death penalty the guards would have paid for doing so. Two of the tortuous ways guards were put to death for leaving their posts or falling asleep was by being crucified upside down and by being stripped of their clothes and burned alive in a fire started by their own garments. It is not reasonable to believe that all the soldiers guarding Christ's tomb left their post or fell asleep with such an unpleasant death threat over their heads. They would have fought to their deaths to protect the tomb . . . if the tomb really had been raided, four dead soldiers would have been left as evidence. But, as history clearly records, the soldiers were alive following the disappearance of Christ from the tomb.

Some skeptics have still asserted that the soldiers all slept at night while the stone was rolled away and the body

MAYBE THE GUARDS FELL ASLEEP (EVEN THOUGH IT WOULD COST THEM THEIR LIVES), THEN HIS FOLLOWERS REMOVED THE TWO-TON STONE AND STOLE HIS BODY WITHOUT WAKING UP THE GUARDS

taken, but this is not possible. Dr. George Currie, a student of Roman military discipline, quoting an eye-witness account from a Roman soldier named Polybius, observed that the "fear of death produced flawless attention to duty, especially in the night watches."[63] If, by chance, the entire unit of guards fell asleep, they would have certainly heard the grating of the huge stone as it was rolled away, and quickly leapt into action. (Since the tomb was carved out of a rock shelf, there was only one way into it . . . through the stone at the door. It is unreasonable to think that the disciples or anyone else could have snuck past sleeping guards and attempted to move the massive stone without the soldiers being awakened by the noise as it was rolled up the incline.)

Even if they awoke to find a stolen body, the grave robbers would have been tracked down and dealt with efficiently. If the Roman military was good enough to conquer the world, they could certainly apprehend a couple grave robbers. As I mentioned before, the Romans would have had major motivation to find the dead body, since the news of His resurrection was causing a large uproar that they would have wanted to quickly silence. They wouldn't have just thrown up their hands, said, "Oh well," and forgotten about it. The news of Christ's resurrection was a major thorn in their side that they would have wanted to remove.

THEORY #2 - THE DISCIPLES STOLE THE BODY

This was at one time the most popular theory in trying to explain how the tomb of Jesus became empty without the intervention of God, but has now been dismissed by the majority of critics due to several serious flaws, including the following . . .

The Disciples Did not Have the Proper Mindset

Past critics have argued that if the body of Christ were stolen from the tomb, the followers of Jesus Christ were most likely to do it. But what many critics ignore or don't understand is the fact that all the disciples had run away to save their lives after Jesus died on the cross. These mentally defeated scaredy-cats would have had to fight off a group of heavily armed Roman guards standing at the tomb's entrance, move the 2 ton stone, steal the body, escape authorities, and eventually die for a known lie. Samuel Fallow said concerning the theft theory that, "It is probable they would not, and it is next to certain they (the disciples) could not (rob Jesus' grave). How could they have undertaken to remove the body? Frail and timorous creatures, who fled as soon as they saw Him taken into custody; even Peter, the most courageous, trembled at the voice of a servant girl, and three times denied that he knew Him. People of this character, would they have dared to resist the authority of the governor? Would they have undertaken to oppose the determination

293

of the Sanhedrin, to force a guard, and to elude or overcome soldiers armed and aware of danger?"[64] Wilbur M. Smith said, "These disciples were in no mood to go out and face Roman soldiers, subdue the entire guard, and snatch that body out of the tomb. I think, myself, if they had attempted it, they would have been killed."[65]

Concerning the Roman seal on the closed tomb, Henry Alford said, "The sealing was by means of a cord or string passing across the stone at the mouth of the sepulchre, and fastened at either end to the rock by sealing-clay."[66] The seal in itself would not keep a potential thief out, but breaking the seal assured that the robber would face the full wrath of Roman law, possibly death. The disciples were in no mood to risk their lives to retrieve a dead body that had been honorably buried. They could have provided no better burial place for Jesus than what He already had received, so they would have had no motivation to remove the body. It certainly wasn't so that they could make it appear that He had risen, and then willingly die for what they knew was a lie.

They Did not Have the Right Understanding

Gregory of Nyssa made this observant statement fifteen hundred years ago concerning the mindset of the disciples, "They did not seem to understand that He was to rise the third day; they certainly were surprised when they found that He had risen. These circumstances negate the thought that they would even contemplate stealing the body to create the impression that He had risen."[67] The disciples would not have sought to make the resurrection seem true when they had no understanding of or belief in it, especially when preaching it would cost them their lives . . . I will talk more about this subject later in the chapter.

The Grave Clothes Provide a Powerful, Silent Witness

Gregory of Nyssa said, ". . . that the disposition of the clothes in the sepulchre, the napkin that was about our Saviour's head, not lying with the linen clothes, but wrapped together in a place by itself, did not bespeak the terror and hurry of thieves, and therefore, refutes the story of the body being stolen."[68]

John Chrysostom, another fourth century writer, made this still-valid point, "And what mean also the napkins that were stuck on with the myrrh; for Peter saw these lying. For if they had been disposed to steal, they would not have stolen the body naked, not because of dishonoring it only, but in order not to delay and lose any time in stripping it, and not to give them that were so disposed opportunity to awake and seize them. Especially when it was myrrh, a drug that adheres so to the body, and cleaves to the clothes, whence it was not easy to take the clothes off the body, but they that did this needed much time, so that from this again, the tale of the theft is improbable."[69]

By Jewish custom, the dead body of Jesus was bandaged tightly from the armpits to the ankles in strips of linen. Between the folds of linen was placed a gummy, aromatic substance which acted as both a preservative and cement that glued the wrappings together into a solid covering that clung tenaciously to the body. The truly amazing thing, as shown by history, is that the grave clothes of Jesus remained in the solid form of a body, but His body was not in it. This is a highly significant fact since it is absolutely impossible for a living or dead man to wriggle out of *tightly wrapped* clothes without disturbing them even slightly . . . in other words, the body of Jesus must have exited the grave clothes in a supernatural manner.

The undisturbed grave clothes serve as a powerful witness against the stolen body theory . . . if someone was determined to steal the dead body of Christ, they would have taken Him, grave clothes and all . . . the grave clothes would not have been in the grave. They certainly would not have taken the time to unwrap the body, strip by strip, then, once the body was removed, to reform the strips into the shape of a body and neatly fold the other parts of the grave clothing, all with a group of armed Roman soldiers standing outside. They or any other supposed thief would have taken the body and split before they were seen. The undisturbed grave clothes provide silent and powerful testimony to the fact of the resurrection.

The Evidence From Hostile Sources is Undeniable

Even Rome and the Jewish religious leaders of the time admitted that to say the body was stolen by an outside party was a lie (Matthew 28:11–15). Other secular sources also admit that this was a lie. James Hastings gave the following commentary on the passage in Matthew, "This fraudulent transaction proceeds upon the admission by the enemies of Christianity that the grave was empty—an admission which is enough to show that the evidence for the empty grave was 'too notorious to be denied.'"[70]

W.J. Sparrow-Simpson noted that, "The emptiness of the grave is acknowledged by *opponents* as well as affirmed by disciples. The narrative of the guards attempts to account for the fact as a fraudulent transaction (Matthew 28:11–15). 'But this Jewish accusation against the Apostles takes for granted that the grave was empty. What was needed was an explanation' . . . This acknowledgement by the Jews that the grave was vacated extends to all subsequent Jewish comments on the point."[71] (The response of the Jewish leaders is not only recorded in Matthew 28:11–15, but also by historians Justin Martyr and Tertullian, demonstrating the known lie that the disciples stole the body persisted among the Jewish people through at least the 2nd century.)

Alexander Balmin Bruce said concerning the Roman guard, "They were perfectly aware that they had not fallen asleep at their post and that no theft had taken place. The lie for which the priests paid so much money is suicidal; one half destroys the other. Sleeping sentinels could not know what happened."[72]

Philip Schaff said, "This infamous lie carries its refutation on its face: for if the Roman soldiers who watched the grave at the express request of the priests and Pharisees, were asleep, they could not see the thieves, nor would they have proclaimed their military crime; if they, or only some of them, were awake, they would have prevented the theft. As to the disciples, they were too timid and desponding at the time to venture on such a daring act, and too honest to cheat the world. And finally a self-invented falsehood could not give them the courage and constancy of faith for the proclamation of the resurrection at the peril of their lives. The whole theory is a wicked absurdity, an insult to the common sense and honor of mankind."[73]

John Chrysostom from Antioch, who lived between A.D. 347–407, made this insightful observation concerning the theft theory: "For indeed even this establishes the resurrection, the fact I mean of their saying that the disciples stole Him. For this is the language of men confessing that the body was not there. When therefore they confess the body was not there, but the stealing of it is shown to be false and incredible, by their watching it, and by the seals, and by the timidity of the disciples, the proof of the resurrection even hence appears incontrovertible."[74]

Based on these and other facts, JP Moreland explained concerning the theory that either the disciples or someone else stole Jesus' body that ". . . no New Testament scholar, regardless of how skeptical he is about the supernatural elements in Christianity, considers this suggestion as remotely possible."[75] If even the skeptics no longer accept this theory, then why should we?

THEORY #3 - THE "SWOON" THEORY

One explanation still used by a few critics today is called the 'swoon theory,' which suggests that Jesus didn't really die on the cross, but simply fainted due to exhaustion and blood loss. After being placed in the cool tomb, those that hold to the theory explain that Jesus was revived by either the coolness or the spice laden grave clothes He was tightly wrapped in. James Hastings said, ". . . myrrh was a drug which adheres so closely to the body that the grave clothes would not easily be removed."[76] He then somehow wriggled out of the grave clothes, took the time to reform them into the shape of His body and neatly folded and placed the napkin that was on his face (John 20:6–7).

Next, He supposedly rolled the two-ton stone up a slotted incline. T.J. Thornburn explained that the stone in front of the tomb was used "as a protection against both men and beasts."[77] Concerning the size of the stones used at that time, he said, "It usually required several men to remove it."[78] Certainly a mostly-dead Jesus could not have removed this stone and pushed it up the inclined slot in front of the tomb, especially without the guards hearing the grating of the stone. He then was said to have either quietly escaped or fought through the soldiers and marched on his merry way.

MAYBE JESUS DIDN'T DIE. MAYBE HE JUST PASSED OUT ON THE CROSS, THEN WOKE UP IN THE TOMB, PUSHED OVER THE TWO-TON STONE, OVERPOWERED THE ROMAN SOLDIERS, AND ESCAPED.

These theorists really expect us to believe that Jesus survived a severe beating and scourging before the crucifixion, six long hours nailed to the cross and a spear wound in his side. Then in the tomb, He withstood 3 days without food or water before performing His escape act. Finally, as E. Hermitage Day said, "A long walk, followed by the appearance to the disciples at Jerusalem, is inconceivable in the case of one recovered from a swoon caused by wounds and exhaustion."[79] If Jesus had only swooned, according to Luke 24:13, He must have walked "to a village named Emmaus, which was about seven miles from Jerusalem." To think that he could have done this in such a weakened condition on feet whose bones, nerves and tendons had been crushed during the crucifixion is ridiculous.

Medical expert Dr. Alexander Metherell, who has thoroughly researched the subject of Christ's crucifixion, when asked if Jesus was definitely dead before He was sealed in the tomb, stated with total confidence, "There was absolutely no doubt that Jesus was dead."[80] Dr. Metherell added concerning the Roman soldiers who oversaw the crucifixion, "They were experts in killing people—that was their job, and they did it very well. They knew without a doubt when a person was dead. Besides, if a prisoner somehow escaped, the responsible soldiers would be put to death themselves, so they had a huge incentive to make absolutely sure that each and every victim was dead when he was removed from the cross."[81] E. Hermitage Day said, "The Roman soldiers were not unfamiliar with the evidences of death, or with the sight of death following upon crucifixion."[82]

Bernard Ramm explained, "Certainly Jesus was put to death in a great public execution known to such historians as Tacitus and Josephus (Tacitus, *Annals, XV*, 44; Josephus, *Antiquities, XVIII*, 3.) The execution was in the capital of the Jewish Commonwealth under the direction of the Roman governor and his soldiers, in co-operation with the highest Jewish authorities, and during one of the greatest religious seasons. Jesus certainly died. The swoon-theory is an outright evasion of the record through willful intention without a shred of historical validation."[83]

When asked about the validity of the swoon theory, Dr. Metherell said, ". . . it's impossible. It's a fanciful theory without any possible basis in fact."[84] Emory University scholar Luke Timothy Johnson said the 'swoon theory' is "the purest poppycock, the product of fevered imagination rather than careful analysis."[85] George Hanson remarked concerning this theory, "It is hard to believe that this was the favourite explanation of eighteenth-century rationalism."[49a] W.J. Sparrow-Simpson, speaking in the 1800's, said that the swoon theory is "now quite obsolete."[86]

While scholars have discounted this theory for at least 200 years, unfortunately, the public has not been made aware of this fact. The public needs to know what Dr. William D. Edwards has observed . . . "Clearly, the weight of the historical and medical evidence indicates that Jesus was dead before the wound to his side was inflicted . . . Accordingly, interpretations based on the assumption that Jesus did not die on the cross appear to be at odds with modern medical knowledge."[87] J.P. Moreland related the fact that due to overwhelming evidence, "Almost no one of reputation today holds that Jesus did not die on the cross or that the disciples went to the wrong tomb."[88]

Surprisingly, it was resurrection skeptic David Friedrich Strauss who delivered what is considered to be the knockout punch to the theory in the 1800's when he declared, "It is impossible that a being who had stolen half-dead out of the sepulcher, who crept about weak and ill, who required bandaging, strengthening and indulgence, and who still at last yielded to His sufferings, could have given to the disciples the impression that He was the Conqueror over death and the grave, the Prince of Life, an impression which lay at the bottom of their future ministry. Such a resuscitation could only have weakened the impression which He had made upon them in life and in death, at the most could only have given it an elegiac voice, but could by no possibility have changed their sorrow into enthusiasm, have elevated their reverence into worship."[89] The swoon theory has now been abandoned by all who know the historical and medical facts dealing with crucifixion.

If the 'swoon theory' is not the answer, then who else could have moved His body? The Jewish authorities hated Him . . . they wanted Him to die and decay. The last thing they wanted was a resurrection. Moving the body would have been contrary to their wishes. Roman authorities wanted peace—to move the body would have caused strife. The Roman soldiers had the best chance to steal the body, but had no motivation to do so, especially since it would have meant death when they were caught—it wouldn't have been worth it. The women who worshipped Him couldn't even move the massive stone sealing the entrance to the tomb (Mark 16:1–3), so they couldn't have stolen His body. Someone else, a common citizen or foreigner, would have had to fight through the Roman guards, roll back the stone, steal the body, and escape all Roman and Jewish authorities. Breaking the Roman seal on the tomb would have meant immediate death by crucifixion upside down. Who would have risked their life to do this?

Theory #4 - Joseph of Arimathea Buried Jesus' Body in a Different Location

Some have mentioned the possibility that Joseph of Arimathea stole the body of Jesus and buried it in another location to fool the world into believing that He had risen from the grave. This argument holds no weight, and there are only a few scholars that still promote this theory . . . most accept the fact that Joseph of Arimathea was a real person and that Jesus was really buried in his tomb. But for argument's sake, here is some evidence against this lowly regarded theory . . .

300

The theory breaks down when we consider that Joseph had no motivation to bury Jesus in a lesser tomb since his goal was to honor Him by burying Him in his own exquisite tomb. Joseph had one of the best tombs in the area . . . why would He bury Him in a tomb or grave that was second rate? Secondly, he buried him at night, which would have required torches to see . . . foul play would have almost certainly been noticed by someone. Thirdly, the New Testament mentions that women beheld where he lay . . . so they watched the burial . . . they too must have been willing to lie for no good reason. Fourthly, the Roman soldiers were in position in front of the tomb the day after the Sabbath (Matt. 27:62–66), leaving very little time for Joseph to perform his deceitful deed with Nicodemus and the women witnesses.

Fifthly, Joseph, as a devout Jew, also would not have wanted to break the quickly approaching Sabbath, which also happened to be the Passover, the most important holiday in the Jewish calendar. Numbers 19:11–13 makes it clear that whoever touched a dead body during the Sabbath would be considered defiled and unable to participate in the Passover/Sabbath, which is a serious issue for a Jew. Jesus died near 3 P.M, and the Sabbath started at 6 P.M, so Joseph had less than 3 hours to ask Pilate for the body, take it from the cross, wash it, wrap it tightly in strips of linen cemented by spices, and bury it. He would have had to really hustle to bury the body and close the tomb by 6P.M . . . he didn't have the time to even think about stealing the body and giving it a dishonorable burial. Even if Joseph had somehow stolen the body and temporarily fooled the authorities and soldiers, he couldn't have gotten away with it—the Romans knew who had asked to bury the body . . . when they found it missing, they would have confronted Joseph first, punished him if he was the thief, and exposed the hoax.

Some have promoted the theory that the disciples lied in saying Jesus was buried by Joseph of Arimathea when He was actually buried by someone else. This theory also holds no weight. If the gospel writers were trying to lie, they certainly would not have mentioned that Jesus was buried in the tomb of a member of the same Jewish Sanhedrin who helped condemn Him to death. (The Sanhedrin was a privileged group of high priests, scribes and tribunal heads who

The Fingerprints of God

had immense power over the affairs of individual Jews, able to sentence them up to the point of death.) Nearly everyone in the Jewish community knew very well who the members of the Sanhedrin were . . . if Joseph really did not bury Jesus in his tomb, he would have surely made this fact known or someone would have extracted the fact from him. If the disciples had lied about Joseph, the people of Jerusalem would have known about it and Christianity would have been dead. In conclusion, we must agree with the evidence and the overwhelming majority of critics who admit that Jesus was really buried in Joseph of Arimathea's tomb.

On a more personal note, consider that Joseph was also risking his position in society by burying Jesus, and openly professing his faith in Him. He risked being put out of the synagogue, which would have made him a social outcast even among his own family members, who would have treated him like he was physically and spiritually dead. In addition, the considerable wealth, power and respect Joseph had in the Sanhedrin would have gone out the window. Believing in Christ meant social, political and economic devastation for Joseph. But he was willing to give up all this because he truly believed that Jesus was God in the flesh. Do you think Joseph would have willingly given up his powerful social standing and wealth if he wasn't absolutely sure Jesus was who He said He was? Joseph of Arimathea's transformation is excellent proof that Jesus really was and is God.

THEORY #5 - THE WRONG TOMB THEORY

Another important aspect of the fact that Jesus was buried in Joseph of Arimathea's tomb is the truth that many, if not most people in Jerusalem would have known where his tomb was. Just incase someone did not know where Joseph's tomb was, as Ramm indicated, "When Pilate set a watch over the grave, he indicated it's locality to friend and foe alike."[90] Certainly, guarding a tomb was not a common occurrence . . . the Roman guard, along with their exact location would have very likely been noticed by at least some of the Passover crowd in Jerusalem.

302

So the skeptic's assertion that the women, disciples and everyone else visited the wrong tomb is absurd. Concerning the women, (including Joses, Mary Magdalene and Mary the mother of James,) we know that they watched Joseph of Arimathea and Nicodemus prepare Jesus' body and put it in the tomb. Luke 23:55 says they "followed after, and they observed the tomb and how His body was laid." Matthew 27:61 adds that they were "sitting opposite the tomb," and Mark 15:47 states that they "observed where He was laid." To say that the women did not go to the right tomb on resurrection day is simply ridiculous . . . they clearly knew where the tomb was. Would they forget the burial location of the one they loved so dearly . . . would you forget the location of a loved one who you had seen laid in the grave just 3 days earlier?

But this theory states that it was more than just the women who went to the wrong tomb . . . it also declares that the disciples, Roman guards stationed at the tomb, and Jewish authorities all failed to locate the right tomb. Further they must believe that even Joseph of Arimathea forgot where his own tomb was located. The 'wrong tomb' theory is a pitiful attempt at trying to refute the resurrection, and understandably is not esteemed highly by those who know the facts.

(As a sidenote, archaeological discoveries have confirmed that only rich men had the types of tombs that Joseph of Arimathea had. Further, it was characteristic for the tombs of the rich to be located in gardens. In both type and location, archaeology has proven that Jesus' burial site as stated in the New Testament is very historically plausible.)

As I've said before, the theories described above are the best that critics have to offer in trying to refute the fact that Jesus' resurrection involved the power of God. These are the best punches they have to throw, and in my opinion along with the opinions of many others who have studied the subject, they have failed miserably. The evidence clearly points away from the theory that Jesus' tomb became empty by human influence and points towards the only other option . . . that Jesus rose from the tomb by Divine power.

REASON #5 - THE DISCIPLES WERE HONEST IN THEIR REPORTING OF WHAT THEY EXPERIENCED

Some critics have raised the possibility that the disciples of Christ simply made up the resurrection story. In other words, they say that the Bible is just a legendary lie, a tale that we can't trust. But as we've seen above, there are some excellent reasons for believing that the resurrection occurred just as the disciples recorded. Another reason to believe is the fact that the disciples admitted in the New Testament embarrassing facts that would have been detrimental to their cause in spreading the resurrection news. One of these admissions is the mention of women as the first to see the resurrected Christ. As J.P. Moreland noted, "In first century Judaism, a woman's testimony was virtually worthless. A woman was not allowed to give testimony in a court of law except on rare occasions. No one would have invented a story and made women the first witnesses to the empty tomb. The presence of women was an embarrassment . . ."[91] If the disciples were trying to tell a convincing lie to the first century world, they certainly would not have indicated that women were the first to proclaim that Christ had risen. This would have hurt their cause . . . the only explanation for their referral to women as the first witnesses is the honest fact that they were.

The disciples also recorded many other embarrassing facts about themselves in the gospels, including the account in the Garden of Gethsemane, where they all ran away, one of them naked (Mark 14:50–52), the passage relating Peter's three denials of Christ before the crucifixion (Luke 22:54–62), and the report that they were all hiding together for fear of death following the crucifixion (John 20:19). If the disciples were trying to spread a convincing lie, they would have made men the first witnesses, and would have made themselves appear to be great champions of the faith, not faithless cowards. They would have written things that made their story sound good, not bad.

But instead of weakening their claim for the resurrection truth, the mention of women witnesses and embarrassing accounts of themselves actually strengthens the validity of their proclamation.

These passages demonstrate the amazing honesty of the disciples . . . they didn't change the facts even though they were detrimental. Their honest reports of embarrassing facts make them more trustworthy witnesses to the truth of the resurrection.

REASON #6 - WITHOUT THE RESURRECTION OF CHRIST, CHRISTIANITY WOULD NOT EXIST

According to the great historian Phillip Schaff, "The Christian church rests on the resurrection of its Founder. Without this fact the church could never have been born, or if born, it would soon have died a natural death. The miracle of the resurrection and the existence of Christianity are so closely connected that they must stand or fall together. If Christ was raised from the dead, then all his other miracles are sure, and our faith is impregnable; if he was not raised, he died in vain and our faith is vain."[92] H.P. Lydon said, "Faith in the resurrection is the very keystone of the arch of Christian faith, and, when it is removed, all must inevitably crumble into ruin."[93]

Certainly Christianity would have died with the failure of its founder. I can't express the importance of this fact enough. After Christ's death, no one in the world, including His supposed followers, believed that He was the God and Savior of humanity who removed the obstacle of sin so that believers may have eternal life. To them, He was a defeated, false Messiah . . . a phony, and His death proved it. The disciples had already written Him off as a failure, and were likely ready to return to their former occupations to try to scratch out a living. If Christ did not rise from the grave, the mindset of the disciples towards their former leader would not have changed and Christianity would have died in the womb.

If the disciples weren't changed, then Christianity would have died before it began, since they were the ones that Christ had commissioned to carry His resurrection news to the world. If the disciples weren't changed, then no one would have been changed and the Church would not exist. The fact that the Christian church does exist is powerful proof that Christ rose from the grave. Scholars John Ankerberg and John Weldon said, "Could the Christian Church ever have come into existence as a result of what had become after Jesus' crucifixion and death, a group of disheartened, frightened, skeptical apostles? Not a chance. Only the Resurrection of Christ from the dead can account for motivating the disciples to give their lives to preach about Christ and nurture the Christian Church the Lord had founded."[94]

The Disciples Mindset and Behavior Did Change Dramatically

History demonstrates that the mindset of the disciples did dramatically change, leading to behaviors that would have never happened without the Resurrection. One of these resulting behaviors is the fact that the disciples, who were Jews, changed their day of worship. When you recognize that Jews strictly keep the Sabbath from sundown on Friday to sundown on Saturday and that the penalty for not keeping the Sabbath was possible death, the fact that the disciples, as law-abiding Jews, changed their day of worship to Sunday after the resurrection is strong evidence that the resurrection really happened. They would not have changed their day of worship to honor a dead and decaying body, with the possible penalty of death. They changed their day of worship and defied the powerful religious authorities only because they were confident that Jesus had risen bodily from the dead. They would not have willingly died for what they knew was a lie.

Another important point to make regarding the resurrection is the fact that in Palestine during Jesus day, there were at least 50 tombs of dead prophets or other religious leaders which served as sites of worship, but Jesus tomb was not venerated, nor is it even explicitly mentioned beyond the gospels . . . this lack of veneration and mention is powerful evidence that that there was not a dead body in the tomb to worship . . . Jesus' body was not there because He had risen. They were worshipping a risen and victorious Savior, not a dead and decaying body which still lay in its tomb.

Not only did the disciples change their day of worship, site and object of worship, but they and the early church changed their style of worship as well. Pliny the Younger a Roman author and administrator writing to the Emperor Trajan in A.D 112, gave us some insight into the worship practices of the early church in this letter . . . "They were in the habit of meeting on a certain fixed day before it was light, when they sang in alternate verses a hymn to Christ, as to a god, and bound themselves by a solemn oath, not to do any wicked deeds, but never to commit any fraud, theft or adultery, never to falsify their word, not deny a trust when they should be called upon to deliver it up; after which it was their custom to separate, and then to reassemble to partake of food—but food of an ordinary and innocent kind."[95] The changes in their day, site, object and method of worship would have never occurred unless the resurrection really happened. The fact that they did is powerful evidence that it really did happen.

The Disciples Weren't the Only Ones Changed

The disciples weren't the only ones to make this dramatic change in their worship practices, as prominent philosopher Dr. J.P. Moreland explained, "But five weeks after he's crucified, over ten thousand Jews are following him and claiming that he is the initiator of a new religion. And get this: they're willing to give up or alter all five of the social institutions (such as worshipping on the Sabbath only) that they have been taught since childhood, which have such importance both sociologically and theologically. So the implication is that something big was going on. Something *very* big was going on!"[96] "Believe me," he continued, "these changes to the Jewish social structures were not just minor adjustments that were casually made— they were absolutely monumental. This was nothing short of a social earthquake! And earthquakes don't happen without a cause."[97]

By abandoning their cherished family traditions, which were several hundred years old, these 10,000+ Jews were jeopardizing their physical and social well-being, and, as Jews, believed that they were risking the eternal damnation of their souls to Hell if they were wrong in following Jesus. But they were willing to sacrifice their lives for what they knew to be true. If they weren't certain that He had risen from the grave, this large multitude of Jews would not have made such a bold, life-transforming proclamation. If Christ did not rise again, early Christians would not have changed their day of worship. Cowardly apostles (Matthew 26:56, John 20:19), and many others would not have boldly opposed Jewish law to set aside a special day of worship for a dead and decaying body. They had no motivation to do so unless they knew for certain that Jesus had risen from the grave.

Did The Disciples Make up the Gospel and Die for a Known Lie?

Some skeptics have promoted the 'group-lie hypothesis,' which says that the disciples mutually agreed to lie to the world that they had seen the risen Christ, when they actually hadn't. In refuting this very weak argument, Dr. Gary Habermas replied, "Actually there are several good reasons why the disciples couldn't have talked each other into this. As the center of their faith, there was too much at stake; they went to their deaths defending it. Wouldn't some of them rethink the group think at a later date and recant or just quietly fall away? And what about James, who didn't believe in Jesus, and Paul, who was a persecutor of the Christians—how did they get talked into seeing something (the risen Christ)? Further, what about the empty tomb (which even the enemies of Christ don't deny)?"[98] Historian and theologian Carl Braaten remarked, "Even the more skeptical historians agree that for primitive Christianity, the Resurrection of Jesus from the dead was a real event in history, the very foundation of faith, and not a mythical idea arising out of the creative imagination of believers."[99] Prominent British theologian Michael Green said, "The appearances of Jesus are as well authenticated as anything in antiquity . . . There can be no rational doubt that they occurred, and that the main reason why Christian's became sure of the Resurrection in the earliest days is just this. They could say with assurance, 'We have seen the Lord.' They knew it was He."[100] Dr. Habermas concluded his assessment of the 'group-lie hypothesis' by saying, "people just grasp at straws trying to account for the appearances. But nothing fits all the evidence better than the explanation that Jesus was alive."[101]

In further refutation of this theory, let's delve a little bit deeper into the mental condition of the disciples immediately after Christ's death and burial and compare it to their powerfully transformed mentality following Christ's resurrection. To do this, we must first picture the psychological absurdity of a small band of defeated cowards cowering in a hidden room one day, and the next day, being transformed into a company that no persecution could silence—and then, if you're a skeptic, attempting to attribute this dramatic change to nothing more convincing than a miserable resurrection fabrication which they didn't understand (Mark:31–32; Luke 18:31–34; John 20:9) or even believe themselves[102] (Mark 16:9–14; Luke 24:10–11; John 7:5).

The crucifixion was devastating to the disciples . . . they had sacrificed their jobs, homes, families (Matthew 19:27) and lives to follow this man, who they believed was the conquering Messiah. All their hopes were attached to Him . . . when He died as a criminal they were frightened and hopelessly crushed, their lives a wreck. They had no hope of a resurrection, for they did not understand or believe it, nor did they want to. Throughout the last three years, Jesus had rebuked each of the disciples for their unbelief in His future resurrection (Matthew 28:17, Luke 24:25–27, 38, 41; John 20:24–27). They could not have possibly fabricated the gospel story since they had to be convinced of the reality of the resurrection against their wills.

The great historian Philip Schaff explained the mental condition of the disciples following the resurrection and the powerful change that took place only 3 days later by saying, "Christ had predicted both his crucifixion and his resurrection, but the former was a stumbling-block to the disciples, the latter a mystery which they could not understand till after the event. They no doubt expected that he would soon establish his Messianic kingdom on earth. Hence their utter disappointment and downheartedness after the crucifixion. The treason of one of their own number, the triumph of the hierarchy, the fickleness of the people, the death and burial of the beloved Master, had in a few hours rudely blasted their Messianic hopes and exposed them to the contempt and ridicule of their enemies. For two days they were trembling on the brink of despair. But on the third day, behold, the same disciples underwent a complete revolution from despondency to hope, from timidity to courage, from doubt to faith, and began to proclaim the gospel of the resurrection in the face of an unbelieving world and at the peril of their lives. This revolution was not isolated, but general among them; it was not the result of an easy credulity, but brought about in spite of doubt and hesitation; it was not superficial and momentary, but radical and lasting; it affected, not only the apostles, but the whole history of the world. It reached even the leader of the persecution, Saul of Tarsus one of the clearest and strongest intellects, and converted him into the most devoted and faithful champion of this very gospel to the hour of his martyrdom. This is a fact patent to every reader of the closing chapters of the Gospels, and is freely admitted even by the most advanced skeptics."[103].

Dr. Gregory Boyd said, "The writers of the gospel had nothing to gain, and much to lose (including their lives) by writing Jesus' story, and they didn't have ulterior motives such as financial gain."[104] Norman Geisler said, ". . . the witnesses to the resurrection had nothing to gain personally for their witness to the resurrection. Certainly, it would have been much more profitable personally for them to deny the resurrection. Rather, they proclaimed and defended it in the face of death."[105] J.P. Moreland observed, "The disciples had nothing to gain by lying and starting a new religion. They faced hardship, ridicule, hostility and martyr's deaths. In light of this, they could have never maintained such unwavering motivation if they knew what they were preaching was a lie. The disciples were not fools, and Paul was a cool-headed intellectual of the first rank. There would have been several opportunities over 3 to 4 decades of ministry to reconsider and renounce the lie."[106]

Simon Greenleaf, the renowned professor of law at Harvard University expanded on this fact when he wrote, "The laws of every country were against the teachings of His disciples. The interests and passions of all the rulers and great men in the world were against them. The fashion of the world was against them. Propagating this new faith, even in the most inoffensive and peaceful manner, they could expect nothing but contempt, opposition, revilings, bitter persecutions, stripes, imprisonments, torments and cruel deaths. Yet this faith they zealously did propagate; and all these miseries they endured undismayed, nay rejoicing. As one after another was put to a miserable death, the survivors only prosecuted their work with increased vigor and resolution. The annals of military warfare afford scarcely an example of the like heroic constancy, patience and unflinching courage. They had every possible motive to review carefully the grounds of their faith and the evidences of the great facts and truths which they asserted; and these motives were pressed upon their attention with the most melancholy and terrific frequency. It was therefore impossible that they could have persisted in affirming these truths they have narrated, had not Jesus actually risen from the dead and had they not known this fact as certainly as they knew any other fact."[107]

Dr. Bernard Ramm said "That the writers of the gospel were sincere, earnest men of high motivation, writing with no desire to defraud or deceive is admitted by most critics."[108] Even the critics of Christ have recognized the fact that the apostles wouldn't have written, and certainly wouldn't have died for the Resurrection news unless they knew for sure that it was true. Cowards don't die for something they don't understand or even believe, especially when they *KNOW* it's a lie. The facts don't add up if you're still a skeptic.

The Complete Transformation of the Disciples and Others can be Explained Only by the Reality of the Resurrection

Based on the above facts, historians Carol and Roddy Smith said, "One of the greatest testimonies to the truth of the resurrection is the transformation in the lives of Jesus' followers. A ragtag group hiding in a hidden room transformed into a dream team of spiritual activists, some even martyrs. Men who doubted, who denied, who ran away, who hid, found the strength to face mobs, kings, cultures, and creeds with a message of which they were so sure they wagered their eternal existence on it."[109]

It was the resurrection that motivated timid kittens to go everywhere proclaiming the message of a risen Christ like ferocious tigers. The resurrection is the only reason why early Christians would have *willingly* endured being beaten, stoned to death, thrown to the lions, tortured and crucified . . . they would not have done so if

Christ did not rise from the grave. Ten of the eleven original disciples (excluding Judas Iscariot, the traitor of Jesus) were killed for their belief that Christ rose from the dead . . . Peter, Andrew, James, the son of Alphaeus, and Simon were all crucified; Philip was stoned and crucified; Bartholomew was beaten, crucified and beheaded; James, the son of Zebedee was killed with the sword; Matthew and Thomas were thrust through with a spear and Thaddeus was killed by arrows. Historical records indicate that John, the only disciple not to be killed, was boiled alive in a scalding cauldron of oil for his faith in Christ. He was removed just before death, and sent to exile on the Isle of Patmos, with excruciatingly painful third degree burns. With his body essentially one massive blister, John wrote the powerfully prophetic book of Revelation.

Dr. J.P. Moreland made this thought provoking point, "The apostles (disciples) were willing to die for something they had seen with their own eyes and touched with their own hands. They were in a unique position not to just believe Jesus rose from the dead, but to know for sure. And when you've got eleven credible people with nothing to gain and a lot to lose (including their lives), who all agree they observed something with their own eyes—now you've got some difficulty explaining that away."[110]

The Transformations of Thomas and James, the Brother of Jesus

The disciples were willing to be tortured and killed only because they knew for sure that Jesus was alive. This is the only logical conclusion. If He was still dead, certainly not all the disciples would have been dramatically changed and willing to die for Him. Thomas especially would not have been dramatically changed and died a martyr's death unless he saw the physically resurrected Christ. Thomas stated that he would not accept Jesus as God and Savior until He saw physical proof (John 20:24–28). George Matheson said, "The skepticism of Thomas comes out in the belief that the death of Jesus would be the death of His kingdom. 'Let us go, that we may die with Him.' The man who uttered these words had, at the time when he uttered them, no hope of Christ's resurrection. No man would

312

propose to die with another if he expected to see him again in a few hours. Thomas, at that moment, had given up all intellectual belief. He saw no chance for Jesus. He did not believe in His physical power. He had made up his mind that the forces of the outer world would be to strong for Him, would crush Him."[111]

Unless Thomas had put his hands in His spear-pierced side and fingers in His nail-pierced hands and feet, He would not have believed in the resurrection, and certainly would not have died for Him. Yet after seeing Him alive and well following His crucifixion, Thomas proclaimed, "My Lord and my God!"[112] He later died for that proclamation. The transformation and martyr's death of Thomas is powerful proof that Jesus really did conquer death and the grave with His physical resurrection.

James, Jesus' own brother would have been even tougher to change. He openly despised Him, rejected His teachings and likely thought that His actions were ruining the family name before the resurrection. Yet afterward, James declared in James 1:1 that he is "a bondservant of God and of the Lord Jesus Christ."[113] Historical records show that he was willingly thrown off a tall building and then allowed his still alive body to be smashed to death with a large stick for his belief that his brother Jesus rose from the dead. James would not have died for a dead brother who he considered to be a lunatic. The sight of the resurrected Christ is the only thing that could have changed him so completely.

The Transformation of Other Early Christians in the Face of Intense Persecution

Jesus must have risen from the dead to change James and the cowardly apostles. But it was not just James, Jesus' brother and the disciples who willingly died for what they knew to be true . . . other early Christians died horrible deaths as well. The first of the ten periods of persecution against the early church began in A.D 64 during the reign of Roman emperor Nero. His rage against early Christians was so fierce that Eusebius, a historian living at that time, recorded, "a man might see cities full of Christian men's bodies, the old lying together with the young, and the dead bodies of women cast out naked, without reverence of that sex, in the open streets."[114] Nero also got a thrill out of tying Christians to a chariot, setting their bodies on fire, and sending them around the sports stadium until their bodies burnt to a cinder. Watching Christians burn to a crisp was one of the favorite sports at the time . . . probably as popular as football is today.

Tacitus, a secular historian living in the mid first century, wrote this concerning the intense persecution suffered by early Christians under the reign of Nero . . . "Their death was a matter of sport; they were covered in wild beasts' skins and torn to pieces by dogs or were fastened to crosses and set on fire in order to serve as torches . . ."[115] Again we read from Tacitus 15:44 that, "Nero fastened the guilt and inflicted the most exquisite tortures on a class hated for their abominations, called Christians by the populace . . . Mockery of every sort was added to their deaths. Covered with the skins of beasts, they were doomed to the flames and burnt, to serve as a nightly illumination, when daylight had expired."[116]

But the persecution of early Christians did not end there. During the reign of Domitian in A.D 97, and in the years immediately following, John Foxe states that the following occurred . . . "Death was not considered enough punishment for the Christians, who were subjected to the cruelest treatment possible. They were whipped, disemboweled, torn apart, and stoned. Plates of hot iron were laid on them; they were strangled, eaten by wild animals, hung and tossed on the horns of bulls."[117] (In addition, they were stabbed, purposely smeared with honey and stung to death by wasps, boiled alive in hot water, sawn in half, beheaded, crucified, burnt alive, blown up, scourged, hunted down and murdered, forced to drink rancid, filthy oil until they died, stretched by cords until their limbs were ripped off, and dragged through the streets by wild animals until their skulls were crushed and brains fell out. Early Christians endured many other gruesome forms of death as well.) Foxe continued, "After they were dead, their bodies were piled in heaps and left to rot without burial. Nevertheless, the Church continued to grow, deeply rooted in the doctrine of the apostles and watered with the blood of the saints."[118] He added, "For three hundred years (during the first ten persecutions), the strongest and richest rulers in the world had tried to snuff out Christianity, using force, politics, torture and death . . . everything at their disposal. Now all those emperors are gone, while Christ and His church still stands."[119]

Is it Possible that Early Christians Died for a Known Lie?

Is it possible that this group of early believers stood under the weight of Nero's and Domitian's intense persecution, willingly dying for a known lie? If the resurrection news was a lie, then the earliest Christians would have certainly known it, for they could have easily searched Christ's tomb to see if it was empty. Dr. Gary Habermas said, "The Resurrection was undoubtedly the central proclamation of the early church from the very beginning. The earliest Christians didn't just endorse Jesus' teachings; they were convinced that they had seen him alive after his crucifixion. That's what changed their lives and started the church. Certainly, since this was their centermost conviction, they would have made absolutely sure it was true."[120]

The earliest Christians didn't need the apostle's doctrine to prove that Christ rose from the dead, since they had either seen the risen Christ themselves or had excellent evidence right before their eyes in the form of the empty tomb. When they died for their belief in Christ's resurrection, they would have known whether they were dying for a lie or not. If the resurrection news was a known lie, it's unreasonable to believe that so many early Christians would have willingly endured the onslaught of tortuous persecution that they faced under Nero and Domitian. It would be even more incredible to believe the fact that the church grew during this persecution if the resurrection news was a known lie. There was no other motivation for their sacrificial actions unless they knew for sure that Jesus had risen physically from the tomb. Early Christians and the disciples would not have willingly died tortuous deaths for what they KNEW was a lie. Many people throughout human history have died for false beliefs, without recognizing the lie . . . they've died for what they sincerely believed to be the truth. But no one will choose to die for a known lie . . . for claims that are easily checkable and proven to be false. When threatened with death, the disciples and other early Christians would have renounced the known lie and lived. But none of them did. This means they must have genuinely seen the resurrected Christ (or at least evidence for the resurrection through the empty tomb). They didn't die for a known lie, but willingly died for what they had physically seen and knew to be true.

Many scholars who have thoroughly researched the evidence have reached this same conclusion. Norman Geisler said, "As has been pointed out before, men will sometimes die for what they believe to be true but never for what they know to be false. A man becomes extremely honest and truthful under the threat of death."[121] Lee Strobel said, "People will die for their religious beliefs if they sincerely believe they're true (this describes the followers of many world religions), but people won't die for their religious beliefs if they know their beliefs are false. While most people can only have faith that their beliefs are true, the disciples were in a position to know without a doubt whether or not Jesus had risen from the dead. They claimed that they saw him, talked with him, and ate with him. If they weren't absolutely certain, they wouldn't have allowed themselves to be tortured to death for proclaiming that the Resurrection had happened."[122] The unique position of the disciples to know the facts for certain makes Christianity unique among world religions. While followers of those religions can only hope their beliefs are true, Christians can know with concrete certainty that our beliefs are true, resting upon a firm historical foundation.

Did Early Christians Only Hallucinate That They Saw the Risen Christ?

Besides the disciples, the Bible states that Christ also physically appeared to over 500 others (I Corinthians 15:3–8), some of whom were probably non-believing, previously hostile witnesses. Certainly unbelievers, who hated Christ, spit on Him, and yelled obscenities at Him would not have preached about a living Savior after they witnessed His death . . . unless something monumental, like the resurrection, happened to change their perspective. Dr. Gary Habermas makes this excellent point, "Now stop and think about it; you would never include this phrase (concerning the 500 witnesses) unless you were absolutely confident that these folks would confirm that they really did see Jesus alive. I mean, Paul was virtually inviting

316

people to check it out for themselves! He wouldn't have said this if he didn't know they'd back him up."[123] These 500 witnesses were alive and known at the time—certainly some would have cracked under the life-threatening persecution of Nero and the Jewish religious authorities if they were lying—but they chose to die, because they knew what they saw. Something special must have happened to transform their lives. They must have known for certain that Christ had risen from the dead.

Some critics have still suggested that maybe the disciples and 500 others all hallucinated, thinking they had seen the risen Christ, while they really had not. But this 'hallucination theory' cannot be true since it contradicts all the laws and principles that psychiatrists say must be the case for hallucinations to occur. Winifred Corduan confirms this fact by saying, "The problem with this theory is that, in the case of the resurrection appearances, everything we know about hallucinations is violated . . . thus the resurrection appearances could not have been hallucinations."[124]

Scholar Thomas James Thornburn raised this objection to the hallucination theory . . . "It is absolutely inconceivable that as many as five hundred persons, of average soundness of mind and temperament, in various numbers, at all sorts of times, and in divers situations, should experience all the kinds of sensuous impressions—visual, auditory, tactual—and that all these manifold experiences should rest entirely upon the subjective hallucination."[125] Norman Geisler identified the following problems with the hallucination theory, "1) Perhaps the major predicament for this hypothesis is that Jesus appeared to a variety of persons, at various times, places, and under different circumstances. The belief that all of these people were candidates for such a rare combination of hallucinatory phenomena (visual, auditory, and so on) multiplies the improbable and borders on gullibility. 2) Moreover, while hallucinations generally develop from hopeful anticipation, the disciples despaired after Jesus' death and did not expect him to rise. 3) Further, it is highly unlikely that subjective experiences could inspire the disciples' radical transformations, even being willing to die for their faith. 4) What grounds do we have to think that James, the family skeptic, was in the right frame of mind to see Jesus? 5) What grounds do we have to think that Paul the persecutor yearned to see Jesus?"[126]

Philip Schaff said this in refutation of the hallucination theory . . . "The chief objection to the vision-hypothesis is its intrinsic impossibility. It makes the most exorbitant claim upon our credulity. It requires us to believe that many persons, singly and collectively, at different times, and in different places, from Jerusalem to Damascus, had the same vision and dreamed the same dream; that the women at the open sepulchre early in the morning, Peter and John soon afterwards, the two disciples journeying to Emmaus on the afternoon of the resurrection day, the assembled apostles on the evening in the absence of Thomas, and again on the next Lord's Day in the presence of the skeptical Thomas, seven apostles at the lake of Tiberias, on one occasion five hundred brethren at once, most of whom were still alive when Paul reported the fact, then James, the brother of the Lord, who formerly did not believe in him, again all the apostles on Mount Olivet at the ascension, and at last the clearheaded, strong-minded persecutor on the way to Damascus—that all these men and women on these different occasions vainly imagined they saw and heard the self-same Jesus in bodily shape and form; and that they were by this baseless vision raised all at once from the deepest gloom in which the crucifixion of their Lord had left them, to the boldest faith and strongest hope which compelled them to proclaim the gospel of the resurrection from Jerusalem to Rome to the end of their lives! And this illusion of the early disciples created the greatest revolution not only in their own views and conduct, but among Jews and Gentiles and in the subsequent history of mankind! This illusion, we are expected to believe by these unbelievers, gave birth to the most real and most mighty of all facts, the Christian Church which has lasted these eighteen hundred years and is now spread all over the civilized world, embracing more members than ever and exercising more moral power than all the kingdoms and all other religions combined!."[127]

It has been shown that hallucinations occur to individuals, not groups, as would have been the case during the resurrection of Christ. The fact is that Jesus appeared over a 40 day period to far too many people (over 500), in far too many and varied places at too many different times (at least 10) for them all to have hallucinated the same thing. Dr. Gary Habermas recounted the significance of this fact by saying, "That is a big problem for the hallucination theory, since there are repeated accounts of Jesus appearing to multiple people who reported the same thing. And there are several other arguments why hallucinations can't explain away his appearances. The disciples were fearful, doubtful, and in despair after the Crucifixion, whereas people who hallucinate need a fertile mind of expectancy or anticipation. Peter was hard-headed, James was a skeptic, certainly not good candidates for hallucinations. Also, hallucinations are comparably rare. They're usually caused by drugs or bodily deprivation. Chances are, you don't know anybody who's ever had a hallucination not caused by one of these two things. Yet we're supposed to believe that over a course of many weeks, people from all sorts of backgrounds, all kinds of temperaments, in various places, all experienced hallucinations? That strains the hypothesis quite a bit, doesn't it?"[128]

E. Hermitage Day added that, "The seeing of visions, the perception of exceptional phenomena subjectively by large numbers of persons at the same time, necessitates a certain amount of 'psychological preparation,' extending over an appreciably long period."[129] The 500+ who saw Christ did not have this time to prepare.

Hallucinations also require that the seer intensely wants to believe what they come to see . . . the disciples certainly didn't believe and weren't waiting in excited anticipation to see the risen Christ. Day pointed out that, "We may recognize the slowness with which the disciples arrive at a conviction to which only the inexorable logic of facts led them."[130] They needed to concretely touch and see the physically risen Christ before they were willing to believe in the reality of His resurrection . . . this is exactly what they got, and it is these concrete appearances that changed their thinking and lives forever. From that moment on, they were set on fire for Christ. The skeptical scholar Adolf Harnack, admitted this fact, saying, "The firm confidence of the disciples in Jesus was rooted in the belief that He did not abide in death, but was raised by God. That Christ was risen was, in virtue of what they had experienced in Him, certainly only after they had seen Him, just as sure as the fact of His death, and became the main article of their preaching about Him."[131]

Hillyer Straton further added that "Men who were subject to hallucinations never become moral heroes."[132] T.J. Thornburn observed that hallucinations have never "stimulated people to undertake a work of enormous magnitude, and while carrying it out, to lead lives of the most rigid and consistent self-denial, and even suffering. In a word, we are constrained to agree with Dr. Sanday, who says, 'No apparition, no mere hallucination of the senses, ever yet moved the world.'"[133] Yet this is exactly what the resurrection witnesses of Christ did . . . they turned the world upside down with the preaching of the resurrection news.

The hallucination theory is simply wishful thinking for those trying to destroy the fact of Christ's resurrection. George Hanson observed that, "The simple faith of the Christian who believes in the Resurrection is nothing compared to the credulity of the skeptic who will accept the wildest and most improbable romances rather than admit the plain witness of historical certainties."[134]

THE TRANSFORMATION OF SAUL INTO PAUL

Dr. J.P. Moreland said, "Another piece of circumstantial evidence is that there were hardened skeptics who didn't believe in Jesus before his crucifixion—and were to some degree dead-set against Christianity, who turned around and adopted the Christian faith after Jesus' death. There's no good reason for this apart from them having experienced the resurrected Christ."[135] I've already mentioned the changes in the lives of skeptics like Thomas the disciple and James, the brother of Jesus, but perhaps the most striking transformation occurred in the life of Paul.

The dramatic change that occurred in the life of Paul (called Saul before his conversion) is an event that is impossible for resurrection critics to explain away. The conversion of Paul is undoubtedly the greatest moral and mental transformation in world history. As Clarence E. McCartney said, "There are plenty of men who hate Jesus Christ and His Church in the world, today. But not even the worst of them hate Him as bitterly and intensely as Paul hated Him. None of them has said as cruel and false and wicked things about Him as Paul said. None of them has tried to destroy his Church with such desperate energy as Paul did. Yet it was this Christ-hater, this Christian-baiter, this Church-destroyer, this man 'breathing out threatenings and slaughter 'against the Christians, who suddenly became the greatest and most influential friend that Jesus Christ had, or has had, upon the earth; the man from whom comes the most powerful expression of Christian doctrine, and the man whose life affords us the grandest example of fellowship with Christ and consecration to the Cross of Christ!"[136]

McCartney continued, "That the persecuting Saul of Tarsus changed into Paul, the Apostle of Jesus Christ, is a fact of history. You must face it. You must account for it. What changed him? Paul says it was the appearance of the Risen Christ. Jesus raised from the dead and appearing to Paul is a cause sufficient to account for the great effect, the conversion of Paul. Anything less than that will not account for it. Therefore, the conversion of Paul, and the great life which followed that conversion, bears witness to the fact of the resurrection."[137]

Bernard Ramm added concerning Paul that, "The leading foe of the Christian faith who called himself a blasphemer, persecutor and insulter (I Tim 1:13), is miraculously converted to Christianity by the personal manifestation of Christ to him. He then becomes Christianity's greatest apostle, missionary and theologian. All efforts to account for Paul by explaining his conversion medically or psychologically are inadequate . . . The conversion of the great apostle is a singular and remarkable proof both of the supernatural in the New Testament, and the reality of Christ's resurrection."[138]

The great historian Philip Schaff had this to say about the complete transformation that occurred in Paul's life, "The transformation of the most dangerous persecutor into the most successful promoter of Christianity is nothing less than a miracle of divine grace. It rests on the greater miracle of the resurrection of Christ. Both are inseparably connected; without the resurrection the conversion would have been impossible, and on the other hand the conversion of such a man and with such results is one of the strongest proofs of the resurrection. The haughty, self-righteous, intolerant, raging Pharisee was changed into a humble, penitent, grateful, loving servant of Jesus. He threw away self-righteousness, learning, influence, power, prospects, and cast in his lot with a small, despised sect at the risk of his life. If there ever was an honest, unselfish, radical, and effective change of conviction and conduct, it was that of Saul of Tarsus.

While the older apostles were devoted friends of Jesus, Paul was his enemy, bent at the very time of the great change on an errand of cruel persecution, and therefore in a state of mind most unlikely to give birth to a vision so fatal to his present object and his future career. How could a fanatical persecutor of Christianity, "breathing threatenings and slaughter against the disciples of the Lord," stultify and contradict himself by an imaginative conceit which tended to the building up of that very religion which he was laboring to destroy!"[139]

Paul was undoubtedly the most hostile non-believer who saw the risen Christ, and was the chief persecutor of the early church. He hated Christians with a passion and enjoyed killing and imprisoning them (Acts 8:3, 9:1). *Why would the chief persecutor of the early church have been willing to face beatings, stonings, mockery, imprisonment (plus other torture . . . II Corinthians 11:24–27) and finally beheading to spread the false message of a dead man that he hated?* History proclaims that this Christian killer spread the gospel (good news) of the resurrection of Christ from the grave to the heart of Rome, the greatest empire the world has ever known. What caused such an immediate, bold and lasting change in the heart of the Christian killer? Again, the only reasonable explanation is that he must have seen the risen Savior just as he claimed.

PERSONAL TESTIMONIES FROM RESURRECTION RESEARCHERS

There has been much study done on the reality of the conversion of Paul. Two able young scholars, Gilbert West and Lord Lyttleton, were determined to attack two events basic to the Christian faith— the conversion of Paul and the resurrection of Christ, and then write a book to destroy Christianity. After years of study, they met to discuss their findings. Both were sheepish because they had come independently to similar and shocking conclusions. Lyttleton found, on examination, that Saul of Tarsus did become a radically new man through his conversion to Christianity, and West found that the evidence pointed unmistakably toward the fact that Christ did rise from the dead. (The book they wrote is entitled, *Observations on the History and Evidences of the Resurrection of Jesus Christ.*[140] You can still find their book in a large library if you need more proof than I've given.)

A lawyer, Frank Morrison was another who made it his life goal to prove that Jesus could not have risen from the dead. After many years of examining the evidence, researching history books and exploring the various alternative theories for the empty tomb, he concluded that the Bible was correct. Jesus really did rise again in supernatural power on the third day, just as He claimed. Morrison's conclusion drove him to become a Christian. If you're curious, Morrison wrote his analysis of the resurrection in the form of a best-selling book called, *Who Moved the Stone?*[141]

Sir Edmund Clarke, a British High Court judge, proclaimed, following his personal investigation of the Resurrection case, "To me, the evidence is conclusive, and over and over again in the High Court, I have secured the verdict on evidence not nearly so compelling. As a lawyer, I accept the gospel evidence unreservedly as the testimony of truthful men to facts that they were able to substantiate."[142]

Sir Lionel Luckhoo, a brilliant lawyer (whose impressive string of 245 consecutive murder acquittals earned him a place in *The Guinness Book of World Records* as the world's most successful lawyer[143]), conducted a rigorous analysis of evidence for the Resurrection, and finally concluded after several years that, "I say unequivocally that the evidence for the Resurrection of Jesus Christ is so overwhelming that it compels acceptance by proof which leaves absolutely no room for doubt."[144]

The great physiologist Dr. A.C. Ivy boldly proclaimed his faith when he said, "I believe in the bodily resurrection of Jesus Christ . . . I am not ashamed to let the world know what I believe, and than I can intelligently defend my belief."[145]

Dr. Craig Blomberg, nationally renowned as one of the great scholars, has spent many years researching the truth of the gospels, and when asked if his efforts have strengthened or destroyed his faith in God, Jesus and the Bible, replied, "It has strengthened them, no question. I know from my own research that there's very strong evidence for the trustworthiness of the gospel accounts."[146]

Dr. Blomberg continued, "I'll tell you this; there are plenty of stories of scholars in the New Testament field who have not been Christians, yet through their study of these very issues have come to faith in Christ. And there have been countless more scholars, already believers, whose faith has been made stronger, more solid, more grounded, because of the evidence—and that's the category I fall into."[147]

At age 84, Dr. Bruce Metzger, still one the most prominent and highly respected Bible scholars in the world, has been the author or editor of over 50 books. When asked what several decades of intense scholarship and delving research into the minute details of the historical accuracy of the New Testament have done to his personal faith, Dr. Metzger confidently responded, "It has increased the basis of my personal faith to see the firmness with which these materials have come down to us, with a multiplicity of copies, some of which are very, very ancient. I've asked questions all my life, I've dug into the text, I've studied this (historical accuracy of the Bible) thoroughly, and today, I know with confidence that my trust in Jesus has been well placed . . . *very* well placed."[148]

Dr. Edwin M. Yamauchi, professor at Miami University in Oxford, Ohio, has spent more than 40 years of his life researching the facts of ancient history and archaeology. When questioned how his 4+ decades of research have affected his faith, Dr. Yamauchi boldly stated, "For me, the historical evidence has reinforced my commitment to Jesus Christ as the Son of God who loves us and died for us and was raised from the dead. It's that simple."[149]

Many other men and women throughout human history have attempted to disprove the facts of the resurrection in hopes of crushing Christianity, but none have succeeded. The honest seekers have found that "The burden of unbelief is too great to carry,"[150] and have discovered the reality of the Resurrection along with eminent scholars Norman Geisler and Henry Morris. Geisler summarized the evidence by saying, "Evidence for the resurrection of Christ is compelling. There are more documents, more eyewitnesses, and more corroborative evidence than for any other historical event of ancient history. The secondary, supplementary evidence is convincing; when combined with the direct evidence, it presents a towering case for the physical resurrection of Christ. In legal terminology, it is "beyond all reasonable doubt."[151] Morris said, "The fact of the resurrection is the most important event of history and therefore, appropriately is one of the most certain facts in all history."[152] If you haven't been convinced of this truth yet, you will, if you wish to research the evidence even deeper.

CHAPTER 11

Do You Want Eternal Life and Love?

The Risen Christ's Offer of Eternal Life

In chapters 1–8, I've demonstrated that this world did not evolve by pure chance from non-intelligent, lifeless matter that came from nothing and nowhere, but that it was indeed created by an intelligent Creator. Chapter 9 established the fact that the God of the Bible is the only possible Creator, since the Bible has been shown to be the only completely reliable, God-written book in the world. And as we saw in the last chapter, the irrefutable fact of history is that Jesus Christ lives, making Him the only person in human history to rise from the grave. The well proven bodily resurrection of Christ makes Him superior to the founders of all cults and religions. It also substantiates all His teachings and everything He said about Himself in the reliable Bible. In this final chapter, I'd like to further consider the importance of the resurrection of Christ . . . more specifically, I'd like to explore the eternal and personal significance of this astounding fact of history.

The cumulative weight of evidence leads us to believe that God exists as the Creator of the Universe, that His Word, the Bible can be trusted and that Jesus is Who He claimed to be . . . the resurrected God and Savior of humanity. But once you've acknowledged these

327

facts, is that the end? Does God just do His own thing and you do yours? Did He create you to live, die and decay as part of an endless biological cycle? Is the grave all you have to look forward to? Don't you want to believe there is more than this? Fortunately, there is more . . . much more.

Through Jesus Christ, God the Father revealed the Savior of the world and the only way to eternal life. Although history overwhelmingly points to Christ as the one and only resurrected Savior, receiving this eternal life still requires faith on your part that He is your personal Savior. Simply believing the historical fact that He died on the cross and rose from the grave is not enough . . . you must believe that His death and resurrection was personal, and was accomplished as the payment for your sins so that you may live forever.

I realize that some of this may be difficult to understand, but I promise to explain it in more detail later. Before explaining in more detail how you can claim eternal life, I must expose the one that wants to rip away the possibility of eternal life in a perfect place before you can claim it.

Satan's Eternal Offer

Satan (who exists as surely as God) is the one who wants to rip this unclaimed eternal life from you, and he hates you with a fiery passion. He makes Ted Bundy, Charles Manson, Osama bin Laden and Sadaam Hussein combined seem like a soft teddy bear. Put bluntly, he wants to do much more than rip your heart out and stuff it down your throat . . . in fact, it would give him great pleasure to watch you consciously scream in agony as your flesh burns forever. Zechariah 14:12 and Revelation 14:9–11 give a vivid description of what Satan wants you to experience. Ultimately Satan wants you to join him eternally in a place of endless torment called Hell.

To get you there, he will try to deceive you into trading eternal ecstasy for short-term power, pleasure and riches on earth. He wants to make your life so busy, confusing and full of temptation that you don't even have time to think about what God is offering you. Improper sexual thoughts, mind and body controlling drugs and alcohol, God-defaming media, etc . . . are just some of the many weapons he unleashes against humanity. He uses the desire for wealth (not money to pay the bills; God knows we need it—Matt.6:32), increased power and pleasure to motivate your actions. He uses your natural desires in trying to lull you to sleep and make you forget your Creator. Satan's tactics are very deceptive and effective at ripping you away from God before you even truly know Him.

His ultimate goal is for you to die before gaining eternal life. He knows that death without God ends all hope of eternal life in a perfect place called Heaven. He also knows that death following the acceptance of Christ as Savior is only the beginning of a wonderful life that never ends. Don't accept Satan's offer of eternal hatred, agony filled torment and forever separation from God. Hold onto something that lasts longer than a lifetime. God offers a life that never ends in a place where love never dies. He displayed His love for you and the only way to eternal life in a perfect place through the sacrifice of Jesus Christ . . .

The Definiton of True Love

To see true love, you must look to a rugged Roman cross and consider, for a few moments, the path your Savior, Jesus Christ, walked for you almost 2,000 years ago in the hours leading up to and including His crucifixion on the lonely hill of Calvary. The night before the crucifixion, He sweat great drops of blood in Gethsemane as He thought about the torture ahead. (Sweating blood is an actual medical condition called Hematidrosis that occurs under extreme agony, and involves the diffusion of small amounts of blood from miniscule capillaries into sweat glands . . . medical expert Dr. Alexander Metherell said the bleeding from this condition would also "set up the skin to be extremely fragile so that when Jesus was flogged by the Roman soldiers the next day, his skin would be very, very sensitive")[1] He was then betrayed by Judas Iscariot and the rest of His disciples as they fled from Him at His arrest.

Following a series of mocking interrogations, which sent Him around Jerusalem like a pinball, He was finally condemned to death at the request of the crowd to "Crucify Him!" Completely alone, He was scourged by Pontius Pilate, as the crowd cheered. (The Roman scourging whip included long, dumbbell-shaped and lashing pieces of bone, lead and/or other metals, which would greatly lacerate human flesh. Dr. Metherell explained that as a result of scourging, "The back would be so shredded that part of the spine was sometimes exposed by the deep, deep cuts. The whipping would have gone all the way from the shoulders down to the back, the buttocks and the back of the legs. It was just terrible. One physician who has studied Roman beatings said 'As the flogging continued, the lacerations would tear into the underlying skeletal muscles and produce quivering ribbons of bleeding flesh.' A 3rd century historian by the name of Eusebius described a flogging by saying, 'The sufferer's veins were laid bare, tendons were crushed, and . . . the very muscles, sinews and bowels of the victim were open to exposure.'")[2]

After the scourging, He was stripped by soldiers, and a crown of thorns was placed on His head. He was mocked, spit upon and beaten on the head several times with a hard, wooden staff similar to a baseball bat. Each blow drove the crown of thorns deeper into His temples, sending small streams of blood down His face. He was then taken to Golgotha ('place of the skull') to be crucified. The cross was erected between two thieves, who were also mocking Him. The nails were then driven through His hands and feet. [(The Romans drove 5–7 inch long spikes through the wrists and feet, to pin the sufferer to the cross. As the nails were driven through the wrists and feet, it crushed the main nerves running to the hand (called the median nerve) and several nerves running to the feet. When asked to describe how painful this would be, Dr. Metherell said, "Let me put it this way . . . do you know the kind of pain you feel when you bang your elbow and hit the funny bone (ulna nerve)? It's extremely painful when you accidentally hit it. Well, imagine taking a pair of pliers and squeezing and crushing that nerve. The effect would be similar to what Jesus experienced.")][3]

As the day wore on, hunger set in, breathing became more labored, the sun began to burn bare skin, and as His muscles sagged from exhaustion, the nails began to tear flesh from bone, sending shockwaves of excruciating pain up His spinal cord. The scabs on His back were ripped off as His body bled and screamed in pain each time a splinter from the rugged cross would drive into His back. (Upon the cross, Dr. Metherell said Jesus' "arms would have immediately been stretched, probably six inches in length, and both shoulders would have become dislocated."[4] Metherell, now a Christian, explained that, "This fulfilled the Old Testament prophecy in Psalms 22, which foretold the Crucifixion hundreds of years before it took place, and says, 'My bones are out of joint.'"[5] Dr. Metherell continued by saying, "crucifixion is essentially an agonizingly slow death by asphyxiation. The reason is that the stresses on the muscles and diaphragm put the chest into the inhaled position; basically, in order to exhale, the individual must push up on his feet so the tension on the muscles would be eased for a moment. In doing so, the nail would tear through the foot, eventually locking against the tarsal bones. After managing to exhale, the person would be able to relax down and take another breath in. Again, he'd have to push himself up to exhale, scraping his bloodied back against the coarse wood of the cross. This would go

on and on until complete exhaustion would take over, and the person wouldn't be able to push up and breathe anymore.")[6]

Frederick W. Farrar described a crucifixion this way, "For indeed a death by crucifixion seems to include all that pain and death can have of horrible and ghastly—dizziness, cramp, thirst, starvation, sleeplessness, traumatic fever, tetanus, shame, publicity of shame, long continuance of torment, horror of anticipation, mortification of untended wounds—all intensified just up to the point at which they can be endured by all, but all stopping just short of the point which would give to the sufferer the relief of unconsciousness. The unnatural position made every movement painful; the lacerated veins and crushed tendons throbbed with incessant anguish; the wounds inflamed by exposure, gradually gangrened; the arteries—especially at the head and stomach—became swollen and oppressed with surcharged blood; and while each variety of misery went on gradually increasing, there was added to them the intolerable pang of a burning and raging thirst; and all these physical complications caused an internal excitement and anxiety, which made the prospect of death itself—of death, the unknown enemy, at whose approach man usually shudders most—bear the aspect of a delicious and exquisite release."[7]

In death, a spear was driven through His side. To this, Dr. Metherell added, "Even before he died—and this is important too—the hypovelemic shock would have caused a sustained rapid heart rate that would have contributed to heart failure, resulting in the collection of fluid in the membrane around the heart, called a pericardial effusion, as well as around the lungs, which is called a pleural effusion. The spear apparently went through the right lung and into the heart, so when the spear was pulled out, some fluid—the pericardial effusion and pleural effusion—came out. This would have the appearance of a clear fluid, like water, followed by a large volume of blood, as the eyewitness John described in his gospel."[8]

When asked to describe the depth of Christ's suffering before and during the Crucifixion, Dr. Metherell said, "The pain was absolutely unbearable . . . in fact, it was literally beyond words to describe; they had to invent a new word: excruciating. Literally, excruciating means, 'out of the cross.' Think about that . . . they needed to create a new word, because there was nothing in the language that could describe the intense anguish caused during the crucifixion."[9]

Yet, despite this unbearable physical and mental anguish, Jesus was able to utter to those who crucified Him, "Father forgive." (When asked why Jesus would be willing to endure such an agonizing death on the cross, Dr. Metherell concluded, "So when you ask what motivated Him, well . . . . I suppose the answer can be summed up in one word—and that would be *love*.")[10] Jesus willingly endured the pain of the cross for **you**—because He loves and wants to forgive you of your sins, if you will only ask. He came to die, yet He lives, to become "the Way," the way for you to live . . . . forever.

Can you honestly look into the imagined face of this suffering Savior, and say that you hate Him . . . that you are ashamed of Him? Will you love Him? He loves you.

How Can You Claim Eternal Life and Love?

The love described above is great indeed, but God offers you more than His love—He offers eternal life wrapped in the presence of this great love. How can you be certain that you will be among those who live eternally wrapped in the presence of God's great love? *TO SECURE ETERNAL LIFE AND LOVE . . . YOU MUST HUMBLY ADMIT YOU'RE AN IMPERFECT SINNER, BELIEVE WITH ALL YOUR HEART THAT JESUS DIED ON THE CROSS FOR YOU TO PAY THE DEATH PENALTY FOR YOUR SINS AND IN FAITH ASK HIS FORGIVENESS FOR THOSE SINS.* As demonstrated by the reality of the resurrection, Jesus is indeed the only God and Savior of humanity, as He claimed. As the only God and Savior, He is certainly powerful enough to forgive your sins and give you eternal life.

At this point, some of you may still be questioning whether you are really a "sinner." Simply put, unless you're perfect like God, you're a sinner (Romans 3:23). Some may say, 'Okay, I accept the fact that I am not perfect, but what does it mean to be a sinner . . . further, what is sin and why is it so terrible?' Sin is a terrible act that is the cause of moral decay in society, physical death and a hard life involving back breaking work, sickness and disease. Before Adam sinned in the Garden of Eden, sin was a foreign concept and all of creation was perfect. After his sin, all of creation was, and still is plagued with pain, sickness, disease, death, harmful insects and weeds, poisonous animals, school shootings, rampant pornography, terrorism and every other form of natural and moral decay. God promised that, as a result of the original sin of Adam, ". . . the whole creation (would) groan and travail together in pain until now"[11] (Romans 8:22). The imperfections we see in creation are evidence that God's warning is true.

As a result of sin, all of creation is winding down like a giant clock, just as God said in Isaiah 51:6. Creation is growing old like a worn piece of clothing . . . the natural resources of Earth are being quickly depleted. Oil, for example, is estimated to be gone within 50 years, natural gas will be eliminated in 60 years, and all known coal resources will be used by 2225. For more evidence that Earth's clock is ticking as a result of sin, consider that the rotation of the planet has been shown to be slowing about 1.7 seconds per year since 1900, and the sun, as time passes, will become a giant red star, then a supergiant and eventually a supernova explosion. As it enlarges, its diameter will eclipse Earth, burning the planet to a cinder. (Interestingly, burning everything to a cinder is what God will do to this planet when forming a new Heaven and Earth, as described in the book of Revelation.)

Sin is certainly a terrible thing. All humans, beginning with Adam and including you, have sinned, and because of this, creation is imperfect, and all humans are cursed to death and eternal separation from God. But there is a way to avoid this agony-filled death curse and forever separation from a perfect, Holy God, who cannot be in the presence of sin. To avoid the awful and eternal penalty of sin, you must ask God to forgive you for everything you've done wrong . . . you must ask Him to forgive your sins. This is the only way for you to appear blameless before a perfect God. By believing Jesus died for *your* sins, the barrier—sin—between you and God is removed forever, and you are immediately given eternal life. Jesus' death is the bridge that crosses 'Sin Canyon' and gives you immediate and eternal access to the one and only God of the Universe.

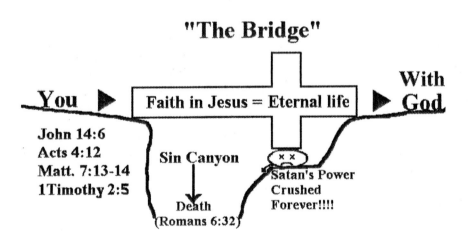

God is giving you a great deal. The eternal life He offers is a free gift; you don't have to and can't do anything to earn it. Being a 'good person' won't save you. (Ephesians 2:8–9) There are no strings attached. Jesus has already paid the price for this gift, so you need

334

8192

only accept it. If you believe that Jesus' death is more than a well proven historical fact, but that He died to wash away the penalty of *your sins*, then you have eternal life—it's as simple as that (John 3:16). It may seem too good to be true, but it's not. If you consider what He's already done (created this awesome world, rose from the grave, etc . . .), it's not hard at all to believe that He can give you eternal life. Jesus is the only hope we have beyond death. I don't know about you, but I'm going to cling to that hope.

What's Next After Eternal Life is Secured?

Faith in Jesus as your personal Savior is more than a feeling—it's a hope and a confidence that remains with you. "Faith is the substance of things hoped for, the evidence of things not seen"[12] (Heb.11:1). With faith, you can boldly look forward to your future, because there are great things ahead. You can be confident that Heaven, as your eternal home, is a place far better than your best dreams (I Corinthians 2:9). (Consider that it took God just 6 days to create all the natural wonders we see around us. He has been preparing an eternal home for almost 2000 years, so we can't even imagine what a wonderful place it will be.)

Even after eternal life is secured, Satan will try to deceive you and make your life miserable. He will tempt you to spend the rest of your earthly life running away from what you need the most—an intimate, personal relationship with Jesus Christ . . . the Lord, Creator and God of this universe. Resist Satan, and he will flee from you (James 4:7). Seize not only eternal life, but the new life Jesus offers. This new life on earth is filled with true satisfaction, eternal joy, hope and peace. Let me tell a true story which beautifully illustrates the unstoppable hope you can have even in the worst trials of life . . .

Philip was an 8 year old child with Downs Syndrome. Because he was different, the other children in his Sunday school class shied away from him. One day, the teacher gave each child a plastic Easter egg that broke apart in the middle. She asked each to find something that is a symbol of new life. One little girl got a flower, another a butterfly. Everyone in the class oohed and aahed. Finally the teacher opened the last egg. It was empty. Everyone laughed. In tears, Philip tugged at the teacher's dress, and struggled to say, "I . . . I did it . . . an empty tomb . . . my new life in Jesus." The room fell silent, and then all the children embraced Philip.

Philip's parents knew that he would live a short life . . . there were just too many things wrong with his small body. That summer, Philip faced death courageously and filled with the hope of eternal life He had through Christ. On his grave, his Sunday school friends laid several empty plastic Easter eggs in memory of the hope Philip had. Since Philip believed that Jesus died on the cross for his sins, was buried and rose again, he was able to live a life and die a death filled with hope, freedom and joy, for he knew that not even death could take away the new life Jesus had given him. (I Corinthians 15:54–57)

This new life Jesus offers is not always easy. God promised life would be hard, so we shouldn't be surprised when it is. Some may lose everything, and God may seem unfair, but who are we to question God, the awesome Creator of the Universe? Please read Job 26:14, 37:5, Psalms 145:3, 147:5, Jeremiah 32:17, 10:12, Isaiah 41:4, 46:11, 48:13, and 55:8–11. He is *GOD*, and has always been in control. We need to trust Him, no matter how bad it gets.

But, no matter how bad it gets, God has promised to be there. The trials and tribulations of this life can't compare with the joy, hope, peace, eternal security and love you have when you believe in Him. You could have your hands and feet cut off, eyes plucked out, be inflicted with 10,000 diseases, and be forced to live in a garbage dumpster . . . still the joys of Heaven will be infinitely greater. The harder your life, the sweeter Heaven will be. (Romans 8:18)

How To Have An Intimate, Personal Relationship With God

The chief purpose of life is to have an intimate, personal relationship with your Savior, Jesus Christ. This relationship can lead to indescribable and unparalleled peace, joy and hope. Jesus doesn't just save you, and then abandon you . . . He wants to give you these indescribable gifts. He also wants to be at the center of your life as an endless source of comfort. I challenge you to take the time to get to know Jesus as your Savior, very best Friend and constant Companion.

336

Invite Him into your heart and ask Him to give you the eternal peace, joy and hope that only He can give. If you're willing to invite Him into your life and truly know Him, you will be positively transformed both now and forever.

How can you know Him? . . . by talking with Him through prayer, which is your hotline to God, and by reading the Bible, which is His love letter to you. Let me give you a general overview of the Bible— its message is simple. There is one problem . . . sin . . . and one solution . . . the Savior Jesus Christ, which unify the pages of the Bible from Genesis to Revelation. Christ is the central figure of the Bible. In the Old Testament, Christ is prophesied; in the Gospels, He is revealed as God in the flesh, to the world; in the Acts and Epistles,

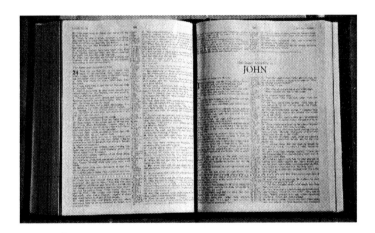

His gospel is spread and explained, and in Revelation, the end of the age is revealed with Christ glorified as King.

To think that this continuous revelation, which confronts some of the most controversial subjects in human history, was harmoniously recorded by 40+ men from various backgrounds over a 1,400 year period is incredible evidence of a Supreme Author. (Old Testament recorders alone admit 3,808 times that they are only human instruments that God used to write His inspired Word.) The Bible is a unique book, because it has a unique Author. I suggest that you begin reading this intriguing book in the Gospels . . . Matthew, Mark,

Luke and John, continue through the New Testament, and then return to the Old Testament later. I hope this helps.

God, through His Word, can stir your heart, *if you let Him,* more than I ever could. If you seriously *study* the Bible, *believing* it to be true, realizing that it is the word of God, written through man, and for man, an indescribable feeling of peace, joy and hope will begin to enter your life.

All God wants is a chance to give you eternal life in a perfect place where love never dies . . . if you haven't already done so, will you give Him that chance now? Will you dare to believe that God's promise is true? Will you cling to Jesus for eternal life, as your only hope? . . . for life without Christ is a hopeless end . . . life with Christ is an endless hope. The French philosopher Pascal said, "The evidence of God's existence and His gift (eternal life through Jesus Christ) is more than compelling, but those who insist that they have no need of Him will always find ways to discount the offer."[13] Please do not discount God's offer . . . at least give Him the chance to give you an incredible eternal future. Will you give God a chance or will you deny His promised gift and accept the eternal agony and hatred that Satan offers?

Now is the moment of truth. What is your verdict? . . . if you've chosen to love Jesus Christ, and trust in Him for your salvation from sin, then all you have to do is simply believe, standing strong through whatever trials life may throw at you, and join the mighty army of Christians who are "Looking for that blessed hope and the glorious appearing of the great God and Savior Jesus Christ."[14] (Titus 2:13)

48 Old Testament Prophecies Fulfilled By Jesus Christ Alone

O.T. Prophecy	N.T. Fulfillment	Subject
BIRTH		
1) Isaiah 7:14/	Matthew 1:22, 23 /	Born of a virgin (Esias is Isaiah)
2) Genesis 3:15/	Galatians 4:4 /	Born from the seed of a woman
3) Micah 5:2/	Matthew 2:1, 5, 6 /	Born in Bethlehem
4) Psalms 2:7/	Matthew 3:17 /	Born the Son of God
5) Psalms 132:11,/ Jeremiah 23:5/	John 7:42, Matthew 1:1 /	Seed of David
6) Genesis 22:18/	Matthew 1:1, Gal. 3:16/	Seed of Abraham
7) Genesis 21:12/	Luke 3:23, 34 /	Son of Isaac
8) Numbers 24:17/	Luke 3:23, 34 /	Son of Jacob
9) Isaiah 11:1/	Luke 3:23, 32 /	Family line of Jesse
10) Genesis 49:10/	Matthew 2:6 /	Born of the Tribe of Judah

11) Psalms 72:10–15 /

               Matthew 2:1, 11 /   Presented w/gifts at birth

12) Daniel 9:24–26 /

               Luke 2:1 /   Birth and death dates

LIFE

13) Hosea 11:1 /	Matthew 2:15 /	To live in Egypt
14) Isaiah 40:3 /	Matthew 3:3 /	John the Baptist will come before Him
15) Isaiah 9:1, 2 /	Matthew 4:12–16, 23 /	Light to Zebulon and Naphtali
16) Isaiah 61:1–2 /	Luke 4:16–21, 43 /	Good News proclaimed
17) Isaiah 42:1–3 /	Matthew 12:17–21 /	Relationship to Gentiles
18) Psalms 78:2 /	Matthew 13:35 /	Secrets to be told
19) Psalms 110:1 /	Matthew 22:43–45 /	Will be called Lord
20) Duet. 18:18 /	Matthew 21:11 /	Will be a prophet
21) Isaiah 33:22 /	John 5:30 /	Will be a Judge
22) Psalms 118:22/	I Peter 2:7 /	Will be the cornerstone

DEATH

23) Zechariah 9:9 /	Matthew 21:4–5 /	To enter Jerusalem on a donkey
24) Psalms 41:9 /	Matthew 10:4:26:47 /	Betrayed by a friend
25) Zechariah 11:12 /	Matthew 26:15 /	Sold for 30 pieces of silver
26) Zechariah 11:13 /	Matthew 27:5 /	Money thrown in God's house

27) Zechariah 13:6–7 /

                   Matthew 26:31, 56 /   His followers
to scatter

28) Psalms 22:18 /   Matthew 27:35 /   Lots cast for
clothing

29) Zechariah 12:10 /

                   John 19:34, 37 /   Body to be pierced

30) Psalms 34:20 /   John 19:33–36 /   No bones broken

31) Isaiah 53:3 /   John 19:5 /   Despised by men

32) Isaiah 53:5 /   I Peter 2:24;
                   Matt.20:28 /   Crushed for
our sins

33) Psalms 35:19, 69:4 /

                   John 15:25 /   Hated without
a cause

34) Psalms. 22:7,109:25 /

                   Matt.27:39,
                   Mark 15:29 /   Mocked in death

35) Isaiah 53:7 /   Matt.27:12–14,
                   Acts 8:32 /   Silent before
accusers

36) Isaiah 53:12 /   Matt.27:38,
                   Mark 15:28 /   Viewed as a
criminal

37) Isaiah 50:6 /   Matthew 26:67 /   Smitten and
spit upon

38) Psalms 22:16 /   Luke 23:33 /   Hands and
feet pierced

39) Isaiah 53:12 /   Luke 23:34;
                   Matt. 26:28 /   Prayed for
persecutors

40) Psalms 38:11 /   Luke 23:49 /   Friends will
stand afar off

41) Psalms 22:17 /   Luke 23:35 /   Stared upon

42) Psalms 69:21 /   John 19:28;
                   Matt. 27:34/   To suffer thirst

43) Psalms 31:5 /   Luke 23:46 /   Committed to
God the Father

44) Psalms 22:14 /	John 19:34 /	Heart burst from agony
45) Amos 8:9 /	Matthew 27:45 /	Darkness to cover the land
46) Isaiah 53:9 /	Matthew 27:57–60 /	Buried in rich man's tomb

RESURRECTION AND ASCENSION

47) Psalms 16:10 /	Acts 2:31 /	Predicted resurrection
48) Psalms 68:18 /	Acts 1:9 /	Will ascend in glory

An Apologetic Outline From Creation to Beyond the Cross

(Christian apologetics is not an "apology" for the truth, but is a defense of Christianity in a postmodern world that opposes truth. As you've discovered in this book, there are many solid reasons to believe in the truth of Christianity . . . it is a defendable faith that is firmly founded upon facts. For your convenience, I've created a simple apologetic outline that summarizes the major logical steps which I've used in this book and which you can use in your defense of Christianity before family, friends, co-workers and others that you associate with.)

1) Evolution is a faith, not a fact because:

    a) The well proven scientific 2nd Law of Thermodynamics directly opposes it

    b) It is statistically and scientifically impossible for life to arise by chance from non-life

    c) It is unreasonable to believe that this incredibly complex and intricately ordered world is the product of lifeless, non-intelligent matter that came from nothing and nowhere

d) The flimsy "finds" of evolutionists make their theory even more doubtful

e) No conclusive transitional fossils have been found in the fossil record . . . these fossils would exist if evolution were true

f) The evidence indicates that we live in a young world

g) The mechanisms of natural selection and mutation fail to explain macroevolution

h) Many former and current evolutionists have admitted the serious flaws and failures of the theory . . . if they doubt their own theory, then why should we believe it?

2) Since evolution is not a fact, and no other conceivable theory has the slightest bit of scientific evidence, Creation is the only viable explanation for our existence

   a) This conclusion is not accepted simply by default since the fact of creation is well- evidenced by the incredibly complex and intricately ordered design that exists from the Universal to the sub-cellular level

3) Since this intricate world was created, there must exist an Intelligent Creator who designed it

4) The intelligent Creator must be the God of the Bible since

   a) The Bible has proven to be the most reliable and only God-written book in the world, as evidenced by historical archaeology, textual criticism and fulfilled prophecy

5) Jesus has proven the truth of His claim to be the only God and Savior of humanity through His exemplary, sinless, miraculous life and bodily resurrection from the grave, which no other man or woman has accomplished

6) The reality of Jesus' supernatural bodily resurrection is demonstrated by, among other things,

  a) The certainty of the New Testament historical record
  b) The confirmation of many New Testament historical facts by ancient secular writings
  c) The lack of any denials by ancient witnesses
  d) The superior safety precautions in place during Christ's death and burial
  e) The undeniable empty tomb, which cannot be explained by any natural cause
  f) The incredible transformation of the disciples, early Christians and enemies of Christ, such as Saul in the face of intense persecution and death
  g) The fact that Christianity exists

7) Since God the Creator really does exist, the God of the Bible is the only possible Creator, the Bible alone is reliable, and Jesus is the only proven God and Savior of humanity, the eternal life He offers is an attainable reality for anyone who places their faith in Him as the ultimate sacrifice for their sins.

Recommended Reading

(From the literature I researched prior to writing this book, I would highly recommend that you read the following books and log on to the following websites for your further personal research. Certainly, this list is not exhaustive . . . there are many more references that confirm what I've said in this book. Except for the Bible, which is by far the most important and reliable, there is no order of preference.)

1) The Bible
2) Answers in Genesis website: *www.answersingenesis.org/*
3) Behe, Michael J.1996. Darwin's Black Box—The Biochemical Challenge to Evolution. The Free Press, A Division of Simon and Schuster Inc., New York, NY., 307pp.
4) Christian Answers Network website—christiananswers.net/
5) DeYoung, Donald B. 1989. Astronomy and the Bible: Questions and Answers. Baker Books, Grand Rapids, Mich., 146pp.
6) Evans, Tony. 1994. Our God is Awesome: Encountering the Greatness of Our God. Moody Press, Chicago. 383pp.
7) Foxe, John, rewritten and updated by Harold J. Chadwick. 2001. The New Foxe's Book of Martyrs. Bridge-Logos Publishers, Gainesville, FL., 442pp.

8) Geisler, Norman and Ron Brooks. 1990. When Skeptics Ask: A Handbook on Christian Evidences. Baker Books, Grand Rapids, Mich. 348 pp.
9) Geisler, Norman L. 1998. Baker Encyclopedia of Christian Apologetics. Baker Books, Grand Rapids, MI. 820pp.
10) Geisler, Norman L. and Ron Rhodes. 1997. When Cultists Ask: A Popular Handbook on Cultic Misinterpretations. Baker Book House, Grand Rapids, Mich. 313pp.
11) Geisler, Norman L. and Thomas Howe. When Critics Ask: A Popular Handbook on Bible Difficulties. Victor Books, a division of Scripture Press Publications, Inc., USA, Canada, England. 580pp.
12) Geisler, Norman L. 1976. Christian Apologetics. Baker Books, Grand Rapids, Mich. 388 pp.
13) Habermas, Gary R. 1996. The Historical Jesus: Ancient Evidence for the Life of Christ. College Press Publishing Company, Joplin, Missouri. 304pp.
14) Ham, Ken. 2000. The Lie: Evolution. Master Books Inc., Green Forest, AR., 185pp.
15) Ham, Ken. 1993. Dinosaurs and the Bible. Answers in Genesis, Florence, KY., 24pp.
16) Ham, Ken. 1998. Is There Really a God? Answers in Genesis, 40pp.
17) Ham, Ken, J. Sarfati and C. Wieland. 2000. The Revised and Expanded Answers Book. Master Books Inc., Green Forest, AR., 274pp.
18) Institute for Creation Research website—www.icr.org/
19) Keller, Werner. 1956. The Bible as History: A Confirmation of the Book of Books. Bantam Books, New York. 515pp. (Second Revised edition published by Barnes and Noble, Inc. by arrangement with William Morrow and Company in 1995.)
20) Kennedy, James D. and Jerry Newcombe. 1994. What if Jesus Had Never Been Born? Thomas Nelson Publishers. 273 pp.
21) Lahaye, Tim and Thomas Ice. 2001. Charting the End Times: A Visual Guide to Understanding Bible Prophecy. Harvest House Publishers, Eugene, Oregon, 141 pp.

22) Martin, Walter, ed. by Hank Hanegraaff. 1997. The Kingdom of the Cults. Bethany House Publishers, Minneapolis, Minnesota, 703 pp.
23) McCartney, Clarence E. 1956. Twelve Great Questions About Christ. Baker Book House, Grand Rapids Michigan.
24) McDowell, Josh. 1999. The New Evidence that Demands a Verdict (Volumes 1 and 2). Thomas Nelson, Inc., Publishers, Nashville, TN. 760pp.
25) McDowell, Josh. 1977. More than a Carpenter. Living Books—Tyndale House Publishers, Inc., Wheaton, IL., 128pp.
26) McDowell, Josh. 2002. Beyond Belief to Convictions. Tyndale House Publishers, Wheaton, Illinois. 322pp.
27) Moreland, J.P. 1987. Scaling the Secular City: A Defense of Christianity. Baker Book House, Grand Rapids, Mich. 275 pp.
28) Morris, John D. 1998. The Young Earth. Master Books, Inc., Green Forest AR. 141pp.
39) Parker, Gary. 1998. Creation—Facts of Life. Master Books, Inc., Green Forest Arkansas. 215pp.
30) Price, Kenneth. 1984. The Eagle Christian. Old Faithful Publishing Company, Wetumpka, AL., 67pp.
31) Ramm, Bernard. 1953. Protestant Christian Evidences. Moody Press, Chicago.
32) Rhodes, Tricia McCary. 1998. Contemplating the Cross: A Pilgrimage of Prayer. Bethany House Publishers, Minneapolis, Minnesota. 189 pp.
33) Sarfati, Jonathan. 1999. Refuting Evolution. Master Books Inc., Green Forest, AR., 274pp.
34) Smith, Roddy and Carol. 2001. The Ultimate Guide to Christian History. Barbour Publishing, Inc., Ulrichsville, Ohio, 435 pp.
35) Strobel, Lee. 1998. The Case for Christ—A Journalists Personal Investigation of the Evidence for Jesus. Zondervan, Grand Rapids, MI. 297pp.

Works Cited and Credited

(A few hundred hours have been spent diligently identifying primary sources, contacting and seeking permission from those sources to use the quotations and some of the facts found in this book. To the best of my knowledge, permission has been granted, where necessary, by the primary sources cited here. If you find that I have improperly cited or credited a source, please contact the publisher and/or author . . . the correction will be made with the next edition.)

Table of Contents

1. DaVinci, Leonardo, as quoted in "Distinctively Human," Moody Discovery Video Series.

Preface

1. Johnson, B.C. 1981. The Atheist Debater's Handbook. Prometheus Books, Buffalo, NY., pg.15.
2. McCartney, Clarence E. 1956. Twelve Great Questions About Christ. Baker Book House, Grand Rapids Michigan, pg. 40.

Chapter 1

1. Permission granted by the Institute for Creation Research

2. Ackerman, Paul D. 1986. It's a Young World After All: Exciting Evidences for Recent Creation. Baker Book House, Grand Rapids, Mich., pg 11.

3. Smith, Robert F., "Origins and Civil Liberties," *Creation Social Science and Humanities Quarterly*, 3 (Winter 1980); 23–24.

4. Bridgman, P.W. 1953. "Reflections on Thermodynamics." *American Scientist*. p.549.

5. Moreland, J.P. 1987. Scaling the Secular City. Baker Book House, Grand Rapids, Mich., pg 37.

6. Asimov, Isaac. "In the Game of Energy and Thermodynamics You Can't Even Break Even," Originally appeared in the Smithsonian Institution Journal (June 1970), p. 6.

7. Geisler, Norman and Ron Brooks. 1996. When Skeptics Ask: A Handbook on Christian Evidences, Baker Books, Grand Rapids, Mich., pg 225.

8. Ross, John. *Chemical and Engineering News*, July 27, 1980, p.40; as cited in Duane Gish, "Creation Scientists Answer Their Critics," Institute for Creation Research, 1993.

9. Asimov, Isaac. "In The Game of Energy and Thermodynamics You Can't Even Break Even," Originally appeared in *Smithsonian* (June 1970) p.6.

10. Asimov, Isaac. Ibid. p. 10.; as cited on pg 82 of the Illustrated Origins Answer Book, 1995. Eden Communications. Gilbert, Arizona.

11. Morris, Henry M. 1967. The Twilight of Evolution. Baker Book House, Grand Rapids, MI. p.35.

12. Parker, Gary. 1994. Facts of Life, (6th ed.—February 1994), Master Books, Green Forest, AR. p.23.

13. See Muncaster, Ralph O. 2003. Dismantling Evolution: Building the Case for Intelligent Design. Harvest House Publishers, Eugene, OR. 254pp.

14. Behe, Michael J. 1996. Darwin's Black Box—The Biochemical Challenge to Evolution. The Free Press, A Division of Simon and Schuster Inc., New York, NY.

15. Ranganathan, B.G. 1998. Origins? The Banner of Truth Trust, Carlisle, PA., p.15.

16. Reprinted by permission of *Nature*, Hoyle, Sir Fred and Chandra Wickramasinghe. "Hoyle on Evolution." *Nature*, November 12, 1981. p.105., Macmillan Publishers Ltd.

17. Hoyle, Wikramasinghe, Ibid.

18. "Continuing Crisis," *American Spectator*, Sept. 1993, p8–9.

19. Sagan, Carl, Francis Crick and L.M. Muchin in Carl Sagan, ed., Communications with Extraterrestrial Intelligence (CETI), Cambridge, MA.: MIT Press, pp45–46.

20. DeYoung, Donald. 1989. Astronomy and the Bible: Questions and Answers. Baker Book House, Grand Rapids, Mich., pg. 37

21. Geisler, N. L., & Geisler, N. L. 1992. *Miracles and the modern mind: A defense of biblical miracles*. Rev. ed. of: Miracles and modern thought. 1982. Baker Book House: Grand Rapids, Mich.

22. Geisler, Norman L. and Paul K. Hoffman, editors. 2001. Why I Am a Christian: Leading Thinkers Explain Why They Believe. Baker Book House, Grand Rapids, Mich.

23. Geisler, Norman and Ron Brooks. 1996. When Skeptics Ask: A Handbook on Christian Evidences, Baker Books, Grand Rapids, Mich., pg 39.

24. From In the Age of Mankind. 1988, p22 by Roger Lewin (Washington, DC: Smithsonian Institution Press) Copyright © by the Smithsonian Institution Press. Used by permission of the publisher.

25. Cosgrove, Mark P. 1987. The Amazing Human Body. Baker Book House, Grand Rapids, MI. pp.106–109.

26. Adler, Jerry and John Carey. "Is Man a Subtle Accident?" *Newsweek*, November 3, 1980.

27. Lubenow, Marvin L. 1992. Bones of Contention, A Creationist Assessment of Human Fossils. Baker Books, Grand Rapids, Mich., pg 7.

28. Lubenow, Marvin L. 1992. Bones of Contention, A Creationist Assessment of Human Fossils. Baker Books, Grand Rapids, Mich., pg.183,199.

29. Morris, Henry M. 1967. The Twilight of Evolution. Baker Book House, Grand Rapids, MI. p.54.

30. Millot, Jacques, "The Coelacanth," *Scientific American*, vol. 193, (December 1955), p.37.

31. Adler, Jerry and John Carey. "Is Man a Subtle Accident?" *Newsweek*, November 3, 1980; Lewin, Roger, "Evolutionary Theory Under Fire." *Science*, November 21, 1980.

32. Singham, Mark. "Teaching and Propaganda," *Physics Today*, vol. 53, June 2000, p.54.

33. Lubenow, Marvin L. 1992. Bones of Contention, A Creationist Assessment of Human Fossils. Baker Books, Grand Rapids, Mich., pg 182.

34. Darwin, C.R. 1872. Origin of Species. 6th ed. John Murray, London, 1902.

35. Simpson, G.G. 1944. Tempo and Mode in Evolution. Columbia University Press, NY., p.106; as cited in Duane T. Gish, Evolution: The Fossils Still Say No! 1995. (El Cajon, CA: Institute for Creation Research) p.334.

36. Kitts, David B. "Paleontology and Evolutionary Theory," *Evolution*, vol. 28, September 1974, p.467.

37. Kay, Marshall and Edwin H. Colbert. 1965. Stratigraphy and Life History. John Wiley and Sons, New York, p.102. Reprinted by permission of John Wiley and Sons, Inc.

38. Barnes, R.S.K., P. Calow, P.J.W. Olive and D.W. Golding. 1993. The Invertebrates: A New Synthesis. Blackwell Scientific, 2nd ed.

39. DuNouy, L. 1947. Human Destiny. The New American Library, New York, p.63.

40. Dawkins, Richard. 1986. The Blind Watchmaker. W.W. Norton and Company, pp.229–230.

41. Geisler, Norman and Ron Brooks. 1996. When Skeptics Ask: A Handbook on Christian Evidences, Baker Books, Grand Rapids, Mich., pg 229.

42. Darwin, Ibid.

43. Gould, Steven J. ed. by J. William Schapf. 1999. The Evolution of Life, chapter 1 in Evolution: Facts and Fallacies. Academic Press, San Diego, CA, p.9. Used by permission of Elsevier.

44. Lee, Robert E. "Radiocarbon Ages in Error," *Anthropological Journal of Canada*, vol. 19, No. 3, 1981, pp.9, 29 as cited in *Creation Research Society Quarterly,* September 1982, 19:117–127.

45. Lubenow, Marvin L. 1992. Bones of Contention, A Creationist Assessment of Human Fossils. Baker Books, Grand Rapids, Mich., pg 247,265.

46. Mackal, R.P. 1987. A Living Dinosaur? In Search of Mokele-Mbembe. E.J. Brill, Leiden, The Netherlands, pp.312–313.

47. Woodward, Scott R. et al. "DNA Sequence from Cretaceous Period Bone Fragments," *Science,* Vol. 266 (November 1994), pp.1229–1232.

48. Bucheim, H.P. and R.C. Surdam. "Fossil Catfish and the Depositional Environment of the Green River Formation." *Geology*, 5(4) p.198.

49. Nilsson, N. Heribert. Sunthetisch Artbildung, pp.1194–1196.

50. Newell, N.O. "Adequacy of the Fossil Record," *Journal of Paleontology*, Vol. 33 (May 1959) p.496. Used by permission of the Paleontological Society.

51. Newell, Ibid. p.495.

52. Nilsson, Ibid. p.1195–1196.

53. Nilsson, Ibid. p.1194–1195.

54. Newell, Ibid. p.492.

55. Ladd, Harry S., "Ecology, Paleontology and Stratigraphy," *Science*, Vol. 129, (January 9, 1959) p.72.

56. Creationism vs. Evolution website: http://www.biblestudymanuals.net/k.33b.htm

57. Nilsson, Ibid. p.1194–1195.

58. From In the Age of Mankind. 1988, p130–131 by Roger Lewin (Washington, DC: Smithsonian Institution Press) Copyright © by the Smithsonian Institution Press. Used by permission of the publisher.

59. Kenyon, Dean H. in an affidavit presented to the U.S. Supreme Court, No. 85–1513, Brief of Appelants, prepared under the direction of William J. Guste, Jr., Attorney General of the State of Louisiana, October 1985, p.A-16.

60. Goldschmidt, R.B. *American Scientist*, 1952, Vol. 40, p.84.

61. Stanley, Steven M. 1981. The New Evolutionary Timetable. Basic Books Inc., New York, p.73. Permission granted by Perseus Publishing Group.

62. Lester, Lane P. and Raymond G. Bohlin. 1984. The Natural Limits to Biological Change. Zondervan Publishing House, Grand Rapids, MI. p.96.

63. Spetner, Lee. 1997. Not By Chance. The Judaica Press, Inc., Brooklyn, NY. p.143.

64. Spetner, Ibid. p.138.

65. Lewontin, Richard C. "Adaptation," *Scientific American* (and Scientific American book, Evolution). September 1978.

66. From In the Age of Mankind. 1988, p26 by Roger Lewin (Washington, DC: Smithsonian Institution Press) Copyright © by the Smithsonian Institution Press. Used by permission of the publisher.

67. From In the Age of Mankind. 1988, p26 by Roger Lewin (Washington, DC: Smithsonian Institution Press) Copyright © by the Smithsonian Institution Press. Used by permission of the publisher.

68. Lewin, Roger. "Evolutionary Theory Under Fire," *Science*, Vol. 210, (November 21, 1980), p.883.

69. Van Flandern, Tom. "Did the Universe Have a Beginning?" *Meta Research Bulletin,* Vol.3, No.3, 15 (September 1994) p.25.

70. Burbidge, Margaret, as quoted by George Schilling. "Radical Theory Takes a Test," *Science*, Vol. 291 (January 26, 2001) p.579.

71. Cline, David B. "The Search for Dark Matter," *Scientific American*, Vol. 288, (March 2003), p.52.

72. Tremaine, Scott, as quoted by Richard A. Kern. "Jupiters' Like our Own Await Planet Hunters," *Science*, Vol. 295 (January 25, 2002), p.605.

73. Cuzzi, Jeffrey N. "Ringed Planets: Still Mysterious—II," *Sky and Telescope*, Vol. 69. (January 1985), p.22.

74. Haynes, Robert C. 1971. Introduction to Space Science. John Wiley and Sons, New York, p.209. Reprinted by permission of John Wiley and Sons, Inc.

75. Matthews, Robert. "Spoiling a Universal 'Fudge Factor,'" *Science*, Vol. 265 (August 5, 1994), pp.740–741.

76. Windhorst, Rogier A., as quoted by Corey S. Powell, "A Matter of Timing," *Scientific American*, Vol. 267 (October 1992), p.30.

77. Abell, George. 1969. Exploration of the Universe, 2nd ed. Holt, Rinehart and Winston, New York, p.629.

78. Robinson. "Review of the Accidental Universe," *New Scientist*, Vol. 97 (January 20, 1983), p.186.

79. Burbidge, G. "Why Only One Big Bang?" *Scientific American*, 266(2), February 1992, p.96.

80. Berman, Bob. "Strange Universe: Bubbleland," *Astronomy*, Vol. 28 (June 2000), p.106.

81. Guest, John. 2002. Amazing Book of Facts. Barnes and Noble, Inc., pg. 119. Copyright currently held by Parragon.

82. Trefil, J. 1988. The Dark Side of the Universe. MacMillan Publishing Company, New York, p.3,55; see also W. Gitt, "What About the Big Bang?" *Creation*, 20(3): (June- August 1998), p.42–44. Reprinted with permission of Scribner, an imprint of Simon and Schuster Adult Publishing group from *The Dark Side of the Universe* by James Trefil. Copyright © 1988 by James Trefil.

83. Tipler, F.J. 1994. The Physics of Immortality. Doubleday, New York, preface.

84. Guest, Ibid. p.132.

85. Wald, George. "The Origin of Life," *Scientific American*. Vol. 190, August 1954, p.46.

86. Associated Press (AP), December 10, 1996.

87. Quotation from Dr. Jerome J. Lejeune, *Creation Magazine*, Volume 18, Number 3, p.49.

88. Bowler, Peter J. Review of In Search of Deep Time by Henry Gee. 1999. Free Press; *American Scientist*, Vol. 88 (March/April 2000), p.169.

89. Hoyle, Sir Frederick, as cited in *Nature*, November 12, 1981, (volume 294, number 5837), pg 105; as cited in Chuck Missler. The Creator Beyond Time and Space. 1996. The Word for Today, Costa Mesa, CA., p.60. Reprinted by permission from Nature, Macmillan Publishers Inc.

90. Dose, K. 1988. "The Origin of Life: More Questions than Answers," *Interdisciplinary Science Reviews*, 13, p.348.
91. Behe, Michael J. 1996. Darwin's Black Box—The Biochemical Challenge to Evolution. The Free Press, New York, pp.185–186.
92. Behe, Ibid. p.186.
93. Behe, Ibid. p.187.
94. Behe, Ibid. pp.252–253.
95. Behe, Ibid. pp.232–233.
96. Darwin, Charles. 1872. The Origin of Species.
97. Darwin, Ibid.
98. Ferris, James P. "Catalyzed RNA Synthesis for the RNA World," in Michael Ruse, ed. 1996. But Is it Science? Prometheus Books. Amherst, NY. p.255.
99. Cohen, J. "Getting All Turned Around Over the Origins of Life on Earth," *Science*, Vol. 267 (1995), pp.1265–66; as cited in Jonathan Sarfati, "Origin of Life: the Chirality Problem," Answers in Genesis website *www.answersingenesis.org*.
100. Cairns-Smith, A.G. 1985. Seven Clues to the Origin of Life: A Scientific Detective Story, Cambridge University Press. Reprinted by permission of Cambridge University Press.
101. Prigogine, I., N. Gregair, A. Babbyabtz. *Physics Today*, 25, p.23–28.
102. Dawkins, Richard. 1987. The Blind Watchmaker. W.W. Norton and Co., New York. p.43.
103. Yockey, Hubert P. 1992. Information Theory and Molecular Biology. Cambridge University Press. p.257. Reprinted by permission of Cambridge University Press.
104. Darwin, C.R. 1872. Origin of Species. 6th ed., John Murray, London, 1902, p.413.
105. Gould, S.J. 1982. Evolution Now: A Century After Darwin. ed. John Maynard Smith. MacMillan Publishing Co., p.140.
106. Simpson, G.G. 1944. Tempo and Mode in Evolution. Columbia University Press. New York. p.105.
107. Raup, D.M. and S.M. Stanley. 1971. Principles of Paleontology. W.H. Freeman and Co., San Francisco, p.306.
108. Clark, A.H. 1930. The New Evolution: Zoogenesis. Williams and Williams, Baltimore, p.189.

109. Goldschmidt, R.B. *American Scientist*, Vol.40, 1952, p.97.

110. Parker, Gary. 1994. Creation: Facts of Life. 6th ed. Master Books, Green Forest, AR.

111. Eldredge, Niles. 1998. The Pattern of Evolution. W.H. Freeman and Co., New York, p.157.

112. Bowler, Peter J. Review of In Search of Deep Time by Henry Gee. Free Press, 1999; In *American Scientist*, Vol. 88, (March/April 2000), p.169.

113. Brues, C.T. "Insects in Amber," *Scientific American,* Vol. 185 (November 1951), p.60.

114. Olson, E.C. 1965. The Evolution of Life. The New American Library, New York, p.180.

115. Lewin, Roger. *Science Magazine*, June 26, 1981. p.1492.

116. Darwin, Charles. My Life and Letters.

117. West, Ronald R. "Paleontology and Uniformitarianism," *Compass*, Vol. 45, 1968, p.216.

118. Smith, Homer W. 1953. From Fish to Philosopher. Little, Brown and Co., Boston, p.26.

119. Charles Darwin to Asa Gray, as cited by Adrian Desmond and James Moore. *Darwin.* 1991. W.W. Norton and Company, New York, pp. 456, 475.

120. Ranganathan, B.G. 1988. Origins? The Banner of Truth Trust, Carlisle, PA. p.22.

121. As quoted in Graham, Keith et al. 1986. Biology. A Beka Book Publications, Pensacola, FL. p.363.

122. Dickerson, Richard E. "Chemical Evolution and the Origin of Life." *Scientific American* (and Scientific American book, Evolution), September 1978.

123. Morris, Henry M. 1967. The Twilight of Evolution. Baker Book House, Grand Rapids, MI. p.91.

124. Rensberger, Boyce. 1986. How the World Works. William Morrow, NY., a division of Harper Collins Publishers, Inc., pp.17–18.

125. Morris, Henry M. 1967. The Twilight of Evolution. Baker Book House, Grand Rapids, MI. p.48.

126. Parker, Gary. 2000. From Evolution to Creation: A Personal Testimony. Answers in Genesis. p.10.

127. Constance, Arthur. 1976. Evolution: An Irrational Faith in Evolution or Creation? Vol. 4—The Doorway Papers, Zondervan, Grand Rapids, MI. p.173–174.

128. Ruse, Michael. "Saving Darwin from Darwinism," *National Post*, May 13, 2000. p.B-3.

129. Ranganathan, Ibid. p.22.

130. Charles Darwin as cited in Wendt, Herbert. 1972. From Ape to Man. The Bubbs Merril Co., New York, p.59.

131. Morris, Henry M. 1967. The Twilight of Evolution. Baker Book House, Grand Rapids, MI. p.90.

132. Nilsson, Ibid. p.51.

133. Behe, Ibid. p.252.

134. Clark, Robert E.D. 1972. Science and Christianity: A Partnership. Copyright © by Pacific Press Publishing Association, Nampa, Idaho, p.154. Used by permission.

135. Morris, Henry M. 1988. Evolution and the Modern Christian. Presbyterian and Reformed Publishing Co., Phillipsburg, NJ. p.19.

136. From In the Age of Mankind. 1988, p26 by Roger Lewin (Washington, DC: Smithsonian Institution Press) Copyright © by the Smithsonian Institution Press. Used by permission of the publisher.

137. Hawking, Stephen. 1988. A Brief History of Time—From the Big Bang to Black Holes. Bantam Books, New York., pp.125, 127.

138. Scientific American, May 1963, p. 53

139. Hawking, Stephen W. 1988. A Brief History of Time—From the Big Bang to Black Holes. Bantam Books, New York., pp.140–141.

140. Morris, Henry M. 1972. The Remarkable Birth of Planet Earth. Institute for Creation Research, San Diego, CA., Preface vii.

141. Horgan, J. "The New Social Darwinists," *Scientific American*, 273(4) (October 1995), p.151.

Chapter 2

1. The Scofield Study Bible, Authorized King James Version, 1945. Oxford University Press, New York.
2. Ibid. above.
3. DeYoung, Donald B. 1989. Astronomy and the Bible: Questions and Answers. Baker Books, Grand Rapids, MI, p.85.
4. DeYoung, Donald B. Astronomy and the Bible: Questions and Answers. Baker Books, Grand Rapids, Mich., pg 40.
5. Cuzzi, Jeffrey N. "Ringed Planets: Still Mysterious—II," *Sky and Telescope*, Vol. 69. (January 1985), p.22.
6. DeYoung, Donald B. 1989. Astronomy and the Bible: Questions and Answers. Baker Books, Grand Rapids, MI, pg 35.
7. DeYoung, Donald B. 1989. Astronomy and the Bible: Questions and Answers. Baker Books, Grand Rapids, MI, pg 47.
8. Newton, Isaac. 1687. Principia—Observations on the Prophecy of Daniel and the Revelation of Saint John.

Chapter 3

1. Newton, Isaac. Ibid.
2. Barnes, Thomas G. "Physics: A Challenge to Geological Time," *Impact*, No. 16, July 1974; as cited on Institute for Creation Research website . . . *www.icr.org/pubs/imp/imp~016.htm*
3. TIME Magazine, April 7, 1980.
4. Margenau, H. and R.A. Varghese. eds. 1992. Cosmos, Bios, Theos: Scientists Reflect on Science, God, and the Origins of the Universe, Life and Homo Sapiens. Reprinted by permission of Open Court Publishing Company, a division of Carus Publishing Company, Peru, IL.
5. Hoyle, Sir Fred. 1982. "The Universe: Past and Present Reflections," *Annual Review of Astronomy and Astrophysics*, 20:16.
6. Greenstein, G. 1988. The Symbiotic Universe. William Morrow, New York, a division of HarperCollins Publishers, Inc., p.27.
7. Hawking, Stephen. 1988. A Brief History of Time—From the Big Bang to Black Holes. Bantam Books, New York, p.125.

8. From: http://physics.nist.gov/constants; Peter J. Mohr and Barry N. Taylor, CODATA Recommended Values of the Fundamental Physical Constants: 2002.

9. Adapted from Ross, Hugh. "Fine-Tuning of Physical Life Support Body," NavPress

10. Ross, Hugh. 1994. "Astronomical Evidences for a Personal, Transcendent God," The Creation Hypothesis: Scientific Evidence for an Intelligent Designer. ed. by J.P. Moreland. Downer's Grove, Ill. Inter-Varsity Press, p.160.

11. Heeren, F. 1995. Show Me God. Searchlight Publications, Wheeling, IL. p. 200

12. Davies, Paul. 1988. The Cosmic Blueprint: New Discoveries in Nature's Creative Abilty to Order the Universe. Simon and Schuster, New York, p.203. Reprinted with the permission of Simon and Schuster Adult Publishing Group from GOD AND THE NEW PHYSICS by Paul Davies © 1983 by Paul Davies

Chapter 4

1. The Scofield Study Bible. Ibid.

2. The Pennsylvania State University. 2001. *Biodiversity—Our Living World: Your Life Depends On It.*

3. Kricher, John C. and G. Morrison. 1988. Peterson Field Guides—Ecology of Eastern Forests. Houghton Mifflin Company, NY., p.100.

Chapter 5

1. Lynch, Wayne. 1996. A is for Arctic: Natural Wonders of a Polar World. Firefly Books Inc., Buffalo, NY., p.19.

2. Cech, Joseph J. Jr. and Peter B. Moyle. 1996. Fishes—An Introduction to Ichthyology (Third Edition). Prentice-Hall Inc., Upper Saddle River, NJ., p.171.

3. Cech, Moyle. Ibid., p.400.

4. Cech, Moyle. Ibid., p.403.

5. Cech, Moyle. Ibid., p.422.

6. Cech, Moyle. Ibid., p.436.

Chapter 6

1. *Urban Forestry News,* 2003, unknown month.
2. Kricher, John C. and Gordon Morrison. 1988. Peterson Field Guides – Ecology of Eastern Forests. Houghton Mifflin Co., NY.

Chapter 7

1. Pitman, Michael. 1984. Adam and Evolution. Rider and Company, London, p.219.
2. Gill, Frank B. 1995. Ornithology (2nd Edition). W.H. Freeman and Company, NY., p.313.
3. Lynch, Ibid. p.46.

Chapter 8

1. DaVinci, Leonardo, as quoted on "Distinctively Human," Moody Discovery Video Series.
2. Ibid. above.
3. Hoyle, Fred and Chandra Wickramasinghe. 1981. Evolution from Space. J.M. Dent and Sons Co., a division of the Orion Publishing Group, London, p.330.
4. Stevens, John K. "Reverse Engineering the Brain," *Byte,* April 1985, pp.287–299, as cited in Richard A. Swenson, 2000. More Than Meets the Eye: Fascinating Glimpses of God's Power and Design. NavPress, Colorado Springs, CO., p.34.
5. Gross, Michael. 1999. Travels to the Nanoworld: Miniature Machinery in Nature and Technology. Perseus, Cambridge, MA., pp.3, 5.
6. Schroeder, Gerald L. 2001. The Hidden Face of God: How Science Reveals the Ultimate Truth. The Free Press, NY., p.189.

Chapter 9

1. Schaff, Philip. History of the Christian Church, Vol. I. William B. Eerdmans, Grand Rapids, Mich., 1910, pg. 175.
2. Wilson, Clifford, as quoted in *Creation Ex Nihilo,* Answers in Genesis, 21(1):15 (December 1998–Feb. 1999).

3. Burrows, Millar. "How Archaeology Helps the Student of The Bible," *Workers With Youth.* April 1948.

4. Sayce, A.H. Monument Facts and Higher Critical Fancies. The Religious Tract Society, London, 1904, pg 23.

5. Information from http://christiananswers.net/q-abr/abr-a009.html

6. Kenyon, Kathleen M. 1981. "Excavations at Jericho," British School of Archaeology in Jerusalem, London, 3:370. © The Council for British Research in the Levant. Used by permission.

7. W.F. Albright, The Archaeology of Palestine and the Bible (Revell, 1935), p. 127.

8. Geisler, Norman and Ron Brooks. 1996. When Skeptics Ask: A Handbook on Christian Evidences, Baker Books, Grand Rapids, Mich., pg 151.

9. Geisler, Norman L. 1998. Baker Encyclopedia of Christian Apologetics. Baker Books, Grand Rapids, MI., p.52.

10. Josephus, Flavius. 1960. Flavius Josephus Against Apion— Josephus' Complete Works, Trans. By William Whiston. Kregel Publications, Grand Rapids, MI., pp.179–180.

11. Davidson, Samuel. 1859. Hebrew Text of the Old Testament. 2nd ed., Samuel Bagster and Sons.

12. Davidson, Samuel. 1859. Hebrew Text of the Old Testament. 2nd ed., Samuel Bagster and Sons.

13. Kenyon, Frederick G. 1941. Our Bible and the Ancient Manuscripts. Harper and Brothers, New York, HarperCollins Publishers Inc., p.38.

14. Bruce, F.F. 1950. Reprints 1963, 1984. The Books and the Parchments: How We Got Our English Bible. Fleming H. Revell Co., Old Tappan, NJ, pg 117.

15. Wilson, Robert Dick. 1926. A Scientific Investigation of the Old Testament. Marshall Brothers Limited, London; Moody Press, Chicago, 1959, pgs 74–75.

16. Wilson, Robert Dick. 1926. A Scientific Investigation of the Old Testament. Marshall Brothers Limited, London; Moody Press, Chicago, 1959, pgs 74–75.

17. Wilson, Robert D. 1926. A Scientific Investigation of the Old Testament. Marshall Brothers Limited, London, pp.64, 7.

18. Geisler, Norman L. 1998. Baker Encyclopedia of Christian Apologetics. Baker Books, Grand Rapids, MI.

19. Green, William Henry. 1895. General Introduction to the Old Testament—The Text. Charles Scribner's Sons, New York, pg 81.

20. Archer. Gleason L. Jr. 1964,1974. A Survey of Old Testament Introduction. Moody Press, Chicago, pgs 23–25.

21. Wilson, Robert Dick. 1926. A Scientific Investigation of the Old Testament. Marshall Brothers Limited, London; Moody Press, Chicago, 1959, pgs 85.

22. Wilson, Clifford. 1977. Rocks, Relics and Biblical Reliability. Zondervan, Grand Rapids; Probe, Richardson, Tex., p.120; cited in Ankerberg and Weldon. Ready with an Answer, p.272.

23. Moreland, J.P. 1987. Scaling the Secular City. Baker Books, Grand Rapids, Mich., pg 136.

24. Geisler, N. L. 1976. *Christian apologetics*. Baker Book House, Grand Rapids, Mich.

25. Geisler, N. L. 1976. *Christian apologetics*. Baker Book House, Grand Rapids, Mich.

26. Geisler, Norman L. and Paul K. Hoffman, editors. 2001. Why I Am a Christian: Leading Thinkers Explain Why They Believe. Baker Book House, Grand Rapids, Mich.

27. Warfield, Benjamin B. 1907. Introduction to Textual Criticism of the New Testament. Hodder and Stoughton, p.12–13.

28. Geisler, Norman L. and William E. Nix. 1980. A General Introduction to the Bible. Moody Press, Chicago, reprint from 1968, p.367.

29. Geisler, Norman L. and Paul K. Hoffman, editors. 2001. Why I Am a Christian: Leading Thinkers Explain Why They Believe. Baker Book House, Grand Rapids, Mich.

30. Kenyon, Frederick C. 1940. The Bible and Archaeology. Harper and Row, New York, HarperCollins Publishers, Inc., p.288.

31. Kenyon, Frederick C. 1948. The Bible and Modern Scholarship. John Murray, London, p.20. Reproduced by Permission of John Murray Publishers

32. Kenyon, Frederick C. 1940. The Bible and Archaeology. Harper and Row, New York, HarperCollins Publishers, Inc., p.288.

33. Geisler, Norman and Ron Brooks. 1996. When Skeptics Ask: A Handbook on Christian Evidences, Baker Books, Grand Rapids, Mich., pg 91.
34. Ramm, Bernard. 1953. Protestant Christian Evidences. Moody Press, Chicago, IL. pg. 85.
35. Ramm, Bernard. 1953. Protestant Christian Evidences. Moody Press, Chicago, IL. pg. 124.
36. Ramm, Bernard. 1953. Protestant Christian Evidences. Moody Press, Chicago, IL. pg. 249.
37. Rev. C.I. Scofield's commentary on II Peter 1:19–21, as found in the Scofield Study Bible. 1945. Authorized King James Version. Oxford University Press, NY.
38. Geisler, Norman L. 1998. Baker Encyclopedia of Christian Apologetics. Baker Books, Grand Rapids, MI.
39. Stoner, Peter W. 1963. Science Speaks. Moody Press, Chicago. Used by permission of Don Stoner.
40. Strobel, Lee. 1998. The Case for Christ: A Journalist's Personal Investigation of the Evidence for Jesus. Zondervan, Grand Rapids, MI. p.184.
41. Strobel, Ibid., p.184.
42. Strobel, Ibid., p.186.
43. Scofield Study Bible, Ibid.
44. Scofield Study Bible, Ibid.
45. Scofield Study Bible, Ibid.
46. Scofield Study Bible, Ibid.
47. Scofield Study Bible, Ibid.
48. Scofield Study Bible, Ibid.
49. Scofield Study Bible, Ibid.
50. Collett, Sidney. All About the Bible. Fleming H. Revell, Old Tappan, N.J., n.d pg 314,315.
51. Collett, Sidney. All About the Bible. Fleming H. Revell, Old Tappan, N.J., n.d pg 314,315.
52. Geisler, Norman L. and William E. Nix. 1968. A General Introduction to the Bible. Moody Press, Chicago pp.123, 124.
53. Lea, John W. 1929. The Greatest Book in the World. Philadelphia, n.p., pp.17–18.
54. Ramm, Bernard. 1953. Protestant Christian Evidences. Moody Press, Chicago, IL. pg. 232.

55. Ramm, Bernard. 1953. Protestant Christian Evidences. Moody Press, Chicago, IL. pp.232–233.

56. *The Daily Review* newspaper, unknown date.

57. Ibid.

58. Ibid.

59. Theodore Roosevelt

60. Ibid.

61. Ibid.

62. Ibid.

63. Geisler, Norman L. and Thomas Howe. When Critics Ask: A Popular Handbook on Bible Difficulties. Victor Books, a division of Scripture Press Publications, Inc., USA, Canada, England.

64. DeYoung, Donald B. 1989. Astronomy and the Bible: Questions and Answers. Baker Books, Grand Rapids, Mich., pg 17.

65. Smith, Joseph. 1978. History of the Church—8 vols. Desert, Salt Lake City, 4:461; as cited in Donald S. Tingle. 1981. Mormonism. InterVarsity Press, Downer's Grove, Ill., p.17.

66. Strobel, Lee. 1998. The Case for Christ: A Journalist's Personal Investigation of the Evidence for Jesus. Zondervan, Grand Rapids, MI. p.107.

67. Taken from: The Facts on the Mormon Church by John Ankerberg and John Weldon. Copyright © 1991 by The Ankerberg Theological Research Institute, Published by Harvest House Publishers, Eugene, OR. Used by Permission.

68. Archer, Gleason L. Jr. 1982. Encyclopedia of Bible Difficulties. Zondervan, Grand Rapids, MI., p.12.

69. Geisler, Norman L. and Ron Rhodes. 1997. When Cultists Ask: A Popular Handbook on Cultic Misinterpretations. Baker Book House, Grand Rapids, Mich.

70. Geisler, Norman L. and Ron Rhodes. 1997. When Cultists Ask: A Popular Handbook on Cultic Misinterpretations. Baker Book House, Grand Rapids, Mich.

71. Geisler, Norman L. and Ron Rhodes. 1997. When Cultists Ask: A Popular Handbook on Cultic Misinterpretations. Baker Book House, Grand Rapids, Mich.

72. Geisler, N. L., & Saleeb, A. 2002. *Answering Islam: The crescent in light of the cross* (2nd ed.). Baker Books, Grand Rapids, Mich.
73. Geisler, Norman L. and Thomas Howe. When Critics Ask: A Popular Handbook on Bible Difficulties. Victor Books, a division of Scripture Press Publications, Inc., USA, Canada, England.
74. Geisler, Norman L. and Thomas Howe. When Critics Ask: A Popular Handbook on Bible Difficulties. Victor Books, a division of Scripture Press Publications, Inc., USA, Canada, England.
75. Strobel, Ibid., pp.86–87.
76. Strobel, Ibid., p.86.
77. Geisler, Norman L. and Ron Rhodes. 1997. When Cultists Ask: A Popular Handbook on Cultic Misinterpretations. Baker Book House, Grand Rapids, Mich.
78. Collett, Sidney. All About the Bible. Fleming H. Revell, Old Tappan, N.J., n.d pg 314,315.
79. Bruce F.F. 1950. Reprints 1963, 1984. The Books and the Parchments: How We Got Our English Bible. Fleming H. Revell Co., Old Tappan, N.J., pg. 88
80. Geisler, Norman L. and Ron Rhodes. 1997. When Cultists Ask: A Popular Handbook on Cultic Misinterpretations. Baker Book House, Grand Rapids, Mich.
81. As quoted in a 1913 edition of *The Brooklyn Daily Eagle*
82. Smith, Joseph. 1978. History of the Church—8 vols. Deseret, Salt Lake City, 4:461; as cited in Donald S. Tingle. 1981. Mormonism. InterVarsity Press, Downer's Grove, Ill., p.17.
83. *Mormonism Unveiled,* 1834. Painesville, Ohio, pg 261.
84. Spoken between 1867–1870 by Horace T. Wentworth
85. William Edward Hatpole Lecky. 1901. History of European Morals from Augustus to Charlemagne. D. Appleton and Co., New York, pg 8.
86. Napoleon Bonaparte
87. Napoleon Bonaparte, as cited in Vernon C. Grounds. 1945. The Reason for Our Hope. Moody Press, Chicago, pg 37.
88. Schaff, Philip. 1913. The Person of Christ. American Tract Society, New York, pg 33.

89. Mead, Frank, ed. The Encyclopedia of Religious Quotations. Fleming H. Revell, Westwood, Ill., n.d., pg 49,

90. Hopkins, Mark, as quoted in Mead, pg 53.

91. Ramm, Bernard. 1953. Protestant Christian Evidences. Moody Press, Chicago, IL. pg. 163.

92. Channing, William E., as quoted in Mead, pg 51.

93. Mead, Ibid., pg 57

94. Strauss, David Friedrich. 1879. The Life of Jesus for the People, 2d ed., Vol. 1. Williams and Norgate, London, pg 412.

95. Ramm, Bernard. 1953. Protestant Christian Evidences. Moody Press, Chicago, IL. pgs. 140–144.

96. Ibid.

97. Ibid.

98. Ibid.

99. Ibid.

100. Ibid.

101. Ibid.

102. Ibid.

103. Geisler, N. L., & Saleeb, A. 2002. *Answering Islam: The crescent in light of the cross* (2nd ed.). Baker Books, Grand Rapids, Mich.

104. Geisler, Norman and Ron Brooks. 1996. When Skeptics Ask: A Handbook on Christian Evidences, Baker Books, Grand Rapids, Mich., pg 98.

Chapter 10

1. Smith, Wilbur. 1945. Therefore Stand. Baker Book House, Grand Rapids, MI., pp.425–426.

2. Green, Michael. 1968. Man Alive. Inter-Varsity Press, Downer's Grove, Ill., p.54.

3. Westcott, B.F. 1868. Gospel of the Resurrection. MacMillan and Co., London.

4. Montgomery, John W. 1971. History of Christianity. Inter-Varsity Press, Downer's Grove, Ill., p.29.

5. Lea, John W. 1929. The Greatest Book in the World. n.p., Philadelphia, pg 15.

6. Geisler, N. L., & Geisler, N. L. 1992. *Miracles and the modern mind: A defense of biblical miracles.* Rev. ed. of: Miracles and modern thought. 1982. Baker Book House: Grand Rapids, Mich.

7. Kenyon, Frederick G. 1901. Handbook to the Textual Criticism of the New Testament. MacMillan and Company, London.

8. Strobel, Ibid., p.230.

9. Strobel, Ibid., p.230

10. Strobel, Ibid., p.231.

11. Strobel, Ibid., pp.232–233.

12. Strobel, Ibid., p.235.

13. Strobel, Ibid., p.220.

14. Strobel, Ibid., p.119.

15. Geisler, Norman L. 1998. Baker Encyclopedia of Christian Apologetics. Baker Books, Grand Rapids, MI.

16. Geisler, Norman L. 1998. Baker Encyclopedia of Christian Apologetics. Baker Books, Grand Rapids, MI.

17. Geisler, N. L. 1976. *Christian apologetics.* Baker Book House, Grand Rapids Mich.

18. Geisler, N. L. 1976. *Christian apologetics.* Baker Book House, Grand Rapids Mich.

19. Geisler, N. L., & Saleeb, A. 2002. *Answering Islam: The crescent in light of the cross* (2nd ed.). Baker Books: Grand Rapids, Mich.

20. Bruce, F.F. 1964. The New Testament Documents: Are They Reliable? Inter-Varsity Press, Downer's Grove, Ill., pp.33, 44–46.

21. Grant, Robert. 1963. Historical Introduction to the New Testament. Harper and Row, New York, HarperCollins Publishers Inc., p.302.

22. Ramsay, Sir William. 1915. The Bearing of Recent Discoveries on the Trustworthiness of the New Testament. Hodder and Stoughton, London, pg 222.

23. Ramsay, W.M. 1962. St. Paul the Traveller and the Roman Citizen. Baker Book House, Grand Rapids, Mich.

24. Geisler, N. L., & Geisler, N. L. 1992. *Miracles and the modern mind: A defense of biblical miracles.* Rev. ed. of: Miracles and modern thought. 1982. Baker Book House, Grand Rapids, Mich.

25. Geisler, N. L., & Geisler, N. L. 1992. *Miracles and the modern mind: A defense of biblical miracles.* Rev. ed. of: Miracles and modern thought. 1982. Baker Book House, Grand Rapids, Mich.

26. Ramsay, W.M. 1962. St. Paul the Traveller and the Roman Citizen. Baker Book House, Grand Rapids, Mich.

27. Sherwin-White, A.N. 1978. Roman Society and Roman Law in the New Testament. Baker Book House, Grand Rapids, Mich., pg 189

28. Bruce, F.F. 1950, reprints in 1963, 1984. The Books and the Parchments: How We Got Our English Bible. Fleming H. Revell Co., Old Tappan, N.J. p. 178.

29. Ramm, Bernard. 1953. Protestant Christian Evidences. Moody Press, Chicago, IL. pg. 231.

30. Greenleaf, Simon. Reprint in 1984. *The Testimony of the Evangelists.* Baker Books, Grand Rapids Mich., pp. 9–10.

31. Geisler, N. L., & Geisler, N. L. 1992. *Miracles and the modern mind: A defense of biblical miracles.* Rev. ed. of: Miracles and modern thought. 1982. Baker Book House, Grand Rapids, Mich.

32. Habermas, Gary. 1996. The Historical Jesus; Ancient Evidence for the Life of Christ, College Press Publishing Company, Joplin, Missouri, pg 250.

33. Babylonia Sanhedrin 43a.

34. Bruce, F.F. 1972. The New Testament Documents: Are They Reliable? 5th Revised Edition. Inter-Varsity Press, Downer's Grove, Ill.

35. Annals XV-44.

36. Ramm, Bernard. 1953. Protestant Christian Evidences. Moody Press, Chicago, IL. pgs. 203,204.

37. McDowell, Josh., as cited in *The Daily Collegian*, Wednesday, March 26, 1997, p.13.

38. Day, E. Hermitage. 1906. On the Evidence for the Resurrection. Society for Promoting Christian Knowledge, London, pgs 33–35.

39. Geisler, N. L. 1976. *Christian apologetics*. Baker Book House, Grand Rapids Mich.

40. *Encyclopedia Britannica*, 15th ed., 1974, p.145, as cited in Josh McDowell. 1979. Evidence that Demands a Verdict—Volume 1. Here's Life Publishers, Inc., San Bernandino California, p.87.

41. Bruce, F.F. 1972. The New Testament Documents: Are They Reliable? 5th Revised Edition. Inter-Varsity Press, Downer's Grove, Ill.

42. Betz, Otto. 1968. What Do We Know About Jesus? SCM Press, pg 9.

43. Ramm, Bernard. 1953. Protestant Christian Evidences. Moody Press, Chicago, IL. pg. 198.

44. Pannenburg, Wolfhart. MCMCXVIII. Jesus—God and Man. Translated by L.L. Wilkins and D.A. Priche. Westminster Press, Philadelphia.

45. Ramsey, Arthur Michael. 1969. God, Christ and the World. SCM Press, London, pp.78–80.

46. Strobel, Ibid., p.220.

47. Strobel, Ibid., p.221.

48. Moreland, J.P., 1987. Scaling the Secular City. Baker Books, Grand Rapids, Mich. p.163.

49. Geisler, Norman L. and Ron Brooks. 1996. When Skeptics Ask: A Handbook on Christian Evidences, Baker Books, Grand Rapids, Mich., pg 204.

50. Stott, John R.W. 1971. Basic Christianity, 2nd ed. Inter-Varsity Press, Downer's Grove, Ill., p.51.

51. *Independent Press Telegram*, (Now Long Beach Press Telegram) Saturday, April 21, 1973, Long Beach, Calif., p.A-10.

52. Green, Michael. 1968. Man Alive. Inter-Varsity Press, Downer's Grove, Ill., p.36.

53. Strobel, Ibid., pp.218–219.

54. Strobel, Ibid., p.223

55. Geisler, N. L. 1976. *Christian apologetics*. Baker Book House, Grand Rapids, Mich.

56. Smith, Wilbur M. 1945. Therefore Stand. Baker Book House, Grand Rapids, Mich., pg 360

57. Smith, Wilbur M. 1945. Therefore Stand. Baker Book House, Grand Rapids, Mich., pg 371.

58. Moreland, J.P. 1987. Scaling the Secular City. Baker Books, Grand Rapids, Mich. p.165.

59. Strobel, Ibid., p.210.

60. Strobel, Ibid., p.212.

61. Smith, William, ed. 1870. Dictionary of Greek and Roman Antiquitie, rev. ed. James Walton and John Murray, London, pgs 250–251.

62. Tucker, T.G. 1910. Life in the Roman World of Nero and Saint Paul. The Macmillan Company, New York, pgs 342–244.

63. Currie, George. 1928. The Military Discipline of the Romans from the Founding of the City to the Close of the Republic. An abstract of a thesis published under the auspices of the Graduate Council of Indiana University.

64. Fallow, Samuel ed. 1908. The Popular and Critical Bible Encyclopedia and Scriptural Dictionary. Vol III. The Howard Severance Co., Chicago, page 1452.

65. Smith, Wilbur M. 1945. Therefore Stand. Baker Book House, Grand Rapids, Mich., pp 367--377.

66. Alford, Henry. 1868. The Greek Testament: With a Critically Revised Text; A Digest of Various Readings; Marginal References to Verbal and Idiomatic Usage; Prolegomena; And a Critical and Exegetical Commentary. Vol I Sixth edition. Deighton, Bell, and Co, Cambridge, pg 301.

67. Gregory of Nyssa, as cited in John F. Whitworth. 1912. Legal and Historical Proof of the Resurrection of the Dead. Publishing House of the United Evangelical Church, Harnsburg, pgs 64–65.

68. Gregory of Nyssa, as cited in John F. Whitworth. 1912. Legal and Historical Proof of the Resurrection of the Dead. Publishing House of the United Evangelical Church, Harnsburg, pgs 64–65.

69. Chrysostom, as cited in Philip Schaff. 1888. A Select Library of the Nicene and Post- Nicene Fathers of the Christian

Church. Vols. IV, X, The Christian Literature Company, New York, pgs 530–531.

70. Schaff, Philip. 1882. History of the Christian Church, Volume 1: Apostolic Christianity, A.D. 1–100. CCEL.

71. Sparrow-Simpson W.J., as cited in James Hastings, John A. Selbie, and John C. Lambert, eds. 1909. A Dictionary of Christ and the Gospels. Vol II. Charles Scribner's and Sons, New York, pg 507–508.

72. Balmin Bruce, Alexander. 1903. The Expositor's Greek New Testament. Vol. 1—The Synoptic Gospels. Hodder and Stoughton, London, pgs 337–338.

73. Schaff, Philip. 1882. History of the Christian Church, Volume 1: Apostolic Christianity, A.D. 1–100. CCEL.

74. John Chrysostom, as cited in G.W. Clark. 1896. The Gospel of Matthew. American Baptist Publication Society, Philadelphia, pg 531.

75. Moreland, J.P. 1987. Scaling the Secular City. Baker Books, Grand Rapids, Mich. p.171.

76. Hastings, James, John A. Selbie and John C. Lambert, eds. 1909. A Dictionary of Christ and the Gospels. Vol II. Charles Scribner's and Sons, New York, pg 507.

77. Thornburn, Thomas James. 1910. The Resurrection Narratives and Modern Criticism. Kegan Paul, Trench, Trubner and Co., Ltd., London, pgs 97–98.

78. Thornburn, Thomas James. 1910. The Resurrection Narratives and Modern Criticism. Kegan Paul, Trench, Trubner and Co., Ltd., London, pgs 97–98.

79. Day, E. Hermitage. 1906. On the Evidence for the Resurrection. Society for Promoting Christian Knowledge, London, pgs 48–49.

80. Strobel, Ibid., p.200.

81. Strobel, Ibid., p.201.

82. Day, E. Hermitage. 1906. On the Evidence for the Resurrection. Society for Promoting Christian Knowledge, London, pgs 46–48.

83. Ramm, Bernard. 1953. Protestant Christian Evidences. Moody Press, Chicago, IL. pg. 186.

84. Strobel, Ibid., p.201.

85. Johnson, Luke Timothy. 1996. The Real Jesus. Harper, San Francisco, HarperCollins Publishers, Inc. p.30.

86. Sparrow-Simpson, W.J. as cited in Samuel Fallow, ed. 1908. The Popular and Critical Bible Encyclopedia and Scriptural Dictionary. Vol III. The Howard Severance Co., Chicago, pg 95.

87. Edwards, William D, WJ Gabel and FE Hosmer. "On The Physical Death of Jesus Christ," *Journal of the American Medical Association*, 265:11 (March 21, 1986), p.1463. Used by permission of the Mayo Foundation for Medical Education and Research. All rights reserved.

88. Moreland, J.P. 1987. Scaling the Secular City. Baker Books, Grand Rapids, Mich. p.171.

89. Strauss, David Friedrich. 1879. The Life of Jesus for the People, 2d ed., Vol. 1. Williams and Norgate, London, pg 412.

90. Ramm, Bernard. 1953. Protestant Christian Evidences. Moody Press, Chicago, IL.

91. Moreland, J.P. 1987. Scaling the Secular City. Baker Books, Grand Rapids, Mich. p.168.

92. Schaff, Philip. 1882. History of the Christian Church, Volume 1: Apostolic Christianity, A.D. 1–100. CCEL.

93. Lydon, H.P. as cited in Wilbur M. Smith. 1945. Therefore Stand. Baker Book House, Grand Rapids, Mich., pg 577.

94. Taken from: Ready With an Answer by John Ankerberg and John Weldon, Copyright ©1997 by Harvest House Publishers, Eugene, OR. Used by Permission.

95. Pliny the Younger, Letters, Translated by W. Melmoth, 10:96. (Pliny was a Roman author and administrator writing to the Emperor Trajan in 112)

96. Strobel, Ibid., p.250.

97. Strobel, Ibid., p.252.

98. Strobel, Ibid., pp.239–240.

99. Braaten, Carl, ed. by William Hordern.1966. History and Hermeneutics, Vol. 2 of New Directions in Theology Today. Westminster Press, Philadelphia, p.78 as cited in Habermas and Flew. Did Jesus Rise from the Dead? p.24.

100. Green, Michael. 1984. The Empty Cross of Jesus. Inter-Varsity Press, Downer's Grove, IL., p.97 as cited in Ankenberg and Weldon. Knowing the Truth about the Resurrection. p.22.
101. Strobel, Ibid., p.240.
102.Paraphrase of Anderson, J.N.D. 1969. Christianity: The Witness of History. Tyndale Press, London, pp5–6.
103. Schaff, Philip. 1882. History of the Christian Church, Volume 1: Apostolic Christianity, A.D. 1–100. CCEL.
104. Strobel, Ibid., p.120.
105. Geisler, N. L., & Saleeb, A. 2002. *Answering Islam: The crescent in light of the cross* (2nd ed.). Baker Books, Grand Rapids, Mich.
106. Moreland, J.P. 1987. Scaling the Secular City. Baker Books, Grand Rapids, Mich., pp.171– 172.
107. Greenleaf, Simon. 1965. The Testimony of the Evangelists, Examined by the Rules of Evidence Administered in Courts of Justice. Baker Book House, Grand Rapids, Mich. pg. 28.
108. Ramm, Bernard. 1953. Protestant Christian Evidences. Moody Press, Chicago, IL. pg. 196.
109. Smith, Carol and Roddy. 2001. The Ultimate Guide to Christian History. Barbour Publishing, Ulrichsville, Ohio, page 75. Used by permission.
110. Strobel, Ibid., p.247.
111. Matheson. George. 1904. The Representative Men of the New Testament. Hodder and Stoughton, London, pg 140.
112. The Scofield Study Bible, Ibid.
113. The Scofield Study Bible, Ibid.
114. Eusebius, as cited in Mattingly, John P. 1961. Crucifixion, Its Origins and Applications to Christ. Unpublished Th.M. Thesis, Dallas Theological Seminary, p. 73.
115. From Tacitus, a secular historian writing near 65 A.D, concerning the intense persecution suffered by early Christians under the reign of Nero.
116. Tacitus 15:44
117. Foxe, John. 1989. Foxe's Christian Martyr's of the World. Barbour Publishing Inc., Uhrichsville, Ohio, p.10. Used by permission.
118. Foxe, Ibid., p.10.

119. Foxe, Ibid., p.21.

120. Strobel, Ibid, p.235.

121. Geisler, N. L. 1976. *Christian apologetics.* Baker Book House: Grand Rapids, Mich.

122. See Josh McDowell. 1977. More Than a Carpenter. Living Books, Wheaton IL., pp60– 71; as cited by Strobel, pp.247– 248.

123. Strobel, p.232.

124. Corduan, Winifred. 1997. No Doubt About It: The Case for Christianity. Broadman and Holman Publishers, Nashville, p.221. Used by Permission.

125. Thornburn, Thomas James. 1910. The Resurrection Narratives and Modern Criticism. Kegan Paul, Trench, Trubner and Co., Ltd., London, pgs 158–159.

126. Geisler, Norman L. and Paul K. Hoffman, editors. 2001. Why I Am a Christian: Leading Thinkers Explain Why They Believe. Baker Book House, Grand Rapids, Mich.

127. Schaff, Philip. 1882. History of the Christian Church, Volume 1: Apostolic Christianity, A.D. 1–100. CCEL.

128. Strobel, Ibid., p.239.

129. Day, E. Hermitage. 1906. On the Evidence for the Resurrection. Society for Promoting Christian Knowledge, London, pgs 51–53.

130. Day, E. Hermitage. 1906. On the Evidence for the Resurrection. Society for Promoting Christian Knowledge, London, pgs 53–54.

131. Harnack, Adolf. History of Dogma, as quoted in E. Hermitage Day. 1906. On the Evidence for the Resurrection. Society for Promoting Christian Knowledge, London, pg 3.

132. Straton, Hillyer, H. "I Believe: Our Lord's Resurrection," *Christianity Today*, March 31, 1968. Used by permission from *Christianity Today.*

133. Thornburn, Thomas James. 1910. The Resurrection Narratives and Modern Criticism. Kegan Paul, Trench, Trubner and Co., Ltd.

134. Hanson, George. 1911. The Resurrection and the Life. William Clowes and Sons, Ltd., London, page 24.

135. Strobel, Ibid., p.248.

136. McCartney, Clarence E. Twelve Great Questions about Christ. Original Printing 1923 by Fleming H. Revell Company; 1956 Edition by Baker Book House, pg. 121–122.

137. McCartney, Clarence E. Twelve Great Questions about Christ. Original Printing 1923 by Fleming H. Revell Company; 1956 Edition by Baker Book House, pg. 122

138. Ramm, Bernard. 1953. Protestant Christian Evidences. Moody Press, Chicago, IL. pgs 29,30.

139. Schaff, Philip. 1882. History of the Christian Church, Volume 1: Apostolic Christianity, A.D. 1–100. CCEL.

140. Green, Michael. 1968. Man Alive. Inter-Varsity Press, Downer's Grove, IL.

141. Morrison, Frank. 1967. Who Moved the Stone? Faber and Faber, London.

142. Stott, John R.W. 1971. Basic Christianity. Inter-Varsity Press, Downer's Grove, IL.

143. McFarlan, Donald. ed. 1991. The Guiness Book of World Records. Bantam, New York, 547.

144. Sir Lionel Luckhoo as quoted in Ross, Clifford. 1991. The Case for the Empty Tomb. Albatross, Claremont, CA., p.112.

145. Smith, Wilbur M. "Scientists and the Resurrection," *Christianity Today*, April 15, 1957, pp.6, 22. Used by permission of *Christianity Today*.

146. Strobel, Ibid., p.52.

147. Strobel, Ibid., p.53.

148. Strobel, Ibid., p.71.

149. Strobel, Ibid., p.90.

150. Ramm, Bernard. 1953. Protestant Christian Evidences. Moody Press, Chicago, IL. pg. 206.

151. Geisler, Norman L. 1998. Baker Encyclopedia of Christian Apologetics. Baker Books, Grand Rapids, MI.

152. Morris, Henry M. 1971. The Bible Has the Answer. Baker Book House, Grand Rapids, MI.

Chapter 11

1. Strobel, Ibid., p.195.

2. Strobel, Ibid., pp.195–203
3. Strobel, Ibid., pp.195–203
4. Strobel, Ibid., pp.195–203
5. Strobel, Ibid., pp.195–203
6. Strobel, Ibid., pp.195–203
7. Farrar, Frederick W. 1897. The Life of Christ. Cassell and Co., Dutton, Dovar, pg 440.
8. Strobel, Ibid., pp.195–203
9. Strobel, Ibid., pp.195–203
10. Strobel, Ibid., pp.195–203
11. The Scofield Study Bible, Ibid.
12. The Scofield Study Bible, Ibid.
13. Pascal, Blaise. 1984. The Provincial Letters, Pensees, Scientific Treatises. In Great Books of the Western World, ed. Robert Maynard Hutchins. Trans. By W.F. Trotter. The University of Chicago, Encyclopedia Britannica, Inc., Chicago, n.p.
14. The Scofield Study Bible, Ibid.

To order additional copies of

THE FINGERPRINTS
OF GOD

Have your credit card ready and call:

1-877-421-READ (7323)

or please visit our web site at
www.pleasantword.com

Also available at:
www.amazon.com
and
www.barnesandnoble.com

Printed in the United States
41844LVS00001B/124-207